FRONT LINES

ALSO BY ALEXIS GREENE

The Story of 42nd Street (with Mary C. Henderson)

Women Writing Plays:
Three Decades of the Susan Smith Blackburn Prize

OTHER PLAYS BY SHIRLEY LAURO INCLUDE

Open Admissions

A Piece of My Heart

FRONT LINES

Political Plays by American Women

Alexis Greene • Shirley Lauro
Editors

THE NEW PRESS

NEW YORK
LONDON

Requests for permission to reproduce selections from this book should be mailed to:
Permissions Department, The New Press, 38 Greene Street, New York, NY 10013.

Published in the United States by The New Press, New York, 2009
Distributed by Perseus Distribution

LIBRARY OF CONGRESS CATALOGING-IN-PUBLICATION DATA

Front lines : political plays by American women / Alexis Greene, Shirley Lauro, editors.
p. cm.
ISBN 978-1-59558-424-3 (pb)
1. Political plays, American. 2. American drama—Women authors.
3. American drama—21st century. I. Greene, Alexis. II. Lauro, Shirley.
PS627.P65F76 2009
812'.60803581—dc22 2009004835

The New Press was established in 1990 as a not-for-profit alternative to the large, commercial publishing houses currently dominating the book publishing industry. The New Press
operates in the public interest rather than for private gain, and is committed to publishing, in
innovative ways, works of educational, cultural, and community value that are often deemed
insufficiently profitable.

www.thenewpress.com

Composition by dix!
This book was set in Fairfield

Printed in the United States of America

2   4   6   8   10   9   7   5   3   1

To the playwrights in our anthology

CONTENTS

FOREWORD

The theater critic Dorothy Parker once mused that the most beautiful words in the English language are "check enclosed." Women theater artists have spent centuries—ten by my count—looking for the respect that comes with a paycheck. Even today, women playwrights receive somewhere around 20 percent of the professional production opportunities nationwide and only about 13 percent in New York City, my hometown and the cultural capital of the world.

We ponder these statistics—and sometimes pound our fists—and promise to effect change. We talk and talk and talk about the need to level the playing field for women theater artists. And yet here we are, still stuck somewhere around 20 percent.

Here's an outrageous suggestion: let's stop talking.

Let's publish more plays by women. Anthologies such as *Front Lines: Political Plays by American Women* dispel dog-eared myths about women playwrights writing only for and about women (would we ever say Albee or Kushner or O'Neill write only for men?) and help women theater artists to achieve the national recognition they richly deserve but rarely receive.

Let's produce more plays written by women in our schools, at our community theaters, and on our professional stages. The more often the plays of women are published and produced, the faster women playwrights will shed their status as emerging artists and be ushered into the respected realm of the emerged and fully formed. The more often the plays of women are published and produced, the faster women playwrights will stop being considered too (put any adjective here) for the average theatergoer. And once they've lost their novelty, women theater artists will stop being marked as women first and will begin being regarded simply as artists.

Let's share responsibility for our current cultural landscape and the artistic legacy we leave to future generations. As audience members, artists, students, and scholars, let's ask our local theaters to produce women playwrights regularly, and then support those productions by buying a ticket and spreading the word to our friends.

Let's insist that our schools include plays written by women across curricula. The work of women artists need not be confined to women's studies courses, and any one of the plays in this volume would surely ignite a stirring debate about the theater, history, government, psychology, or a host of other worthy subjects.

Writing a play is always a political act. Playwrights, female and male, choose which stories to tell. They create the lens—sometimes transparent but more often a little out of focus—through which audiences experience their stories. They boldly and beautifully influence our sensibilities and intellect in order to reel us into their theatrical worlds.

Buying a ticket to the theater or the script of a play is also a political act. There are a scary number of entertainment choices. In New York City alone, there are more than 350 companies dedicated to producing and presenting live theater, and everywhere we find Netflix, Facebook, and Starbucks competing with dance, opera, and live music. The choices are breathtaking, and yet every day we take a breath and choose.

You have chosen to have this book in your hands, and you are about to enter a world of plays that are unrepentantly political and also profoundly innovative, imaginative, and insightful. Relish in the extraordinary ride you will take while reading them. And when you're done reading, choose to take it one step further and produce them or pass them on to those who will. That's one way to ensure that more women theater artists find the "check enclosed," and we can level the playing field at last.

Julie Crosby
Producing Artistic Director
Women's Project, New York City

PREFACE

Justice is a woman. The Greeks called her Goddess Themis; the Romans, Goddess Justitia. Both civilizations sculpted statues of her in flowing gowns, carrying sword in one hand to kill the unjust, scale in the other to measure equality, and sometimes a book of law to help determine guidelines for fairness. Often the statues were blindfolded, signaling all would be treated evenhandedly. Through the ages in a myriad of cultures, this embodiment of justice has survived nearly intact, emerging in modern times as Lady Justice, the iconic symbol of fairness and equality throughout the world. She is a statue, a photo, an emblem. She graces parks, stands before courthouses, palaces, government buildings, archways to law schools; her likeness is imprinted on letterheads and books. Sometimes she holds an olive branch and scepter or a book of law. Sometimes she is blindfolded with her scales of justice in one hand, her sword in the other. Sometimes she sits and sometimes she stands. But clear eyed or blindfolded; sitting or standing; scales, sword, or book in hand—justice is a woman.

Alexis Greene and I were drawn to edit this anthology because we feel there *is* something special and unique about women and justice. Georgia O'Keeffe once said: "Something remains unexplored about women that only a woman can explain." This anthology, for us, speaks to that "something" as regards justice. Much of our own work as author and playwright, respectively, does as well. The playwrights, each from her own angle of vision, have created characters or chosen figures searching for fairness and equality as they are thrust into the writer's vision of an unjust world.

From diverse points of view the struggle for justice is the focal point for our writers: *No Child . . .* , flinging open the door on the inequality of education in our inner cities; *Hot 'n' Throbbing*, exposing the blatant violation of rights inherent in domestic and sexual violence; *The Exonerated*, laying bare the scandal of imprisoning the innocent; *Words of Choice*, examining bias and inequality in women's right to choose; *Clarence Darrow's Last Trial*, unveiling the enormity of the American upper-class white power structure over our legal system; *Mrs. Packard*, exploring women's daunting quest to stand as independent-minded, equal partners with their husbands; and *Elliot, a Soldier's Fugue* . . . lyrically depicting the unjust impact of war on a family.

In the book we hope you will hear our playwrights' special clarion call as they seek justice.

Shirley Lauro
New York City
2008

ACKNOWLEDGMENTS

The editors wish to thank the Daryl and Steven Roth Foundation for its generous support of this book. We also want to convey our deep appreciation to the theater company Voice & Vision for their significant help. The editors would like to thank The New Press for its editorial expertise and our agent, Joe Veltre, head of The Veltre Company, for his guidance.

All of our playwrights' agents and their assistants have been extraordinarily helpful in enabling us to secure the material for this book: Peter Hagan of the Abrams Artists Agency; John Buzzetti; Carl Mulert of the Gersh Agency; Peter Franklin and Val Day of William Morris Agency; and Bruce Ostler of Bret Adams Limited.

The idea for our book evolved from a panel discussion we initiated under the auspices of the League of Professional Theatre Women in collaboration with Marymount Manhattan College, and the support of Dr. Mary Fleischer, Marymount's theater department chair. The concept for our book was nourished by an article we published in the Dramatists Guild magazine, *The Dramatist*.

Finally we express our gratitude and affection to our respective husbands, Dr. Gordon R. Hough and Dr. Louis Lauro, who have stood beside us with great patience and encouragement from the beginning.

INTRODUCTION

Playwrights have a responsibility to address the social and political issues of their time.

So thought the ancient Greeks, and so concluded many of the women whose dramas may be found in the canon of American plays. From Mercy Warren's eighteenth-century satires on the greed and incompetence of the British Tories to Lorraine Hansberry's revolutionary 1959 drama *A Raisin in the Sun* and beyond, women have been setting pen to paper, fingers to keyboards, to expose the social and political ills they both experience and observe.

The history of women in the United States has been one of continuous marching on the front lines to raise their voices in protest. Women have fought: for independence from British rule; for the abolition of slavery; for the right to vote; for sexual freedom and reproductive rights; for equal rights in every arena of American work and life. And ever since the country came into being, women have waged the battles for these rights in the pages of their plays and on the stages where those plays were performed. Feminist scholarship has revealed that many more American women plied the playwriting trade than traditional historians ever recognized.

Still, there is no doubt that, since the 1970s, when the second wave of feminism swept across the United States and many of the world's democracies, women's playwriting has accelerated as a means for social and political expression. In the United States, this has occurred despite an increase in conservatism at all levels of government and a retrenchment in public funding for the arts, two developments that make a career for a woman in theater more challenging than it ever was—and it was never easy.

Several of the dramatists represented in this anthology lived through the decade of women's liberation. All have benefited from it. Long gone are the doubts and self-consciousness about subjects that a woman should or should not tackle, the language and the forms that a woman should or should not employ, and the separatist idea that a woman must only create work for, with, and about other women. In *Elliot, a Soldier's Fugue,* Quiara Alegría Hudes dramatizes the experiences of three generations of men who go to war. Shirley Lauro puts the attorney Clarence Darrow at the center of her play. Jessica Blank has collaborated with Erik Jensen to forge *The Exonerated,* their unsettling indictment of the U.S. system of justice.

Indeed, the reader will find a range of subjects and styles within this volume. But while the dramatists come to theater with both a fierce sense of personal commitment and acute awareness of the flawed public world about which they write, finally their work is theatrical, not polemical. They are artists, not stump speakers. These plays are to be relished for their imagination and craft as well as their content.

The Exonerated, by Jessica Blank and Erik Jensen, is based on interviews with sixty men and women who were arrested, convicted, and subsequently imprisoned on death row for crimes they did not commit. Some remained in prison for as long as twenty-two years, until their convictions were reversed.

The play that emerged from Blank and Jensen's conversations offers stories of despair, anger, and sorrow, told mostly in the words of the people whom the playwrights interviewed. But the play's larger story is one of racism on the part of those in power, and manipulation of the U.S. judicial system, again by those in power.

Cindy Cooper's *Words of Choice,* a compilation of first-person accounts, satiric sketches, and poems, illuminates the many angles from which Americans approach the issue of reproductive choice, especially the choice of whether or not to have an abortion. Among other things, the play is intended as a warning about the consequences of reversing the 1973 Supreme Court decision in the case of *Roe v. Wade*, which made abortion legal in the United States. A father describes how his daughter was assaulted and raped one Fourth-of-July evening, as she walked home through Washington, D.C. When his daughter became pregnant, he encouraged her to have an abortion. There is an excerpt from entertainer Kathy Najimy's stand-up comedy show *Parallel Lives* and a sprightly riff about an imaginary "morning-after burrito" from Taco Bell. There is also nurse Emily Lyons's account of being blown nearly apart by a bomb, which antiabortionist Eric Rudolph exploded at a Birmingham, Alabama, women's clinic in 1998. "I've been to war," Lyons says. "I've gone to hell, and I've come back."

The private hell endured by soldiers in more traditional wars is the subject of *Elliot, a Soldier's Fugue,* Quiara Alegría Hudes's drama about three Latino men, fathers and sons, who served respectively in the Korean and Vietnam wars and the most recent Iraq war. For each generation, war brings fear, loneliness, horror, and possible death. Yet, as Hudes shows, each man has kept his wartime experiences to himself, and so each generation must come of age through war all over again. And thus, the play implies, wars occur again and again, generation after generation.

In *Clarence Darrow's Last Trial,* Shirley Lauro takes us to the Territory of Hawaii in 1932 for her dramatic interpretation of the notorious Massie trial. The aging Darrow is famous for defending John Scopes's right to teach human evolution in Tennessee and for successfully representing African Americans at a time when they rarely received justice in U.S. courts. Now, however, he agrees to serve as counsel for wealthy white defendants in a racially charged murder trial in Honolulu.

To his dismay, Darrow finds that he is prevented from carrying through the groundbreaking insanity defense he had hoped would cap his risk-taking career. Added to that personal disappointment is his realization that the defendants have colluded with the court to avoid the sort of proper justice to which he has dedicated his career. Faced with a misuse of political and judicial power that he cannot condone or control, Darrow abandons the trial. But as the play's final words indicate, he never abandons his "undying faith in the institutions of this land" and his commitment to help the "wretched, the forgotten of this earth."

Going further back in time, to Illinois during the early 1860s, Emily Mann dramatizes the case of Mrs. Elizabeth Packard, whose husband, a Calvinist minister, incarcerated her in a lunatic asylum for publicly disagreeing with his sermons.

Mrs. Packard, which received its world premiere at McCarter Theatre Center in Princeton, New Jersey, in 2007, draws on Elizabeth Packard's diaries and on court records, but the characters and the story have been elaborated upon and shaped by the playwright. At the center is a woman who staunchly upholds her right to voice her beliefs in the face of a legal system that allows a man to commit his wife to an insane asylum without proof of her insanity. Unwilling to sacrifice her mind in order to obtain her freedom, Packard ultimately finds a way to affirm her sanity and extricate herself from her husband's control, but at enormous personal cost. The play illuminates a dark episode of women's history in the United States. It has contemporary resonance for a United States still wrestling with the granting of habeas corpus to political and military prisoners.

As a young actor, Nilaja Sun frequently taught theater in some of New York

City's most troubled public schools. She witnessed the struggles of students who were handicapped by difficult circumstances at home and, at school, by insufficient funding for public education. Often the very buildings in which she taught were crumbling around her.

In response, Sun created *No Child . . .* —a one-woman play that takes its title from the No Child Left Behind Act of 2001, which promised quality education to every American student. Arriving at the fictional Malcolm X public high school, "Miss Sun" really does bring a valuable educational experience to her sometimes rambunctious, sometimes unmotivated class. Despite moments when she feels like running away from it all, Miss Sun leads her students to put on one performance of Timberlake Wertenbaker's *Our Country's Good*—a drama about English convicts who are transported to Australia in the late eighteenth century to establish a penal colony and, upon arriving, stage a play.

The final entry in this anthology is a revised version of Pulitzer Prize–winning dramatist Paula Vogel's *Hot 'n' Throbbing*, published for the first time.

Domestic violence forms the core of *Hot 'n' Throbbing*. But obscenity is also an issue. The central character, Charlene, supports herself and her two teenage children by writing fiction that she calls "adult entertainment," to stimulate women's sexual fantasies. Is that fiction obscene? Or is it obscene that Charlene's ex-husband, Clyde, once nearly beat her to death and now invades her home and threatens her again?

In its original version, *Hot 'n' Throbbing* received its first major production in 1994, staged by Anne Bogart at the Hasty Pudding Theater in Cambridge, Massachusetts. "After I saw that," Vogel has said, "the thing I wanted to redo is that it's not the erotic which is scary. It's not the erotic that's the danger. It's the living room that's the danger." She changed the focus for the 2005 production, which was directed by Les Waters at Signature Theatre Company in New York City.

The new version also introduces the theme of Herman Melville's novel *Moby-Dick,* which Charlene's fifteen-year-old daughter, Leslie Ann, is supposed to be reading for school. A voice-over device, which Vogel uses in the play to suggest both Charlene's inner voice and the voice that writes her fiction, occasionally quotes some of the descriptions of the white whale's bloody demise, possibly to foretell Charlene's own ending and possibly to suggest a parallel with the novel's obsessive, destructive male quest.

Finally, Vogel has added a kind of coda to *Hot 'n' Throbbing*, during which we see that Leslie Ann, now a grown woman, has become the self-reliant feminist that her mother could never quite achieve. It is an optimistic, if bitter-sweet, ending.

Vogel's play brings this collection back to where it started with *The Exonerated*—back to the question of power.

The plays in this volume dramatize how women and men confront institutions and situations more powerful than them, be it a misused judicial system, a broken educational system, or a husband's brutality.

Perhaps not surprisingly this question of power is also the theme that permeated Mercy Warren's prorevolutionary plays in the eighteenth century. More than two hundred years later, the dramaturgy may be more sophisticated, the specific causes different. But the underlying political issue—the drive to preserve an individual's freedom—remains.

Alexis Greene
Walton, New York
June 2008

THE EXONERATED

by Jessica Blank and Erik Jensen

Richard Dreyfuss and Sara Gilbert in the New York premiere of *The Exonerated*
(Photo: © Carol Rosegg)

JESSICA BLANK AND ERIK JENSEN

The Exonerated, *by Jessica Blank and Erik Jensen, won Drama Desk, Lucille Lortel, Outer Critics Circle, Ovation, Fringe First, and Herald Angel awards. It has been extensively produced around the world, and translated into French, Spanish, Italian, and Japanese. The play was subsequently adapted by Blank and Jensen for a Court TV movie, starring Susan Sarandon, Danny Glover, Aidan Quinn, Delroy Lindo, and Brian Dennehy. Living Justice, Blank and Jensen's book on the making of* The Exonerated, *was published by Simon & Schuster in 2005. Blank's* Liberty City, *co-written with April Yvette Thompson, received nominations for Drama Desk, Lucille Lortel, and Outer Critics Circle awards. Her first novel,* Almost Home *(Hyperion, 2007) has been optioned for a feature film, with Blank and Jensen adapting. Blank's second novel,* Karma for Beginners, *is forthcoming from Hyperion in 2009. In addition to playwriting, Blank and Jensen are actors. Blank has appeared on television in* The Bronx is Burning, Law & Order: CI, Rescue Me, One Life to Live, *and* Guiding Light. *Her film credits include* The Namesake, The Exonerated, *and the indies* On the Road with Judas *and* Undermind. *Jensen has co-starred in over twenty feature films and has appeared on television in* CSI, Alias, Law & Order, *and* Love Monkey. *He played Yankee legend Thurman Munson in* The Bronx is Burning *and co-stars in* Virtuality, *the new project by the creators of* Battlestar Galactica.

INTRODUCTION

Over the summer of 2000, we traveled across the United States, sat in people's living rooms, and listened as they told us what it was like to be wrongly convicted and on death row. They were from vastly different ethnic, religious, and educational backgrounds. Their views on the world varied greatly. The only thing they held in common was that they had each been sentenced to die, spent anywhere from two to twenty-two years on death row, and subsequently had been freed by the state. We interviewed forty people on the phone and twenty in person. Six of these interviews form the core of *The Exonerated.*

That spring, we had gotten the idea for the play at a conference on the death penalty at Columbia University. We brought the idea to producer Allan Buchman, a friend of ours from the downtown theater community in New York.

Governor George Ryan of Illinois had just declared a moratorium on the death penalty in his state, and another George was running for high office—

with more executions carried out under his watch as governor of Texas than in any other state since the reinstatement of the death penalty in 1976. The issue was very much in the news. Allan told us we could have his theater for three nights in the fall if we could have something up before the elections. So we hit the road. We went as far north and west as Chicago, as far south as Texas and Miami, and just about everywhere in between to meet the people whose stories appear in this play.

We returned from the interviews with hours and hours of tape, which became several hundred pages of transcripts. We're both primarily actors, which means we have lots of talented and underemployed friends. We enlisted them to come workshop the transcripts with us and began the process of shaping hundreds of pages of everyday speech into a play. At the same time, we called director Bob Balaban and asked him to direct three readings of the play at Allan's theater that fall. Bob brought his highly trained eye to the material we were developing, as well as helped us assemble a cast for the readings that included Gabriel Byrne, Ossie Davis, Vincent D'Onofrio, Charles Dutton, Cherry Jones, David Morse, Susan Sarandon, Tim Robbins, Debra Winger, and many other extraordinary actors. They performed an initial version of the play that consisted of the stories of twelve exonerated people, taken entirely from the interviews we had conducted.

After three readings at the Culture Project and a performance at the United Nations, we hit the road again. It was clear to us, Bob, and our audiences how the exonerated people felt about what had happened to them; what was still unclear was how it could've happened in the first place. So we went through the extremely difficult process of paring down the number of stories in the play, in order to tell each one more fully. Additionally, we dug into the court transcripts and case files of the people whose stories we were telling. We spent countless hours in dusty courthouse record rooms, pawing through thousands of microfiche files and cardboard boxes full of affidavits, depositions, police interrogations, and courtroom testimony. The court employees assumed we were law students—and we did nothing to discourage that belief. With a few exceptions, each work spoken in this play comes from the public record—legal documents, court transcripts, letters—or from an interview with an exonerated person. The names of the exonerated people are their own; some names of auxiliary characters have been changed for legal reasons.

The vast majority of the piece is as it was said two, five, ten, and twenty years ago by the actual participants. At the time we conducted these interviews, there were 89 people who had been exonerated from death row. As of this writing there are now 102. We consider every one of their stories to be part of this play.

Jessica Blank and Erik Jensen
2004

THE EXONERATED was originally presented in Los Angeles by the Actors' Gang (Tim Robbins, artistic director), in association with the Culture Project, on April 19, 2002. It was directed by Jessica Blank and Erik Jensen with supervision by Bob Balaban.

KERRY . . . . .Ken Palmer
SUNNY . . . . .Adele Robbins
SUE, SANDRA . . . . .Victoria Cunningham
DELBERT . . . . .Richard Lawson
ROBERT . . . . .Ken Elliott
MALE ENSEMBLE #1 . . . . .Kelly Cole
MALE ENSEMBLE #2 . . . .Jon Kellam
MALE ENSEMBLE #3 . . . .Terrell Tilford
FEMALE ENSEMBLE . . . . .Blaire Chandler
DAVID . . . . .Ben Cain
GARY . . . . .Brian Powell
GEORGIA, JUDGE, DARLA,
STATE PROSECUTOR . . . . .Yolanda Snowball
Set Design: Richard Hoover
Original Music and Sound Design: David Robbins
Costume Design: Ann Closs-Farley

THE EXONERATED premiered in New York City at 45 Bleecker Theatre on October 10, 2002. It was produced by the Culture Project, Dede Harris, Morton Swinsky, Bob Balaban, Harit Allan Buchman, Patrick Blake, David Elliott, Jane Bergere, Ruth Hendel, and Cheryl Wiesenfeld. It was directed by Bob Balaban.

KERRY . . . . .Richard Dreyfuss
SUNNY . . . . .Jill Clayburgh
SUE, SANDRA . . . . .Sara Gilbert
DELBERT . . . . .Charles Brown
ROBERT . . . . .David Brown Jr.

MALE ENSEMBLE #1 . . . .Bruce Kronenberg
MALE ENSEMBLE #2 . . . .Phil Levy
DAVID . . . . .Curtis McClarin
GARY . . . . .Jay O. Sanders
GEORGIA, JUDGE, DARLA,
STATE PROSECUTOR . . . . .April Yvette Thompson

CHARACTERS

DELBERT TIBBS—African American, 60. A seminary dropout, radical, and poet. His whole personality is like an old soul song: smooth, mellow, and with an underlying rhythm that never lets up. Actors playing Delbert should take care to find his substantial sense of humor, in addition to his obvious depth.

SUNNY JACOB—White, 50. A bright, pixie-ish yoga teacher from California; her lightness and positivity contrast with moments of great depth and clarity.

ROBERT HAYES—African American, 30s. A former horse groomer from the deep South; hardened but not lacking a sense of humor. Deep rural Mississippi accent.

GEORGIA HAYES/FEMALE ENSEMBLE 1—African American, 30. Robert's wife, also Southern; outspoken and extremely warm. She and Robert have a lovingly contentious relationship. Loves to speak her mind.

GARY GAUGER—White, 45. A Midwestern hippie and organic farmer. Clearly was in his element in the late 1960s and early 70s. He is generally good-natured, friendly, and quite smart.

KERRY MAX COOK—White, 45. A nineteen-year-old trapped in a forty-five-year-old's body, born and bred in Texas. Kerry was imprisoned for twenty-two of his forty-five years, and is eager to rediscover the world. Always wants to make sure he connects with whomever he is talking to. Strong Texas accent.

DAVID KEATON—African American, 40. A gentle, sad man, born and raised in northern Florida (otherwise known as Southern Alabama). Has a very strong spiritual sense and had aspirations to the ministry before being put on death row at eighteen. He is continually engaged in a battle between resignation and hope.

SANDRA COOK/SUE GAUGER/FEMALE ENSEMBLE 2—White, 40. SANDRA is married to KERRY. Sweet, nurturing, loves Kerry dearly and has a great sense of humor about him. She has a strong Texan accent. SUE is married to GARY. Salt of the earth; she is also an organic farmer. She has a *strong* upper Midwestern accent—think *Fargo*.

MALE ENSEMBLE 1 and 2—Both white, 35–50. MALE ENSEMBLE 1 and 2 play police officers, attorneys, suspects, and other supporting characters. Both actors should be good with dialects and characterization, and different from each other in build and appearance. Both roles require highly versatile, commanding actors.

MALE ENSEMBLE 1—Plays WHITE COP 1, KERRY'S DEFENSE, SHERIFF CARROLL, JESSE, COURT ATTORNEY, DAVID'S PROSECUTOR, VOICE-OVER/INMATE, WHITE GUARD, JEFF, CELLMATE, EX-BOYFRIEND, and FARMER.

MALE ENSEMBLE 2—Plays WHITE COP 2, KERRY'S PROSECUTION, RHODES, DEPUTY, SOUTHERN WHITE GUY, ROBERT'S JUDGE, DAVID'S DEFENSE, DOYLE, and THE PROSECUTION.

FEMALE ENSEMBLE 1 (GEORGIA)—Also plays STATE ATTORNEY, KERRY'S JUDGE, and DARLA.

FEMALE ENSEMBLE 2 (SANDRA/SUE)—Also plays FEMALE LAWYER.

The roles of BLACK COP, BLACK GUY 1, and BLACK INMATE—Are played by the actor who plays DAVID.

The role of BLACK GUY 2—Is played by the actor who plays ROBERT.

(*Open on a stage, bare except for ten plain, armless chairs. These chairs can be used variously to set up scenes throughout the piece. The entire play can be performed using only these chairs. No further set pieces are necessary, although tables and other set pieces might work, too. The play is seamless: there are no blackouts during the performance, and no intermission. Unless otherwise noted, the exonerated people deliver their monologues to the audience.* DELBERT *can see the other exonerated people; unless otherwise noted, none of the other exonerated people see each other or* DELBERT. *At various points in the play we may see "scenes" illustrating the stories being told by the exonerated. These scenes exist in the exonerated people's memories, and unless otherwise noted, should take place behind or beside the character telling the story.*

DELBERT *functions as a sort of Chorus, fading in and out of the action. He is a black man in his late fifties. His personality is like an old soul song: smooth, mellow, but with a relentless underlying rhythm. He has a great sense of humor. He's from Chicago.*)

DELBERT: This is not the place for thought that does not end in concreteness;
    it is not easy to be open or too curious.
    It is dangerous to dwell too much on things:
    to wonder who or why or when, to wonder how, is dangerous.
    How do we, the people, get outta this hole, what's the way to fight,
    might I do what Richard and Ralph and Langston 'n them did?
    It is not easy to be a poet here. Yet I sing.
    I sing.

(*Lights up on* SUE *and* GARY. SUE *is* GARY's *wife. Farmer woman, salt of the earth. She has a very strong upper Midwest accent—think* Fargo.

GARY *is a Midwestern hippie in his midforties. He is an organic farmer. He was clearly in his element in the late 60s and early 70s. He is generally good-natured and quite smart.*)

GARY: Gary Gauger. This is my wife, Sue. (*Beat;* SUE *waves.*)
    So my case—the day before, I had gone to work here, you see our workshop is a little building right over there. And it is about ninety-two percent recycled.
SUE: Even the shingles and the foundation are recycled.
GARY: So anyway, I start my plants out there, and then in mid-March we move

'em out front to the hot beds. So I would come over here in the morning and work all day, and I'd go back for supper at night.

So anyways, that day, I went to work, my folks weren't around.

SUE: But they had been planning a trip to Sugar Grove.

GARY: I just thought, "No big deal, they go away sometimes." By night, they didn't get home, I was worried about 'em. I said, "Jeez, they must've gotten in a car accident." But what do you do, call hospitals?

SUE: Oh, ya can't. Ya can't. Not between here and Sugar Grove.

GARY: And the police, I knew, wouldn't investigate until they'd been missing for twenty-four hours. So I just basically stayed by the phone till midnight, went to bed.

Next morning, I got up to call the police, and a customer came walkin' up the driveway, looking for motorcycle parts, and in the back room where we thought the part might be is where we found my father's body.

Now, it looked to me like he'd suffered a stroke, because he was facedown in a pool of blood. And he obviously . . . was dead. I felt his pulse.

So, all of a sudden, here's my father's body, my mom's been missing. So I called the paramedics, who called the police, who told me they suspect foul play.

About an hour and a half later, they find my mother's body in a trailer out in front of the house. She had been killed and covered with rugs and pillows. (*Pause.*) They had been hidden, and their throats were slashed.

Two and a half hours after I found my parents, they had me arrested.

(*Lights down on* GARY *and* SUE, *up on* DELBERT.)

DELBERT: It is not easy:
    you stand waiting for a train
    or a bus that may never come
    no friend drives by to catch a ride
    cold, tired:
    call yourself a poet
    but work all day mopping floors and looking out for thieves . . .

(*Lights down on* DELBERT; *up on* ROBERT *and his wife* GEORGIA. ROBERT *is a black man in his midthirties, hardened but not lacking a sense of humor, with a deep rural Mississippi accent.* GEORGIA *is also Southern; outspoken, earthy, contentious, and extremely warm. Loves to speak her mind. The two of them overlap, finish each other's sentences, and otherwise play off each other whenever they appear together.)*

ROBERT: Robert Earl Hayes. This here's my wife—

GEORGIA: Georgia Hayes.

ROBERT (*Sotto voce*): Baby, they know your last name—

GEORGIA: I know, I just wanted to introduce myself. Go ahead.

ROBERT: Now, at the time that all this happened I was working around the racetrack, takin' care of the horses you know. And at that racetrack, this white girl, she gets raped and killed. And you know, she be dating the black guys, and when she got killed, they ask me have I ever had sex with the girl. I told them yeah, they said—

WHITE COP 1: Well, were you having sex with her that night?

ROBERT: I said no. Then they said—

WHITE COP 1: Well, why does she like hanging out on the black side of the track?

ROBERT: So I said, "I don't know why she like hanging out back there, I guess we more fun."

But this girl, she got killed. And the cop came to my job the next morning, they said—

WHITE COP 1: We gotta talk to you.

ROBERT: I said okay, I went to the police station. And they kept saying—

WHITE COP 2: We know what happened—

WHITE COP 1: We know you asked her for a date, and she hit you—

WHITE COP 2:—and you hit her back—

WHITE COP 1:—and you didn't *mean* to hit her that hard.

(*Lights down on* COPS.)

ROBERT: They just came right after me. This white girl, me and she had dated, and you know people 'round here don't like that too much. And in my first trial I *knew* I was going to prison—I had eleven whites and one black on that jury.

GEORGIA: And do you think, seriously, now be honest, if the roles had been reversed, if it had been a black woman and a white man, it woulda been like that?

ROBERT: Right, 'cause let's go to another high-profile case.

GEORGIA: Oh, here we go—

ROBERT: Now within all y'all's hearts—now be honest—within your *heart*, do you really think O.J. committed that crime?

GEORGIA (*Laughing*): Well, but O.J., you know, I'm black and I *still* think he guilty, I'm sorry—I don't care what they say. I say, if the DNA put you there, O.J., you guilty.

(*Lights down on* ROBERT *and* GEORGIA, *up on* KERRY *and* SANDRA. KERRY *is an eager nineteen-year-old trapped in a forty-four-year-old's body, white, with a Texan accent.* KERRY *is an "up-talker"—he ends many of his sentences with a question mark.* SANDRA *is* KERRY's *wife, also Texan, very pregnant, very sweet, takes care of* KERRY.)

KERRY: Kerry Max Cook. (*Beat.*)

SANDRA: Sandra Cook.

KERRY: It actually started when I was in the ninth or tenth grade: me and my friends would, you know, act like we were going to school and then run out the back door and start trying to find a car with the keys in it. And I had the misfortune that one of the cars that I stole, in my adventures to conquer the world, was the sheriff deputy's car and I, ah . . . wrecked it—driver's ed I didn't take—and, make a long story short, the deputy beat me for it.

And that was pretty much it—after that, any robbery, any broken window, any cat up a tree, everything was just *my fault*, as far as the sheriff was concerned.

And then fast-forwarding, I'm nineteen, and I'm at this apartment complex in Texas called the Embarcadero—there's a swimming pool there, it's where all the hip people hang out. And I was an attractive guy, I dressed real nice. It was the seventies, you know, man: I bought my clothes from the hippest place, like the Gap, and I had my hair styled real long, platform shoes and bell bottoms. I looked tight. And I was walkin' towards the swimming pool, and there was this beautiful gorgeous girl, man.

(*To* SANDRA.) Not as pretty as you.

SANDRA: Go on.

KERRY: But really *gorgeous*, man—just nude and fondling herself, right there in the window. So I look up and I go, "Oh my god, man . . . wow," 'cause I had lived a very sheltered, naive life, I'd never even been to a strip club before, and I'm seeing this total complete mature woman, and I'm goin' "okay, yeah, that's cool, man."

And so anyway, a couple days go by, and I'm back at the pool and there's this chick, layin' out there. To make a long story short, we started talking, told her I was a bartender in Dallas—'course I was working at a gay bar, but I didn't tell her that—I'm just stretching everything as much as I can because I want to be all that plus a bag of potater chips. Anyway, we end up going back to her apartment . . . we . . . uh . . . you know . . . made out.

SANDRA (*To audience*): But not—all the way.

KERRY: Oh, no, no, no. I was in there for about maybe thirty, forty-five minutes, whatever, and I got cold feet because she was so aggressive, and I left.

And I didn't ever see or hear from her ever again until I'm arrested for her murder three months later, August of 1977.

(SFX: *gavel. Lights up on* KERRY'S DEFENSE, PROSECUTION, *and* JUDGE. *They speak facing the audience.*)

KERRY'S DEFENSE: Since June 10, 1977, Tyler, Texas has been screaming and crying for *someone* to answer to this crime—

KERRY'S PROSECUTION (*Thick Texan accent*): The state of Texas would object to that being far beyond the scope of this case—

KERRY'S JUDGE: I am going to sustain that objection.

(*Courtroom freezes.*)

KERRY: They had found a fingerprint of mine on her door frame.

SANDRA: And they had a fingerprint guy whose knowledge of fingerprints at that point was a six-month correspondence school—

(*Courtroom back in action.*)

PROSECUTION (*Overlapping*): The lieutenant here is an expert fingerprint technologist. He will testify that he found a fingerprint belonging to the defendant, Kerry Max Cook. It is as clear, ladies and gentlemen, as the day when you put your footprint on your birth certificate. That officer didn't have any reason to lie. He will narrow the time element of the leaving of those fingerprints—

DEFENSE: Objection, Your Honor.

KERRY (*To audience*): You *can't* date a fingerprint, it's scientifically impossible.

DEFENSE: It cannot be proven what time those prints were made. This would place in the minds of the jurors that the defendant was there at the time of the murder!

JUDGE: Is that all you have?

DEFENSE: Yes, ma'am.

JUDGE: Your motion is overruled.

KERRY: That judge let them say, all through my trial, that I left that fingerprint there at the time of her murder.

And this next part has all been hidden for twenty years: Debra, the victim, had been having an affair with Professor Whitfield, a professor of sciences over at the university, and *everyone* had just found out about it, he was fired from his job, lost his wife, lost his kids, whole big mess. And her roommate, Darla, had seen somebody in the apartment the night of the murder, who she said had silver hair, medium short, touching the ears fashion, wearing white tennis shorts. Just like Whitfield.

In her police report, Darla says she sees Whitfield in the apartment that night and says—

(Lights up on DARLA.)

DARLA: Don't worry, it's only me.

KERRY: —and goes to bed. But at the trial she turns around and says—

DARLA *(Pointing)*: That's the man right there.

KERRY: —and points at me.

(Lights down on DARLA and courtroom.)

KERRY: And my lawyer didn't even argue with that. My attorney was the former DA who jailed me twice before. He was paid five hundred dollars, and in Texas, you get what you pay for.

(Lights down on KERRY and SANDRA; up on DELBERT.)

DELBERT: It's not easy to find some quiet place.
      Some grace. No time
      to talk about dreams
      in this world
      where ice
      is everywhere.

(Lights down on DELBERT; *up on* DAVID.)

DAVID: David Keaton.

  At the time they pulled me in, I was in high school. I had a lotta thoughts of what I was gonna do, where I was gonna go, where I should be, ten years from there, you know. I was, as some might say, I was called to the ministry.

  But I mean the way they picked me up—me and some friends was comin' from a movie that day and we saw a big commotion, and we said, "man, what's goin' on?" So we run down, and the cops are all round here, shinin' their lights up on my grandmother's house.

  And we was just standin' there watchin', and the cop says—

(Lights up on DEPUTY.)

DEPUTY: Do any of y'all know David Keaton?

DAVID: And boy, here I am like a nut, "I am he."

  So they took me down to the station and interrogated me, askin' me about this robbery, and I just kept sayin' to them over and over, "I don't know what you're talkin' about. I don't know what you're talkin' about. I don't know what you're talkin' about." But they locked the doors, they held me incommunicado, as you might say.

  When they first brought me into the jail, one of the deputies asked the sheriff at that time—

(Lights up on CARROLL.)

DEPUTY *(Southern accent)*: You gonna keep him?

DAVID: And the sheriff said—

SHERIFF: *(Thick Southern accent)*: You're goddamn right, we gonna keep him.

DAVID: The sheriff was running for reelection at the time, and this was a big unsolved crime, so he had to bring somebody in for it. And they're tellin' me what happened in the crime, who was standin' where and all of that, and I mean I don't even know what the store looks like, and they're yellin' at me, tryin' to get me to describe it.

(Lights dim slightly on DAVID *throughout the following.)*

DEPUTY: This interview is being given with Deputy Sheriff H.M. Carroll. Mr. Carroll, if you will, explain to me the events that took place at Luke's

Grocery on September 18, 1970, as they relate to the case of David Keaton.

CARROLL: Well, about 2:30 Officer Khomas Revels and myself went in, I went over to the tobacco counter to get some chaw and he walked on back toward the milk case. And then I heard a nigger tell him, "Get on over there, I ain't got no time to fool with you," so I walked on around to where Khomas was at. And this boy, he had a gun, just said, "Don't give us no trouble." And he had ah, kind of an Afro haircut, not a full Afro, but he looked like he was tryin to grow him some Afro hair. And he had a little mustache, best I can remember, I mean everything was goin' so fast there. And the other one that was standin' over where they had about five or six customers tied down, he was around six foot tall. And the third sonofabitch—on his forehead, looked like he had, I don't know, you've seen them with kind of a scar sometimes?

DEPUTY: Oh yeah.

CARROLL: Anyway, they told us to give them our money. So we did, 'bout thirty-two dollars, and then they said we want them watches too. Well, we didn't either one of us pull our watches off.

And they told us to lay down. So we did, and one of them, he reached over to get him some panty hose to tie us up with—but myself and Khomas, we came up and tackled them. Ain't nobody gonna be tyin' me up with no panty hose. And so the other one, he come running down shooting at us.

They must have shot eighteen or twenty bullets during the ruckus there, and the two hit me, and the two hit Khomas. And I could see that he was dead. (*Extended beat.*) And the niggers, they just disappeared.

DEPUTY: Mr. Carroll, in listening to these people talk in the store, did they have any type of accent, did they sound like local people or were they from out of state?

CARROLL: Naw, they just sounded like regular niggers to me.

(*Lights down on* DEPUTY *and* CARROLL; *full up on* DAVID.)

DAVID: And I was just eighteen, I didn't know the rules. And they kept on talkin', and they were threatenin' me, and all that. And I was afraid. I mean they could go in there and beat you up, mess you up, hang you up, nobody'd ever hear nothin' else about you. And so I say, okay, to prevent that, I'm gonna go ahead and confess to the crime. I know I'm tellin the truth, and the witnesses are gonna know too, 'cause I just wasn't there and they would have seen that. So I'm like, I'm gonna let them go ahead, they gave me all the information already, all I do is put some names to the spots and then we all can be free.

(*Lights down on* DAVID; *up on* SUNNY.)

SUNNY: Sunny Jacobs. (*Beat.*)

In 1976, I was sentenced to death row, which for me wasn't a row at all because I was the only woman in the country who had the sentence of death. So *I* suggested they put me in the same cell as my husband!

But let me start at the beginning. (*Beat.*)

When I was twenty-six, Jesse and I had been together for three years. We weren't officially married, but I considered him my husband, you know. Our daughter had just been born, and Jesse said he was gonna get himself a regular job, maybe painting murals or something, but he just needed to go to Florida one last time to do a little deal.

Now, I didn't want to know about this deal, because I knew it wasn't positive; it wasn't violent, but it wasn't positive. And finally he calls and says that the deal fell through, and not only is he broke and has no way home, but he's staying with some *girl*! So, of course, me, instead of saying, "well, when you get it together, me and the kids will be here waiting for you," I said, "I'll be right there to getcha!"

My son Eric was nine, and I was driving, shifting, singing, and nursing Tina all at the same time. It was like driving through the ten plagues, you know, the first being the oil leaking all over the road, and the final one—you know those love bugs that smash themselves on your window?

So anyway, we get there, get Jesse, the car dies, and we're all stuck in Florida. And so Jesse says he'll ask this guy he knows if we can stay with him until we can scrape the money together to get home.

And that's when I met Walter Rhodes.

So we're all stuck in Florida, staying at Walter Rhodes's apartment. And it was a real sleazebag place; it sure seemed like he was doing illegal activities.

(*Lights up on* JESSE *and* RHODES.)

JESSE: Hey Rhodes, we're gonna take off. Could you give us a lift to my friend's over in Broward County?

RHODES: I don't know, man, it's late—I don't know if I want to be on the road—

JESSE: Come on, man, nothing ever happens in Broward.

(*Lights down on* JESSE *and* RHODES.)

SUNNY: And it was so weird—my son Eric woke up screaming in the middle of the night. He had this nightmare that something terrible was going to happen to us. And it did.

DELBERT: It's not easy
to feel good in winter winds
when ice is everywhere
and you just wanna sing . . . Copyright 1997, Delbert Tibbs. (*Beat.*) I'm Delbert Tibbs.

I'm a child of the sixties and the seventies, right? So, much of the philosophy that people were motivated by during those times I was, and continue to be, motivated by. I have an ongoing—an *abiding* interest in things philosophical and/or metaphysical; I won't say religious . . .

And so, you know, in 1972, I went to seminary for a year and a half, but the racism there was so pervasive you could cut it with a knife. So I decided that the seminary wasn't gonna take me where I wanted to go, so I dropped out, and started roaming America. We called it *tunin' in*. Tune in, turn on, an' drop out. And I haven't turned off for a long time.

So that's where I was at—and I happened to be in Florida when some crazy stuff happened, a guy was killed, a young woman was raped, and I happened to be in Florida.

And I knew that some folks were gonna say—

(*Lights up on* WHITE GUY 1.)

SOUTHERN WHITE GUY: Now what's this nigga doin here, and who is he, an' why is he here?!

(*Lights down on* SOUTHERN WHITE GUY.)

DELBERT: —and so forth, but my attitude was fuck that, you know? I'm an American citizen, and I've served in the Armed Forces of the United States, and all that kinda shit.

The point I'm trying to make is that, in my mind I decided that I was gonna be free in terms a my movements. That I was gonna go wherever I wanted to go, in these United States, an' whatever came out of that, if there was trouble, then I would deal with it when it came. And sure enough . . . (*Chuckle*) sure enough, trouble came.

(*Beat.*) Because this *crime* had occurred, and I was on the highway in Florida, so I was stopped and questioned, and the captain wrote me out a note sayin—

(*Lights up on* WHITE COP 1.)

WHITE COP 1 (*Fast robotic monotone*): This person was stopped by me on this date and I'm satisfied that he's not the person wanted in connection with the crimes that occurred in Southern Florida.

(*Lights down on* WHITE COP 1.)

DELBERT: Now, initially, the girl who survived the thing described the murderer as a black man about five-six, very dark complexion, with pock-marked skin, and a bush Afro. (*Beat.*) Now that don't fit me no matter how you draw it—except racially. That's the only thing we had in common: we're both black men.

But now it's like two weeks or something after the crime has occurred, and they gotta find *somebody,* cause the small town is in hysterics, you know? There's a nigger running around killing white men and raping white women, and you can't have that. (*Beat.*) Understandably.

So anyway, the cops stopped me again, and I said no, I'm not. I said I was stopped in Florida—

(*Lights up on* WHITE COP 1.)

WHITE COP 1 (*Again, unnaturally fast robotic monotone*): This person was stopped by me on this date and—

(*Lights down on* WHITE COP 1.)

DELBERT (*Interrupting*): —and to the satisfaction of the Florida Highway Patrol, I'm not the person that you're looking for. He says, in effect:
WHITE COP 2: Bullshit.

DELBERT: He says—

WHITE COP 2: You're Delbert Tibbs, I have a warrant for your arrest.

DELBERT: And they arrested me in Mississippi.

(Lights down on DELBERT and WHITE COP 2, up on ROBERT and GEORGIA.)

ROBERT *(To GEORGIA)*:—I mean, I might as well be wearin' a sign that says, "arrest me, I'm black."

GEORGIA *(To audience)*: It's always somethin'. I mean it's not all police officers, it's not all white people, but it's those few that make the rest of them look so bad—

ROBERT *(To audience)*: But I mean, hypothetically speaking, if me and a white woman have an altercation, the cop gonna say; well, it's okay for her. But for me, all she got to say is he touched my breast, he touched my booty, and there go the wildfire.

GEORGIA: It's not only just whites, it's blacks, too—

ROBERT *(interrupting)*: Not to cut you off, but one night, me and a white guy, we were sitting at a gas station. We were just sitting there talking, and a white cop came back around to talk to us.

(Lights up on WHITE COP 1 and SOUTHERN WHITE GUY.)

ROBERT: And he didn't ask me was I having a problem, he asked the white guy was *he* having a problem. He says—

WHITE COP 1: I see both you guys talking and moving your hands.

ROBERT: —and you know, the black person talk with his hands, if you guys haven't noticed. The white guy, he said—

SOUTHERN WHITE GUY: No, me and Robert just sitting up here talking.

ROBERT: And the cop said—

WHITE COP 1: Do you know Robert?

SOUTHERN WHITE GUY: Yeah, I been knowing him for the longest.

ROBERT: But the cop said—

WHITE COP 1: Oh, I thought he was harassing you.

GEORGIA: Okay?!

(Lights down on COP and SOUTHERN WHITE GUY.)

ROBERT: I mean, God put everyone on earth, God put the ass, he put the fleas, but there's a lot of white people that make me upset. But I'm not gonna call them crackers and go and get my cousin and all that.

GEORGIA (*Sotto voce, overlapping*): No, don't get your cousin; your cousin *crazy*.

ROBERT: I think if anyone have anything against anyone in this country, it should have been the Indians. But I do think now, these days, it's a lot better, especially in Mississippi because if it wasn't, I'd be sittin' here saying, "yes ma'am, Miss Daisy." Maybe it's goin' away—

GEORGIA (*Interrupting*): But Robert— (*To audience.*) Okay, in my opinion, you never gonna get rid of it. My father taught me, things are passed down from generation to generation, and if the older generation teach the younger generation, then it ain't never gonna go away.

(*Lights down on* ROBERT *and* GEORGIA; *up on* DELBERT.)

DELBERT: No time in this world to talk about dreams,
        no space to place words in some lovely configuration;
        deliberation is not the method
        for passage through these woods
        cold, tired
        if you dream in this world
        it is dangerous.

(*Lights down on* DELBERT, *up on* SUNNY.)

SUNNY: My son Eric couldn't sleep because of the nightmare, and I just couldn't stay with Rhodes another night. So finally Rhodes agreed to give me, Jesse, and the kids a ride.
        And we left, but the traffic got bad and it was getting late, so the decision was made to pull off the road until morning.

(*Dim light up on* BLACK COP, JESSE, *and* RHODES.)

SUNNY: And according to the police reports, the cops came to do a routine check on the rest area. And when they look in the window, they see a gun between Rhodes's feet. They order him out of the car and ask for his ID. The policeman calls in the ID information, and then tells Rhodes:

BLACK COP: Stand over there, I'm finished with you.

SUNNY: And then they ask my husband Jesse to get out.
        And then the police radio comes back with the announcement that Rhodes is on parole—and possession of a gun is a parole violation.

And that changed everything. The policeman drew his gun. He said—

BLACK COP: Okay, the next one to move is dead.

SUNNY: It all happened so fast, you know. I just ducked down to cover the kids.

(SFX: *four loud gunshots.*)

SUNNY: And then it was silence. I mean *dead silence*. There wasn't an earthly sound.

And then Rhodes runs around the front of the police car with a gun in his hand, and he's saying—

RHODES: Come on, we're gonna take the police car!

SUNNY: I mean, Rhodes had just killed two policemen, had a gun, and was telling us to get in the police car. And, you know, people say, "Why didn't you just refuse to go?" And I think, you've never been at the other end of a gun, have you?

So we get in the police car. We couldn't speak.

(SFX: *cars honking/helicopters.*)

SUNNY: We were kidnapped at that point, and we just didn't dare.

But then all of a sudden, the traffic gets terrible, and you can hear the helicopters, and I know there must be a roadblock. "Hey, we're gonna be *rescued*! Help is on the way, you know, the cavalry!"

And out of nowhere Rhodes makes a sharp left to try and avoid the roadblock—

(SFX: *heavy gunfire.*)

SUNNY:—and this whole line of policemen opens fire on the car. The car was literally bouncing with all the bullets. So again I cover the kids. And finally we crash.

(SFX: *crash/sirens.*)

SUNNY: And a bunch of cops surround us, and I'm trying to explain that we were kidnapped, but they just wouldn't listen.

(*Lights shift: we are now in* SUNNY's *interrogation room.*)

WHITE COP 1: All right. Sonia, or do you want me to call you Sunny?

SUNNY: It doesn't matter.

WHITE COP 2 (*Interrupting, to* SUNNY): Do you know what the date today is?

SUNNY: I think it's the twentieth.

WHITE COP 2: Is it Friday?

WHITE COP 1 (*jumping in*): Let me inject one thing here. Are you aware of the fact that you have been charged and arrested on first-degree murder?

SUNNY: (*beats*) You just told me now.

(*Lights down on* SUNNY *and* COPS, *up on* GARY.)

GARY: I took a polygraph test around midnight. They wouldn't let me sleep, wouldn't let me lie down—and the polygraph examiner said he cannot pass me because of flat lines due to *fatigue*. Well, *duh*, it's midnight, I'd been under questioning now for six hours, and my parents had just been *murdered*.

About one A.M., they got three or four photos of my parents with their heads pulled back, you could look down their throat, and the detective's yelling—

(*Lights up on* COPS.)

WHITE COP 1: How could you do this?

WHITE COP 2 (*Overlapping*): How could you kill this woman?

WHITE COP 1 (*Overlapping*): The person who gave birth to you!

(*Lights down on* COPS.)

GARY: And this is how the interrogation went. I was in such a vulnerable and suggestible state from finding my parents and not knowing what happened. I was emotionally distraught, I was physically exhausted. I was confused. I had fifteen cups of coffee. I was spaced out. And the police used that. They said they had all the evidence, they didn't even *need* my confession. They said they had bloody fingerprints, the weapon, everything.

I was brainwashed, man. They told me—

WHITE COP 1 and WHITE COP 2 (*In unison, very friendly*): We can't lie to you, or we'd lose our jobs.

GARY: They seemed very sincere too. Very believable. They started making me think I had a blackout and actually done it. I said, look, if I killed my parents I want to know about it.

So I said, okay, if I could construct the situation in my mind—[*Small beat.*] I finally volunteered to give what they call a "vision statement"—a hypothetical account of what I would have done if I had killed my parents—

COPS: To try and jog your memory.

GARY:—to try and jog my memory.

(*Lights down on* WHITE COP 2. GARY *begins "vision statement," trying to put it all together.*)

GARY: Well, I guess I would've gotten up that morning—

WHITE COP 1: (*Testifying on the stand. Sure of what he's saying. His lines overlap tightly with* GARY's—*in the following section, the actors should speak over the ends of each other's lines.*) The defendant stated that he got up that morning—

GARY: And my mom would've been out in the trailer—

WHITE COP 1:—and that he looked outside and saw his mother in the trailer.

GARY: Then I woulda gotten dressed—and I would've had to have a knife in my pocket or something—

WHITE COP 1: And he indicated he put his pants on, and he had a knife in his pants pocket.

GARY: I guess I would've gone over to the trailer she was in—

WHITE COP 1: Then he walked up to the trailer and stepped onto the porch.

GARY:—and walked in—

WHITE COP 1: He said he opened the door, he walked in.

GARY: I would've had to have reached out toward my mom—

WHITE COP 1: He reached up and he grabbed his mother with his left hand and cut her throat with his right.

(*Lights down on* WHITE COP 1.)

GARY (*Beat*): I never would've hurt her.

(*Lights shift.*)

GARY: They used that vision statement for a *confession*.

And they wouldn't let me say anything besides how I would've done it. Any time I tried to say anything else, they would just holler at me, and holler at me, and holler at me.

After I made the statement about my mom, I cried for about three minutes, and then I told them how I would have killed my father. And then I said, I *told* them, this is just hypothetical. I have absolutely no memory of any of this.

The autopsies showed that everything I said in those statements was wrong. But nothing was written down, nothing was recorded. At the trial, they said that I was never under arrest, I was free to go at any time, that I had voluntarily "chatted" with them for *twelve hours*, and then suddenly blurted out facts that only the killer would know.

(*Lights down on* GARY, *up on* DELBERT.)

DELBERT: Well, yeah, man, it definitely has an effect on you for people to lock you up: first of all, it shows you they have the power to do it, and then they tell you they're gonna kill you, you know, and you're inclined to believe them. (*Chuckles.*) So it definitely messes with your sense of personal power, you know what I'm saying?

(*Lights up on* SUNNY.)

SUNNY (*To audience*): So I actually did at first try to lie, and I told the cops I didn't know these people, I was just a hitchhiker. Stupid. Because of course they think you're lying because you did something. But I was just scared.

(*Lights shift: we are back in* SUNNY's *interrogation room.* COPS *keep the pressure intensely, relentlessly high on* SUNNY *throughout the following.*)

WHITE COP 2: Let me ask you point blankly: Who shot the highway patrolman and the other officer?
SUNNY: I don't know.
WHITE COP 1: Did you shoot the highway patrolman?
SUNNY: No!
WHITE COP 2: Sunny, did you shoot anyone?
SUNNY: No.
WHITE COP 1 (*Yelling*): DO YOU KNOW IF SOMEONE WAS SHOT?!
SUNNY: I'm *sorry*. People were shot. The patrolmen were shot and that's what this is all about—I don't know—

WHITE COP 2 (*Jumping down* SUNNY's *throat*): Well, how do you know that the two policemen are dead?

SUNNY: You said. That's what we're here for.

WHITE COP 2: Okay. We advised you that they were dead because we had— (*Continues to talk over* SUNNY's *next line.*)

SUNNY: I didn't see. I didn't see—

WHITE COP 2 (*Talking over her*):— we had to read you your rights and it's imperative that you relate the facts of this to the best of your ability. Something caused you to be very disturbed. What was that something?

SUNNY (*Breaking down*): This is very upsetting because how does—this guy, he told—he just told us to sit in the car, you know—and I'll stay here and I won't make any calls and I—I haven't done anything except the wrong choice of people and I—

WHITE COP 1 (*Very close to* SUNNY): But you do want to cooperate with the state of Florida?

SUNNY: Yeah, I—

WHITE COP 2: You're not *being* too cooperative because you're saying a lot of things you don't even remember and yet you were there. You were there, Sunny.

SUNNY: I'm sorry, I—I know but I never had anything like this happen to me before. I just—I don't want to be blamed for something that I had nothing to do with and I don't want them to take the kids away and I—'cause the baby's crying and crying and crying and Eric's scared and I—I do want to help. I—

WHITE COP 1: All right, Sunny, I want you to help us.

SUNNY: Because I don't—I don't know what this guy was up to and I don't want to be pulled into it, but do you understand I'm trying to cooperate with—

WHITE COP 1 (*Condescending to her*): Yes, sweetheart, I fully understand this.

SUNNY: And if I can't tell you everything you need to know, please don't be angry with me.

WHITE COP 2: Okay, okay. (*Beat.*) Is there anything you care to add to your statement at this time?

SUNNY: I can't think of anything, but if I do I will.

WHITE COP 1 (*An accusation*): All right, are the answers you've given true and accurate to the best of your knowledge? (*Beat, as* SUNNY *considers whether to tell the truth. Then, yelling:*) ANSWER ME!

SUNNY: (*Lying*) Yes.

(Lights down on COPS; *we are out of* SUNNY'S *interrogation room.)*

SUNNY: And what I didn't know, was at the same moment I was being questioned and Jesse was being questioned, what that Rhodes, from his hospital bed, was negotiating a deal. He'd been in prison before, he knew how the system worked. And so he was claiming that he didn't do it— we did.

STATE ATTORNEY: Okay, Mr. Rhodes. Who had the gun in their hands when the first shot was fired?

RHODES *(Overly helpful)*: When the gun first went off, Sonia was the one holding the gun. *(Then, scrambling)*: This is to the best of my knowledge, I am not one hundred percent sure. To the best of my knowledge, she fired two shots, I believe then Jesse pulled the gun from her and shot him one more time and then he shot the other cop twice.

STATE ATTORNEY: Let me recap this now. To the best of your recollection, Sonia fired?

RHODES: First.

STATE ATTORNEY: It is your testimony here that Sonia fired the first three shots at the Florida highway patrolman?

RHODES: Either the first two or three.

STATE ATTORNEY: Two, or three?

RHODES: Two for sure.

STATE ATTORNEY: And then what took place?

RHODES: Then I started to go toward my car, to get in, it didn't even enter into my mind, but Jesse said get in the police car, we have got to get out of here or something and I said, "No," you know, "what happened?!" Anyway I did get in the police car, I was damn near in shock myself.

STATE ATTORNEY: Thank you.

RHODES: No problem.

(Lights down on RHODES *and* ATTORNEY, *up on* DELBERT.)*

DELBERT: So I'm sitting there in Mississippi. After a couple days of being locked up, I decided I would waive extradition. Now this was because of my spiritual growth. A friend of mine has something he calls his "nigger radar," right, which sort of alerts him when, as he quotes Darth Vader, when there's a "disturbance in the force."

But I'm operating on another thing, you know, cause a lotta the *tension* I had felt regarding race had sorta been washed away. I had achieved some sort of spiritual . . . plateau, if you will, by living out on the road.

I wasn't expecting any problems. I had been befriended by all kinda people—mostly white folks, cause there weren't no black folks around. I hitchhiked across Texas, which is as big as Russia, you know what I'm sayin? And I got *one* ride from a brother. Brother picked me up, he said—

(*Lights up on* BLACK GUY.)

BLACK GUY 1: Man, you know brothers don't hitchhike out here too much.
DELBERT: I know, but I don't have any money, what am I gonna do?

(*Lights down on* BLACK GUY.)

DELBERT: Anyway, I waived extradition to Florida, meaning I voluntarily went back. If I hadn't done that, I don't think I would've ever gone to death row, 'cause the state of Florida really didn't have a case. Nobody had seen me there, there was no connection between me and the place where the crime occurred, fingerprints, none a that—cause I wasn't there.

And in Florida, as in most places, the jury is chosen from the voting records—and this is 1974, black people had only had the right to vote since 1965, and this is a backwater town where it's run sorta like a plantation and the folks in charge are the folks in charge, right?

And as I sometimes tell people, if you're accused of a sex crime in the South and you're black—you probably shoulda done it, you know, 'cause your ass is gonna be guilty. And they found me guilty.

(*Lights up on courtroom;* SFX: *gavel.*)

ROBERT'S JUDGE (*Thick Southern accent*): [*Bangs gavel*] Gentlemen, you have the right to remain silent. Anything you say can and will be used against you in a court of law. If you cannot afford an attorney, one will be appointed for you. Does everyone understand that? (*Beat.*)

You can answer that question. (*Small beat.*) Yes? (*Murmurs from seated group.*) Good. Robert Hayes.
COURT ATTORNEY: He's in the first chair, Your Honor.
JUDGE: Mr. Hayes. (*No response. Beat.*) Mr. Hayes.

ROBERT (*Very softly; head down*): Yeah.

COURT ATTORNEY: Your Honor, he hears the court. He just doesn't want to
    show his face to the cameras, which is—

JUDGE: I want him to respond to me. Mr.—

ROBERT (*Looking up*): I *said* yes.

JUDGE: Okay. Mr. Hayes, you're charged with murder in the first degree. We
    find probable cause the accused committed the offense. He'll be held
    on no bond.

COURT ATTORNEY: Your Honor, Mr. Hayes has indicated that he does not wish
    to speak to anyone from law enforcement without an attorney present.

JUDGE: Okay, Mr. Hayes, can you afford a lawyer?

ROBERT: No.

JUDGE: Are you employed?

ROBERT: I *was.*

JUDGE: Do you own any property?

ROBERT: No.

JUDGE: Do you have any bank accounts?

ROBERT: No.

JUDGE: Do you have an automobile?

ROBERT: No.

JUDGE: The court will find that Mr. Hayes is indigent. Appoint the public de-
    fender to represent him

(SFX: *gavel.*)

COURT ATTORNEY: Thank you.

(*Lights down on courtroom.*)

DELBERT: This is a weird country, man, it really is. It always amazes me when
    I talk about this. I say, "How do you figure this, now: all these guys, they
    been to Vanderbilt and to Yale and to Princeton and Harvard and shit,
    they look at the same information and they come up with diametrically
    opposite conclusions. Figure that out."
        So it doesn't have anything to do with one's intelligence, it has to do
    with one's preconceptions, with one's *tendencies,* and how one looks at
    other human *beings*—you see, *that's* what it's about.

(*Lights down on* DELBERT; *up on* KERRY *and his* PROSECUTION.)

KERRY: So they had a lead that the victim's boyfriend, Professor Whitfield, might have done the murder. But they didn't go after him, they went after me. They said the crime was done by a homosexual maniacal murderer who hated women. The prosecution accused me of bein' a homosexual—before the jury—

PROSECUTION (*Thick Texan accent*): A young woman lies in her grave not far from this courtroom, butchered, because of Kerry Max Cook's warped homosexual lust for blood and perversion—

DEFENSE: Objection, Your Honor. The defendant's alleged homosexuality has nothing to do with the allegations in the murder indictment.

JUDGE: Objection will be overruled.

DEFENSE: We would then request an instruction to the jury that they cannot consider—

JUDGE:—that motion is also overruled—

DEFENSE: We would then request the Court to declare a mistrial in this case—

JUDGE:—*Overruled*. Proceed, Counsel.

PROSECUTION: Thank you. Your Honor.

(*To audience: with crescendoing fervor*) Ladies and gentlemen of the jury. I would be remiss in my duty if I did not show you every last grotesque detail, because the killer sits right before you in this courtroom and it is time for twelve good people from this country to put that man on the scrap heap of humanity where he belongs. He has a warped perversion and he will not reason with you. The victim was a young woman just beginning to realize her dreams and he butchered her body. This is the kind of sick perversion that turns Kerry Max Cook on.

You people have no right to even submit prison guards to the kind of risk that man poses. Think about it. Do you want to give this pervert his butcher knife back? Now, we must look upon it as putting a sick animal to sleep. Kerry Max Cook has forfeited his right to walk among us. He no longer has rights.

So let's let all the freaks and perverts and murderous homosexuals of the world know what we do with them in a court of justice. That we take their lives.

(*Lights out on* KERRY *and* PROSECUTION; *up on* SUNNY.)

SUNNY: My husband Jesse was tried first, and he had a past record, from when he was seventeen years old, and his trial lasted four days. We both had, of course, no good attorneys, no dream team, no expert witnesses, and so he was convicted, and sentenced to death.

My trial came later. I thought, surely that won't happen to *me*, I mean, I was a hippie, I'm one of those peace-and-love people, I'm a *vegetarian*! How could you possibly think I would kill someone?

And so I thought I'd go in, they'd figure out I didn't kill anyone, and they'd let it go. But that's not how it works. There was prosecutorial misconduct, there was hiding of evidence that would have proven I didn't do it; the jury wasn't even allowed to know that Rhodes accepted a plea bargain of three life sentences in exchange for his testimony! Now, I don't think three life sentences is a bargain. Nobody *I* know would think it's a bargain . . .

And I didn't have any investigators, I didn't have any expert witnesses, I didn't have thousands of dollars. My parents said, "Well, you know, we were told we could try and get you a better lawyer, but you *have* a lawyer, they've *appointed* you one, so it's okay." We didn't know.

(Lights down on SUNNY; *up on* DAVID, *his* PROSECUTION *and* DEFENSE, *sparring verbally.)*

DAVID'S PROSECUTION: The state respectfully submits to this jury that in that grocery store, David Keaton actually fired at Sheriff Carroll in order to come to the assistance of his co-defendant, who was in the process of cold-bloodedly murdering and killing Officer Khomas Revels. It's just as clear and simple as that. As a matter of fact, that is actually the truth.

DAVID'S DEFENSE: It was a quiet and peaceful Sunday night before David Keaton, then eighteen years old, was speedily whisked away to Quincy Jail. He was not told the reason for his arrest, nor was his family informed.

PROSECUTION: They're gonna tell you that all of Keaton's answers were suggested by the officers, that he was framed. Not by one officer, now; not by two officers; but by three or more state and county law enforcement officers.

DEFENSE: He was questioned without benefit of counsel, despite his request to his interrogators to call his mother and obtain legal assistance. At eleven P.M. Keaton was taken to the jail in Tallahassee, where questioning resumed and continued until the next morning.

PROSECUTION: Now, Keaton could have said in his statement anything he wanted to. There was nobody making those defendants say anything, and this jury knows anyway that of course that would be impossible, impractical. You just can't *make* somebody say something; nobody can!

DEFENSE: There is a law in this state that any person arrested shall be taken without delay and have the charges read in open court. The defendant was arrested on a Sunday. Well, this courthouse is open on Monday, and it's open on Tuesday, Wednesday, Thursday too. The defendant was not taken before a judge until Friday, although he had been arrested the Sunday before.

Now, I have nothing but respect for the deputy sheriffs, but I recognize, too, that it was a member of their staff that was killed. Wouldn't it be understandable for them to be more—*emotionally involved* in the investigation?

(Lights down on DAVID, PROSECUTION, *and* DEFENSE; *up on* SUNNY.*)*

SUNNY: They tell you exactly how they're gonna do it. They're gonna send 2,200 volts of electricity through your body until you're dead. And then they ask you if you have anything to say to that, and really, it's kind of dumbfounding. So after the judge read the sentence, I just said, "Are you finished?" I didn't have anything to say. What do you say? How can you say anything to that?

(SFX: cell door slamming shut.)

DELBERT: I don't remember any of my dreams from when I was on death row. I almost never recall my dreams, which I am absolutely fascinated by.

When I was at the University of Chicago, I took part in a laboratory experiment. They were running a test to see if creative people's dreams differ from those who are less creative. And so, of course, it appealed to the ego in me, thinking somebody thought I was creative.

So you go to bed in the lab and they are monitoring your respiration and your REM and so forth. And they would wake me up over the microphone and it always sounded to me like one of the Nazi doctors, 'cause he had an accent, you know, he would be like, "MISTA TIBBS, YOU VERE DREAMINK." And I wanted to say, "No shit."

But the fascinating thing was, when the motherfuckers hooked me up—they put the receptors by your ears, right exactly at the same place they do when they're getting ready to execute your ass.

(Lights down on DELBERT, *up on* SUNNY.)

SUNNY: Instead of sending me to be Jesse's cellmate, they decided to clear out an entire disciplinary unit at the women's prison. It's a very old prison, it's like a dungeon-type place. It was six steps from the door to the toilet bowl—you could stretch out your arms and touch both walls. They take your clothes, they give you a number, so basically they're taking—who you *are* from you. You no longer have a name, you're a number, you're locked inside this *tomb*. It's like you're thrown to the bottom of the well.

(Lights down on SUNNY, *up on* DAVID.)

DAVID: There was one woman, lived across the street when I was a little boy, she had a goiter on her neck. And I was sayin', "Lord, if I only had the power of the Spirit, I would go lay my hands on her and her illness would disappear." And that's all I want, just to let the Spirit be operatin' through me, whether it be knowledge, discernment, speak the word or whatever. *(To God.)* I would love to just do that before I die.

I had a relationship to God when I got in here, but somehow I've lost it. I guess I'm still reachin' out to find it—you know, I said some nights now I wanna light me a couple candles, lay back and just meditate, 'cause they say the kingdom of God is within you, isn't it? You know, everybody lookin' for something outward, but then, that light's *within* you, that voice we speak to . . . *(Whispering God's voice.)*: "C'mon, boy."

Give you the chills when I say that, right?

(Lights down on DAVID, *up on* KERRY.)

KERRY: You know, when I was in there, I saw 141 guys go down. All's I got to do is pick up the newspaper, turn on the news, "such and such becomes the two-hundred-twenty-second inmate executed resulting from capital punishment"—and I hear the name and I say, "Oh my God," 'cause I know him, I mean, I don't just *know* him, I *ate* with him, I *cried* with him, we used to play basketball and talk about, "man, you're gonna go free."

You know, I got a book, a book about Texas death row, and seriously, this book is what, five years old, and everyone in here has been executed. I can go through that book, one by one, and point out every face in here that's gone.

VOICE-OVER/INMATE: Executed.

(SFX: *switch being thrown.*)

VOICE-OVER/INMATE: Executed.

(SFX: *switch being thrown.*)

VOICE-OVER/INMATE: Executed.

(SFX: *switch being thrown.*)

KERRY: And you know, at a capital trial, the prosecutors always say, "He's dangerous, he's a maniac, the sick, twisted murderer." But I'm no different from you—I mean, I wasn't a street thug, I wasn't trash, I came from a good family—if it happened to me, man, it can happen to anyone.

(*Lights down on* KERRY, *up on* GARY.)

GARY: I was in X-house—the execution house. That place was like somethin' out of a movie. There were no guards. They would just open your cell door and let you run around. I guess they figured, you were gonna die anyway, so why not.

So you can walk around through this dimly lit series of corridors, and through the observation room, into the execution room. That's where the phone was that all of us used. Which was also the phone that the governor would use to call in and stop an execution.

The whole place was run by gangs, you know, there was ongoing warfare between the different factions. And the only gang open to white guys was the Northsiders—which is basically made up of the Aryan Nation and the Skinheads. So I had no gang protection. So I kept to myself a lot. Killed a lot of time on my own.

One way I killed time, was I found a sewing needle stuck in a concrete wall. Somebody had smuggled it in. So I taught myself embroidery.

You'd take extra clothing—the blue jeans made real good blue thread. And I was lucky—I had kept my old yellow jumpsuit that they gave me to wear when I first went in. So that gave me yellow. You take your sheet apart, that gives you white. So I had three colors of thread, just from unraveling cloth. I made myself a tote bag I'd take to chow hall, and I embroidered flowers on it. I put bell-bottoms on a couple of my prison blues, made a Calvin and Hobbes patch I put on my hat. They confiscated that one.

(Lights down on GARY, up on ROBERT.)

ROBERT: The electric chair was downstairs and I was upstairs, and every Wednesday morning they cranked that electric chair up and you could hear it buzz.

And when they served breakfast, you gotta have sharp ears to hear that front door open, 'cause if you oversleep, the roaches and the rats come and eat your breakfast, and that's the God's honest truth.

And the guards—I think nine times out of ten, the average person that became a guard, the only way I can see it, when he grew up he was a little runt and then the bigger guy would mess with him and all of that. And then they grow up and they wanna do that, too.

When I was in there, one day, this officer was harassing my neighbor and I was a witness. And the other inmate, he wanted to write the officer up, he asked me—

BLACK INMATE: Hey Robert, would you sign this statement?

ROBERT: I said, I told him, yeah.

But a couple of days later, the officer came back to work, and something just told me to pay attention to him.

(Lights up on WHITE GUARD.)

ROBERT: And sure enough, this officer, he read that statement, he gonna get back at me. He gonna spit off in my tea. And I *seen* him spit off in my tea. And so I said—*(To guard)*: "Now why would you do that?"

WHITE GUARD: Do what? I didn't do that.

ROBERT: Hold on, I'm gonna prove it to you.

(To audience): And I went and got me a piece of toilet paper—*(Miming)*: twisted it up, and put it directly on top of that tea. And I went 'round it. And I said—

(To guard): "Now what is that? You can have my tea. You can take that shit back. MOTHERFUCKER."

(Lights down on GUARD; lights shift on ROBERT.)

ROBERT *(With increasing intensity)*: Robert E. Hayes, #95-19817, May 21, 1996.

Judge Kaplan,

I am writing to you in regards to some matters which I am having in this jail. The superintendent declines to answer any of my grievances so I am makin' you aware of this before I get charged this time for something I DID do. The problem is this Officer Santiago, who has constantly been provoking me. He come into my cell and toss my legal papers around, just tryin' to provoke me to fight him.

And today, he got classification to relocate me to the day room of a special wing for drug offenders. And by law they isn't supposed to have anyone sleeping in the day room no matter what wing it's in.

With my luck, some other inmate, some snitch, will get one of my legal briefs while I am sleeping, call the state, say Robert Hayes confessed to me so he can get himself a deal, and say "if you let me out I'll testify against him." And you, Judge Kaplan, will believe that fuck shit.

So Judge, I am askin' you to grant me an order stating that me and the stated officer be kept away from one another, because I am *not* goin' to take *any more* of his *bullshit*!!!

(Small beat.) But thank you for your time. I'm sure I'll see you on another charge if you refuse to keep Santiago away from me.

Robert Hayes.

(Light up on GEORGIA.*)*

GEORGIA: And, okay, some snitch *did* get a hold of one of his legal briefs. Just like Robert said.

(Lights down on ROBERT *and* GEORGIA; *up on* KERRY.*)*

KERRY: So, uh, they accused me of bein' a homosexual, and that got into the media that got to death row even before I got there, so in prison, uh, uh—I was uh, uh—*(Pause.)*—I had three guys pull a train on me . . . and they raped me, and sodomized me, and they carved "good p-u-s-s-y" on my behind. And it's there all over my body, its cut so deep I can't, plastic surgery won't remove it, it's not a tattoo, and I attempted suicide a couple times with this whole little war I was fighting: on the one side, the criminal justice system, and then on the Western front I'm fighting with fear of my life with these inmates every day.

(*Lights up on* DELBERT.)

DELBERT: Needless to say, Job is one of my favorite Biblical figures.

(*Lights down on* KERRY.)

DELBERT: I don't know if I have the patience of Job—but I hope I have his faith. Even if you got a teeny weeny bit, it's big. The shit is hard to come by, you know what I'm sayin'?

But faith or not, I realized a long time ago, if I internalized all the anger, and all the pain, and all the hurt, I'd be dead already—they wouldn't even have to execute me.

(*Lights down on* DELBERT, *up on* DAVID.)

DAVID: When I was inside, one time, I felt this feelin' came over me where I felt the longin' of God for his people, I felt his love for his people, his desire for his people not to be cast aside. You know, I felt all this, and here I was on death row. It was so heavy. God, it was a burden on me.

And I was feelin' all this, and we went outside for recreation, and in the yard out there you have a little basketball court, shuffleboard court, and there's a curtain up with the electric chair showin'. You look right up there, you can see the chair. You know, even if you playin', they gotta remind you that you still gonna die, 'cause here's the chair.

(SFX: *thunderclap and rain.*)

DAVID: But then it starts stormin', man—

I looked up, raise my hand and I said, "In the name of Jesus, I command this rain to stop."

(SFX: *"swoosh" and rain stops.*)

This guy says, "Man, you do it one more time, I'm gonna become a believer!" So it started again—

(SFX: *thunder and rain.*)

So I said it again, "In the name of Jesus, I command this rain to stop."

(SFX: *"swoosh" and rain stops.*)

It stopped. He said, "Man, you do it *one more time*—"
So it started back . . . same thing.

(SFX: *thunder and rain.*)

"In the name of Jesus, I command this rain to stop."

(SFX: *"swoosh" and rain stops.*)

But this time he didn't say nothin. He just looked at me like "Hmmm,"
you know.

But it didn't rain anymore, until we finished playin', and we had to go
back inside. And when the last man stepped through the door, the whole
world just burst open.

(SFX: *thunder and rain.*)

It rained for the rest of the night.

(*Lights down on* DAVID, *up on* SUNNY. *Rain fades slowly over the beginning of*
SUNNY's *speech.*)

SUNNY: I have fifteen years' worth of letters between me and Jesse. I saved not
only the letters, but the envelopes, because anything that he touched, or
that he wrote on, or that he licked with his tongue, I was keeping. I
didn't even read his letters when I first got them; I would carry 'em
around with me for a while. Just to hold it. I'd see if he put the stamp on
right side up or upside down. That was part of his message too.

And then I'd open it and I wouldn't read it for content; I would just
look at it to see: did he look like he was happy when he wrote it, or sad.
Did the writing slant upward or downward. Oh, it's big round open letters, he must have been having a good day. Oh, it's very tight writing, I
can see he must have been having some problems. I would just savor the
whole thing, and *then* I'd read it.

We carried on a fairly full life in our letters, actually, including our sex
life. Oh yeah. (*Laughter.*) You know, you have to send your letters out
unsealed so that they can read them to see that there's no escape plans

or whatever. So we got ourselves little Japanese dictionaries, and we used the Japanese language for our lovemaking, because we wanted to have some privacy.

(*Lights up on* JESSE.)

JESSE: September 30, 1976
My Dearest Sunny,
I love you. It's about 11 P.M. now. I'm sitting here on my bunk. The TV is on with the sound off and on the channel that is just fuzzy so that I can use it for light. I'm reading *King Lear* and *Hamlet*, if you can believe that. I've been studying too much law lately and need to give my head something relaxing too. I received your beautiful letter and . . . two pictures of the kids. We're so lucky. I love you so much. You're my woman, as close as my breath. You're the strongest female I've ever known. Hand and glove, you know?
     Never be lonesome, we're only separated by miles. This won't last either, believe that. I sure would like to speak to you alone, let's say for a few hours—
Hito banju kimyo ikasatai.
Kimito ito tsuni nandi tai.
My place or yours. And don't worry, I'm on the case, lover.
I love you, Mama.
Jesse

(*Lights down on* JESSE.)

SUNNY: And so we had this life, you know; this little world together. I existed on those letters.

(*Lights down on* SUNNY, *up on* KERRY.)

KERRY: I was holding on for my brother—I can't tell you how close we were, he wasn't just a big brother. I *worshipped* him, he was my *role model*, he was everything I wasn't—he didn't smoke pot, he made straight A's in school—and I was the black sheep of the family. My brother was always trying to rescue me, very strict on me—

(*Lights up on* DOYLE.)

DOYLE: No, Kerry. I'm gonna *lose* you, I'm gonna *lose* you, you're gonna get hurt—

KERRY: —and then there I was, sitting on death row.

He was taking up for me my whole life. I was just always a real soft sensitive person, you know, and I guess I had so many girlfriends cause I was so sensitive, I don't mean girlfriends like girls *sexually*, I mean friends that are girls.

And so my brother—the last time I touched him was at the Smith County jail—he reached in and held my hand and was crying and said—

DOYLE: It's not over, Kerry, 'cause you're not gonna die, you're gonna get out.

KERRY: I was the baby of the family and my brother would come visit me and I would have these black eyes and stuff, you know, and he said—

DOYLE: I want you to tell me who did this to you, I'm going to talk to the warden.

KERRY (*To* DOYLE): "You don't understand, you'll get me killed, that's called snitching, that's the worst thing you can do."

(*To audience.*) So I forced my brother—when he thought he could help me, I took that away from him, too, saying, "you can't help me, I'm on my own now." And so, uh—[*Pause.*]—he started drinking.

The guy had it all, man, he was a senior supervisor at this huge corporation company, and he fell into a bottle, lost his wife, lost his kids, he'd sit around in a dark room and get drunk and talk about his little brother, why isn't he coming home. He put himself right on death row with me.

And he's workin' as an assistant manager at a McDonald's in downtown Jacksonville, and there's this guy named Jeff works there. Jeff said that my brother liked him because my brother told him—

JEFF and KERRY: You're a lot like my little brother Kerry.

KERRY: —and that's how they got to be friends.

So anyway, one night after work they go to this club in Tyler, Texas, and they're shooting pool. You know how you get when you're drinking beer and you're hot with the stick.

And right now it's closing and my brother's running the table on this one last guy—and he says to Jeff—

DOYLE: You go, I'll be out there in a minute.

KERRY: And Jeff's walking out of the club, and there were these two black guys sitting on the table, and one of them's wearing sunglasses, and Jeff reaches up—he's just playing—takes the glasses and puts them on—

(JEFF *mimics Stevie Wonder.*)

KERRY: —and mimics Stevie Wonder. And the guy says—

BLACK GUY 2: Say, what's up on you, man?

KERRY: —and this guy jumps off the table and gets real aggressive, and he's like—

BLACK GUY 2: I'm gonna bring a world of hurt to him.

KERRY: And so about this time my brother walks up and says—

DOYLE: Hey, hey, man—

KERRY: My brother's really laid-back, you know, he wasn't a violent dude—I mean, he was a real laid-back, compassionate person. But Jeff just says—

JEFF: Man, fuck these people.

KERRY: And walks out. So my brother follows him outside.

(Beat. Lights shift.)

KERRY: It's December 27, 1997, it's really cold that night, and my brother and Jeff are both trying to get in the car but the locks are frozen, and this pickup truck pulls up behind my brother, and Jeff says—

JEFF: Hey—watch out!

KERRY: My brother turns around and this guy, he got out of the truck with his hand behind his back and he says—

BLACK GUY 2: Whatcha gonna do for me, white boy, you gonna call me nigger? Whatcha gonna do for me?

KERRY: There was all kinds of people standing around, and my brother told him—

DOYLE: Hey, look man, we've all been drinking tonight—this is nothin' to have no misunderstanding about, tomorrow morning you're gonna wake up and laugh about this.

KERRY: And he says—

BLACK GUY 2: Fuck you, man.

KERRY: —and he brings from around his back a big ol' forty-four magnum and he shoots him—

(SFX: loud, long gunshot.)

KERRY: —and uh, uh, my brother—so weird, man—he rose up and stood up, and Jeff walked over to him and he couldn't even tell he was shot, his eyes were fixated looking straight ahead, and Jeff said—

JEFF: Man, you okay? Man, you okay?

KERRY: —and blood started pouring out of my brother's nose and he fell . . . and he died on that parking lot.

And uh . . . [*Pause.*] with me being on death row, the DA was reluctant to take it to trial—she said the defense would claim that my brother had bragged that he had a brother on death row and he was bad.

And so they got my mom and dad to agree to a plea bargain, and the guy who killed my brother got ten years. And he got out in three.

My mother would look me in the eye and tell me that I'm responsible for my brother's murder. That if it weren't for me going to death row, he'd still be here. She would tell me that. I know it's going to sound corny there, but—and I mean it—every day that goes by I wished I could tell him how much I love him. So while you've got it, man, never take it for granted, 'cause you never know.

(*Lights down on* KERRY, *up on* SUNNY.)

SUNNY: First I had to decide: "this is bullshit, I am not going to let them do this to me." 'Cause if you sit there, rubbing two sticks together and crying on your sticks, they're never gonna make a spark. But, you know, if you stop feeling sorry for yourself, just because you're determined not to believe in hopelessness, then a spark happens, and then you just keep fanning that little spark until you got a flame.

And I realized that it was like a big trick. That I wasn't just a little lump of flesh that they could put in a cage. And I decided that I would have faith, that there was some power out there greater than them, to which I could make my appeal.

Now, you people that don't believe, you could say I was like Dumbo and I put this feather in my nose and I flew because I could fly anyway.

Or you could say that there is really something out there and that if we have faith in it and we appeal to it, it will answer us—and maybe we're both right. I don't know.

(*Lights down on* SUNNY, *up on* ROBERT.)

ROBERT: Well, see, before I went to prison, I had a dream about prison—and I seen death row, I seen the inside, and I seen myself get out. And 'cause a that dream, I always said, I'm gonna get a new trial. And sure enough, one day, I get awakened by all this commotion. All the inmates, they get up in the vents, hollerin—

ALL MEN (*Ad lib*): Man, you got a new trial! Damn, Robert, you gonna go free! You on the radio! Turn on the radio! [*Etc.*]

CELLMATE: Put the radio on!

ROBERT: Well, I put the radio on.

> And later that day, my lawyer came, and she said to me—

FEMALE LAWYER: Now, you know, Robert, if you lose, you can go back to death row.

ROBERT: And I said—(*To lawyer*): "Well, now, accordin' to that dream, I'm gonna go free."

> And she said—

FEMALE LAWYER (*To ROBERT*): You gonna put all your trust in a dream?

ROBERT: And I said, "Yep." (*Small beat.*)

> My lawyer had found a record that said that in the girl's hand when she died was some white people hair, red hair, sixteen inches long. So they said—

PROSECUTION: When you were strangling this girl, she reached up and pulled her own hair!!!

ROBERT: (*To PROSECUTION*): Hold on.

> [*To audience.*] Now, when you come up behind me and you strangle me, are you gonna pull your own hair? Or are you gonna pull the hair of whoever back there behind you?

GEORGIA: Okay?!

ROBERT (*To PROSECUTION*): You can have a seat.

(*PROSECUTION sits down.*)

ROBERT (*To audience*): And we all knew this white guy, her ex-boyfriend. He had been asking the girl for a date, telling her—

EX-BOYFRIEND: Why you keep hanging out with all them blacks?

ROBERT: And he asked her that *same night*—

EX-BOYFRIEND: We gonna go out?

ROBERT: And she said, "We ain't."

> And so my lawyer, she found out the cops had that hair, she found the guy. He got up and testified at my appeal.
>
> So my lawyer ask him—

FEMALE LAWYER: Back in 1990, what color was your hair, and how long was it?

ROBERT: And by then he had short hair, salt and pepper, you know, and he said—

EX-BOYFRIEND *(On the stand)*: My hair was the same color and length back
    then as it is now.

ROBERT: And my lawyer said—

FEMALE LAWYER: Are you sure?

EX-BOYFRIEND: Of course I'm sure.

ROBERT: So my lawyer pulls out this envelope. And she said—

FEMALE LAWYER: Again in 1990, do you remember having your picture taken
    near the racetrack?

EX-BOYFRIEND: Uh, yeah.

ROBERT: And then she pulled that big ol' photograph picture out and showed it
    to him. And there he was, his hair red and brown and sixteen inches long
    on the picture.

(ROBERT looks to GEORGIA.)

ROBERT and GEORGIA: Okay?!

(Lights down on ROBERT, GEORGIA, EX-BOYFRIEND, and LAWYER; up on KERRY.)

KERRY: So then after I've been on death row for twenty-two years, they find
    this DNA evidence, you know, and the prosecution says that this will be
    the final nail in Kerry Max Cook's coffin: "We'll show the world once and
    for all that he committed that murder." And then the results come in and
    it did just the opposite, it finally took the nail out of my coffin, told the
    world the truth—that that was Professor Whitfield's DNA they found
    on that girl. And he's still out. They never even went after him. He's been
    walking around a free man, laughing at the system for twenty-two years.
        Twenty-two years.

(Lights down on KERRY, up on GARY.)

GARY: About halfway through my time on death row, a lawyer named Larry
    Marshall took on my case. He's at Northwestern, he works with a bunch
    of law students on wrongful convictions. My twin sister found out about
    him and went down there literally through a blinding snowstorm to see
    if he would take me on. And he said yes.
        Man, that was like the cavalry coming.
        Once he started working on it, Larry found out about this motorcycle
    gang called the Outlaws. Guys gained entrance into the gang by per-

forming violent acts: they killed a bunch of people, they bombed the Hell's Angels—they just did a lot of stuff. And the federal government, the ATF, was running wiretaps on them. Well, in 1995, the ATF got a videotaped confession from an Outlaw guy saying he killed my parents. But I wasn't released until 1996. And that whole year in between, they were fighting my appeal. They fought it all the way to the Illinois Supreme Court.

The two guys who killed my parents were just found guilty last year.

But I've been adamant that those guys not get the death penalty. Some people think that's stupid, but why would I want them to die? It's not gonna bring my parents back. No good's gonna come from it.

(Lights down on GARY; *up on* SUNNY *and* RHODES.*)*

SUNNY *(To audience)*: In 1979, Walter Rhodes wrote the following letter to the judge.

RHODES: I, Walter Norman Rhodes, hereby depose and say that I am under no duress nor coercion to execute this affidavit. This statement is made freely and voluntarily, and to purge myself before my Creator.

Briefly. On February 20, 1976, at approximately 7:15 A.M. I did, in fact, shoot to death two law enforcement officers with a 9 mm Browning pistol.

I state emphatically and unequivocally that my previous testimony against Jesse Tafero and Sonia Jacobs was *false* and part of the statements I was instructed to make by the Assistant State Attorney, who did coerce me into lying.

I took a polygraph examination relative to this case, but owing to the fact that I am a student of Yoga and Karaté, and have been for the last ten years, I passed it. And can pass any such test, in my opinion.

The foregoing statements are true and correct to the best of my knowledge and belief. I so swear.

Walter Norman Rhodes, Jr., 9 November 1979.

(Lights down on RHODES.*)*

SUNNY: Keep in mind that I wasn't released until 1992.

So I'll just give you a moment to reflect: from 1976 to 1992, just remove that entire chunk from your life, and that's what happened. *(Long pause, the length of a six count.)*

But after all that, one day, the guard came into my cell and told me I was getting out. I thought he was trying to trick me.

(SFX: *cell door opening;* SUNNY *takes it in.*)

SUNNY: And it was just so *joyous.* I mean, I know a lot of people are angry, and I was angry some, but I didn't want to waste my time be-ing mad.

At first I did everything that Jesse and I said we were going to do together. I went to New York City, I went to the bookstore we said we were going to go to, I bought the book we said we were going to buy to make our Japanese gardens. I was doing it all for both of us.

(*Lights down on* SUNNY; *up on* DELBERT.)

DELBERT: When I first got out, I was numb. I didn't sleep for the first three days. I couldn't. And on death row, I had slept like a baby every night.

My first day home, they threw a party at my brother's house. My brother. He gave me his bed for the night, you know with a red velvet coverlet on it and everything. And one of the sisters from the defense committee—she spent the night with me—which was nice, you know.

But I just couldn't get the fuck to sleep, man, and I guess around the third night I began hallucinating, and one of my friends said, let me call my pastor and ask him to pray for you. And I talked to the pastor, and he said some kind of prayer and I laid down and went straight to sleep. I haven't had any problems sleeping since then.

After that, the main adjustment was just learning to feel again. You know, when you're in prison, you can't allow yourself to feel too much. So when you get out, you've gotta practice. I had to practice a bunch to be human again. To remind me.

(*Lights down on* DELBERT, *up on* DAVID.)

DAVID: Maybe I'm still in there, in a way. 'Cause after I was out, I would go to work, I would come home, I would shut the door, and I would lock it. Just like in prison. Go to work, go to the store, come home, lock the door, click. Then one day I saw. "What're you doing, lockin' the door?" I say. "Don't you know you're free now? You're not in lockup anymore, man— you're free!"

Prison took away that—spark for life, okay, 'cause in my old pictures from high school, I can see in my face—I'm smilin, you know. And now that's somethin' people round here don't see me do too much, smile.

(SFX: *Rain.* DAVID *looks up, acknowledges the rain. Halfheartedly:*)

In the name of J—

(*Rain does not stop. Another half try:*)

In the name of Jesus—

(*Rain does not stop. It continues softly under the following and slowly fades.*)

Prison really did somethin' to me.

And now, I do a lot of things—like I may drink, okay, and I smoke some marijuana—to cocaine, to crack cocaine. A perfect day, to me, would be, just to get plastered, you know, to forget. 'Cause now I'm tryin' to find out who I am, and if I smoke a joint of reefer, it takes me to that point where I can sit down and write me some poetry or whatever, just like I useta do.

But what are you gonna do? I mean, if they're in power and you have no power, then you're through. Bein' little is like bein' up next to a large oak tree and you just a little small pine. (*Beat.*)

That's why, like I said, I really gotta get back into a spirituality thing and focus on findin' that light within . . . 'cause that's all I really got, you know.

(*Lights down on* DAVID; *up on* KERRY *and* SANDRA.)

SANDRA: Actually, I am not a bleeding-heart liberal at all, as a matter of fact I had a family member murdered and I was always a believer in the death penalty—

KERRY: She's a scientist—

SANDRA: But I was on the board of directors at the Dallas Peace Center and a guy from Amnesty approached me one day and told me he wanted me to help Kerry get integrated into society.

So we were supposed to meet at this conference, and this *boy* walks in, I mean, he had on some jeans and any piece of clothing that had a zipper—you know, from the seventies—it had to have a zipper or he didn't want it, he had grown his hair out and he dyed it—because, you know, he's really nineteen at heart . . . he couldn't look at anyone, he looked down, his leg was shaking the whole time.

KERRY: Especially with a female, man, I was super traumatized about that. Very shy.

SANDRA: He got up and used the bathroom probably about twenty times because he was so nervous—

KERRY: Aw, man, don't tell 'em that—

SANDRA: But then I thought—and I'm ashamed to have had this thought— what did he do to get himself in that situation? That's how I looked at it . . . 'cause you know, I was very conservative—(*beat.*) and also very stupid. But he gave me the evidence, the hardcore evidence, and it dawned on me, oh my god, how could this have happened? And he would get so close to you, and then look down—

KERRY: The state of Texas executed me over a thousand times, man, and it just keeps on doin' it. I get nightmares—sometimes I forget I'm really here. And every day when I get in the shower I'm reminded of it, 'cause I cannot avoid the scars all over my body. This is the only woman I've been with since I've been free, 'cause of that, and I married her. Think I'm gonna keep her.

But I'll be honest with you: the price of being here, alive, in this room, is really extraordinary—because when I'm alone, man, especially at night—(*Beat.*) Talk about a mental trip, huh?

(*Lights down on* KERRY *and* SANDRA, *up on* ROBERT *and* GEORGIA.)

ROBERT: I been out now three and a half years, goin' on four. And we got married, what?

GEORGIA (*Proud*): Two years, 'bout two years—

ROBERT: And she be wanting me to come home, you know at night, and I don't want to come home, I wanna stay out, you know, 'cause if I come home—(*Joking.*)—it makes me feel like I *still locked up.*

(GEORGIA *responds.*)

ROBERT: And you know, there's a lotta times when she go to the store, and she had to knock on the door to let me know she coming in.

GEORGIA: Yeah, he jumps! When I first moved in, I just be walking in, walking out, and he just jump up, 'cause he's just in that mode! I'm like, okay, he has to take a minute to calm down 'cause he's just used to that. You know, stuff like that plays with your mind.

ROBERT: Yeah, I was in there seven and a half years and it ain't ever gonna go away, far as I'm concerned. Lost my relaxation. Lotta other things, too. You know, you can't really put your thoughts on what you could have lost, or what you *have* lost. I said I could have been a millionaire, or I could have been the police chief. I could have been one of the famous black horse trainers—

GEORGIA: And they won't even give him his license back.

ROBERT: The Trotting Association, they wouldn't even give me my racing license back.

GEORGIA: Can you believe that?

ROBERT: I went to the county, I passed my test with flying colors. They asked me have I ever been convicted of a crime. I put down on the application no, because the Supreme Court, they overturned it. Well, they wrote me back and told me I lied.

GEORGIA: Tell 'em what you told your cousin.

ROBERT: So I told my cousin, I said, well watch. I can go to a gun shop around here, I'm gonna see if they're gonna deny me. I went and got the gun. But the racing commission wouldn't give me my license back. I can legally get a gun, but I can't get a license to drive a horse.

GEORGIA: He can't do something he *likes* to do.

ROBERT: Can't do something I like to do.

And you know, all I want is, I would like to have me this woman here, a nice piece of land in the country, a nice barn, tractor, and a couple of horses. I don't ask for much. But they sayin' I can't. [*Small beat.*] Because of their mistake.

(*Lights down on* ROBERT *and* GEORGIA, *up on* GARY *and* SUE.)

GARY: What's the matter?

SUE: (*To* GARY): I had an incident at the market today, and, and I don't know why it upset me so much, but it really upset me. Some—well—

Well, it was awful. It was—it was about you.

GARY: What, at the market? Somebody didn't like the produce?

SUE: No . . . (*To audience.*) I mean, this has been over three years now, and this guy was like, you know—(*To* GARY.) It started out he just wanted to buy beets. Said—

(*Lights up on* FARMER.)

FARMER: I want a bushel of beets.

SUE: And I told him—(*To* FARMER): "Well, all of our produce is certified organic."

    And he says—

FARMER: Oh, you grew all of this just in water?

SUE: I'm like—(*To* FARMER): "No, that's hydroponic."

    And he asks me—

FARMER: Where do you farm?

SUE: And I told him. So he said—

FARMER: *Oh*, so you farm with that guy that was in all that trouble.

SUE: Oh, you mean Gary? Yeah, he's my husband.

FARMER: Yeah, that was sort of a fishy case, wasn't it?

SUE: Well, you know, two bikers just confessed and were convicted.

FARMER: Well, Gauger confessed, too. You know, the paper *said*.

(*Lights down on* FARMER.)

GARY: (*To* SUE): There's gonna be idiots. I mean, that guy, you know, he's living a lie, just like the newspapers or the prosecutors or whatever. Everyone perceives things in their own way, so which one is the reality, you know? Is the reality your perception? Or is it a composite of everybody's perception, or what?

    [*To audience.*] I mean, what is reality? We're all light beams, you know.

SUE: Oh, Gary, don't go there—

GARY: We're all light beams. People wonder, how could God create miracles? Well, because God moves at the speed of light, and time stops, you see. Once you get to the speed of light, you got all the time in the world to change things and create miracles.

SUE (*Bemused*): Oh, so you're an expert now?

GARY: It's all there on a molecular level, you know. Once somebody told me God is DNA, and you look how tenacious that stuff is, you start to wonder.

(*Lights down on* GARY *and* SUE, *up on* SUNNY.)

SUNNY: You see, I got another chance, because I looked for it. I looked to turn a pile of manure into flowers. I didn't even get lemons, I got manure. (*Laughs.*)

I mean, I'm not glad for what happened to me—when I was in there my parents died, my children grew up without a family . . . and my husband was executed—very, very brutally. Jesse's execution was known worldwide. The chair malfunctioned and made a mess of it. And— (*Pause.*) they had to pull the switch three times.

And he didn't die. It took *thirteen and a half* minutes for Jesse to die. Three jolts of electricity that lasted fifty-five seconds each. Almost a minute. *Each.* Until finally flames shot out from his head, and smoke came from his ears, and the people that came to see the execution, on behalf of the press, are still writing about it. *Ten years afterwards.*

Why do we do that?

(*Lights down on* SUNNY, *up on* DELBERT.)

DELBERT: Mahatma Gandhi said that once he discovered who God was, all fears left him regarding the rest of the world, you know, and it's *true*, you know. If you're not harboring any kind of malice, any kind of stuff like that in your heart, there really ain't too much to be afraid of.

And I understand why people are afraid, I mean, I do think the world itself, if you think about it, can be quite frightening—[*Pause.*]—I mean, just like getting up every day, you know, I understand.

But you can't give in to that. 'Cause as they say in the cowboy pictures, nobody's gonna live forever, you know what I'm sayin'? And if you have to go, then you might as well go being about the highest thing that you can be about. And that means learning not to fear other people, man, on a *human* level, white or black or *whatever*.

I mean, it's a real struggle not to lump all white people—you know, if you're locked up in a room and a guy comes in wearin' a gray suit and he hits you every time he walks into the room, afterwards you gonna have a thing about people with gray suits, I don't give a fuck who they are.

But I try not to look at the world monolithically like that, and that's what has helped me to survive. I mean, I think the American criminal justice system is totally fucked up—I think some things about our *country* are fucked up—but I also think it's a great country, you know, I really do.

But I mean, the fact that you can have people who probably knew that a lotta folks were innocent—but *they* were not gonna be the ones to lose their jobs, jeopardize their kids' college education, blow their new SUV or whatever, for some abstraction like justice. (*Beat.*) That's fucked up.

And I know America gets tired of all of these people talking about what they don't have and what's wrong with the country. Folks say, "Well, what's right with the country?" Well, what the fuck? To make things *better*, we ain't interested in what's *right* with it, we're interested in what's *wrong* with it. You don't say, "What's *right* with my car?" What's *wrong* with it is what we better deal with.

(*Lights up on* SUNNY.)

SUNNY: I want to be a living memorial. When I die I want 'em to plant tomatoes on me, or apple trees or something, so that I can still be part of things. And while I'm still alive, I'm planting my seeds everywhere I go, so that they'll say, "I once heard this woman, and she didn't let them stop her, and she didn't get crushed, and if that little woman person can do it, then I can do it." And *that's* my revenge. That's my legacy, and my memorial.

You know, I've never been to Jesse's grave, and for a long time it was a bone of contention between his mother and me. But I explained to her, I said that grave is not where Jesse really is. I said, that grave is your monument, and this is mine. My life is my monument.

DELBERT: This
is the place for thoughts that do not end in concreteness.
It is necessary to be curious
and dangerous to dwell here, to wonder why
and how and when is dangerous—
but *that's* how we get out of this hole.
It is not easy to be a poet here.
Yet I sing.
We sing.

(SFX: *rain slowly fades in.*)

DELBERT (*To* DAVID, who does not see him. Lights glow on DAVID) Sing.

(DAVID *raises his hand to stop the rain. It does. He smiles to himself as* DELBERT *watches. Blackout.*)

End of Play

WORDS OF CHOICE

Created by Cindy Cooper
Co-adapted with Suzanne Bennett

Safiya Fredericks and Rebecca Mills in *Words of Choice*
(Courtesy Cindy Cooper)

CINDY COOPER AND SUZANNE BENNETT

Cindy Cooper's How She Played the Game *was produced off-Broadway by The Women's Project and Primary Stages, and at 100 other venues in the United States, Canada, and Europe. Other works include* Strange Light, The Outermost House, Slow Burn, Sisters of Sisters, *and* Sentences and Words. *A journalist, book author, and former practicing lawyer, Ms. Cooper has twice received the Jerome Fellowship. Suzanne Bennett, co-adapter, is a director and dramaturg who has served as director of Special Programs for Women's Project and Productions in New York; artistic director of Eureka Theater in San Francisco; and as a consultant for the Fund for Women Artists. Her directing assignments have taken her to the Women's Project, Immigrants' Theatre Project, Lark Theatre, Theatre Rhinoceros, and Santa Rosa Repertory, among others. She is a founding member of New Shoe Theatre.*

Words of Choice received a pilot performance in Washington, D.C., on January 2004. It was directed by Suzanne Bennett. The cast consisted of Elisha Bartels, Lynn Neal, and Tom Tomlinson.

Words of Choice was originally produced in New York City in September 2004. It was directed by Suzanne Bennett. The cast consisted of Safiya Fredericks, Ryan Jensen, and Rebecca Mills.

NOTES ON THE SCRIPT

Words of Choice is a compilation culled from diverse contributing writers (see below). The works are adapted and arranged to create a theatrical journey, while presenting a panorama of stories related to women's rights and reproductive freedom. The play is performed by an ensemble cast with a minimum of three actors (two women, one man) who play multiple roles. It may be performed by as many as seven actors. Diversity in casting is encouraged.

The stage is set minimally with three (or more) chairs and the actors sit on stage when they are not performing. A light pool in front of the chairs defines the playing area. One or two tables may be placed on the stage for props and costume items; alternatively, each actor's chair area may be set with the necessary items. The play is meant to be performed flexibly in a variety of venues.

Each selection moves fluidly into the next with a simple sound bridge of a triangle, gong, bell, or other musical instrument played by an actor or stage manager. There are no blackouts. Performances are followed by a discussion. See www.wordsofchoice.org. Dedicated to Anne Hale Johnson.

LIST OF SCENES:

1-Roe v. Wade *by Justice Harry Blackmun* (excerpt)
2-My Good Friend Roe *by Sherica White*
3-A Father's Story *by Angela Bonavoglia* (excerpted and adapted)
4-Haunted House of Hell: A Parody *by Words of Choice*
5-Approximating Mother *by Kathleen Tolan* (excerpts)

6-You're on Your Own *by Michael David Quinn*

7-They Say *by Gloria Feldt* (excerpt)

8-What I Said, *Testimony to the United States Congress* (excerpted and adapted)

9-Tru Luv *by Cindy Cooper*

10-She Said—Before 1973 *by Judith Arcana* (excerpts)

11-Remembering *by Emilie M. Townes*

12-SCHIPS on Their Shoulders: A Parody *by Cindy Cooper*

13-Kathy: "My Mother" *by Angela Bonavoglia* (excerpt): *and* "Parallel Lives" *by Kathy Najimy* (excerpt)

14-To Hell and Back: Emily Lyons, R.N.: a compilation of Web site material by *Words of Choice* and "To Hell and Back" *by Emily Lyons* (excerpt)

15-Taco Bell: A Parody *by The Onion* (excerpt)

16-blessed *by Alix Olson* (excerpt)

1

Roe v. Wade: An Opinion of the United States Supreme Court (excerpt)
BY JUSTICE HARRY BLACKMUN

(The speaker delivers this text as if reading a poem. The other actors may join in to create a vocal round of the text that resonates and rings from the stage.)
The "right of privacy . . .
founded
in the Fourteenth Amendment's
concept of personal liberty . . .
is broad enough
to encompass
a woman's decision
whether or not to terminate
her pregnancy."
Justice Harry Blackmun
Roe v. Wade
1973

(Sound bridge: gong.)

2

My Good Friend Roe
BY SHERICA WHITE

(The Ensemble sings a robust "Happy Birthday to You" at the outset. At the beginning of the third round, one actor, BIRTHDAY GIRL, speaks.)
BIRTHDAY GIRL: In 2008,* *Roe v. Wade* and I are both celebrating birthday
number (35*).

*(Singing fades. *Adjust date and age to reflect the actual year: Roe was decided January 22, 1973.)*
We're sitting in one of those ritzy Georgetown pubs and reminiscing

about the last three decades. We're toasting girl power, the third wave, hypothesizing about what the rest of the twenty-first century will bring.

But what am I thinking? This is not the time for frivolous birthday parties. If you read the magazines and papers, you know that *Roe* isn't the healthiest person around.

She still faces clinic violence, waiting periods, TRAP regulations, fetal protection laws, international censorship, declining access, and numerous other attempts to stifle her. But, why—after all these years— is she fighting for her life?

In Washington, D.C., where I live, Medicaid patients are unable to obtain elective abortions as part of their health care services. Many doctors are afraid to practice as a result of death threats by protectors of "life."

And let me tell you about these self-proclaimed defenders of the unborn. I met up with a few of them some years back. As I approached a D.C. abortion clinic—confused, afraid, and shaken by their protests,— two of them vowed to help me through my pregnancy and with my baby.

After 2000-plus diaper changes, fourteen babysitters, and a half-dozen ER visits . . . I'm still waiting for their help.

Well, leave *Roe*—and me—alone.

(*BIRTHDAY GIRL raises her glass, toasts the others.*)

As we celebrate our birthday, I wish that *Roe* be allowed to flourish and grow. Then maybe my children and my grandchildren also will be able to celebrate choice, and many more birthdays for *Roe v. Wade.*

(*Singing picks up with final line of "Happy Birthday to You."*)

(*Sound bridge: gong.*)

3

A Father's Story (the story of a journalist who asked to be anonymous)

FROM *THE CHOICES WE MADE*: 25 WOMEN AND MEN SPEAK OUT
ABOUT ABORTION BY ANGELA BONAVOGLIA
(4 WALLS 8 WINDOWS, 2001)

FATHER:

(The FATHER *is a man of forty-five. He sits, as if addressing a small group, feeling certain, if uncomfortable with the idea of talking about himself and his family, unease that he tries to hide at first. The time is 2004.)*

This may be ten—more—years ago, but my story feels like yesterday.

This is one of those sad family stories that normally you don't find fathers talking about in public, or even very much with close friends. It's a personal story with general implications. The general implications appear whenever I pick up a newspaper to read that a House of Representatives committee voted to abolish abortions in family-planning funding overseas, even when the pregnancy is the result of rape; or refuses to consider what their votes mean when they eliminate abortion for poor women on the same basis.

Now the decision to eliminate abortion for poor women who are raped was not a question of cutting the budget. Abortion costs for poor women who are raped do not amount to a large sum. Rather it was a question of morality. Republican Congressman Henry Hyde of Illinois and the Moral Majority types who follow him around were convinced that abortion is wrong even when the woman who wants one wants it because she has been raped. So I didn't think it would be very long before Henry and his friends came after the *un*poor.

So let me tell you my story.

(With a sense of determination and resolve, he stands.)

Some years ago, my daughter attended an enormous Fourth of July celebration at the Washington Monument. It was a free show with fireworks and flags and entertainment, and, according to the newspaper account, the large crowd behaved well.

But as my daughter strolled alone off the monument grounds and entered a side street, a car rolled up next to the sidewalk. Three men emerged from it, seized her roughly, and, before she could do more than utter a half-stifled cry, put her into the backseat, where two more men held her to the floor.

She was tied, gagged, and taken to a house, the location of which she cannot now identify. She was kept in the house for the rest of the night, during which time she was repeatedly beaten and raped.

The next morning she was blindfolded, driven back to the monument grounds, and shoved out of the car. Eventually, sometime around mid-day, she made her way home. During the time she was gone, there was, of course, a great deal of worry and anxiety at that home. And, I must confess, anger. Her arrival was followed by various interviews with policemen who tried to be helpful to a hysterical girl but couldn't be, because the hysterical girl could only estimate the time she had been in the car, describe the inside of a house, and sob out some meaningless first names.

That's really the end of the story. Except, of course, that within a very short time, my daughter knew that she was pregnant.

Now I wanted to ask Congressman Hyde what he would have been if he had been the father of the girl. I know what I did. And I can promise the congressman and the Moral Majority and all the shrill voices of the right-to-life movement that no matter what law they may pass and how stringent the penalty, I would do it again.

(Sound bridge: gong.)

4

Haunted House of Hell: A Parody
BY WORDS OF CHOICE

(JESSIE stands, as if busy at a desk or at a crafts table. JESSIE is straightforward and sincere, thoroughly upbeat. LUCILLE, high strung and plastically pleasant, enters, carrying some literature. Her voice and manner reflect that the writing is a parody.)

JESSIE: Can I help you?
LUCILLE: You work at the church?
JESSIE: I volunteer with the youth program.
LUCILLE: Wonderful. And you are?

(*SHE motions LUTHER to enter.*)

JESSIE: Jessie.
LUCILLE
(*Shakes JESSIE's hand. LUTHER nods a silent hello.*)
    My friend and I are with the Bountiful Life Christian Ministry in Texas,
    and we're visiting various churches in your town because we know that
    you are sick of the pro-homosexual, pro-abortion, devil-worshipping cul-
    ture of death that infests our communities.
JESSIE: Actually, we're Unitarian.

(*LUCILLE and LUTHER gasp, but hold on. LUTHER motions to hand over literature
anyhow.*)

LUCILLE: We at the Bountiful Life Christian Ministry are reaching out by of-
    fering our acclaimed "Haunted House of Hell" skit and costumes for
    Halloween. Our "Haunted House of Hell" is set up like a typical
    haunted house, but our visitors are guided by Lucifer through the In-
    ferno that awaits sinners. The "Haunted House of Hell" package gives
    you everything you need to create the best Hell outside of Hell. And it's
    only $299.
JESSIE: We do a candy toss for Halloween.
LUCILLE: Our kit has been used—successfully—by six hundred churches
    across the nation to unmask evil in seven pretested scenes.
JESSIE: I'm busy.
LUCILLE:
(*Listing them to see which one hits a nerve*)
    "Scene 1—SATANISM."
    "Scene 2—HOMOSEXUALITY."

(*LUTHER points to LUCILLE's pad.*)

    "Scene 3—ABORTION—"

JESSIE: Look, I'm not interested.
LUCILLE: Well, I'll just leave this with you. We'll be around.

(*LUCILLE and LUTHER turn away, smiling, and leave the literature, which JESSIE picks up.*)

JESSIE: "Scene 3—Abortion: the chilling tale of the killing of a human life!"?

(*JESSIE suddenly becomes a character in a fantasy envisioning of scene 3, as it leaps out around her. LUCI, LUCIFER's assistant, grabs JESSIE and brings her to LUCIFER.*)

LUCIFER: Welcome to HELL! Ha-ha-ha. Bring her in!
JESSIE (*Pushed by LUCI*): Stop!
LUCI: It's Jessie! And I've got her number! She's a baby killer!
JESSIE: I am not.
LUCIFER: Oh dear. That's so sad. Well, ha ha, this is your "CHOICE," Jessie. (*In a This Is Your Life kind of tone.*) We've got big sur-PRIZES in store for you! (*They continue a back-and-forth pushing of JESSIE as if she were a rag doll and not a person.*)
LUCI (*Looking longingly at JESSIE*): It all started innocently enough.
LUCIFER: Ohh: One Britney song in the basement. (*Crooning.*) "Oops, I did it again."
JESSIE: No, it wasn't like that.
LUCI: One soft breeze on a sandy beach. First a kiss, then a touch, then a rub.
LUCIFER (*As if JESSIE's date*): "Don't you know sex is c-o-o-l, baby. Nothing bad will happen! I even have a condom that I got for FREE at a SEX-ED CLASS!"

(*LUCIFER hoists a balloon with a funny shape and bright color—very un-condomlike.*)

JESSIE: You don't know what you're talking about.
LUCI: Next thing, she's walking into a Death Clinic.
JESSIE: No, I didn't . . .
LUCIFER: A voice called her: "Mommy, mommy, mommy, don't kill me. I'm your baby." SHE IGNORED IT! (*Shoves JESSIE hard.*)
JESSIE: No! I talked to a counselor . . .
LUCI: "Just give us your money and shut up!"

JESSIE: I'd like some literature.

LUCIFER: "Read all you want. It's NOW OR NEVER!"

JESSIE: The doctor . . . I'd like to see the doctor!

LUCIFER: I am the doctor! Ha ha ha. And I call the shots! Give her a shot! And make sure you draw blood. I love to see bloooood. (*LUCI attends to JESSIE.*)

JESSIE: It doesn't hurt, does it?

LUCI: It hurts like HELL!

LUCIFER: Get me the giant Hoover! She's a big girl. Hurry! I don't have much time. I have lots of other babies to destroy!

JESSIE (*Screams*): Stop! I changed my mind!

LUCI: Too late now, Jessie! Drug addiction, suicide, post-traumatic stress, BREAST cancer! It's only the beginning!

LUCIFER: Mental illness, infirmity, infertility. You'll never have a BABY again!

LUCI: We've fixed that!

JESSIE: No, no, no!

LUCI: Oh, grow up, Jessie.

LUCIFER: Flames, burning bodies, thumbscrews, the rack! Jessie, You've won ETERNAL DAMNATION! (*To LUCI, with high five.*) Congratulations!

LUCIFER and LUCI (*Both, to JESSIE*): AND have a good time in HELL! (*LUCIFER and LUCI laugh manically, move off.*)

JESSIE (*Returns to present and continues with letter*): The Bountiful Life Christian Ministry also offers Additional Enhancements for the "Haunted House of Hell" Evening of Enlightenment including: *Spirit High!* A Christian CD of the Hallelujah Chorus sung by the Beautiful Bountiful Children's Choir.

ACTORS 2 AND 3 (*The actors previously playing LUCI/LUCILLE and LUCIFER/LUTHER, turn, step forward, and sing, sweetly.*)

"Hallelujah"!

JESSIE: Only $19.00!

(*Sound bridge: gong.*)

5

Approximating Mother (excerpts)

BY KATHLEEN TOLAN

(From scene 6 of Approximating Mother. JEN, *a teenager of about fifteen years of age, and* SYLVIA, *a counselor, sit in* SYLVIA'S *office.* JEN *is about six months pregnant.)*

JEN: I didn't use anything.

SYLVIA: Uh huh.

JEN: Didn't think we'd do it.

SYLVIA: Right.

JEN: I thought about it a lot while we were doing it, thought I should say something but I guess I felt shy so I kept putting it off. And then I thought, well, he won't go all the way without asking if I'm on the pill or getting some rubbers or something. And then he was inside me and I kept putting it off and didn't want to interrupt and then he came inside me and I thought, "shit." But then I thought, well, I'm not so regular anyway, so who knows when I'm going to be ovulating. Think of all the times I *haven't* done it this month. The odds are really good that I was ovulating one of those times.

SYLVIA: Hmm.

JEN: SO when my period was late, I thought, "Shit—"

SYLVIA: Hm.

JEN: —but then, well, it's been late before and I just tried not to think about it. And I started feeling really bloated and my breasts started getting really tender and big but I really just tried not to think about it. Finally I couldn't zip my jeans and I faced the fact I had to do something so I called my girlfriend Brena and she helped me find a clinic and we went to the doctor and he said I was pregnant and I said I wanted an abortion and he said I had to have permission from my parents and I said I didn't want to tell them.

SYLVIA:

(Pause. JEN *shifts in her chair.)*

And now you say you want to keep the baby.

JEN: Yeah.

SYLVIA: What made you decide that?

JEN: Um. Well, they wouldn't give me permission to have an abortion and here I am stuck with it. I mean, I know I could give it up but I don't want to do that. That'd be really . . . I don't know, I don't want to do that.

SYLVIA: Mm hm.

JEN: And anyway, here I am and I can't go back home—

SYLVIA: They want you to come back. As soon as the baby is born. They just can't handle the baby.

JEN: Yeah, well, that's just . . . I don't want to.

SYLVIA: Uh huh. It's a tough decision.

JEN: Uh huh.

SYLVIA: So let's ask the tough questions, okay?

JEN: Okay.

SYLVIA: Who's gonna pay the medical bills?

JEN: I don't know.

SYLVIA: Your parents gonna pay them?

JEN: No.

SYLVIA: No insurance, right?

JEN: I don't know.

SYLVIA: The father's not going to pay. You got a friend maybe with some money?

JEN: No.

SYLVIA: Okay. Let's just skip that one for now. Let's say you get out of the hospital. How you gonna support yourself and the baby?

JEN: I'll get a job.

SYLVIA: Okay. And who's gonna take care of the baby?

JEN: I don't know. I'll get a babysitter.

SYLVIA: Okay.

(*Beat.*)

I've seen a lot of girls go through this place. Some of them choose to give their babies up for adoption, go back home, finish high school, get training, or even go on to college, eventually get married and have a family. The ones who keep the children . . .

(*Beat.*)

It's a hard road. Most cases, the father's long gone, they end up on welfare or doing some lousy job while their kids are in some kind of nightmare childcare situation and there's no way out.

(*Beat.*)

You know how it feels to work all day at a job you hate, come home, to a screaming baby? Never go out, never get a break.

(*Beat.*)

You know that most abusive mothers started to have kids when they were teenagers? They beat their kids. Because teenagers are bad? No way. It's hard. They're frustrated. They lash out. But they're ruining more than their own lives, understand?

JEN: I heard the heart beat. I hadn't been thinking of it being, you know, alive. And the doctor let me listen and I heard this thump, thump, thump . . . I couldn't believe it. And it's starting to move around . . .

SYLVIA: Uh huh. Well. Just think about it. I know you'll make the right decision, okay?

(SYLVIA *pats* JEN, *and the two move apart as the scene shifts to what is scene 8 from* Approximating Mother. JEN *gets up and switches her chair and sets up another stage-created setting, this a home for pregnant women. In some cases, the actor who plays* SYLVIA *will also play* BRENA, *and she changes her hairstyle, picks up a bag of items, and strips to a tank top or makes other costume adjustments. Optionally, a third actor may address the audience to provide these stage directions:* "One month later, a home for pregnant women. JEN's *friend* BRENA *comes to visit.*")

(JEN *sits, uncomfortably pregnant.* BRENA *enters with exuberance, carrying items with her. They greet each other warmly.*)

BRENA: Uh oh. I hope I didn't give that house lady one of the hash cookies. I was going to put some regular ones in . . .

JEN (*Taking a cookie*): Right.

BRENA: I thought you needed a little fun in here. That lady was so uptight. I had to really lay it on thick, talk about Jesus and shit.

JEN: God. She's gonna get really stoned.

BRENA: She'll just think it's the flu.

JEN: They'll kill me if they find out. They're so uptight. It's like a prison. I feel like Hansel or Gretel or whoever it was the witch was fattening up for the roast. I mean they're like nice to us in this really fake way but you know as soon as they get their hands on it we'll see if they remember us.

(BRENA has pulled out a bottle of soda. They pass it back and forth.)

BRENA: I saw your mother the other day.

JEN: "How nice." She's going through this whole God trip, hate the sin but love the sinner but you know she's thinking "you slut, you disgusting pig, didn't I tell you to keep those pricks out of your pants?!" But she'd never let me come back with the baby, for all her friends and neighbors to know I was so disgusting.

(Pause.)

I always feel like two people, you know?

BRENA: Uh-huh.

JEN: The person who had these feelings, these secret feelings and it's about feeling good, you know, from when you're little and you get that people don't like to see you rubbing yourself up against stuff to feel good, know what I mean?

BRENA: You're bad.

(They laugh.)

JEN: So you like go underground . . .

BRENA: You better!

JEN: and then when a guy kisses you or feels your tit or says something in your ear and you feel really hot and silky . . . and on top of it, really intense, riding a wave. And . . . it's so far from your life, the rest of your regular life. And it's fabulous. And it has nothing to do with, like, sex education—

BRENA: Huh?

JEN: Like everybody says, you asshole, why didn't you use anything—

BRENA: Who said that?

JEN: Anyway, everybody's thinking it. And they talk about how it makes *guys* feel . . .

BRENA: Uh huh.

JEN: Like *they* have this, like urge, these strong feelings but nobody wants to like admit—like they're scared or something that girls have these really hot feelings—

BRENA *(Sarcastic)*: They don't.

JEN: So all they talk about is it's up to the girls to not let the guys into their pants—

BRENA: That's right.

JEN: And don't get pregnant and watch out for diseases and getting raped and, shit, I know there are a lot of assholes out there and I don't want to get diseased or raped but—shit.

BRENA: Yeah.

(Pause.)

JEN *(Putting her hand on her stomach)*: Hey, hey, hey!

BRENA: What?

JEN: She's kicking me.

(To stomach.)

Don't you listen to this, baby. God. She sure is lively.

BRENA: How come you call it a she?

JEN: 'Cause they did an amnio.

BRENA: What's that?

JEN: It's when the adopters want to know if it's going to be a boy or a girl. It's a girl.

BRENA: Wow. Cool.

(Pause.)

JEN: I got a letter from the lady that wants to adopt her.

BRENA: Wow.

JEN: She lives in New York City. She isn't married. I thought that'd be good 'cause I'm not married. And the kid wouldn't grow up with a lot of arguing and stuff.

BRENA: Right.

JEN: She has some kind of job that she does in an office but she can do it at home if she wants.

BRENA: Wow.

JEN: Editing.

BRENA: Huh.

JEN: She lives in an apartment and she also has a house in the countryside in Massachusetts that she goes to sometimes on weekends and summer vacation. She has a garden.

BRENA: Wow.

JEN: I wonder what you have to do to get to be an editor.
BRENA: Yeah.

(JEN *pulls out a letter, reads.*)

JEN: She says she's thirty-eight years old.
BRENA: Wow.
JEN: And she thinks that's good because she had a lot of time to get to know what she wanted to do in her life and have fun.
BRENA: Huh.
JEN: She says, "There's nothing I can think of that would be as gratifying as to bring up a child. To nurture and guide and teach and love."
BRENA: Huh.
JEN: Sounds good.
BRENA: Yeah.

(*Pause.*)

JEN: I had this thought. That I could write her and say, okay, you can have the baby if you take me too.
BRENA: She's not going to want you.
JEN: I know, but maybe.
BRENA: No way.
JEN: She sounds so nice.
BRENA: She wants your baby.
JEN: Yeah. It's weird. Like, sometimes I think about Frankie, like, what if he knew about it, what would he do, and what if he comes through the restaurant again and I'm there. I mean, maybe she's gonna look like him or something.
BRENA: Yeah.
JEN: Then I think, what if I could get a hold of him and maybe he'd lend me some money, just to get me started, just 'cause maybe he wouldn't want to give away his kid or something.
BRENA: Yeah.
JEN: It would just be so cool to have a baby and, like, you'd never feel alone anymore and if you ever needed a reason to, like, work hard or if you just felt, what's the point, just look over at her and that's it.
BRENA: I don't know.
JEN: But I don't even know his last name. I'm such a fool.

(Pause.)

You never saw him again after that night, did you?
BRENA: Uh uh.
JEN *(To stomach)*: Hey, hey, easy does it. We're talking about your daddy, the
    fuck.

(They laugh.)

No,—not really. I'll always say he was a cool guy, like, you don't want to
    grow up thinking your daddy was a shit.
BRENA: Right.
JEN: I'll just say he lost my number or something.
BRENA: Yeah.

(Sound bridge: gong.)

6

You're on Your Own
BY MICHAEL DAVID QUINN

*(All of the actors take stage, each adopting a character, such as a preacher, a
parishioner, a protestor, a choir member. The actors are encouraged to musicalize
the text either with inflection or musical improvisation. The actors may all share
the verses, or one actor may read the lead verses and be joined by the others on the
"chorus" verses that begin with "You're on your own.")*

Yes, all the womb's a stage once the performer takes his place,
And the mother's just the theater that is renting out the space.
The drama of your life begins when sperm encounters egg,
So pull yourself together and go out and break a leg.

It's a limited engagement biological revue,
And we swear we won't let critics close it down before it's through.
But once you take your final bow, you better move along,
Cause another act is hitting town—that's why we sing this song:

You're on your own, yeah
You're on your own.
We'll stand with you till you're born.
After that you stand alone.
Till you join this world of strife,
Lord, you got a right to life—
But after that, well, I'm afraid you're on your own.

We'll mother you and nurture you and shield you from attack,
Until you take one step beyond the amniotic sac.
'Cause while you're still an embryo, you're innocent and sweet,
But once you are a baby, you'll become a welfare cheat.

Your mommy didn't count on you when she went out to play,
But count on us to see that you're the price she'll have to pay.
Because of us you're free to live whatever life you please—
As long as you don't start to think that food stamps grow on trees.

You're on your own, yeah
You're on your own.
We'll stand with you till you're born.
After that you stand alone.
Till you join this world of strife,
Lord, you got a right to life—
But after that, well, I'm afraid you're on your own.
Our love of life is ridiculed by baby killing cynics.
We'll show them our sincerity by blowing up some clinics.
We hope you aren't hurt when the explosion goes KERPLOW!
But with what your mother plans to do, you're a goner anyhow.

Well, the Lord works in mysterious ways, his wonders to reveal
Perhaps someday we'll meet while you are scrounging for a meal.
But a soul that knows no hardship is a soul that goes unfed—
The only perfect people are the unborn and the dead.

Still we ask that Jesus shelter you with loving hands so mild
From undesired pregnancy to undesired child
To juvenile delinquent to a death row prison cell
And when you walk that final mile, you'll know it all too well.

You're on your own, yeah
You're on your own.

We'll stand with you till you're born.
After that you stand alone.
Till you join this world of strife,
Lord, you got a right to life—
But after that, well, I'm afraid you're on your own.

(*Sound bridge: gong.*)

7

They Say

FROM *THE WAR ON CHOICE* BY GLORIA FELDT
(BANTAM BOOKS, 2004)

(*A single actor,* NARRATOR, *addresses the audience.*)

NARRATOR: In her book *The War on Choice*, Gloria Feldt, then the president of the Planned Parenthood Federation of America, exposes the scare tactics used in abstinence-only education.

(*As if reading a headline.*)

"The Consequences of Premarital Sex":
ENSEMBLE:
(NARRATOR *is joined by the other actors, who take turns reading the lines, physically characterizing the word or phrase as they do so.*)
Pregnancy,
fear of pregnancy,
AIDS,
guilt,
herpes,
disappointing parents,
chlamydia,
inability to concentrate on school,
syphilis,
embarrassment,
abortion,

shotgun wedding,
gonorrhea,
selfishness,
pelvic inflammatory disease,
heartbreak,
infertility,
loneliness,
cervical cancer,
poverty,
loss of self-esteem,
loss of reputation,
being used,
suicide,
substance abuse,
melancholy,
loss of faith,
possessiveness,
diminished ability to communicate,
isolation,
fewer friendships formed,
rebellion against other familial standards,
alienation,
loss of self-mastery,
distrust of complementary sex,
viewing others as sex objects,
difficulty with long-term commitments,
aggressions toward women,
ectopic pregnancy,
sexual violence,
loss of a sense of responsibility toward others,
loss of honesty,
jealousy,
depression,

(*Beat.* ACTORS, *in unison.*)

—death.

(*Sound bridge: gong.*)

8

What I Said to the Congress of the United States
(about the proposed ban on so-called partial-birth abortion)
EXCERPTED AND ADAPTED FROM ACTUAL TESTIMONY

(The gong merges with the sound of a gavel. The setting is a hearing room of the House of Representatives, and the audience is composed of members of Congress and the general public. One actor steps forward, and, setting up a podium, calls for attention.)

MEMBER OF CONGRESS: Quiet; please, may I have quiet? The House of Representatives will continue now with further testimony on the proposal titled as the Ban on Partial Birth Abortion.

(MEMBER OF CONGRESS moves away and sits down.)

CLAUDIA:
(CLAUDIA, a woman who is forty years of age, steps to the podium and begins to address the assembly. She may have notes or papers in her hand, to which she refers from time to time. CLAUDIA is slightly nervous and knows that the topic is a difficult one for her, but she tries to contain her emotions.)
Thank you.

Seven years ago, I had a perfect pregnancy. *I thought* I had a perfect pregnancy. I decided, along with my doctor, not to have an amniocentesis. At thirty-three, there seemed to be no need.

Then one day, feeling anxious, I went to my doctor. There was no basis for my anxiety; it was just an instinct. To set my mind at ease, my doctor sent me to a radiologist to have an ultrasound. "Don't worry," my doctor told me, "he can see a vein out of place."

The radiologist spent a long time conducting the exam. He said that he wanted to review the images. He said he would call.

The next day, when my husband, Richard, and I returned from Rosh Hashanah services, there was a message on the answering machine. "I'd like you to come back in so that my partner can take a look at your ultrasound. Please don't worry. I don't think it's anything," he said.

You can't tell a pregnant woman not to worry.

His partner determined there was a sac of fluid in my baby's brain. He called it a Dandy Walker Syndrome. He said that many people are born with Dandy Walker Syndrome. On the other hand, it could be more serious. He referred us to a perinatologist for a more expert opinion. The doctor put his hand on Richard's shoulder and told him not to lose hope and that everything could be okay.

You don't console someone if nothing is wrong.

The perinatologist arranged to see us the next day. She prepped me for an ultrasound and within thirty seconds, she announced, "I concur with your doctor."

Concur with what? We had no idea.

In addition to Dandy Walker Syndrome and a fluid-filled non-functional brain, our son had a malformed heart with a large hole between the chambers that was preventing normal blood flow. He had also developed an extremely large cyst filled with intestinal matter, and hyperteloric eyes, another indication of severe brain damage. These symptoms added up to trisomy 13, a fatal chromosomal disorder.

With each new bit of information, the tears flowed. Richard was holding me. What were we going to do? This was our son. We loved this baby. We wanted this baby desperately.

We asked question after question. Could a cardiologist fix our son's heart? Could a neurosurgeon repair his brain? Could an eye surgeon help him to see? Was there anything that could be done? The answers were no, no, no, no. Even if my son survived the pregnancy, he had no chance of life. Every day meant pain and torture for him.

Away went the baby name books. Away went the first birthday party, the baseball games, the bar mitzvah. Away went our dream.

We went through our options. I could carry to term. I could have a Cesarean. I could induce premature labor. All posed risks for me. The doctors chose a procedure that would be the most appropriate.

The entire process took three days.

Ironically, the final day of the procedure was Yom Kippur, the holiest day of the Jewish year. On Yom Kippur, we are asked to mourn those who have passed and pray to God to inscribe us into the Book of Life. I prayed more than one person can pray. I was praying for all of us.

Thank you.

(CLAUDIA *nods, stands for a moment, looks out, steps away.*)

(*Sound bridge: gong.*)

9

Tru Luv

BY CINDY COOPER

(*The setting is a contemporary American home, a cozy modern place with a progressive* MOM, *a liberal* DAD, *and an enlightened teen,* MARLA, *all cohabiting comfortably in mutual happiness and deep regard for one another. Life is wonderful.* MOM *and* DAD *are sitting in the living room when* MARLA *enters.*)

MARLA (*Enters*): Mom, Dad . . .

DAD: What is it, honey?

MARLA: I've got something I want to say. It's a little scary. I'm afraid after I tell you, you won't love me anymore.

MOM: You can tell us anything, dear.

DAD: Absolutely, tootsie pop.

MARLA: Well, I'm in love.

DAD: That's wonderful.

MOM: Anyone we know?

MARLA: No.

DAD: Then tell us who it is . . .

MARLA: I don't know.

MOM: Oh, sweetie, are you worried it's someone we won't like?

MARLA: It's hard to tell.

DAD: If you're worried that it's someone of another race or religion or background, that's really okay with us, as long as you are happy. Is it someone you met at school?

MARLA: No.

MOM: We accept all people into our lives. A same-sex relationship is all right with us. Is it someone that works at the hospital where you are volunteering?

MARLA: Kind of. Okay. Here goes. Lately, at the hospital, I've been helping in the lab area—filling orders, tracking samples . . .

MOM: Yes, so you've said.

MARLA: Mom, Dad: I fell in love with a stem cell.

(*Pulls out a container.*)

Look.

DAD: But . . .

MOM: It's so . . . little . . .

MARLA: You think just because it's little, it isn't alive. You think because it's a stem cell, it doesn't have feelings and concerns.

DAD (*Looking at container*): I can't actually see anything.

MOM (*To* DAD): It's that little dot . . . there . . . like a piece of pepper. Or salt.

MARLA: It's so-o cute! I can't wait for it to be implanted in a womb and become a zygote and then some day an embryo and then a fetus. And when it's finally born, we can go off together . . .

MOM: Honey, wouldn't that be robbing the cradle?

MARLA (*Grabs the container back*): I *knew* you wouldn't understand. We're leaving!

(*She drops the container.*)

Oh no! My stem cell! My love!

(*She sobs.*)

DAD: Honey, don't worry, there's more than one fish in the sea.

MARLA: I'll never find another stem cell like that. Never! Never never. I was in love with a stem cell and now that stem cell is gone. My life is over!

(*She exits.*)

MOM and DAD (*Looking on the floor, swapping lines, quickly and overlapping*): (D) Maybe we can find it. (M) It's got to be here somewhere. (D) It wasn't bad looking, if you could see it. (M) I never said it was bad looking. (D) Oh the truth is, we've failed as parents!

(They hug.)

(MOM) We'll keep trying. We'll get it right, darling, we will.

(Sound bridge: gong.)

10

She Said—Before 1973
BY JUDITH ARCANA
(EXCERPTS *CALYX 17:3*, WINTER 1998)

(One actor takes the stage and addresses the audience. The actor speaks as a NEWSPAPER COLUMNIST, *along the lines of Studs Terkel. The actor may be separate from the remaining piece, or may be part of it.)*

NEWSPAPER COLUMNIST: The story of "Jane" is the story of the struggle by a diverse group of women in the Chicago area to create access to abortion. A feminist group, Jane offered a safe alternative to dangerous back-alley abortions at a time when abortion was illegal. Jane operated in private apartments throughout the city and had an impeccable safety record. So trusted were the Jane members that it was used as a referral source by police, social workers, clergy, hospital staff, and friends of friends. Over 11,000 women of all backgrounds were helped by Jane in the years leading up to *Roe v. Wade*.

(The remaining portion of the piece is performed by two actors, or three. If three, one actor reads the statements in italics and the other actors alternate in reading the standard text; if two, the actors alternate in their readings of the italicized portions and the standard text. The italicized portions are spoken by a counselor or worker at the Jane service—all of the Jane service counselors and workers are women.)

On the phone she said, I have a friend who's got a problem, but she couldn't get to a phone so I'm calling for her. Do you know what I mean? Is this the right place?

When we were putting in the speculum, she said, Oh, I had breakfast before I came. I know I wasn't supposed to but I was so hungry I just ate everything in sight, is that ok?

Later she said, I think I have to throw up.

Sometimes she said, Can I see it before you throw it away?

But another time she said, I don't want to look at it, ok? When it comes out, I'll just close my eyes, and you take it away, ok?

She stood on the back steps outside the counselor's apartment and said, This is mi prima, my cousin, from Mexico. Can you talk Spanish to her? Habla un poco? Un poquito? Si, gringa! We will do this.

No, I'll keep it on, I'm not hot, it's ok, I'm fine. *She was wearing her boyfriend's baseball jacket in the kitchen. She said,* Just tell me what I have to know.

When we told her she should pay whatever she could afford, she was quiet a minute and then said, I think I can get nine dollars.

He doesn't like me to talk to my mother. Him and his mother, they don't let me go home to visit. *She put the tiny baby in her mother's arms and said,* We sneaked to come for this appointment. He doesn't know I'm pregnant again. My baby is so new, I can't have another one right away. He wouldn't even want it really, he thinks this one makes too much noise. He doesn't like me to do anything without his permission.

Why do you do this? *She looked around the small bedroom and said,* You're not rich. With what you charge, you can't be doing this for the money. What's it all about? Are you a bunch of women's libbers? Is that it?

I'm not nervous. I think you are good women. I'm never nervous, maybe cuz I'm always tired. *She was so tired that when the woman beside the bed rocked her shoulder softly to wake her up, she said,* It's over? I'm sorry, I just closed my eyes after the shot you gave me down there. I'm sorry, but I was real tired, I had to work a double shift and din have no time between work and here.

She gulped some water in the kitchen and said, Oh thank you, you'll never know what this means to me, thank you so much. I can't thank you enough, I'm sure. I know some people say it's wrong, abortion, that you shouldn't take a life. And maybe you did take a life. But it's all give and take, isn't it? My mother always said that everything always comes down to give and take. So the baby, today, that was the taking—and me, me, my own life, I think that was the giving.

(Sound bridge: gong.)

11

Remembering

BY EMILIE M. TOWNES

(Delivered by one actor, or two who rotate.)

> i remember the stories the older women
>   told us when we came "of age"
> the stories that warned us to keep our
> legs together
>   and stay out of corners
>   never wear red
>   never pierce your ears
>   never wear an anklet
>   because that's what whores do
>   i listened and sifted out the
>   half true
>   and the true true
> i remember other stories the older women
>   told us when we came "of age"
> the stories that were told in
> hushed mournful tones
>   of things botched
>   infected
>   body parts destroyed
>   and finally . . .
>   . . . and she died
>   . . . and her daddy don't talk no more
>   . . . and her mamma just sits
>   and rocks
>   and i listened and sifted out
>   denial
>   blocked access
>   no choices
>   except death
> i don't think these stories
>   these last stories

told in hushed mournful tones
were so much about choice
but more about power
sashaying about with a
mimed and deceitful holiness
these are some of the old southern stories
the memories
the realities
that came to me as i
listened to these stories
and sifted out
the lives of the women i've known
for the
sometimes true
the half true
and true true
. . . and sadly
they are not just southern stories

(*Sound bridge: gong.*)

12

SCHIPS on Their Shoulders: A Parody
BY CINDY COOPER

(*An actor crosses to audience and begins shaking hands with members of the audience. The actor is portraying* TOMMY THOMPSON, *former secretary of Health and Human Services, in a fantasy scenario.*)

TOMMY: Doctors: Hello! How are you? Tommy Thompson, *former* secretary of Health and Human Services. Hi, Hello. Tommy Thompson.
I'm really pleased to be able to speak with you doctors directly.
I am so proud to tell you about some of the great accomplishments in my tenure. Because of my efforts, and doctors, I don't have to tell you, this wasn't easy, you may now sign up all new zygotes, embryos, and fetuses for SCHIPS—the State Child Health Insurance Program! As unborn children, all services to fetuses are completely covered!

(*Beat.*)

Regrettably, pregnant women can no longer be covered.

There are many, many benefits for you under SCHIPS! And too many doctors simply have not taken advantage of them. So to help you, I've prepared a list of NINE REASONS—one for every month that a fetus is a fetus—on why a fetus is a better patient than a pregnant woman.

Reason Number Nine: Fetuses do not ask about your medical school education, the number of deliveries that you have done, or your thoughts about natural childbirth, midwives, water deliveries, home deliveries, and doulas.

Eight: Fetuses do not get into chatty conversations about this 'n that with the nurses or paraprofessionals, undermining your productivity and billing.

Seven: Fetuses do not drop saltine crackers on the waiting room carpet.

Six: Fetuses do not obsess endlessly: Am I too fat? Have I gained too much weight? Why am I always hungry?

Five: Fetuses do not throw up in the examination room.

Four: Fetuses do not bother you about having a video camera, a friend, a husband, or a playwright in the delivery room.

Three: Fetuses do not ask embarrassing questions about sexual activity during pregnancy.

Two: Fetuses do not ask to pee when their feet are in the stirrups.

And the Number One reason why fetuses are better patients than pregnant women—is: Pregnant women are women—and a fetus might be a boy!

So doctors, get out there now, and get going with with SCHIPS! Also, please remember I am available for all of your consulting needs. Thank you So Much!

(HE *exits.*)

(*Sound bridge: gong.*)

13

Kathy

EXCERPTED FROM *THE CHOICES WE MADE: 25 WOMEN
AND MEN SPEAK OUT ABOUT ABORTION* BY ANGELA
BONAVOGLIA (4 WALLS, 8 WINDOWS, 2001)
AND *PARALLEL LIVES* BY KATHY NAJIMY

(Two women step forward and, turning chairs, kneel on the seat, facing the audience. Before they start to speak, one, KATHY, stops the action, and steps out. The other woman stops abruptly, relaxes, looks at KATHY occasionally, waiting as if indulging KATHY.)

KATHY *(Pointing to the setting of chairs)*: The biggest challenge for me in the show *Parallel Lives* is doing the abortion monologue.

Growing up, I was completely against abortion. I grew up in the Catholic church. Sex outside of marriage was a sin. Birth control was a sin. Abortion was murder. In fact, in the seventh grade, at thirteen or fourteen, I wrote a poem that got published in our school paper. It was called "Murder." When I heard my friend was going to get an abortion, I was horrified, so I wrote this poem and gave it to her. I didn't *know* anything then. I think she still had the abortion.

I never really told my mom about my abortion in college. She's a Catholic, Lebanese woman; she's not political; she's not the most liberal, vocal woman. But her last time in New York she saw my show, *Parallel Lives*, a lot, and I think it hit her what the abortion piece was about.

She never sends me a clipping unless I'm in it, but after she left she sent me a clipping from "Dear Abby." She said, "Thought you might be interested in this." The clipping is just a little letter from a Midwestern woman saying, to all the anti-choice people: "I'm so tired of hearing you talk about abortions and how women shouldn't get them. I personally wouldn't get an abortion, but that's my personal choice. I would never make a law saying other women can't."

It really meant a lot to me. It was her way of saying that my being pro-choice was okay.

(KATHY returns to the chair and the other actor continues the scene.)

This is from that show—*Parallel Lives*.

(KATHY *becomes* TINA *and the other actor becomes* TERI. *Both* TINA *and* TERI *are on their knees and are side by side, but they look straight ahead. The timing in their interactions requires a constant symbiosis and impeccably quick responses, as if each knows the other's thoughts, and can think them and finish them.*)

(*"First Confession"*)

(TERI *and* TINA *simultaneously, in identical mimicry, fold their hands in front of them to pray.*)

TINA: Bless me, Father, for I have sinned. It has been about . . .

TERI: . . . fourteen years since my last confession. Okay, let's see—that puts me in about . . .

TINA: . . . the tenth grade. Okay, the tenth grade. Let's start there. Well, I must have done something. I probably cheated in math, I knew I wouldn't use it. I smoked . . .

TERI: . . . dope. I let Mark Richard touch my breast. I started a rumor about . . .

TINA: . . . Cissa Potts stuffing her bra.

TERI: I took speed, I masturbated.

TINA: I used a fake ID . . .

TERI: . . . to buy Schlitz Malt Liquor talls.

TINA: I lied.

TERI: I lied.

BOTH: A lot.

(*A sound of church bells, low.*)

(*"Pregnant Monologue"*)

TERI: Please, God, please don't let me be pregnant. I swear to you G . . . , you I'll never have sex without birth control again, ever. I'm serious God, if you make me not pregnant this time I'll never even have sex again. I know I've said this before but this time I won't even kiss again. Who needs kissing? Look here. It's an application to the Sisters of Charity convent. I swear to you if you make me not pregnant, I'll send it in.

(*"Second Confession"*)

TINA: And then I cheated on my math final. Well, that puts me at twenty-one.

TERI: Oh, that was a bad year, twenty-one.

TINA: I hit and run—an ice cream truck.

TERI: I had a three-way, I think.

TINA: I had an abortion. I did cocaine.

TERI: I lied . . .

TINA: . . . about my student loan.

TERI: I lied . . .

TINA: . . . about my disability insurance.

TERI: I lied . . .

TINA: . . . about the weight on my driver's license.

TERI: I lied . . .

BOTH: . . . a lot.

(Sound of church bells, low.)

("Abortion Monologue")

TINA: No, no, I don't remember feeling bad. Well, no, I do, I remember not letting myself feel bad. That would be like giving in, you know? And if I let
myself feel bad, it might make those people who are so against it think
that they're right. Like, I'm proof. A chance for them to say, "You feel
awful—therefore you shouldn't have done it you are wrong." And the
last thing I wanted to do when I was going through the whole ordeal is be
a part of anything that would make them think that we don't have a
choice. So you don't think about it, 'cause if you think about it then you
might feel bad or guilty and have to give up your choice. So, no, I don't
remember feeling bad. It was too scary for me to feel. Because then
maybe they would seem right. And they're not right. You see, when you
do something like that, you do it because for you it is your only choice.
The sad thing is you want to be able to feel bad about it, without feeling
wrong. But no, I don't remember feeling bad.

("Third Confession")

TINA: Well, that was last year. That brings us up to . . .

TERI: . . . now. Well, I might as well go for the gold. I had sex . . .

TINA: . . . with a married man.

TERI: I had sex . . .

TINA: . . . with a married woman.

TERI: A lot of sex.

TINA: I never visit or write my relatives ever.

TERI: I cheat on my taxes.

TINA: I think bad thoughts about people . . .

TERI: . . . all over the place. I lie . . .

BOTH: I lie a lot.

TERI: Well, that's about it, Father.

TINA: I feel ever so much better. I really feel cleansed.

TERI: What is my penance Father?

TINA: Two Hail Marys and three Our Fathers?

TERI: For fourteen years of sin?

(They look at each other in amazement.)

(Sound of church bells, low.)

(Sound bridge [gong] may be omitted.)

14

To Hell and Back: Emily Lyons, R.N.

A COMPILATION OF WEBSITE MATERIAL BY WORDS OF CHOICE AND SPEECH BY EMILY LYONS, R.N., WWW.EMILYLYONS.COM

(An actor, COMPUTER SURFER, sits, as if at a computer. A second actor, who is EMILY LYONS, enters later.)

COMPUTER SURFER: Enter your search terms.

(Types in search terms.)

"Emily Lyons."

(Reads from the screen.)

Welcome to the Prayer Adoption Website: Targeted Prayer Fighting the Culture of Death.

As Christians, we have a duty to pray for our families, our neighbors, our friends. We also have a special duty to pray for our enemies.

Unborn children, however, can't pray for their enemies. It is our duty to take on the task they cannot do themselves. We must pray for their enemies. This page is devoted to promoting "adoption" of some of the biggest enemies of the unborn.

Click on the name of the Death Promoter to learn about Emily Lyons's Role in the Culture of Death.

Prayer Adoption for Emily Lyons.

Emily Lyons is the nurse who was injured in the Birmingham, Alabama, abortion mill bombing. Rather than turn to God after her brush with death, she has become a high-profile promoter of abortion.

Links. TO HELL and BACK: Emily Lyons's speech to Planned Parenthood.

(A second actor, EMILY, *emerges.* COMPUTER SURFER *watches quietly for a moment, and then shifts to the chairs in the background.)*

EMILY:
*(*EMILY *is attractive, solid. She has a slight Southern accent and a sense of humor. She is not visibly damaged, except possibly for a slight discomfort in her leg.)*

I have been a registered nurse for twenty years. I was trained to provide reproductive services. I've been a labor-and-delivery nurse, a reproductive counselor, and for four years I worked in a clinic that provided a variety of services, including abortions.

I am often asked what my injuries were. I usually respond, "How much time do you have?" I had first-, second-, and third-degree burns. The trauma surgeon described it by saying that I had hundreds of wounds. He had served in Desert Storm and had seen others who had been bombed. He was shocked to see a bombing victim back in the United States.

Metal tore my left eye to the extent that it had to be removed. Metal also shot into my right eye. After several operations and months of waiting, I am able to see well enough to read a little, but my sight will never be like it was. My face, eye sockets, and teeth were broken, my left eardrum was ruptured, my right hand was mangled, a hole about the size of a fist was torn in my abdomen, exposing my intestines. Both knees were so full of nails that they had to be opened and the nails cleaned out before they would move again.

The skin was torn off both shins, exposing bone and requiring skin grafts. Both bones in my lower left leg were shattered, and the doctors feared amputation of one leg. I had dozens of complete nails inside my body, and hundreds of metal fragments and other debris. The blast was so strong it shredded my clothing and blew my shoes off.

I have had twelve operations this year, and expect many more. As a result, I am a trained nurse with twenty years experience who cannot write, read, or stand for long periods of time.

Prior to this, I did not feel like I was in a war. That has all changed. And, the war has not stopped.

I will continue to speak out and speak up for the right for women to make their own reproductive decisions.

Once you've been blown up, there's not much to intimidate you. I don't put up with crap from anyone anymore. Some of our hate mail tells me I'm going to burn in a lake of fire. I just laugh it off. I've been to war, I've gone to hell, and I've come back.

(Sound bridge: gong.)

15

Taco Bell Launches New Morning-After Burrito (excerpt)
BY *THE ONION*, MARCH 1999

(Two actors take the stage. One actor reads the copy as a television anchor person. The second actor reads all of the portions "quoted" in character. Other actors may also be used to read the "quoted" persons.)

TV ANCHOR PERSON: PURCHASE, NY—Hot on the heels of last week's FDA approval, on Monday PepsiCo subsidiary Taco Bell launched its controversial "morning-after" burrito, a zesty, Mexican-style entree that prevents unwanted pregnancies if ingested within 36 hours following intercourse.

Developed by a team of top Taco Bell gynecologists, the $1.99 "ContraceptiMelt" burrito creates an inhospitable environment within the womb, causing fertilized ovum tissue to be flushed from the body.

Also available are ContraceptiMelt Supremes, featuring sour cream and extra cheese. Taco Bell officials are excited about the offering.

ACTOR TWO (GRANT LESKO): "In the past, before *Roe v. Wade*, young women literally had to 'make a run for the border' to terminate an unwanted pregnancy . . ."

TV ANCHOR PERSON: . . . Taco Bell public relations director Grant Lesko said.

ACTOR TWO (GRANT LESKO): "But now, women can make that same run for the border at over 7,300 convenient locations right in their own hometowns."

TV ANCHOR PERSON: Possible side effects of the new birth-control snack item include weight gain, stomach upset and gas, the same as with all other Taco Bell products.

ACTOR TWO (GRANT LESKO): "The new ContraceptiMelt is a safe, effective alternative to traditional forms of birth control that must be administered before intercourse . . ."

TV ANCHOR PERSON: . . . Lesko said.

ACTOR TWO (GRANT LESKO): "Plus, it's delicious."

TV ANCHOR PERSON: Customers who wish to purchase a ContraceptiMelt will be required to meet briefly for consultation with a registered Taco Bell counselor/cashier. The counselor will ring up the customer's order and collect money for it, then provide change, before being allowed to administer the ContraceptiMelt.

Additionally, a five- to ten-minute waiting period may be necessary during high-volume "busy periods" in the restaurant, depending on the length of the line.

ACTOR TWO or ACTOR THREE (COUNSELOR/CASHIER): "Late afternoon, like 3 P.M., is usually a good time to come in . . ."

TV ANCHOR PERSON: . . . said Gerry Frankel, an Arlington, Virginia, Taco Bell counselor/cashier.

While the new burrito is legal and available in all 50 states, parental-consent laws in 37 states require minors who wish to purchase the ContraceptiMelt to obtain permission from a parent or legal guardian—unless they order a side of Cinnamon Crisps and a large beverage.

Taco Bell vice-president of product research Marvin Sekuler expects the new product to be tremendously successful.

ACTOR TWO or ACTOR THREE (MARVIN SEKULER): "All of our test marketing indicates that among 14- to 22-year-old females, there is great demand for a quick, relatively painless termination of unwanted pregnancy via spontaneously induced rejection of fertilized, pre-fetal tissue from the uterine canal . . ."

TV ANCHOR PERSON: . . . Sekuler said.

ACTOR TWO or ACTOR THREE (MARVIN SEKULER): "Plus, 14- to 22-year-olds love delicious, Mexican-style fast-food products."

TV ANCHOR PERSON: Sekuler noted that the decision to terminate a pregnancy is an individual one. But, he said, every ContraceptiMelt comes with a special guarantee.

ACTOR TWO or ACTOR THREE (MARVIN SEKULER): "If any customer becomes pregnant after consuming our new burrito, the Taco Bell Corporation will, guaranteed, hire that person for $6.25 per hour . . ."

TV ANCHOR PERSON: . . . he said.

ACTOR TWO or ACTOR THREE (MARVIN SEKULER): "Taco Bell's above-minimum-wage salaries; flexible schedules; and fun, team-oriented atmosphere make it an ideal place for a young, single mother."

TV ANCHOR PERSON: Pending FDA approval, Taco Bell plans to follow up the ContraceptiMelt with the RU-486 MexiCarriage Deluxe. The Mexi-Carriage Deluxe costs $1.59 if purchased during the first MexiMester, $1.79 during the second, and $1.99 during the third.

    Olé!

(Sound bridge: gong.)

16

blessed (excerpt)
BY ALIX OLSON

(All actors take the stage. The selection is performed by GIRL, *who may be joined in various parts by one or more actors.* ALL ACTORS *join in unison on the final line.)*

GIRL: she was blessed with a family that threw her up high, said flap your brains girl it's time we test drive the sky and she did not know where she was headed, but it had to be more than what she was leaving behind so she grabbed her life by the scruff of its years she let loose the reins and she went for a ride and it helped that she was friendly cause she'd smile when she'd say what she'd say so she felt armed to be a hero, the impossible kind with the big dagger flaw and the world loomed like a tragedy, she'd never seen one up so close before there was daunting poverty, and

there was haunting wealth and the narrator warned her to keep to herself the people were petty, and precious, their faces were preserved in
stone and the chorus insisted she leave them alone. so, she peeked behind the curtain at the mainstream stage everything there was colorful
and strange, cellphones patrolled the streets connecting fools from
brain to brain and she put one hand on her head and the other on her
heart and she swore to all she knew that she would never be able to tell
them apart and she says, i guess that i am prey to all these things that i
condemn and i confess perhaps that's why i am as pissed off as i am. so
i'll keep one hand on my head and the other on my heart and i'll swear to
all i know that i will never be able to tell them apart. and yeah, she is just
one citizen with her hands tied behind her back and this is why she
chooses to use her teeth and tongue to attack. this is why you gotta use
your mouth to fight back. cause you got one hand on your head and the
other on your heart, and you're swearing to all you know that you will
never be able to tell them apart. you're swearing to all you know that they
will never be able to tear them apart. but we are blessed with this family,
that has thrown us up and i say flap your brains, it's time we test drive
the sky and we may not know where we are headed, but it has got to be
more than what we're leaving behind so let's grab our lives by the scruff
of their years, let's let loose the reins and let's go for this ride. let's go for
this ride.

(*All actors join on last line, in unison.*)

End of Play

CONTRIBUTING WRITERS:

Judith Arcana ("She Said: Before 1973") is a poet and a former member of Jane in Chicago; her books include *"What if your mother?"* and *Our Mothers' Daughters.*

Harry Blackmun ("Roe v. Wade") wrote the decision in *Roe v. Wade* in 1973 while serving as a justice on the United States Supreme Court.

Angela Bonavoglia ("A Father's Story" and "Kathy: My Mother") is the author of *The Choices We Made: Twenty-Five Women and Men Speak Out About Abortion* and *Good Catholic Girls.*

Gloria Feldt ("They Say") is the past president of Planned Parenthood Federation of America, the author of *The War on Choice* and, with Kathleen Turner, *Send Yourself Roses.*

Emily Lyons ("To Hell and Back") is a former reproductive health nurse in Alabama, and the co-author, with Jeff Lyons, of *Life's Been a Blast.*

Kathy Najimy (*Parallel Lives*) is a movie and theater actress who co-wrote and co-starred in the Obie-award winning *Kathy and Mo Show.*

Alix Olson ("blessed") is an award-winning spoken-word artist. She is the editor of *Word Warriors: 35 Women Leaders in the Spoken Word Revolution.*

The Onion ("Taco Bell, A Parody") is the nation's premier comedy newspaper.

Michael David Quinn ("You're On Your Own") is a playwright and satirist living in Brooklyn.

Kathleen Tolan (*Approximating Mother*) is a widely produced playwright whose other works include *Memory House, A Girl's Life,* and *A Weekend Near Madison.*

Emilie Townes ("Remembering") is a poet and the Andrew W. Mellon Professor of African American Religion and Theology at Yale Divinity School.

Sherica White ("My Good Friend Roe") is a mother in Washington, D.C. who was born at the same time that *Roe v. Wade* was decided.

ELLIOT, A SOLDIER'S FUGUE

by Quiara Alegría Hudes

Armando Riesco in *Elliot, a Soldier's Fugue* at the Culture Project
(Photo: Monique Carboni)

QUIARA ALEGRÍA HUDES

Elliot, a Soldier's Fugue *was a Pulitzer Prize finalist in 2007, and has been performed throughout the United States and abroad.* In the Heights, *for which Hudes wrote the book, received the 2008 Tony Award for Best Musical. Off-*

Broadway, In the Heights *received the Lucille Lortel and Outer Critics Circle awards for best musical and garnered Hudes an HOLA Award for Outstanding Achievement in Playwriting. Her play* 26 Miles *received its world premiere at Atlanta's Alliance Theatre in March 2009. She is currently writing a musical entitled* Barrio Grrrl! *for the Kennedy Center, and her first children's book is being published by Scholastic, Inc. Hudes is a resident playwright at New Dramatists.*

Elliot, a Soldier's Fugue was produced by Page Seventy-three Productions at The Culture Project on February 4, 2006.

Cast:
GRANDPOP . . . . .Mateo Gomez
GINNY . . . . .Zabryna Guevara
ELLIOT . . . . .Armando Riesco
POP . . . . .Triney Sandoval
Director: Davis McCallum
Set Design: Sandra Goldmark
Costume Design: Chloe Chapin
Lighting Design: Joel Moritz
Original Music: Michael Friedman
Sound: Walter Trarbach, Gabe Wood

CHARACTERS

ELLIOT—Serving in Iraq, 1st Marine Division, 19

POP—Elliot's father, served in Vietnam, 3rd Cavalry Division, various ages

GRANDPOP—Elliot's grandfather, served in Korea, 65th Infantry Regiment of Puerto Rico, various ages

GINNY—Elliot's mother, served in Vietnam, Army Nurse Corps, various ages

SET

The set has two playing areas. The "empty space" is minimal. It transforms into many locations. It is stark, sad. When light enters, it is like light through a jailhouse window or through the dusty stained glass of a decrepit chapel.

The "garden space," by contrast, is teeming with life. It is a verdant sanctuary, green speckled with magenta and gold. Both spaces are holy in their own way.

PRODUCTION NOTES

Fugues
In the "fugue" scenes, people narrate each other's actions and sometimes narrate their own. For instance:

ELLIOT: A boy enters.

(*ELLIOT enters.*)

GRANDPOP: Clean, deodorized.
     Some drops of water plummet from his nose and lips.
     The shower was ice cold.

(*ELLIOT shivers.*)

Elliot's action should mirror what the narrator, Grandpop, says. The narrator steps in and out of the scene as necessary.

Pop's Letters
Pop's letters are active and alive. They are not reflective, past-tense documents. They are immediate communication. Sometimes the letters are shared dialogue between Pop and Grandpop, but it should always be clear that it is Pop's story being spoken.

Music
Flute. Bach, danzónes, jazz, études, scales, hip-hop beats. Overlapping lines.

Other
Please do not use actual barbed wire or vines in the wrapping scenes. The stage directions in these moments are an important part of the soul of the piece, but should not be staged literally.

1

Fugue

(The empty space, very empty. A pair of white underwear is on the ground. That's all we see.)

GINNY: A room made of cinderblock.
A mattress lies on a cot containing 36 springs.
If you lie on the mattress, you can feel each of the 36 springs.
One at a time.
As you close your eyes.
And try to sleep the full four hours.
POP: A white sheet is on the mattress.
The corners are folded and tucked under.
Tight, like an envelope.
GRANDPOP: Military code.
The corner of the sheet is checked at 0600 hours, daily.
No wrinkles or bumps allowed.
ELLIOT: A man enters.

(ELLIOT enters in a towel. It's 2003. He's 18.)

GRANDPOP: Clean, deodorized.
Some drops of water plummet from his nose and lips.
The shower was ice cold.

(ELLIOT shivers. HE picks up the underwear.)

GINNY: He performs his own military-style inspection.

(ELLIOT looks at the front and back of the underwear. No apparent stains. HE sniffs them. They're clean.)

ELLIOT: Nice.

(ELLIOT puts them on under the towel, removes the towel.)

POP: There's little bumps of skin on his arm.
    His pores tighten.
    His leg hair stands on end.
    Cold shower spray.

(ELLIOT *drops to the ground and does ten push-ups.* HE *springs to his feet and seems invigorated.*)

ELLIOT: One two three four five six seven eight nine ten. Rah!
POP: The mirror in the room reflects a slight distortion.

(ELLIOT *peers into the mirror—the audience.*)

GINNY: The chin.
    The teeth.
    Uppers and lowers.
    The molars.
    The one, lone filling.

(HE *clenches his jaw, furrows his eyebrows. Holding the face, he curls a bicep, showing off a round muscle.*)

ELLIOT (*To the mirror adversary*): What? You want to step? You're making Sub-
    way hoagies. I'm a marine. Who are you?

(*He shakes out that pose. Now, he smiles like a little angel into the mirror.*)

ELLIOT (*To the mirror mommy*): Mami, quiero chuletas. Pasteles. Morsilla.
    Barbecue ribs. Sorullito. Macaroni salad. Sopa de fideo. When I make it
    back home, you gonna make me a plate, right? A montón of ribs. But no
    pigs feet. Ain't no other Puerto Rican on this earth be cookin no pigs
    feet.

(ELLIOT *shakes out that pose.* HE *leans in, an inch away from the mirror. He pops a pimple. He wipes it on his underwear. He scrutinizes his face for more pimples. There are none. He fixes his nearly shaved hair. He stands in a suave posture, leaning sexy. He blows a subtle kiss to the mirror.*)

ELLIOT: You know you like it. Navy nursee want mi culito?

(HE *turns around, looks at his butt in the mirror. He clenches his butt muscles and releases. Then he does this about ten times in quick succession, watching the mirror the whole time. He stops.*)

POP: Blank.
    He's nervous about something.
GRANDPOP: He will board the ship to Iraq at 0700 hours.

(ELLIOT *starts to put on his uniform under . . .*)

(*The room is empty. A towel is on the floor.*)

GINNY: A room with steel doors.
    Steel walls, steel windows.
    The room sways up and down.
    Hammocks on top of hammocks swing back and forth.
GRANDPOP: The room is inside a boat.
    That's on the ocean to Vietnam.
GINNY: The floors of the USS *Eltinge* are inspected at 0530 daily.
POP & GRANDPOP: Military code.
    No dirt allowed.
GINNY: But the floor is wet.
    It's the Pacific Ocean, seeping inside.
POP: A young man enters.

(POP *enters. It's 1966. He wears a uniform and catches his breath.*)

GINNY: The 0400 deck run was hot.
    The shower will be warm.
    640 muscles will relax.
GRANDPOP: Military code.
    No bare chests.

(POP *untucks his shirt, unbuttons it, throws it to the floor.*)

POP: (*Imitating a drill sergeant under his breath. Faux Southern accent.*) Keep up the pace, Ortiz. You can't hear me, Ortiz? Are you deaf, Ortiz? Corporal Feifer, is Corporal Ortiz deaf?

GRANDPOP: Military code.
  No bare feet.

(He takes off his boots, peels off his socks.)

POP: You're the best damn shot in the marines, Ortiz. You could kill a fly. Does
  your momma know what a great shot you are?
GINNY: Reflect honor upon yourself and your home country.

(He peels off his undershirt.)

POP: Where are you from, Ortiz? What's your momma's name? Eh? Is she fat
  like you? Your momma got a fat ass, Ortiz?

(ELLIOT is fully dressed. HE salutes the mirror.)

ELLIOT: Lance Corporal Elliot Ortiz Third Light Armored Recon Battalion
  First Marine Division. Mutha fucka.

(POP finds a paper and pencil. HE taps the pencil, thinking of what to write.

(ELLIOT checks inside his duffel bag.)

GINNY: The duffel is heavy full of boots and pants.
  A map of Iraq.
  A Bible with four small photographs.
GRANDPOP: Military code.
  No electronic devices.
ELLIOT: Got my Walkman.
GRANDPOP: Military code.
  No valuables.
ELLIOT: My Nas CD. Jay Z. Slow Jams. Reggaetón 2002.
POP: April 12, 1966 . . .

(ELLIOT opens a little green Bible, looks at photos.)

ELLIOT: My photos. Mom. In your garden.

(He kisses the photo. Finds a new one.)

Grandpop. Senile old head.

(Taps the photo. Finds a new one.)

Pops. With your beer-ass belly.

POP *(Writing)*: Dear Pop . . .

ELLIOT *(Still to the photo)*: When I get home, we gonna have a father and son. Chill in mom's garden. Drink some Bud Light out them minicans. I don't want to hear about no "leave the past in the past." You gonna tell me your stories.

(ELLIOT puts on headphones and starts bobbing his head to the hip-hop beat.)

(POP continues to write under . . .)

(The room is empty. A towel is on the floor.)

GINNY: A tent.
    No windows, no door.
    Walls made of canvas.
    A floor made of dirt.
    The soil of Inchon, Korea, is frozen.

GRANDPOP: Sixteen cots they built by hand.
    Underwear, towels, unmade beds.
    Dirty photos.

GINNY: That is, snapshots of moms and daughters and wives
    That have dirt on them.

GRANDPOP: A boy enters.

(GRANDPOP enters. It's 1950. He's wearing heavy soldier clothes. He rubs his arms for warmth. He puts on additional clothing layers.)

GINNY: His breath crystallizes.
    His boots are full of icy sweat.
    The 0500 swamp run was subzero.

(GRANDPOP blows into his hands for warmth. He bends his fingers.)

GRANDPOP: One two three four . . . five. My thumb is as purple as a flower.

(He pulls a black leather case from his cot. He opens it, revealing a flute. He pulls out pieces of the flute, begins to assemble them, cleaning dirt from the joints.)

    Ah, this Korean dirt is too damn dirty. We lost another man to frostbite
    this week. These guys deserve some Bach. Light as a feather,
POP *(Finishing the letter)*: Your son,
GRANDPOP: free as a bird.
POP: Little George.

(GRANDPOP puts the flute to his lips, inhales, begins to play. The melody of a Bach passacaglia.)

(POP folds up the letter, puts it in an envelope. Addresses the envelope.)

GINNY: Military code.
    Make no demands.
    Military code.
    Treat women with respect.
    Military code.
    Become friends with fellow soldiers.
    No rude behavior.
    Pray in silence, please.

(POP drops the letter, lays down, sings himself to sleep. It overlaps with GRANDPOP's flute and ELLIOT's head-bobbing.)

POP: 1, 2, 3, 4
    We're gonna jump on the count of four
    If I die when I hit the mud
    Bury me with a case of Bud
    A case of Bud and a bottle of rum
    Drunk as hell in kingdom come
    Count off
    1, 2, 3, 4.[1]

(ELLIOT skips forward a few tracks on the Walkman. He finds his jam. Head bobbing, feeling it.)

---

[1] Based on traditional military cadences

ELLIOT: Uh, uh.
    And when I see ya I'ma take what I want so
    You tryin to front, hope ya
    Got ur self a gun
    You ain't real, hope ya   POP
    Got ur self a gun   1, 2, 3, 4
    Uh, uh, uh, uh.   We're gonna charge on the count of
    I got mine I hope ya . . . uh, uh   four
    You from da hood I hope ya . . .   If my heart begins to bleed
    You want beef I hope ya . . .   Bury me with a bag full a' weed
    Uh, uh, uh, uh.   A bag full a' weed and a
    And when I see you I'ma   Bottle of rum
    Take what I want so   Laugh at the devil in kingdom come
    You tryin to front, hope ya . . . Count off
    You ain't real, hope ya . . .   Bud bud bud bud
    Uh, uh, uh, uh.[2]   Bud bud bud bud

(It is three-part counterpoint between the men. Lights fade, counterpoint lingers.)

2

Prelude

(The empty space. A flashbulb goes off.)

SPORTSCASTER VOICE: Thanks, Harry. I'm standing outside the Phillies locker room with hometown hero Lance Corporal Elliot Ortiz. He'll be throwing out tonight's opening pitch.
ELLIOT: Call me Big El.
SPORTSCASTER VOICE: You were one of the first marines to cross into Iraq.
ELLIOT: Two days after my eighteenth birthday.
SPORTSCASTER VOICE: And you received a Purple Heart at nineteen. Big El, welcome home.
ELLIOT: *Philly!*

---

[2] From Nas, *Got Yourself A Gun*

SPORTSCASTER VOICE: You're in Philadelphia for a week and then it's back to Iraq for your second tour of duty?

ELLIOT: We'll see. I got until Friday to make up my mind.

SPORTSCASTER VOICE: Did you miss the city of brotherly love?

ELLIOT: Mom's food. My girl Stephanie. My little baby cousin. Cheesesteaks.

SPORTSCASTER VOICE: Any big plans while you're home?

ELLIOT: Basically eat. Do some interviews. My mom's gonna fix up my leg. I'm a take my pop out for a drink, be like, alright, old head. Time to trade some war stories.

SPORTSCASTER VOICE: I hope you order a Shirley Temple. Aren't you nineteen?

ELLIOT: I'll order a Shirley Temple.

SPORTSCASTER VOICE: Big Phillies fan?

ELLIOT: Three years in a row I was Lenny Dykstra for Halloween.

SPORTSCASTER VOICE: A few more seconds to pitch time.

ELLIOT: Hold up. Quick shout out to North Philly. Second and Berks, share the love! To my moms. My pops. I'm doing it for you. Grandpops— videotape this so you don't forget! Stephanie. All my friends still out there in Iraq. Waikiki, one of these days I'm going to get on a plane to Hawaii and your mom better cook me some Kahlua pig.

SPORTSCASTER VOICE: Curveball, fastball?

ELLIOT: Wait and see. I gotta keep you on your toes. I'm gonna stand on that mound and show y'all I got an arm better than Schilling! Record lightning speed!

3

Prelude

(The garden. GRANDPOP *opens a letter and reads.* POP *appears separately.)*

GRANDPOP & POP: May 24, 1966

POP: Dear pop,
    It's hot wet

GRANDPOP: cold muddy

POP: miserable. Operation Prairie has us in the jungle, and it's a sauna.

GRANDPOP: One hundred twenty degrees by 1100 hours,

POP: you think you're gonna cook by 1300. Then yesterday it starts to rain.

GRANDPOP: Drops the size of marbles—

POP: my first real shower in weeks. Monsoon. They said,

GRANDPOP: "Get used to it." Corporal shoved a machete in my hand and told me to lead.

POP: He's the leader, but I get to go first!

GRANDPOP: I cut through the vines, clear the way. We get lesions,

POP: ticks,

GRANDPOP: leeches.

POP: At night we strip down, everybody pulls the things off each other. We see a lot of rock ape.

GRANDPOP: They're bigger than chimps and they throw rocks at us.

POP: They've got great aim! You just shoot up in the air, they run away.

GRANDPOP: At night you can't see your own hand in front of your face.

POP: I imagine you and mom on the back stoop, having a beer. Uncle Tony playing his guitar. My buddy Joe Bobb,

GRANDPOP: from Kentucky.

POP: He carries all his equipment on his back, plus a guitar, and he starts playing these hillbilly songs.

GRANDPOP: They're pretty good.

POP: I think Uncle Tony would like them. I pulled out your flute and we jammed a little. C rations, gotta split,

POP & GRANDPOP: Little George.

4

Prelude

(GINNY *in the garden.*)

GINNY: The garden is twenty-five years old. It used to be abandoned. There was glass everywhere. Right here, it was a stripped-down school bus. Here, a big, big pile of old tires. I bought it for one dollar. A pretty good deal. Only a few months after I came back from Vietnam. I told myself, you've got to *do* something. So I bought it. I went and got a ton of dirt from Sears. Dirt is expensive! I said, when I'm done with this, it's going to be a spitting image of Puerto Rico. Of Arecibo. It's pretty close. You can see electric wires dangling like right there and there. But I call that "native Philadelphia vines." If you look real close, through the heliconia you see antitheft bars on my window.

Green things, you let them grow wild. Don't try to control them. Like people, listen to them, let them do their own thing. You give them a little guidance on the way. My father was a mean bastard. The first time I remember him touching me, it was to whack me with a shoe. He used to whack my head with a wooden spoon every time I cursed. I still have a bump on my head from that. Ooh, I hated him. But I was mesmerized to see him with his plants. He became a saint if you put a flower in his hand. Secrets, when things grow at night. Phases of the moon. He didn't need a computer, he had it all in his brain. "I got no use for that." That was his thing. "I got no use for church." "I got no use for a phone." "I got no use for children." He had use for a flower.

There are certain plants you only plant at night. Orchids. Plants with provocative shapes. Plants you want to touch. Sexy plants. My garden is so sexy. If I was young, I'd bring all the guys here. The weirdest things get my juices going. I sit out here at night, imagine romances in the spaces between banana leaves. See myself as a teenager, in Puerto Rico, a whole different body on these bones. I'm with a boyfriend, covered in dirt.

When I was a nurse in the Army Nurse Corps, they brought men in by the loads. The evacuation hospital. The things you see. Scratched corneas all the way to a guy with the back of his body torn off. You get the man on the cot, he's screaming. There's men screaming all around. Always the same thing, calling out for his mother, his wife, girlfriend. First thing, before anything else, I would make eye contact. I always looked them in the eye, like to say, hey, it's just you and me. Touch his face like I was his wife. Don't look at his wound, look at him like he's the man of my dreams. Just for one tiny second. Then, it's down to business. Try to keep that heart going, that breath pumping in and out, keep that blood inside the tissue. Sometimes I was very attracted to the men I worked on. A tenderness would sweep through me. Right before dying, your body goes into shock. Pretty much a serious case of the shakes. If I saw a man like that, I thought, would he like one last kiss? One last hand on his ass? Give him a good going-away party.

Just things in my mind. Not things you act on.

With George, though. We had a great time when he was in the evacuation hospital. I stitched his leg up like a quilt and we stayed up all night smoking joints. Everyone in the hospital was passed out asleep. The first time George got up and walked to me. I took his head in my right hand and I kissed him so hard. That kiss was the best feeling in my body. Ooh.

You see so much death, then someone's lips touches yours and you go on vacation for one small second.

Gardening is like boxing. It's like those days in Vietnam. The wins versus the losses. Ninety percent of it is failures but the triumphs? When Elliot left for Iraq, I went crazy with the planting. Begonias, ferns, trees. A seed is a contract with the future. It's saying, I know something better will happen tomorrow. I planted bearded irises next to palms. I planted tulips with a border of cacti. All the things the book tells you, "Don't ever plant these together." "Guide to Proper Gardening." Well I got on my knees and planted them side by side. I'm like, you have to throw all preconceived notions out the window. You have to plant wild. When your son goes to war, you plant every goddam seed you can find. It doesn't matter what the seed is. So long as it grows. I plant like I want and to hell with the consequences. I planted a hundred clematis vines by the kitchen window, and next thing I know sage is growing there. The tomato vines gave me beautiful tomatoes. The bamboo shot out from the ground. And the heliconia!

(SHE *retrieves a heliconia leaf.*)

Each leaf is actually a cup. It collects the rainwater. So any weary traveler can stop and take a drink.

5

Prelude

(*The garden.* GRANDPOP *opens a letter and reads.* POP *appears separately.*)

POP: October 7, 1966
GRANDPOP: Dear dad and all the rest of you lucky people,
POP: Got my next assignment. All those weeks of waiting and boredom? Those are the good old days! They marched us to Dong Ha for Operation Prairie 2. I'm infantry. Some guys drive, go by tank. Infantry walks. We walk by the side of the tank. Two days straight, we've been scouting for body parts. You collect what you find, throw it in the tank, they label it and take it away. Where they take it? You got me. What they write on the label? It's like bird watching. You develop your eye.

GRANDPOP: Don't show this letter to mom, please. And don't ask me about it when I get home. If I feel like talking about it I will but otherwise don't ask.

POP: Today this one little shrimp kept hanging around, chasing after the tank. Looking at me with these eyes. I gave him my crackers I was saving for dinner. I made funny faces and he called me dinky dow. That's Vietnamese for crazy, I guess. Dinky dow! Dinky dow! He inhaled those crackers then he smiled and hugged my leg. He was so small he only came up to my knee.

6

Fugue

(*The empty space. Two wallets are on the ground.*)

GINNY: In my dreams, he said.
Everything is in green.
Green from the night vision goggles.
Green Iraq.
Verdant Falluja.
Emerald Tikrit.

(*ELLIOT enters. HE puts on night vision goggles.*)

ELLIOT (*To imaginary night patrol partner*): Waikiki man, whatchu gonna eat first thing when you get home? I don't know. Probably start me off with some French toast from Denny's. Don't even get me near the cereal aisle. I'll go crazy. I yearn for some cereal. If you had to choose between Cocoa Puffs and Count Chocula, what would you choose? Wheaties or Life? Fruity Pebbles or Crunchberry? You know my mom don't even buy Cap'n Crunch. She buys King Vitaman. Cereal so cheap, it don't even come in a box. It comes in a bag like them cheap Jewish noodles.

GINNY: Nightmares every night, he said.
A dream about the first guy he actually saw that he killed.
A dream that doesn't let you forget a face.

ELLIOT: The ultimate Denny's challenge. Would you go for the Grand Slam or the French Toast Combo? Wait. Or Western Eggs with Hash Browns?

Yo, hash browns with ketchup. Condiments. Mustard, tartar sauce. I
need me some condiments.

GINNY: Green moon.
 Green star.
 Green blink of the eye.
 Green teeth.
 The same thing plays over and over.

(ELLIOT's attention is suddenly distracted.)

ELLIOT: Yo, you see that?

GINNY: The green profile of a machine gun in the distance.

ELLIOT: Waikiki, look straight ahead. Straight, at that busted wall. Shit. You
 see that guy? What's in his hand? He's got an AK. What do you mean, "I
 don't know." Do you see him?

(ELLIOT looks out.)

We got some hostiles. Permission to shoot.

(Pause.)

Permission to open fire.

(Pause.)

Is this your first? Shit, this is my first, too. Alright. You ready?

GINNY: In the dream, aiming in.
 In the dream, knowing his aim is exact.
 In the dream, closing his eyes.

(ELLIOT closes his eyes.)

ELLIOT: Bang.

(ELLIOT opens his eyes.)

GINNY: Opening his eyes.
 The man is on the ground.

ELLIOT: Hostile down. Uh, target down.

(ELLIOT *gets up, disoriented from adrenaline.*)

GINNY: In the dream, a sudden movement.
ELLIOT: Bang bang. Oh shit. That fucker moved. Did you see that? He moved,
    right? Mother f. Target down. Yes, I'm sure. Target down.
GINNY: Nightmares every night, he said.
    A dream about the first guy he actually saw that he killed.

(POP *enters, sits on the ground. He's trying to stay awake. He looks through
binoculars.*)

GRANDPOP: In my dreams, he said.
GINNY: Walking toward the guy.

(ELLIOT *walks to the wallet.*)

GRANDPOP: Everything is a whisper.
GINNY: Standing over the guy.

(ELLIOT *looks down at the wallet.*)

GRANDPOP: Breathing is delicate.
GINNY: A green face.
GRANDPOP: Whisper of water in the river.
GINNY: A green forehead.
GRANDPOP: Buzz of mosquito.
GINNY: A green upper lip.
GRANDPOP: Quiet Dong-Ha.
GINNY: A green river of blood.

(ELLIOT *kneels down, reaches to the wallet on the ground before him. It represents
the dead man. He puts his hand on the wallet and remains in that position.*)

GRANDPOP: Echo Vietnam.
POP: Joe Bobb. Wake up, man. Tell me about your gang from Kentucky. What,
    back in the Bronx? Yeah, we got ourselves a gang, but not a bad one. We
    help people on our street. Like some kids flipped over an ice cream

stand. It was just a nice old guy, the kids flipped it, knocked the old guy flat. We chased after them. Dragged one. Punched him till he said sorry. We called ourselves the Social Sevens. After the Magnificent Sevens.

GRANDPOP: Nightmares every night, he said.

A dream that doesn't let you forget a voice.

The same sounds echoing back and forth.

POP: Guns? Naw, we weren't into none of that. We threw a lot of rocks and bottles. And handballs. Bronx Handball Champs, 1964. Doubles and singles. Hm? What's a handball?

GRANDPOP: The snap of a branch.

POP: Shh.

GRANDPOP: Footsteps in the mud.

POP: You hear something?

GRANDPOP: Three drops of water.

A little splash.

(POP *grabs his binoculars and looks out.*)

POP: VC on us. Ten o'clock. Kneeling in front of the river, alone. He's drinking. Fuck, he's thirsty. Joe Bobb, man, this is my first time. Oh shit. Shit. Bang. (*Pause.*) Bang.

GRANDPOP: Whisper of two bullets in the air.

Echo of his gun.

A torso falling in the mud.

POP: Got him. I got him, Joe Bobb. Man down. VC down.

(POP *rises, looks out.*)

GRANDPOP: Hearing everything.

Walking to the guy.

Boots squishing in the mud.

(POP *walks to the second wallet.*)

GRANDPOP (*Standing over the guy*):

The guy says the Vietnamese word for "mother."

He has a soft voice.

He swallows air.

A brief convulsion.

Gasp.
Silence.
Water whispers in the river.
POP & ELLIOT: Military code.
Remove ID and intel from dead hostiles.

(POP *kneels in front of the wallet. It represents the dead man.* HE *reaches out his hand and touches the wallet.*)

(ELLIOT *and* POP *are in the same position, each of them touching a wallet. They move in unison.*)

POP: The wallet
The body
The face
The eyes

(ELLIOT *and* POP *open the wallets.*)

ELLIOT: The photo
The pictures
Bullet

(ELLIOT *and* POP *each pull a little photo out of the wallets.*)

POP: Dog tags
The wife
ELLIOT: The children

(*They turn over the photo and look at the back of it.*)

Black ink
POP: A date
POP & ELLIOT: Handwriting
A family portrait

(*They drop the photo. They find a second photo. Lights fade.*)

7

Prelude

(The empty space. A flashbulb goes off. ELLIOT *is in a TV studio. Harsh studio lighting is on him.)*

PRODUCER VOICE: ABC evening local news. And we're rolling to tape in three, two . . .

ELLIOT *(Tapping a mike on his shirt collar)*: Hello? What? Yeah. So where do we start?

(He presses his fingers against his ear, indicating that a producer or someone is talking to him through an ear monitor.)

My name? Elliot Ortiz.

(Listens.)

Sorry. Lance Corporal Elliot Ortiz, 3rd Light Armored Recon Battalion, 1st Marine Division.

(Listens.)

What? How was I injured?

PRODUCER VOICE *(Impatient)*: Someone fix his monitor. Don't worry, Mr., uh, Ortiz. Just tell us the story of your injury, would you?

ELLIOT: Okay. Well. I was on watch outside Tikrit. I don't know. I feel stupid. I already told this story once.

PRODUCER VOICE: You did?

ELLIOT: Just now. In the screen test.

PRODUCER VOICE: Right, right. That was to acclimate you to the camera.

ELLIOT: It loses the impact to repeat it over and over.

PRODUCER VOICE: Was it scary?

ELLIOT: People say, oh, that must be scary. But when you're there, you're like, oh shit, and you react. When it's happening you're not thinking about it. You're like, damn, this is really happening. That's all you can think.

You're in shock basically. It's a mentality. Kill or be killed. You put every-thing away and your mentality is war. Some people get real gung ho about fighting. I was laid back.

PRODUCER VOICE: Yes, Mr., uh, Ortiz. This is great. This is exactly it. Let's go back and do you mind repeating a couple sentences, same exact thing, without the expletives?

ELLIOT: Say what?

PRODUCER VOICE: Same thing. But no shit and no damn.

ELLIOT: I don't remember word for word.

PRODUCER VOICE: No problem. Here we go. "But when you're there, you're like, oh shit, and you react."

ELLIOT: But when you're there you're like, oh snap, and you react.

PRODUCER VOICE: "You're like, damn, this is really happening."

ELLIOT: You're like, flip, this is really happening.

PRODUCER VOICE: Flip? Do people say "flip" these days?

ELLIOT: You're like, FUCK, this is really happening.

PRODUCER VOICE: Cut!

ELLIOT: It's a marine thing.

8

Prelude

(GRANDPOP *in the garden.*)

GRANDPOP: Of everything Bach wrote, it is the fugues. The fugue is like an ar-gument. It starts in one voice. The voice is the melody, the single solitary melodic line. The statement. Another voice creeps up on the first one. Voice two responds to voice one. They tangle together. They argue, they become messy. They create dissonance. Two, three, four lines clashing. You think, good god, they'll never untie themselves. How did this mess get started in the first place? Major keys, minor keys, all at once on top of each other. (*Leans in.*) It's about untying the knot.

In Korea my platoon fell in love with Bach. All night long, firing eight-inch howitzers into the evergreens. Flute is very soothing after the bombs settle down. They begged me to play. "Hey, Ortiz, pull out that pipe!" I taught them minor key versus major key. Minor key, it's melan-choly, it's like the back of the woman you love as she walks away from you. Major key, well, that's more simple, like how the sun rises. They understood. If we had a rough battle, if we lost one of our guys, they said, "Eh, Ortiz, I need a minor key." But if they had just got a letter from home, a note from the lady, then they want C major, up-tempo.

"Light as a feather, free as a bird." My teacher always said the same thing. Let your muscles relax. Feel like a balloon is holding up your spine. He was a gringo but he lived with us rural Puerto Ricans. Way in the mountains. He was touring in San Juan with his famous jazz combo, fell in love with a woman, never left. We accepted him as one of our own. He was honorary Boricua. "Light as a feather, free as a bird." I said, you know, if I get any lighter and freer, I'll float to the moon. But that's how you learn. By repeating. Over and over. At Inchon my right hand was purple with frostbite, I developed a technique for left hand only. In Kunu-Ri? Every night we took our weapons to bed, like a wife. One night I shot myself in the shoulder. So I mastered the left-hand method.

Elliot always wanted to know. "Abuelo, tell me a story." About life in the service, about Puerto Rico. "Abuelo, how old were you when? How old were you when this, when that?" Carajo, I don't remember! All I know is what music I was playing at the time. When I started school, when I was a boy, helping mom in the house, it was études and scales. The foundations. The first girl I "danced with," it was danzónes around that time, mambo with a touch of jazz. But in Korea, I played Bach only. Because it is cold music, it is like math. You can approach it like a calculation. An exercise. A routine.

At the airport, I handed the flute to little George. I thought, he needs a word of advice, but what is there to say? I sent him to boot camp with a fifty-dollar bill and a flute. That he didn't know how to play. But without it my fingers grew stiff. I started losing words. Dates. Names of objects. Family names. Battles I had fought in. I started repeating words as if I was playing scales. Practice. Bookmarks to remind myself. "Inchon, Inchon, Inchon." "Korea, Korea." "Bayamón." "Howitzer." "Evergreen."

9

Prelude

(The garden. GRANDPOP opens a letter and reads. POP appears separately, in a good mood.)

POP: November 30, 1966
>   Did you ever notice a helmet is an incredibly useful item? I got a wide
>   range of artistic and practical uses for mine.

GRANDPOP: Today I took a bath, if you want to call it that, out of my helmet.
>   The newer ones have two parts.

POP: If you take the metal part out, you can cook in it. Tonight we had two
>   cans of tuna. A hamburgers in gravy. Hess's contribution?

POP & GRANDPOP: Ham with lima beans.

POP: Everyone empties out their cans. Make a little blue campfire with some
>   minor explosives. Voila,

GRANDPOP: helmet stew.

POP: So that's our Thanksgiving feast. The guys are singing carols. They're in
>   the spirit!
>   Jingle bells
>   Mortar shells
>   VC in the grass
>   Take your Merry Christmas
>   And shove it up your ass

10

Fugue

(The empty space. Two cots are there.

*ELLIOT lies on the ground. GRANDPOP, GINNY, and POP wrap ELLIOT's legs in barbed
wire. They entangle ELLIOT in this position, trapping him. ELLIOT lies helpless.)*

GINNY: A road outside Tikrit.
>   A mile short of Saddam's hometown.

GRANDPOP: Cars are allowed out, but not back in.

POP: The boy was standing guard.

GRANDPOP: He saw an incoming car.

GINNY: The headlights approached.

POP: He fired into the car.

GRANDPOP: The horn sounded.

POP: The car collided into the barricade.

GINNY: The concertina wire slinkied onto his legs.

GRANDPOP: Two seconds ago.

ELLIOT: Sarge! Sarge! Waikiki!

GINNY: Seventy four thorns dig deep into his skin.

POP: Seventy-four barbs chew into his bone.

GRANDPOP: It is not a sensation of rawness.

GINNY: It is not excruciating pain.

POP: It is a penetrating weakness.

GRANDPOP: Energy pours out of his leg.

GINNY: Like water from a garden hose.

ELLIOT: Sarge!

POP: The boy knows he is trapped.

GRANDPOP: He doesn't know he is injured.

GINNY: He does a military-style inspection.

(ELLIOT *reaches up his pants leg.*)

GRANDPOP: His hand enters the warm meat of his calf.

ELLIOT: Oh shit. Stay calm. Put the tourniquet on. Lay back. Drink a cup of water.

(ELLIOT *pulls a strip of cloth from his pocket. He wraps it like a tourniquet around his thigh. Tight.*)

GINNY: Forty-one percent of all injuries are leg wounds.

POP: Military code.

GRANDPOP: Carry a tourniquet at all times.

GINNY: Instructions in the event of rapid blood loss.

GRANDPOP: One.

ELLIOT: Stay calm.

POP: Two.

ELLIOT: Put the tourniquet on.

GRANDPOP: Three.

ELLIOT: Lay back.
     Four . . . Four?

GINNY: Drink a cup of water.

ELLIOT: Someone get me a cup of water.

POP: Stay

GRANDPOP: Calm
     Put

POP: Tourniquet

GINNY: Lay

GRANDPOP: Back

Drink

POP: Cup

GINNY: Water

ELLIOT: Hello? Stay calm. Put a beret on. Fall away. Drink a hot tub. Fuck. Stay with me, Ortiz. Big El going to be okay. Hello? Big El okay. Right?

POP: Fast forward pictures.

GINNY: Mom

POP: Pop

GRANDPOP: Grandpop

POP: Fast forward.

GINNY: Grandpop

GRANDPOP: Pop

POP: Mom

GINNY: Rapid shutter motion.

GRANDPOP: Frames with no sound.

GINNY: Moving lips, no words.

ELLIOT: Mom

POP: Pop

GRANDPOP: Grandpop

ELLIOT: Stay calm. Lay back. Smoke a cigarette.

(He pulls a cigarette out of his pocket.)

Anyone got a light?

(He smokes the unlit cigarette.)

POP: Instructions if wounded while alone.

GRANDPOP: Call for help.

POP: Signal commander.

GINNY: Call for your corpsman.

POP: Identify yourself.

ELLIOT: Sarge! Waikiki! Big El down. Big El down.

POP: His blood congeals in the sand.

GRANDPOP: His fingertips are cool.

GINNY: He enters a euphoric state.

GRANDPOP: The boots,

ELLIOT: Beautiful.

POP: The barbed wire,

ELLIOT: Beautiful.

GINNY: The stars,

ELLIOT: Beautiful.

GINNY: In the event of extended blood loss.

    Reflect on a time you were happy.

    When have you felt a sensation of joy?

ELLIOT: Mom . . .

    Pop . . .

(ELLIOT remains injured under . . .)

(POP enters and lays on a cot.)

GRANDPOP: An evacuation hospital.

    Made of a Vietnamese monastery.

    Ancient windows with no glass.

GINNY: Through the window, views of Vietnam.

    That look like views of Puerto Rico.

    Mountains.

ELLIOT: Mountains.

GRANDPOP: Waterfalls.

ELLIOT: Waterfalls.

GINNY: All different colors of green.

    Rock formations.

    A few bald spots from the bombs.

GRANDPOP: The wood floor is covered with cement.

    The cement is covered with water and blood.

    The cement is cool.

    The blood is cool.

ELLIOT: Cool.

(ELLIOT nods off, going into shock.)

GINNY: A woman enters.

(GINNY enters, approaches POP's cot.)

    Hey.

POP: Nurse Ginny. Still on duty?

GINNY: Shh. Don't wake the babies.

POP: Can't sleep?

GINNY: Yeah.

POP: Me too.

GINNY: Nightmares. Weird stuff, I kept seeing your leg. I thought I should check up on you.

POP: It itches, but you know. The guy next to me's got no left leg at all.

GINNY: I was thinking, a private physical therapy session.

POP: Sounds good.

GINNY: Clean you up.

(GINNY *lifts up his pant leg. There is a big gauze patch there. She slowly pulls back the gauze.*)

POP: That's as far back as it goes. The rest is stuck to the gauze.

GINNY: We're all out of anesthetic. I'll be gentle.

(*She works on his wound. He is clearly in physical pain.*)

Twenty-eight stitches.
Two diagonals.
The first time she touched the man's wound,
A pain pierced up through her index finger.
Through her knuckle.
Wrist.
Forearm.
Elbow.
Humerus.
Shoulder.
The pain jolted in her veins.
Exploded in her vital organs.
Pancreas, lungs, brains, spleen.
Planted itself between her legs.
She touched the blood on his skin and had the desire to make love to the wounded man.

POP: Ay dios mio. Fuck.

GINNY: Think of the time in life you were happiest.

POP: Why?

GINNY: You forget the pain.
POP: It's not pain. It fucking itches!
GINNY: Sorry.
POP: Sorry.

(Pause. GINNY covers the wound. She pulls down his pant leg. She sits on top of him.)

GINNY: Is it too much weight?
POP: Please, crush me to death.
GINNY: There's too many bells and whistles in hospitals. To be a nurse is easy. Give a dog a bone.
POP: Reach into my pocket.
GINNY: Lance Corporal Ortiz.
POP: Go ahead.

(She puts her hand into his pocket. She feels around.)

GINNY: What am I looking for?
POP: You'll know when you find it.

(She removes her hand from his pocket. She's holding a joint.)

Medicine.
GINNY: Anesthetic.

(GINNY lights the joint. They pass it back and forth. Between inhales, they touch each other.)

GRANDPOP: Through the window, views of Vietnam.
That look like views of Puerto Rico.
Mountains.
Green.
Stars.
Bamboo.
Little huts up the mountainside.
POP *(Stoned)*: I got one. I was a little boy in Puerto Rico. Bayamón. I had this ugly scrappy dog. We used to run around scaring my dad's roosters. One of the roosters got pissed and poked the dog's left eye out.

GINNY: What was his name?
POP: Jimmy.
GINNY: Jimmy? Jimmy!

(ELLIOT *shivers.*)

ELLIOT: Ugghhh . . .
POP: Shh. Did you hear something? The operating room.
GINNY: No, it's the monkeys. There's a whole family of them that live in the
     tree.
POP: They're not rock ape are they?
GINNY: What's rock ape?
POP: Big, brown, and ugly.
GINNY: Rock ape!

(*They laugh. She suddenly gets off of him and walks to a far corner of the room.
She still has the joint.*)

GINNY: Tonight you're going to do like Jesus did. You're going to get up and
     walk on water. Defy all the odds. And I'm going to do like a circus tamer.
     Like someone who trains dogs or exotic animals. If you're a good tiger
     and you do your trick and you don't bite, you get a reward. If you do your
     dolphin tricks, I give you a fish.
POP: Seafood is my favorite.
GINNY: Walk to me. See if you can make it.
POP: Not even a hand out of bed?
GINNY: If you want a taste of this ripe avocado, you got to pick it off the tree all
     by yourself.

(POP *struggles to get up. This is a difficult, painful process. He slowly makes his
way across the room.*)

POP: Shrapnel.
     In the ligaments.   ELLIOT:
     In the soft-hard knee cap.   Stay
     In the spaces between stitches.
     Shrapnel from a mortar bomb.   Back
     Splinters that fragment within you.   Lay

Wobbling within your guts.
Creating ripples in your bloodstream.   Home

(POP *arrives at* GINNY. *He falls into her. They kiss.*)

Signal
Elliot Ortiz

(GINNY *and* POP *stop kissing.*)

POP: Do you heal all your patients this way?

Elliot Ortiz.

GINNY: Let's go outside and watch the monkeys.
POP: No, really. You do this a lot?

Elliot Ortiz.

GINNY: Think you can make it outside?
POP: Give me a hand this time.

Ortiz.

GINNY: There's a gorgeous view of the moon.

(*They exit, slowly, carefully, in each other's arms. They pass in front of* ELLIOT, *who is shivering.*)

ELLIOT: Mom?
    Pop?

11

Prelude

(*The empty space.* ELLIOT *wears big radio station headphones.*)

RADIO VOICE: You're listening to WHYY, member-supported radio, welcome
    back. I'm having a conversation with Elliot Ortiz, a North Philadelphia
    native who graduated from Edison High in 2002. So, Elliot, you're sev-
    enteen years old, just finishing boot camp, and the president declares
    war. What was going through your mind?
ELLIOT: I was like, okay then, let's do this.

RADIO VOICE: You were ready. Is it exciting to be a marine?

ELLIOT: People say, oh, it's like a video game. Oh, it's like the movies. Naw. Base is the most depressing place ever. You wake up, go outside, you see rocky sand mountains. That's it. Rocks. Sand. You gotta drive thirty minutes to find a Wal-Mart. I just mainly stay on base, rent a lot of movies.

RADIO VOICE: But not base, let's talk about Iraq. Did you see a lot of action?

ELLIOT: Yeah.

RADIO VOICE: Were there times you were scared?

ELLIOT: The first time I heard a mortar shell. That scared the crap out of me. Literally.

RADIO VOICE: And you were injured. Tell me about that.

ELLIOT: It's a long story.

RADIO VOICE: What sticks out in your mind? About the experience?

ELLIOT: I got two corrective surgeries. They'll send me back if I want.

RADIO VOICE: To Iraq? Will you go?

ELLIOT: I mean, my leg is still messed up but. I'm not trying to stay here and work at Subway hoagies. "Pardon me, sir, you want some hot peppers with that roast beef?"

RADIO VOICE: What do the troops think about politics? Do they support the war?

ELLIOT: Politics? Nobody cares about that. People drink their sorrows away. You hear people running down the hallway like, "F this!" "F that!" "Kill raghead!"

RADIO VOICE (*Slightly changed tone*): Editor flag last remark. (*Back to interview.*) Both your father and grandfather served in the military.

ELLIOT: My pop was in Vietnam, marine corps. Three purple hearts.

RADIO VOICE: It must be something else to trade war stories with your father.

ELLIOT: He doesn't bring up that stuff too much.

RADIO VOICE: Some say there's a code of silence after returning home.

ELLIOT: My mom's got a box of his old letters, his uniform, dog tags. Our basement flooded and everything is in piles down there. But I was like, Mom, you gotta find that stuff.

RADIO VOICE: What about your grandfather?

ELLIOT: He was in Korea. He was a flute player. He'll be like, "I played Mozart in the north when everyone had frostbite." He's got two or three stories that he just tells them over and over. He's got old-timers.

RADIO VOICE: Alzheimer's?

ELLIOT: Right.

RADIO VOICE: You must have felt a great deal of pressure to enlist.

ELLIOT: Naw, I didn't even tell them. I just went one day and signed the papers.

RADIO VOICE: Just like that.

ELLIOT: Dad was actually kind of pissed, like, "The marines is no joke. The marines is going to mess with you."

RADIO VOICE: So why go then?

(No answer.)

Why did you enlist?

ELLIOT: I was like, dad was a marine. I want to be a marine. I really did it for him.

12

Prelude

(The garden. GINNY *holds a large yellow envelope stuffed full of papers. She pulls out one sheet at a time.*

GRANDPOP *appears separately, reading a letter.*

POP *appears separately. He is incredibly happy, slightly drunk.)*

POP: April 4, '67
    To my pop back in the Bronx aka "Little P.R.,"
    The evac hospital was like Disney Land. Real beds.

GRANDPOP: Clean sheets.

POP: Fresh pajamas. The women there? I met this one nurse, Ginny. Nurse Ginny. So let me ask you.

GINNY: "Nurse Ginny."

POP: How old were you when you fell for mom?

GRANDPOP: Did you know right away she was your woman?

POP: I'm serious, old man, I want answers. Got back to the platoon this morning. The guys were still alive, which is a good feeling. We had a big celebration.

GINNY: "Helmet stew."

POP: Hess's mom sent a package with wood alcohol. Stuff she made in the bathtub. Awful stuff.

GRANDPOP: We got drunk.

POP: Joe Bobb pulled out his guitar. I pulled out your flute. I made a big official speech, told them the whole story. You're a decorated veteran,

GINNY: "Bird watching."

POP: you served in Korea, back when they kept the Puerto Ricans separate. How you played the same exact flute to your platoon. Then when I enlisted you handed me the flute and said,

GRANDPOP: "You're a man. Teach yourself how to play."

POP: Joe Bobb showed me a hillbilly song. I showed him a danzón. The keys are sticking, it's the swamp. Low D won't budge, two of the pads fell off. Here's my little plan I'm putting together.

GRANDPOP: Get home safe.

POP: Marry nurse Ginny.

GINNY: "C rations."

POP: Have a son, give him the flute. One flute, three generations. Aw man, right now Joe Bobb is throwing up all over. The smell is bad. It's the wood alcohol.

GRANDPOP: Tell mom my leg is okay.

GINNY: "Date unknown."

POP: And sorry I didn't write for so long.

13

Prelude

(The garden, at night. ELLIOT stands in the garden. POP's letters are on the ground.)

ELLIOT: My little green Bible. Every soldier has something you take with you, no matter where you go, you take that thing. Waikiki had a tattoo of his mom. Mario had a gold cross his grandma had gave him. He wore it around his neck even though it was against the rules. I kept the Bible right inside my vest pocket. I had a picture of Stephanie in it, like a family portrait with all her cousins. My senior prom picture with all the guys. A picture of mom and pop. I looked at those pictures every day. Stared at those pictures. Daze off for like two hours at a time. (*Pause.*) The first guy I shot down, I kept his passport there.

One night, I don't know why, I was just going to kill my corporal. He was asleep. I put my rifle to the corporal's head and I was going to kill him. All I kept thinking was the bad stuff he made us do. He was the kind of guy who gets off on bringing down morale. Like making us run with trench foot. Trench foot is when your feet start rotting. Because of chemical and biological weapons, we didn't take our boots off for thirty-six days straight. When I finally took my boots off, I had to peel my socks from the skin. They were black, and the second they came off, they became instantly hard. Corporal made us run with trench foot. Run to get the water. Run to get the ammo. Everyone was asleep and I was ready to pull the trigger. Waikiki woke up and saw what I was doing. He kicked my arm like, "Eh, man, let's switch." So I looked at my pictures and slept, he went on watch. The next day me and Waikiki were running to get the water and he was like, "Eh, man, what were you doing last night?" I was like, "I don't know." He was like, "It's alright. We'll be out of here soon."

After I got injured, when my chopper landed in Spain. They pulled me out of there. They cut. My clothes were so disgusting they had to cut them off my body. My underwear was so black. The nurse had to cut it up the sides and take it off me like a Pamper. The second she did that, it turned hard like a cast of plaster. You could see the shape of everything. Everything. It looked like an invisible man was wearing them. She threw it like a basketball in the trash. When the guys had finally found me, they had stuffed my leg full of cotton rags. The nurse counted one two three then ripped all the cotton out. I thought I was gonna die. I broke the metal railing right off the stretcher.

They didn't have underwear to put on me so they put a hospital gown instead. The kind that opens in the back and you can see the butt. I was still on the runway. The chopper took off, my gown flew up over my face, but my hands were tied down so I couldn't do nothing. I was butt naked in the middle of everybody. Next thing I know, someone pulled the gown away from my face and I saw this fine female looking down at me. When I saw her, it was like angels singing. (*He imitates angels singing.*) Like, *aaaaaaah.* So what's the first thing that's gonna happen to a guy? She saw it. I was so embarrassed.

The sponge baths I got while I was over there? They give you a sponge bath every other day. The first time. Once again, it was another fine female. It was four months since I seen one. Most female officers, out in the field, they don't look like this one did. So something happened, you know what happened. She was sponging me down and saw it and was like, "You want me to leave the room?" After three days she got used to it. She would be chatting, changing the subject. When you catch a woody with an officer, who you have to see everyday in Spain? The day I left she was like, "Yo, take care of your friend."

When I first landed in Philly, Chucky and Buckwheat met me at the airport. They came running up to the gate like, "Did you kill em? Did you kill em? Did you have a gun? Did you have a really big gun?" I was like, nah, don't you worry about none of that. Don't think about those things. I was trying to forget, but that's how they see me now. That's what I am. That's how Stephanie sees me. And the guys.

On the airplane flying home. All I could think was, I have to talk to pop. Hear his stories. He used to tell stuff from the war but looking back, it was mostly jokes. Like he swallowed a thing of chewing tobacco and puked for three days. He took a leak off a tank and a pretty Vietnamese lady saw him. He never sat me down and told me what it was like, for real. The first night I got here, I was like, pop, I need to hear it from your mouth. That was Monday. He was like, we'll talk about it Tuesday. Wednesday rolled around, I'm like, pop, I'm only home a week. Did you have nightmares, too? Every single night? Did you feel guilty, too? When you shot a guy? Things he never opened up about. Finally I got him real drunk, I'm like, now's the time. I was like, did you shoot anyone up close? Did you shoot a civilian? Anything. He threw the table at me. Threw his beer bottle on the steps. Marched up the stairs, slammed the door.

Seeing mom, it takes so much stress off. She laid me down, and worked on my leg in an old-fashioned way. Went to the herb store, got all her magic potions. The gauze bandage, it hardly came off. I could peel it back like a inch. The rest was infected, stuck to the gauze. At night, it itched so bad I had to scream. Mom laid me down in her garden, she told me to relax. Breathe in. Breathe out. Breathe like a circle. She told me to close my eyes and imagine the time I was happiest in my entire life. Then I felt her fingers on my leg. That felt so good. Hands that love you touching your worst place. I started to cry like a baby. I don't know why. It's just, I forgot how that feels. Like home. The tears were just coming. She put aloe and all sorts of stuff in there. I could tell she was crying too. She knows I been through a lot. She understands.

(GINNY *enters. She begins to braid vines around* ELLIOT'S *body, from the garden. She wraps his body in intricate, meticulous ways. She adds leaves and other flora. This is a slow process. It lasts until the end of the scene.*)

It's a hard question. Of every second in your life, nail down the best one. I started playing memories, like a movie in my mind. The prom. Me all slicked out with the guys, in our silver suits. Matching silver shoes. Hooking up with Stephanie. All the different places me and Steph got freaky. In her mom's house. On top of the roof for New Year's. This one time I took Sean fishing down the Allegheny. He farted real loud. He ripped a nasty one. All the white dudes, in their fisherman hats, they were like, "Crazy Puerto Ricans. You scared the fish away."

The first time I ever went to Puerto Rico. With mom and pop. We drove around the island with the windows rolled down. I was like, damn, so this is where I come from. This is my roots. This one time we stopped at Luquillo beach. The water was light light blue, and flat like a table, no waves. Mom was like, "Pull over, George, and teach me to swim." We swam in there like for five hours. Pop was holding mom on the surface of the water. He would hold on, like, "You ready? You ready?" She was like, "Ay! Hold on, papi! I'm gonna sink!" And he would let go and she would stay, floating, on the top. She was so happy. It looked like they were in love. Then you could see the moon in the water. It was still day but she floated on the moon. I could live in that day forever. See them like that every day.

After mom fixed my leg, she was like, "I got a gift for you. Something important." She gave me a fat yellow envelope. Crusty and old. She was like, "Burn this or read it. It's up to you." I sat out in the garden, started pulling letters out of the envelope. It was all of pop's letters from Vietnam.

(POP *enters the garden.*)

POP: Date unknown
ELLIOT: I read every one. All night, I didn't hardly move.
POP: Dad,
    I just want to say I'm sorry.

ELLIOT: I was like, pop, I fucking walked in your shoes.

POP: I threw your flute away.

ELLIOT: Pop, we lived the same fucking life.

POP: All these thoughts were going through my head like thinking about the Bronx, you, mom.

ELLIOT: It's scary how much was the same. Killing a guy. Getting your leg scratched up. Falling in love.

POP: They got Hess and Joe Bobb.

ELLIOT: Nightmares. Meds. Infections. Letters to your father.

POP: One instant. Their bodies were covered with dust. Tree bark. Their eyes.

ELLIOT: Even ripping them up, taping them back together. It was like the feeling from Puerto Rico, but not a peaceful feeling.

POP: It was like shoot someone, destroy something. I threw your flute in the river.

ELLIOT: You see all the shit you can't erase. Like, here's who you are, Elliot, and you never even knew.

POP: You can't sit around and feel sorry for yourself or you're gonna die. I had to do something, so that's what I did.

(POP's *letter is done.*)

ELLIOT: Pop's up on the second floor, got the AC on, watching TV. Probably smoking weed. Probably doesn't even know I seen his letters. I know he won't even come to the airport tomorrow. He'll just be like:

(POP *speaks directly to* ELLIOT.)

POP: Well, you chose it, so good luck with it. Don't do anything stupid.

(ELLIOT *is tangled in vines. Lights fade.*)

14

Fugue

(The empty space. Three duffel bags are on the floor.)

GINNY: A runway.
 The Philadelphia airport tarmac.
 July 2003 is dry and windy.
 Two seagulls fly even though the ocean is miles away.
 Luggage carts roll in one direction,
 Taxiing planes in another.
 The windows are sealed to airtight, noisetight.
 People crowd around the departure monitors.
ELLIOT: A man enters.

(ELLIOT enters.)

 Cologne is sprayed on his neck.
 A clean shave.

(ELLIOT looks at his watch.)

 0700 hours.
 Thinking in military time again.
 He fixes his short hair.

(ELLIOT fixes his short hair.)

 Grabs his life.

(ELLIOT picks up a duffel bag.)

 Inside his bag are two fatigues his mother ironed this morning.
 Fresh sorullito from grandmom.
 Still warm, wrapped in two paper towels.
 Grease-sealed in a plastic bag.
 A naked photo from Stephanie.
 In the photo she is smiling and holding in her stomach.

Her skin is brown.
The hair on her body is brown.
She is blinking, her eyes half closed.
GINNY: San Juan Bay.
A boarding ramp.
A transport ship to South Korea
Via Japan via Panama Canal.
September 1950 is mild.
The water is light light blue.
And flat like a table, no waves.
GRANDPOP: A boy enters.

(GRANDPOP *enters. He stands beside* ELLIOT *and picks up another duffel bag.* GRANDPOP *waves goodbye to his family, offstage.*)

Slacks pressed.
Hair combed.
Family standing at the rails.
His wife wears a cotton dress.
Sweat gathers in her brown curls.
On her hip, Little George.
His five-year-old son.
A boarding ramp.
Corrugated steel.
His first ride on the ocean.

(GRANDPOP *picks up his duffel and freezes.*)

GINNY: A runway.
The Newark airport tarmac.
August 1965 is unseasonably cool.

(POP *enters. He stands beside* ELLIOT *and picks up a duffel bag.*)

POP: A boy enters.

(*He looks at his watch.*)

9:15 A.M.
He will never get used to military time.

He grabs his life.
At the bottom of his duffel, good luck charms.
A red handball glove.
A bottle of vodka from the Social Sevens.
Two pencils and paper.
A long corridor.
A gray carpeted ramp.
A plane to Parris Island
To a ship to Vietnam.

(POP *picks up his duffel and freezes.*)

ELLIOT: The bag
 The duffel
 The photo
 Stephanie
 Teeth
 Jazz
 Calvin Klein
 Fubu
 Flute
 Helmet
 36 springs
 Ink
 Heliconia
 Handwriting

(ELLIOT *grabs his duffel, steps forward.*)

He walks down the gray carpeted ramp.
Boards the plane to Camp Pendleton.
Where he will board his second ship to Kuwait.
Where he will cross the border north into Iraq.
Again.
Happy he has an aisle seat.
Going back to war.

End of Play

CLARENCE DARROW'S LAST TRIAL

A play in two acts by Shirley Lauro

John Felix as Clarence Darrow in *Clarence Darrow's Last Trial* at the New Theatre, Coral Gables, Florida. (Photo: Eileen Suarez)

SHIRLEY LAURO

Clarence Darrow's Last Trial *has been honored with a National Endowment for the Arts Access to Excellence Award and also was a 2006 Carbonell nominee as Best New Play in Florida, where it enjoyed its world premiere at New Theatre. Lauro's latest play,* Madame Marie Sklodowska Curie, *recently received an EST/Sloan Commission, while another new play,* All Through the Night, *was an 2006 Jeff nominee as Best New Play in Chicago and will premiere in New York at Red Fern Theatre, Fall 2009.* A Piece of My Heart *opened Manhattan Theatre Club's 20th Anniversary Season, has enjoyed over one thousand productions around the world, and recently was selected by V.W. Veterans, Inc., as "the most enduring American play about the Vietnam War."* Open Admissions, *which marked Lauro's Broadway debut, garnered one Tony nomination, two Drama Desk nominations, a Theatre World Award, and the Dramatists Guild Hull Warriner Award. She subsequently adapted the play for CBS, starring Jane Alexander and Estelle Parsons. Her novel,* The Edge, *was a Literary Guild choice. Lauro is a Guggenheim Fellow, twice recipient of a National Endowment for the Arts Grant, and a New York Foundation for the Arts Award winner. She has served twelve years on the Dramatists Guild's Council and Steering Committee, and is a director of the Dramatists Guild Fund. Affiliations: Ensemble Studio Theatre, Actors Studio (Playwrights Unit), PEN, Writers Guild of America, Authors Guild, League of Professional Theatre Women.*

Clarence Darrow's Last Trial held its world premiere January 21, 2005, produced by New Theatre, Coral Gables, Florida. Raphael de Acha, artistic director.

Cast:
Clarence Darrow . . . . .John Felix
Ruby Darrow . . . . .Susan Dempsey
Mrs. Montegu . . . . .Angie Radosh
Lieutenant John Ramsey . . .John Bixler
Naniloa Whitefield Chan . . .Tara Vodihn
Dr. David Stein . . . . .William Schwartz
Reporter Tom Lou . . . . . . .Ricky J. Martinez
Director: Raphael de Acha
Set Design: Rich Simon

Costume Design: Estela Vranocovich
Sound Design: M. Anthony Reimer

CHARACTERS

CLARENCE DARROW—Seventies. Rambunctious, strong, brilliant, egocentric, stubborn, but in his seniority. Extremely vulnerable time in his life and career. Tall, craggy, American looks. Wears red galluses, string tie, white shirt, crumpled gray linen suit, hat of the era.

RUBY DARROW—Young middle age. Younger than DARROW. His second wife. Was his secretary. Totally dedicated to him, shares his opinions and causes. His true helpmate. Pretty, bright, steady, intuitive. Simple print dress of the period, small heels, hat, chenille robe at start.

MRS. MONTEGU—Fortyish. Lieutenant Ramsey's mother-in-law; Theodie Ramsey's mother. Very aristocratic. WASP, Southern accent. Southern matriarch from wealthy Old Atlanta plantation family. Charming, grand in manner, great hostess, especially at Oyster Bay, Long Island, their summer residence. Seductive with men in Southern way. Underneath is steel. Silk dress of the period, pearls, small heels.

LIEUTENANT JOHN RAMSEY—Late twenties. Handsome. "All-American" in looks and manner. A naval officer, 1st Lieutenant, who bears himself as such. Sense of authority, in control of himself and others. Perhaps too much? Speaks with Southern accent.

THEODORA (THEODIE) RAMSEY—Very early twenties. Lieutenant Ramsey's wife, Mrs. Montegu's daughter. Aristocratic, elegant WASP: blonde, attractive. Southern accent. A little of the "'20s flapper" and "Southern flirt." Bubbly, "little girl" aura. Slightly eccentric with dramatic flair, but hints of deep wound, from long ago. Wears long chartreuse chiffon scarf around neck that trails down.

NANILOA WHITEFIELD CHAN—Thirties. The prosecuting attorney. Mixed blood: white, Chinese; from a Royal Hawaiian Ali'i family. Bears herself as such. Extremely intelligent, strong, regal. A freethinker. Beautiful and passionate. Wears dark crepe dress of the period and a Hawaiian lei.

DR. DAVID STEIN—Middle aged. Jewish. An avant-garde doctor in new field of psychiatry. As a resident knew Darrow. Testified, helped with Leopold-Loeb case: "Insanity as mitigating circumstance in the defense." Vest, doctor's white coat, glasses/pince-nez, smokes pipe.

TOM LOU—Thirties. Mixed blood: Asian, Hawaiian, white. Ambitious, bright, assertive with perception and humor. Wears mix of Hawaiian/American/Asian clothes. Straw hat.

PLAYWRIGHT'S NOTES

Clarence Darrow's Last Trial is suggested by events surrounding and occurring in the last major criminal court trial Darrow fought. But the play and characters are fictional except for Clarence and Ruby Darrow.

The play is a style piece. All design elements conform to this. Abstracted, suggested, part for whole. Nothing in text should be illustrated or literally rendered from the design standpoint. Play can adapt to simple or more formal, elaborate design concept. Use of unit set with platforms, lights, sound, music, projections, and other visuals indicated in the script are an effort to suggest stylistically how changes of times, place, and ambience might be implemented on stage. Sense of transience, swirling movement, then stops, then movement again—as if the characters and the telling of their story are caught for critical moments in the glare of the light of history.

The Research and the External Services Department at the University of Hawaii at Manoa, Honolulu, Hawaii; the Research Library at the William S. Richardson Law School of the University of Hawaii; Honolulu; and the Research Departments of both the Law School Library and the Bobst Library of New York University have been of invaluable help in the research phases of this project.

The places of the play: Chicago and the Territory of Hawaii.

The time is 1931 and onward . . . dawn of celebrity as Lindbergh Baby is kidnapped. Dawn of technology—phones, radios—immediate international communication. Transient, fluid movement throughout the world—as World War II looms ahead . . .

ACT ONE

(Abstracted sounds of railroad station: train whistles, chugging train wheels. Shadowy—isolated feeling. Swirl of smoke as if billowing from trains. Now, as if caught in spot searchlight, a MAN, seventyish, enters. Stooped, weary, HE wears 1930s fedora hat, carries overcoat, briefcase. This is CLARENCE DARROW. HE goes to a phone booth, and makes a call. SOUND of phone ringing. Lights up on corner of DARROW's Chicago apartment living room. Humble. Sparse. DARROW's wicker rocker by window. Frayed reddish rug. Bookcase with books overflowing onto the floor. RUBY enters, tying robe, answers phone on a desk.)
RUBY: Hello?

(SHE then looks at DARROW as if they were in same room. Not realistic. CHARAC-TERS do not hold receivers but directly speak to each other as if in same room.)

DARROW: Rube?
RUBY: Dee?
DARROW: I'm out of the case, Rube.

(Sound of train station.)

CAN YOU HEAR? FORCED OUT! THE SCOTTSBORO CASE!
RUBY: You still there?
STATIONMASTER (V.O.): NASHVILLE, LOUISVILLE, CHICAGO! NOW BOARDING, TRACK FIVE!
DARROW: THE TRAIN STATION DOWN HERE.

(Talks louder.)

TAKIN' THE CHICAGO SLEEPER HOME! BE THERE 8 A.M.
RUBY: What happened, Dee?

(More train sounds: whistles, wheels chugging, DARROW talking louder and louder.)

DARROW: COMMUNIST LAWYERS FROM NEW YORK GOT A STRAN-GLEHOLD ON THE CASE.

RUBY: CAN HARDLY HEAR YOU! WHAT?

DARROW: "Scottsboro Boys're represented by us now!" They said. "But always an honor to have *you*, Mr. Darrow—if you can get rid of that NAACP who sent you. Just *assist us* instead!" "ASSIST?" says I. Good-naturedly, mind you. "Nine colored boys from Scottsboro accused of gang-raping two white girls? Why that's my very cup of Lipton Tea, boys," says I.

RUBY: You out of the case? Oh Lord!

DARROW: But I was calm at that point, Rube. I was *calm!* "You know though, boys, I did 'the' breakthrough racial rape case in this nation! First time a colored man convicted of raping a white woman got life instead of death—and I got him that!"

RUBY: I'm so sorry Dee—they wanted you to *assist?*

DARROW: "Isaac Bond! Chicago, 1906!" says I. "Remember it by any chance, boys? Annals of American history—law schools—journals—encyclope- dias, boys?" But they're sitting there, Rube, lookin' twelve years old— starin' at me like I was some kinda jackass talkin' about defendin' Micky Mouse!

(SHE *turns away from facing him:* HE *is nearly overcome with grief at this point.*)

So then—then, Rube?

(SHE *turns back to him.*)

RUBY: I'm here, Dee. Little hard to hear though.

DARROW: I—gave 'em the highlight of that landmark plea then:

(HE *launches into speech as if in courtroom.*)

"If a human life is worth anything, it is worth saving!"

RUBY: Anybody at the station with you, Dee?

DARROW: What are you talkin' about? You aren't listenin' bird one!

(HE *hangs up. Lights down on* RUBY. HE *picks up case, moving into shadows as suddenly camera flashes.* DARROW *whirls around, startled, as camera flashes again.* DARROW *looks enraged as flash goes off again and again.*)

Get that damn thing away from me, will you?

(*DARROW exits. Lights up on* RUBY *at table, in corner of living room. Gray, winter morning, snow seen falling outside window.* RUBY *is filling pen from inkpot, then writing in large ledger checkbook open before her.*)

RUBY (*Reading*): "Pay to the Order of" (*SHE checks spelling then writes:*) "Horace B-a-y-l-o-r, M.D.—"

(*DARROW bursts into room brandishing newspaper.*)

DARROW: RUBY!!
RUBY: I'm right here, dear—you get a little sleep on the train?

(*SHE rises to embrace him, but he charges past her into room.*)

DARROW: See this? They caught me at the train station.

(*HE brandishes paper.*)

"DARROW DISMISSED"! Mug shot a mile high. Like a mad dog, Ruby! Like a-
RUBY (*Interrupting*): Stop! You'll make yourself sick!

(*SHE takes paper from him, tries to take off his coat.* HE *pulls away from her.*)

DARROW: Why don't they print the truth? "FORCED OUT"! Asked for their $1,000 retainer back too—I tell you that? And there's no $5,000 fee of course . . .

(*SHE turns away, shocked, angry, frustrated.*)

What's wrong?
RUBY: The one thousand's gone! Back rent—grocery bills for two months— electric—

(*SHE looks down at ledger.*)

And Dr. Baylor? I swore to him: "The $800 for that surgery will be-"

(*SHE stops short.*)

RUBY (Cont'd):

Well, we'll pay it off. Don't worry. Look—it's the Depression—every-body's in debt . . .

(SHE *detaches check from ledger.*)

DARROW: Pro bono all my life! And now? Seventy-six years old for cryin' out loud. And I can't pay my doctor bill!!

RUBY: Dee, don't do that to yourself!

DARROW: Scottsboro would've solved it all! Money—colored boys free—my legacy like a rock!

(HE *is imagining this scene as* HE *speaks:*)

Old warrior, high in the saddle—ridin' off—

RUBY (*Softly laughing, amused*): Ole Cowhand Dee?

DARROW: You think it's *funny?* My hat's on the *hook,* Ruby! I am yesterday's newspaper!

(HE *takes newspaper, tearing it up.* SHE's *gone back to checkbook, adding up fig-ures.* HE *notices, takes checkbook, tearing it up too.*)

Not in *front* of me!

(HE *goes to sideboard, pours whiskey shot, downs it.* SHE *goes there, shoves whiskey decanter into sideboard cupboard, slams door.*)

RUBY: Well, not in front of *me!*

(HE *looks at her, gets idea, starts rummaging through his books, pulling one out, putting it in briefcase.*)

DARROW: There's one!

RUBY: Now what's that for?

DARROW: The appraiser.

RUBY: Appraiser?

DARROW: Gonna sell all these autographed books. Pay off Dr. Baylor, and everybody else! Just decided: I'm sellin' off my office desk, chairs, book-cases, lamps, sign on the door, too! Givin' up the damn office. Why the hell pay rent two places when I can work here?

(HE'S *trying to jam several books in his small briefcase. They don't fit.* SHE *fills pen again, secures cap on ink bottle, smoothes ledger pages, then closes it. Begins writing figures on pad again.*)

RUBY (*Casually*): Chester called.

DARROW: Chester Hawthorne? Here?

RUBY: From New York. His law office.

DARROW (*Sarcastically*): Condolence call for Scottsboro? Saw my puss in the *New York Times?*

RUBY: He—

DARROW (*Interrupting*): So damn smug since he left here! Deeper the Depression, deeper the pockets of "Wall Street Chester, Ink!"

RUBY: Chester's your good friend, Dee. You two travel back very far in time.

DARROW: A forgotten time! 'Cause he travels now with hoity-toity New York tycoons.

RUBY (*Casually*): He'll be calling back.

DARROW: To gloat?

RUBY: Wants you to reconsider that Hawaiian case. That family in Hawaii doesn't want to use their Honolulu lawyers for their defense.

DARROW: HAWAII? Christ, I turned that a while ago. And down it *stays*! It's *his* client's family up on the murder charge in Hawaii. That's why he called.

(HE'S *trying books one way, then another, packing, repacking.*)

RUBY: He said he thinks the trial could be "an historical moment in time" for you, Dee—if it was argued right.

DARROW: "Historical moment in time"? Every moment's historical in time. What the hell's he mean by that?

RUBY: The international spotlight'll be on the trial is what he meant. "They're broadcasting live from the courtroom all around the world first time in history!" he said. Reporters from *Le Monde—Der Berliner—*the *London Times.* "Clarence would be center stage again with a significant case" is what he meant.

(SHE *is adding numbers, figuring their balance.*)

DARROW: Center stage wrong side! There're race issues. I can't touch that case with a ten-foot pole! We went over and over that already. Don't you re-

DARROW (Cont'd):
> member? How can I begin to defend white rich aristocrats in Honolulu for killing a Hawaiian??

RUBY: They're rich all right . . . they . . . they're offering you a fortune—$30,000 fee, Chester said—lodgings at the Royal Hawaiian Hotel—and a stateroom on a fancy boat to cruise down there. If you can imagine us "cruising"!

(DARROW *looks at her.* THEY *both smile a little.* SHE *goes back to adding figures,* HE *keeps looking at her. Then:*)

DARROW: Somethin' like that trip'd be milk and honey for you though, huh?

(HE *chucks her under chin.*)

> Puttin' up with me all these years, for God's sake!

RUBY: Trip'd be a treat for anybody. Have to be a fool not to relish something like that. But it's not the reason to go, Dee . . . for us.

(SHE *looks around room.*)

> Depression times or not, we're both pretty used to how we live, huh—so you can do what you do. Reason to go would be: the case is right for you.

DARROW: Well, it's not!

(*Beat.*)

RUBY: Chester did remind me—you felt the family was probably innocent—when you considered it before. From all the documents—papers—everything else he and the Honolulu lawyers sent—

DARROW: Damn it, I know they're innocent! And you know that's not why I turned it down.

RUBY: But then too, you had the choice of Scottsboro at that time.

(HE *turns away.*)

> Maybe you should just rethink a little? Remember?

(HE *turns back, looks at her.*)

A naval lieutenant's wife's gang-raped by Hawaiian thugs—but then at
the trial—

DARROW (Interrupting, remembering): The jury splits on racial lines.
five/seven, wasn't it?

RUBY: Four Orientals to acquit. Eight whites to convict . . . as I recall . . .

(THEY *are both getting caught up in story:*)

DARROW: No! Five Orientals to acquit—and seven white to convict! So—they
cannot reach a verdict! One hundred hours of deliberation! Bailiff
shouting, yelling in the jury room—and no verdict!

RUBY: So the judge dismisses the case and—

DARROW (*Jumping in*): No! No! How could he dismiss the case, for God's
sake? He declares a mistrial—and the Hawaiians go on probation—
waiting for the new trial—scared for their lives. And then-

RUBY (*jumping in*): The DA tells the family: "The Hawaiian gang leader just
sent word"—

DARROW: Privately—discreetly—

RUBY: Before retrial happens—he wants to sign a confession—for a plea bargain—but not in the courthouse or legal office-

DARROW (*Jumping in*): Secretly—so his gang doesn't know he's going state's
evidence—

RUBY: In the family's house

DARROW: Where he feels safe to turn on his gang-

RUBY (*Jumping in*): But he turns on the *family* instead—with a knife!

DARROW: And the family shoots *him* in defense!

(*Silence as* THEY *think about the case.*)

RUBY: "Highly intriguing case"! Chester reminded me those were your exact
words when—

(*Phone rings.*)

Oh, I bet that's him—

DARROW: Let it ring.

(*Phone rings again.*)

RUBY: I told him you'd be home by now.
DARROW: Tell him I left.

(*HE starts off. Ring stops as* RUBY *speaks looking at person:*)

RUBY: Hello?

(*Spot on* RAMSEY *looking at her from corner of deck of boat. Far away.* THEY *speak loudly.*)

RAMSEY: Is this the Darrow residence, ma'am?

(DARROW *stops, turns, looks at him.*)

RUBY: Yes. This is Mrs. Darrow.
RAMSEY: Honor, ma'am. Lieutenant John Ramsey here. From Pearl Harbor? Our family's legal counselor in New York—Chester Hawthorne?
RUBY: Yes?
RAMSEY: I told him I wanted to call myself. Plead my case to Mr. Darrow directly. If I might speak with him, please, ma'am?
RUBY: Dee—Hawaii! The Lieutenant!

(*To* RAMSEY.)

Just a minute, please? Here's Clarence Darrow now!
RAMSEY: Mr. Darrow, sir?

(DARROW *reluctantly joins conversation.*)

DARROW: Yes?
RAMSEY: Privilege, sir. Lieutenant John Ramsey, here. My wife's the one got assaulted down here—and now her mother and I are incarcerated on a boat—accused of murdering the gang leader and-
DARROW: I know all about it, Lieutenant. But I'm afraid I'm gonna have to turn your case down *again*. I'm sorry.
RAMSEY: Good God, you don't think we're guilty, sir?
DARROW: Look, son—I think you were most probably tricked by a Hawaiian thug who almost murdered you all! It's just I'm not so good unless I'm fighting for the underdog—

RAMSEY: But you saved Leopold and Loeb! They were white, wealthy—and guilty! And their victim was a child!

DARROW: Everyone there was white and wealthy: their victim and Leopold and Loeb. What saved 'em was I argued they were "mentally unstable."

(A beat. Two.)

RAMSEY: Didn't know that, sir.

DARROW: Pleaded 'em guilty of murder, then brought Temporary Insanity in as cause . . . mitigating circumstance. Let me open the door a little more to insanity as a legitimate plea! God, I loved that chance!

(Beat.)

RAMSEY: Of course—

DARROW: Your Honolulu lawyers'll do a good job for you all, I'm sure. And I wish you all the luck—

RAMSEY *(Interrupting)*: Mr. Darrow? Listen? Please? Local lawyers here aren't good. First trial? My wife was even given a bad prosecutor from the DA's office! Incriminating evidence tainted, botched, suppressed—critical witnesses not called. Her mistrial was because of that, sir. Not racial Top Dog–UnderDog issues. Good lawyers and we'd've won.

(Beat.)

DARROW: Be that as it may, I—

RAMSEY *(Interrupting)*: My mother-in-law's life and mine are on the line down here, sir—we're desperate—

DARROW: I just can't!

(A beat. Then two.)

RAMSEY: Look, Mr. Darrow—I panicked and blanked when he pulled his knife and said he'd rape my wife again! I went crazy! Wild in the moment— shooting crazy wild—an accident that I shot him—

(HE looks at DARROW.)

We wanted him brought to justice legally! That's what inviting him to the villa to sign the confession was about!

(A long silence: DARROW's *thinking of something.)*

DARROW: That ever happen to you before, son?
RAMSEY: What?
DARROW: "Blanking"? "Panicking"—Going "crazy wild in the moment?"

(Beat, then softly.)

RAMSEY: I've blanked before . . . lost time . . . after my wife Theodie was . . .
    assaulted—and—
DARROW: What?

*(*RAMSEY *looks around deck to see if he's being overheard. Then a whisper:)*

RAMSEY: Happened on the submarine I command too. After my wife's
    assault—I pretended a migraine—was relieved of duty—

(Again a lengthy silence.)

DARROW: See a doctor, son?
RAMSEY *(Ashamed)*: Private psychiatrist—
DARROW: Have trouble like this—before Hawaii?

(Silence. Then:)

RAMSEY: Annapolis—
DARROW: What happened there?
RAMSEY: Couldn't separate what was happening from what I thought was
    happening—ended up in the infirmary—

(Silence.)

DARROW: When did you say the trial starts?
RAMSEY: Five weeks—
DARROW: Wouldn't give a lawyer time enough to tie his shoe! Takes a week to
    get down there, doesn't it?
RAMSEY: You're thinking about coming? Oh my God.
DARROW: Thinking about—just thinking—
RAMSEY: Look—the Honolulu lawyers have done all the groundwork already

and Chester will send you the whole background of the first case—you'd
   have every possible kind of help. Oh my God, Mr. Darrow! There's a
   chance?

DARROW: Get all your medical records to me fast as you can. Don't forget Annapolis.

RAMSEY: Yes sir—

DARROW: If I came—*if* I came—I'd be coming for the chance to go for a Temporary Insanity plea, Lieutenant. Highly experimental—

RAMSEY: I—I see—

DARROW: You willing to take the stand on that plea, son?

RAMSEY: I—I—what's the risk?

DARROW: Reputation—career—all that—

RAMSEY: I—I—yes . . .

DARROW: I'd need to see a psychiatrist friend of mine, first. Helped me with
   Leopold and Loeb.

(*Blackout on* RAMSEY. DARROW *to* RUBY:)

   Call David at Chicago Psychiatric, will you, Rube?

(HE *puts on hat.*)

   Let him know what I'm thinking of doin'?

(*Starts walking. Over shoulder to* RUBY:)

   Should be there by noon—tell him I want his advice—

(*Blackout on* RUBY. *Lights up, corner of* STEIN's *office.* DARROW *walks in.* STEIN *at
desk, going over papers.* HE *rises.*)

STEIN: Clarence!

(THEY *shake hands.*)

DARROW: Ruby called?

STEIN: I think it's there's a damn good shot with this, Clarence.

(*Several beats.* DARROW *mulling this over, smiles at* STEIN.)

DARROW: Would you come testify to that, David?

(*Beat.*)

STEIN: Other side of the world, Clarence . . . just lost my best resident—
    there're good psychiatrists there, Clarence—I don't think—
DARROW: Trust some Local Yokel? I never would've saved Leopold or Loeb
    without you on board. Now you've experience—credentials! I think we
    can get the plea established with this. Might help you start your own
    clinic—like that Karl Menninger friend of yours has—
STEIN: Well that'd be the ticket—wouldn't it?

(*Beat.*)

DARROW: Well?
STEIN: I—I'll try to come—
DARROW: What the hell kind of answer is TRY?

(*DARROW starts from area.*)

STEIN: Count me in!

(*Blackout on* STEIN, *as* DARROW *enters his home area, sits, thinking.*)

DARROW: Ruby?

(*RUBY enters, studying him a moment, then:*)

RUBY: Stein's agreed and you're taking the case!
DARROW: I am.
RUBY: Not worried about the race issues like you were before then?
DARROW: Mental illness is universal, Rube. I'll cross all color lines with a plea
    like this.

(*HE is pacing, thinking.*)

RUBY: Maybe I'm playing devil's advocate now—but there *are* race issues—
    natives who don't want us there taking over their people—their
    language—their land . . .

(HE *continues thinking, not really listening.*)

And the Lieutenant's navy! Sailing their waters every day he goes to work. All of it could get into the trial, you said—you felt that pretty strongly before, in fact—

DARROW: I don't think that anymore, all right? It's like Chester said before:

(*Pacing again, thinking.*)

Times change . . . Hawaiians're Americans now—thousands of new jobs, schools—medical system we got going down there. Democratic legal system we helped 'em set up . . . why the Lieutenant's part of *their* navy, Rube! Risking *his* life protecting *them*!

(HE *stops a minute.*)

RUBY: But the race issues are still there, aren't they? They—

DARROW (*Interrupting*): Christ, I want to go! I've got the chance to establish a new plea. At my age, for God's sake! "Temporary Insanity." My name will be on it in the courts for all time! Good will come out of this for the future.

RUBY: Well—I hope so. Still there's a race issue, Dee. There's—

DARROW (*Interrupting*): So what if there's a little hostility around? Think I haven't handled that before? God, it's in my bones to go now, Rube! In my bones!

(HE *starts pacing again. Then:*)

I'm gonna ask for a signed agreement from the family before I accept. Hardly ever done but I'm in a position to ask for it and get it! Powerful people like this? A fella has to protect himself every step.

(*Paces, thinking.*)

Get this down?

(SHE *gets pen, paper, starts writing.*)

"It is agreed Clarence Darrow will control all trial decisions—including but not exclusive to choices of jurors, witnesses, and nature of their tes-

DARROW (Cont'd):

timony. And he shall control including but not exclusive to all pleas, strategies, appeals—before, during and after trial." We'll fill in more details later.

RUBY: Then the trip is on?

DARROW: They give me that power and control in writing? The trip is on!

(*Lights change. A bright, clear, sunny day. Pure blue sky. In distance, ukulele Hawaiian music sounds. Grows louder as we see projections of Hawaiian Harbor as it was in the era. Festive atmosphere. Projections of Hawaiian girls dancing hula. Music loud as* DARROW *comes down boat ramp docked in harbor, wearing lei. Applause, cheers.* TOM LOU *appears: flash of his camera.*)

TOM LOU (*Calling*): Aloha! Couple more photos, sir?

(*Camera flashes again. Sounds of people close by. Camera flash again.*)

Care to give us your opening statement about coming to Hawaii, sir?

DARROW (*Looking around*): Outstanding scenery: those hula girls over there, huh? Uh, the palm trees! The palm trees is what I meant.

(ALL *laugh.*)

TOM LOU: Care to comment on the case, sir?

DARROW: We've had a whole winter in Chicago struggling with eighteen below, nine inches of snow . . . weather's wonderful here! So I sure hope my wife brought my summer suit for court. She's already in the car that's waiting—

(HE *waves toward car, starts to move,* TOM LOU *snaps shot of* DARROW, *then blocks him.*)

Guess I'll just go on over there and ask her. If you'll excuse me?

(HE *waves toward car, tries to go but* TOM LOU *keeps blocking. Scene takes on "stop/start" quality.*)

TOM LOU: Have you decided on a "Code of Honor" plea? The "Unwritten Law," as it's sometimes called. It's what the family wants, we hear— "Code of Honor"—"Unwritten Law"?

DARROW: I always aim to please—so I just may have decided on that plea. I just may have!

TOM LOU: It's what we hear in the native neighborhoods, too—

DARROW: You represent some native paper?

TOM LOU: Yes sir: *Honolulu Sun*!

DARROW (*Smiling*): Native newspapers are the ones with the real bead on the news. Don't want anything to get around of course—about a Code of Honor plea—

TOM LOU: We don't want that plea! Natives, I mean. Hoping you won't go with it, sir—"that a person can take the law into their own hands if they can't get justice in the courts"? That's a posse. Spells trouble for the natives, sir.

DARROW (*Waving to* RUBY *in waiting car*): We sure don't want trouble. We sure don't!

(HE *starts walking to new area, as simultaneously, lights up on incarceration boat at Pearl Harbor,* RAMSEY *pacing on deck. As* DARROW *walks to area, up gangplank ramp.*)

RAMSEY (*Waving, calling down*): Hallooo down there!

(DARROW *looks up, waves back.*)

Welcome to Pearl Harbor—Mr. Darrow?

(DARROW *comes onto deck.*)

Honor, sir!

(THEY *shake hands.*)

DARROW: Lieutenant!

RAMSEY: So glad to meet you in person, sir. Here—here, this way—so appreciate your coming to Pearl Harbor—and so soon, too.

(HE's *leading* THEM *to cabin lounge area,* DARROW *looking around.*)

Just an old navy incarceration boat—

(*THEY enter cabin lounge area.*)

Here—sit—make yourself comfortable, sir—

(*THEY sit. DARROW offers cigarette.*)

DARROW: Smoke?
RAMSEY: Thank you, sir.

(*THEY light up.*)

So grateful you've taken us on, sir.
DARROW: You know how much I sympathize with all your family's been through.
RAMSEY: *We* know it's a high-risk case for you, sir—pleading for people like us.
DARROW: Gonna knock everybody's socks off with that plea, son. I-

(*MRS. MONTEGU makes a grand entrance. THEODIE with her. The MEN stand. MRS. MONTEGU offers hand to DARROW.*)

MRS. MONTEGU: My dear Mr. Darrow.
RAMSEY: My wife's mother, Mrs. Montegu.
DARROW: Honor to meet you, Mrs. Montegu.
MRS. MONTEGU: The honor is mine!
DARROW: Chester Hawthorne? Spoke to him before we sailed—he sends regards.
MRS. MONTEGU: Dear Chester! My daughter, Mr. Darrow? Theodie Montegu-Ramsey.
THEODIE (*Shaking his hand*): Mr. Darrow—
DARROW: And Chester's daughter, Bunny, sends regards to you, Mrs. Ramsey.
THEODIE: Bunny Hawthorne? My stars, I went to boarding school with old Bunny Hawthorne!
MRS. MONTEGU: And regards to Mrs. Darrow. Please tell her I trust the stateroom on the boat and the suite at the Royal Hawaiian were reasonable choices.
DARROW: Excellent choices! She loves it all!
MRS. MONTEGU: Because in spite of everything, we so want you to have some enjoyment—in your free hours. As best you can.

DARROW: Always love to enjoy myself, madam! In my free hours—as best I can.

(HE *smiles at her.* EVERYONE *laughs.*)

MRS. MONTEGU: Well? Let's sit! Sit! Everybody sit!

(THEY *do.*)

> You know, Mr. Darrow, Claudine Durham wants to give a little party in your honor? At the Oahu Club? She'll want you to say a few words. "Lionizing the Lion," she's calling her evening—if you're "game"?
> DARROW: "Lionizing the Lion?"

(HE ROARS, *imitating lion.* THEY *all laugh.*)

> I'm "game." You see? I'm fair "game."

(THEY *laugh, more.*)

MRS. MONTEGU: You are too funny Mr. Darrow.
DARROW (*Immediately rising to occasion*): I'll say something light!

(*As if at a dinner table:*)

> "Folks," I'll say . . . I'm gonna call 'em "folks" . . .
> MRS. MONTEGU: Claudine will simply adore that: "folks"!
> DARROW: "I've got thirty-seven pair of galluses!" I'll say, "Different colors—and I brought 'em all along!" Then I'll open my jacket—

(HE *opens jacket, displaying pair of bright-red suspenders. Hooks his thumb in them.* THEY *laugh.*)

> I'll be wearin' two, three pairs though. Oughta get me a laugh.
> MRS. MONTEGU: A positive hoot! A veritable "lion's roar!" She's a Pineapple Durham, of course.
> DARROW (*Chuckling, bewildered*): Pineapple Durham?
> THEODIE (*Laughing lightly*): Mummer means the Durhams grow pineapples. And practically own Hawaii!

MRS. MONTEGU: I do wish I could be there. But neither Johnny nor I can leave this boat incarceration—of all the ridiculous notions! Admiral's said he'll accompany Mrs. Darrow though. And Theodie, maybe, you'll let Mr. Darrow escort you?

THEODIE: I once did a wicked Charleston, Mr. Darrow. Top of the table? But Johnny said:

(*Imitating* RAMSEY:)

"Conduct unbecoming an officer's wife!"

(SHE *salutes, giggles, rearranging scarf.* RAMSEY *goes to her good-naturedly, arm around her shoulder.*)

RAMSEY: If you want to Charleston with Mr. Darrow, sweetheart, I'd be delighted!

MRS. MONTEGU: Well then—let's ring for coffee?

(SHE *rings bell.*)

Their Kona beans, Mr. Darrow, make a tantalizing brew.

DARROW: Thanks, but . . . but a little hot for coffee, ma'am.

MRS. MONTEGU: Oh, I do wish we had a more warm weather refreshment to offer you as we have in our summer home—in Oyster Bay? Something minty, lemony. We are in such reduced circumstances, as you will understand, dear Mr. Darrow, imprisoned on this boat. Still it is a mercy the navy could arrange even this—spared us that sordid Honolulu jail at least!

(*A beat.*)

THEODIE: Mr. Darrow?

DARROW: Ma'am?

THEODIE: I wanted you to know the very thought of testifying again makes me about to swoon, Mr. Darrow . . .

DARROW: Look, ma'am, I'm gonna try my best to make all this suffering only a dim memory for everybody.

THEODIE: Oh, please God!

DARROW: Let me tell you what I'm plannin' then? I know the law here's "one innocent, all innocent"—so I'm figurin' to just to plead the Lieutenant, because he has cause and motivation. Not gonna put anyone else on the stand at all.

THEODIE: Answer to a young girl's prayers, sir.

MRS. MONTEGU: I won't have to take the stand then, either, Mr. Darrow?

DARROW: No, ma'am.

MRS. MONTEGU: Oh thank heaven! Because I do feel so hideously responsible, Mr. Darrow—Johnny was in no state, you see—so I drove. If only I'd taken the other turn at that intersection—Kalani might've lived! I keep going over and over it all in my mind 'til I feel about to burst, Mr. Darrow.

RAMSEY: Kalani's the Hawaiian.

DARROW: Yes, I know.

MRS. MONTEGU: You see—that mountain villa I rented is so far out from the Honolulu hospital—and I was going at such breakneck speed to get Kalani there—and was such a stranger to the roads—I turned left instead of right. And suddenly we were on the cliff road!

RAMSEY: Where they stopped us for speeding—found Kalani not breathing. And—arrested us!

MRS. MONTEGU: I get shaky even talking about it, Mr. Darrow.

DARROW: I give my word neither you or your daughter will have to relive this on the stand!

MRS. MONTEGU: Thank God you've come!

(DARROW opens briefcase.)

DARROW: As to the plea? Let me go over just a few of the facts tonight. The Lieutenant—

RAMSEY: Please call me Johnny, sir.

DARROW (Smiling): Johnny. You had been under cruel and unusual mental strain before the incident at the villa. For how long would you say?

RAMSEY: Close to five months. Theodie's injuries were so severe—and Mother M. was under such tremendous stress—coming down here to nurse Theodie all the way from Atlanta! I bore the brunt myself . . . like anyone would, sir.

MRS. MONTEGU: Theodie was in the most hideous pain, Mr. Darrow. Jaws wired together from the beating . . . only able to sip through a straw—

RAMSEY: And—then—she had to undergo a curettage from the assaults. She'd become pregnant along with everything else. Complications followed—we—we don't know if we can even have children now. We—

THEODIE: Johnny—

(*THEODIE takes* RAMSEY's *hand. A beat.*)

DARROW: And all the while commanding a submarine, Johnny? Responsible every minute down there for the whole crew? You told me you were at the breaking point . . . how long would you estimate you stayed there?

THEODIE: Johnny started not to be himself the minute I was assaulted.

DARROW: From that time on you started seeing the local psychiatrist?

MRS. MONTEGU: What?

DARROW: I'd better ask him to have his appointment book ready with all dates—

(DARROW *makes a note of this.*)

MRS. MONTEGU: Psychiatrist's records?

DARROW: For the Temporary Insanity plea. Hasn't Johnny told you?

MRS. MONTEGU: No!

RAMSEY: I thought you'd want to present the plea to everyone, sir.

(*Beat.*)

MRS. MONTEGU (*Smiling*): But Johnny's the most steadfast man on earth, Mr. Darrow. Anyone would be a bit trembly with what he went through!

DARROW: Fortunately past records reveal more than "trembling," ma'am.

MRS. MONTEGU: *Fortunately?*

DARROW: Annapolis to start . . .

MRS. MONTEGU: Ancient history! Buried deep in the sands of time!

DARROW: Lord, I don't want it buried!

(*Beat.*)

MRS. MONTEGU: Well, of course, you're the best judge—but a Temporary Insanity plea? Extremely damaging! We are a military family, you see. And we have confidence Johnny has a brilliant future ahead in the navy—once we get past this.

RAMSEY: Please, Mother M., I—

MRS. MONTEGU: Don't be shy, Johnny, for Lord's sake! He's already commander of a submarine here, Mr. Darrow. Our newest, most dangerous military weapon—as you may know. Why, a plea like this would simply destroy his climb to the top. To say nothing of wrecking our family name!

THEODIE: Mummer!

MRS. MONTEGU: Theodie hush! We are looking for a Code of Honor plea, Mr. Darrow.

JOHNNY: Mother M. I-

MRS MONTEGU (*Interrupting*): Johnny? Please! Well then—Mr. Darrow—I'd thought you'd indicated that plea in the local papers. I'd actually planned discussing it tonight. My husband, the Colonel, wants it. The Admiral here at Pearl wants it—the local team of lawyers wants it—and a great many of our naval and American community on the islands want it too! You see, it would give Johnny the right to take the law in his own hands if he couldn't get justice and-

DARROW (*Interrupting*): Never! I spread it around the papers for strategy—that's all!

MRS. MONTEGU: But my dear Mr. Darrow—

DARROW (*Interrupting*): Your husband—the Colonel—signed the agreement putting all decisions in my hands. I'm hoping to establish Temporary Insanity in the courts with this case.

MRS. MONTEGU (*Aghast*): Our case?

DARROW: Bring an expert witness down here, if you'll agree to his fee. Steep but worth it. Dr. David Stein. Brilliant psychiatrist.

MRS. MONTEGU (*Weak little laugh*): An expert—at our expense—to "certify" to the world Johnny's insane? You either must be joking—or a bit overcome with our tropical heat?

DARROW: Like I said—we agreed—in writing—all the legal decisions are mine.

MRS. MONTEGU: We all didn't *really* agree to anything, Mr. Darrow. You see, down here in the Territory—end of the world—words on paper are very cheaply bought and sold.

DARROW (*Looking at her sharply*): Not my words!

MRS. MONTEGU: Admiral would simply blanch at the very idea of his commanding officer declared insane in court—and he's so very influential—

DARROW (*Interrupting*): Admiral's not on trial for his life, ma'am—you are!

MRS. MONTEGU: The Colonel's a very—

DARROW: And the Colonel's not the defense lawyer, ma'am—I am! Don't any of 'em know how much trouble you folks are in? There's a powerful circumstantial case against you, Mrs. Montegu.

MRS. MONTEGU: They haven't got one witness to what happened!

RAMSEY: Mother M.? Listen to Mr. Darrow. Please!

DARROW: The dead body was in the backseat when your car was stopped. Both of you in front—a bullet in Kalani from your gun—found in your Villa—with yours and Johnny's prints.

MRS. MONTEGU: We all know Johnny handled it and it was *my* gun—but purchased months ago. I was just so terrified staying alone up there in the mountains!

DARROW: Johnny pulled the trigger—left his prints. The rest is only your word—and you told me just now how "words are cheap" down here!

MRS. MONTEGU (*Rising*): I'm afraid I've become dreadfully unnerved by all of this! In pieces, to be honest. I simply cannot discuss any of this a moment more—so—if you'll excuse me?

(SHE *starts out.* RAMSEY *and* DARROW *rise.* DARROW *shakes hands with her.* SHE *smiles, trying to pull herself together.*)

MRS. MONTEGU: Good night? And I trust you will think it all over, dear Mr. Darrow? So we'll all be in harmony with whatever you choose?

DARROW: Of course . . .

(SHE *exits.*)

Her life's on the line too, whether she acknowledges it or not! God, I wish you'd told her and got it settled before I came!

RAMSEY: I'm sorry sir. I should've—but—well, we've just been beside ourselves—

(*Beat.*)

Look—here's a thought Mr. Darrow—

DARROW: What?

RAMSEY: Does she really have to know for sure you're going ahead with the insanity plea?

(THEODIE *and* RAMSEY *link eyes, extremely excited at idea of this little plot.*)

DARROW: I think so. There's the question of the psychiatrist's fee. I have to wire him $2,000 right away and she's footing all the bills, isn't she?

(*Beat.*)

THEODIE (*Excited*): I have discretionary funds, Mr. Darrow. I can arrange the doctor's fee.

(SHE *takes* RAMSEY's *hand.*)

RAMSEY: And I'll be prepping alone and not with Mother, won't I, sir?

DARROW: Yes—

RAMSEY: And you agreed you wanted her in agreement with "whatever you chose."

DARROW: I guess I did—

THEODIE: Then why can't Mummer think you're reconsidering? That it's all up in the air? Daddy and the Admiral can think that too. And the local lawyers.

DARROW: I don't know—I sure don't want to lie—mislead the folks on our side—

RAMSEY: It's just postponing the telling. Not lying. Or misleading.

DARROW: I—I just don't know as I'm comfortable with that—'specially your mother.

THEODIE: Mummer's all to pieces now and can't think straight. But that's just a temporary and unusual circumstance, Mr. Darrow.

RAMSEY: Sheltered woman. Protected life. And put through the mill with everything down here. And the tensions tonight meeting you. She'll come around, for my sake and Theodie's. She always has.

THEODIE: By the time we're in trial Mummer'll be back to her old self, standing right by us. She'll manage to forget what she thought was right. She has that way about her: forgetting what she thinks is right—

(DARROW *shuts briefcase.*)

DARROW: So then—we start prep tomorrow in your cabin?

RAMSEY: "Temporary Insanity plea." Thank you, sir.

(THEY *shake hands on it.*)

THEODIE: I'll leave with you, Mr. Darrow—Johnny?

(THEODIE *kisses* RAMSEY *with some passion, tosses scarf over shoulder, joins* DAR-ROW. THEY *walk down ramp from boat as* RAMSEY *takes out pack of cigarettes, begins to smoke, pacing on deck in nervous, almost "quick-march" step, then exits.*)

THEODIE: I come every day. Johnny likes candy so much I bring him coconut
   drops every time—

(*THEY* stand, *SHE* *looks at him, giggling, a little mischievous.*)

DARROW: I think it's worth your every effort to help him. He's a good man,
   ma'am.

(*THEY* start walking. Following scene occurs as they stop, then walk, then
stop, etc.)

THEODIE: Well—I am trying to help—and don't I just know what a good man
   he is—

(*SHE* fingers her scarf, looks away, starts walking ahead, *DARROW* following.
Comes beside her.)

DARROW: I felt fatherly to him right off the bat? Smart—friendly—respect-
   ful—practical! Grasps the situation completely, doesn't he?
THEODIE: Oh, he does grasp it all, Mr. Darrow. Very well.
DARROW: Gonna make me a good witness. Feel it in my bones!
THEODIE: Well, that's wonderful.
DARROW: All that military discipline's gonna carry him right straight through
   on the stand.

(*HE* stops walking as does *SHE*.)

   You know, you just can't shake up a military man!
THEODIE: No sir, you really can't! It's carried him through everything!

(*SHE* stares at *DARROW* then starts walking again. *HE* follows suit.)

DARROW: More worried about your mother. Like a vote of confidence from her
   100 percent.
THEODIE (*Laughing*): She'll cooperate—but like everyone says—we aristo-
   crats don't give our real confidence to anyone—except each other!

(*Long beat as* *SHE* *stops, scrutinizing him.*)

I'm an exception though: I give my confidence to any person I trust.
DARROW: Wonderful I can count on that!
THEODIE: I confide things? Important things?

(*Silence.*)

You know—on the boat? When I come here every day?
DARROW: Yes?
THEODIE: I set out the candy and then play three-handed bridge with them.

(*Looks back at* DARROW, *then somewhat confidential:*)

Done that since I was little—three-handed bridge, I mean. My Daddy—the Colonel? He taught me.

(SHE *keeps focusing on* DARROW.)

You see I was his "special girl"—only child—my—my Daddy? He—he—taught me lots of things.

(SHE *laughs, a little hysterical? Maybe. She then begins fussing with her scarf, arranging, rearranging it.*)

DARROW: I'm sure.
THEODIE: Like riding his great big horse—you know about that?

(SHE's *staring at him.*)

DARROW: Not that—

(HE's *studying her.* SHE *twirls her purse, her scarf.* THEY *start walking.*)

THEODIE: How could you? Well, he was an expert horseman . . . my Daddy . . .
DARROW: I see.
THEODIE: Roughrider. Went to Santiago with Teddy Roosevelt. Cavalry. We're distant relatives of Teddy. Daddy named me for him—Theodora.

(SHE *smiles.*)

THEODIE (Cont'd):
> Thomas Edison's my grand uncle. Mummer's side. They used to say: Edison side of the family is always "lit up!"

(*DARROW laughs.*)

> Family joke . . .

DARROW: Distinguished family to be proud of, Mrs. Ramsey.

(*THEY stop and SHE looks at him, then nervously smiling.*)

THEODIE: Father shot a bullet through the headboard of a freshman's bed at Yale. While the boy was asleep. Almost killed him.

(*Laughs again, nervously.*)

> Hazing. His fraternity. They expelled him and he went on to West Point instead. Start of his brilliant military career!

(*SHE looks dead-on at DARROW.*)

> Now? He has a direct line to President Hoover!

(*Again her nervous laugh.*)

> Well. All the men in the family seem to get caught for one wild, violent thing or another!

(*DARROW looking at her.*)

Then? (*Another nervous laugh.*)

> They just get themselves "reinstated" . . . like they hadn't done anything at all.

(*SHE laughs again. Long pause. SHE turns away.*)

> Mr. Darrow?

DARROW: Yes?

(*SHE doesn't answer. Instead looks at her watch.*)

Yes, ma'am, what is it?

THEODIE (*A new tone, glancing at watch*): It's so late—I'm never out this late in Pearl Harbor—

DARROW: Escort you back to Honolulu?

THEODIE: No—no, thank you—

(SHE *looks at him again, slightly confidential.*)

You see I drove the car.

DARROW: Tonight?

THEODIE (*Seems confused*): What?

DARROW: You drive alone at night now, I mean. Tonight.

(*Beat as* SHE *looks at him.*)

THEODIE: Huh? Oh . . . oh, no—not tonight! Not anymore at all in fact. Tonight was the exception—to greet you, Mr. Darrow. I'll be fine—highway from Pearl's always busy . . .

(SHE *takes both* DARROW'S *hands in hers, laughs lightly, and smiles.*)

Delightful meeting you, Mr. Darrow—at long last.

(SHE *exits.* DARROW *starts off as* TOM LOU *appears. Flash of his camera shooting Darrow.*)

TOM LOU: Evening, Mr. Darrow. Statement after visiting your clients for the first time, sir? Have you decided tonight on the unwritten law as the plea?

DARROW: Well, sir—the way I see it, there are too many written laws now. A fella can't really keep track of all of 'em he's supposed to abide by. The Prohibition Law for example? Makes it too darn hard for a fella to get a drink!

(TOM LOU *laughs.*)

But I do like Unwritten Laws!

(DARROW *exits one way,* TOM LOU *runs to new area: corner of his office. Lights up on desk with typewriter, phone, mike. Morse Code beeps. Then* HE *types and speaks words as, possibly; they also roll across top of proscenium:*)

TOM LOU: "DARROW MEETS CLIENTS. HINTS STRONGLY AT UN-
WRITTEN LAW PLEA"

(HE *continues typing as lights up: brilliant sunshine. Possibly projections: shots of Waikiki Beach. Honolulu. Festive ambiance. Hawaiian (ukulele) and calliope music mix, possibly twirling carousel horse descending on pole while helium bal-loons drift on as Morse Code beeps.*)

TOM LOU (*Picking up text*): Good morning! Tom Lou here at WHLU, your native news, Honolulu. April 3, 1932. And a bright and beautiful morning
as the Montegu-Ramsey Trial begins jury selection.

(HE *leaves desk, begins strolling towards courthouse area, observing the sights, speaking directly to audience.*)

Downtown—a flood of world travelers—adventurers—sensation seek-
ers. A "carnival" atmosphere. Always happens with Mr. Darrow's trials;
they say—Leopold and Loeb—Scopes trial particularly . . . but surely
unexpected here—

(*In courthouse area:*)

In front of the courthouse now, folks—new telegraph lines up to radio
broadcast this trial to the mainland—LIVE—an historic first! *Special
passes* given to those with what they call "legitimate interests" to go in
but . . . *barricades* up to hold back the rest of the people?

(HE *looks around, surprised.*)

Everyone's searched for *bombs*, folks!! *Guns!* There's a fear of native hostility towards this trial! *Shocking!* But true—

(HE *steps closer.*)

Very near the courthouse now: desks, typewriters, telephones being hauled into courtroom for international reporters—

(DARROW *enters area, looks around,* TOM LOU *watching, moving to side where* DARROW *doesn't see him.*)

Thirty-six years ago? The courthouse was the Hall of Chiefs—the *Ali'i*—our royal advisors to Queen Leliuokalani—they met here to serve the *Hawaiian people!*

Across the courtyard? Iolani Palace—home of our queen and courtiers. Now? *Office of the American Governor for "The American Territory"!*

(DARROW *before a statue with inscription.* NANILOA *enters, watching.* TOM LOU *to audience, sadness now in voice:*)

King Kamehameha's statue is before the courthouse, folks. Arms outstretched to our people. His words at its base . . .

(HE *moves off slowly, looking back at* DARROW, NANILOA.)

I'll be back when trial begins—

(HE *exits.*)

NANILOA (*To* DARROW): "*Ua mau ke ea o ka aina I ka pono.*"

(DARROW *looks at her.*)

"The Life of the Land is perpetuated by righteousness" is what it means. Mr. Darrow? Sir?
DARROW (*Doffing hat*): Yes?
NANILOA: Aloha!
DARROW: Aloha, ma'am.
NANILOA: I am Naniloa Whitefield Chan.
DARROW: Ma'am?
NANILOA: The prosecutor, Mr. Darrow.

(SHE *offers hand;* HE *seems not to see it or hear what* SHE'S *said.*)

DARROW: Yes, madam?

NANILOA: Deputy district attorney, sir. For the people of the territory, sir.

DARROW: Prosecutor?

NANILOA: Against your clients, sir.

DARROW (*HE shakes her hand, barely looking at her*): Madam.

NANILOA: I am so honored to meet you, Mr. Darrow, A privilege to serve on the same case—

DARROW (*Baffled by conversation*): Of course—of course—

NANILOA: You are such an idol for me, sir—all your pioneer work—for the colored, the poor, the underprivileged!

DARROW: Prosecutor?

NANILOA (*SHE smiles, bows slightly in Asian manner*): Miss Naniloa Whitefield Chan.

DARROW: Chan?

NANILOA: My father was an importer from Shanghai—and "Naniloa"? For my maternal grandmother—a Hawaiian chiefess. An *ali'i*—royal advisor— to our Queen.

DARROW: Chiefess?

NANILOA: Naniloa *Whitefield* Chan. That's for my maternal grandfather— Jonas Whitefield. Missionary from Massachusetts. Died serving the lepers of Molokai. I am called simply "Naniloa."

DARROW: You're the Prosecutor?

NANILOA (*Smiling, bowing head slightly again*): "Young Portia of Honolulu" my nickname when I won a case for natives' water rights—

DARROW: Against who?

NANILOA: Plantation owners draining it for themselves! I began in civil law. I will do anything—devote my life, Mr. Darrow, to helping the underdogs of my country—the suffering people of this earth. As you do.

DARROW: Well—noble ambition—to be sure—

NANILOA: Educated at Stanford, sir—*Law Review*.

DARROW: You don't say—

(*Sound of gavel is heard.*)

NANILOA (*Smiling, slightly bowed head. Offers hand*): A pleasure to meet you, Mr. Darrow.

(*THEY shake hands as NANILOA looks around.*)

But such a "carnival atmosphere," sir, you bring to Honolulu! Strange for a murdered *Hawaiian's* trial?

(*HE looks at her.*)

Aloha, Mr. Darrow—sir—

(*Smiles, bowing head,* SHE *exits as gavel sounds.* DARROW *exits. Spot on* TOM LOU *at desk typing, Morse code beeps. He speaks into mike:*)

TOM LOU: WHLU, Tom Lou at the end of day one of jury selection. And—we have *three* jurors, folks! THREE! Everyone in court now hurrying out—to fresh air.

(*As* HE *speaks,* DARROW *enters new area: hotel bar, darkish. Sits at table, takes flask from pocket; pours into glass, belts it. Lights cigarette.*)

And—the beach and cold refreshments—I'll be back in court with you tomorrow, folks. Tom Lou from WHLU signing off . . .

(*Morse Code beeps.* HE *exits as* DARROW *belts another shot, sits silent, isolated, mood dark.* RUBY *enters, looking for him. Sees him, stops, watching. Then:*)

RUBY: Dee? Dee?
DARROW: Huh? What?
RUBY: It's late. We're missing one of those parties—Mrs. Montegu's friends.

(*Silence.*)

I couldn't figure out where you went—so I sent regrets.

(SHE *looks around dark bar.*)

Come on out of this dark bar? Please? You can relax upstairs in our room—beautiful light streaming in this time of day—
DARROW: I don't know who the hell I just chose for jurors! Must've spoken six different mother tongues. I don't know if they understand English at all! And their accents? So thick I couldn't out make if they were saying "yes" or "no"! And oh my God, the odd faces!

DARROW (Cont'd):

(HE *begins seeing jurors before him:*)

> Japanese, Portuguese—which they tell me's not exactly Caucasian white—but working-class white—whatever the hell that's supposed to mean. Or look like! Then Hawaiians, Chinese, Polynesian, Japanese, Siamese. Then the "mixed bloods." They're the worst! Can't tell whose side they're on or what they believe. And then? Their crazy, peculiar behavior!

RUBY: What're you talking about?

DARROW: Half of 'em kept smiling—bowing to me—for no damn reason! Whatever I asked—

(HE *half rises, imitating this.*)

> A smile and a little bow!

RUBY (*Chuckling*): Well, it really is the "Inscrutable East" then, huh?

DARROW: You know I hate stereotyping! Stop that!

RUBY: Exactly what *you're* doing, Mr. Darrow, sir! Even imitating them? Really, Dee, can't you just keep your sense of humor about it all?

DARROW: I don't find it funny. That all right with you?

(*Beat.*)

RUBY: How'd the prosecutor choose his jurors?

DARROW: First off? He's a she!

RUBY: What?

DARROW: As we say in Chicago: "A Lady Law"! And distinguished—and young and beautiful to boot!

RUBY: Really?

DARROW: Worse: she's one of them.

RUBY: Who?

DARROW: "Mixed bloods." Like I told you—the worst of the worst to figure out. She's Hawaiian, Chinese, white. *"Hapas,"* they call 'em. Looks like 'em. Thinks like 'em. *Is* one of 'em. Knew exactly what how to pick jurors, too. And I couldn't read how she was doin' it dime one! Scares me to death!

RUBY (*Laughing a little*): Scared of a young lady prosecutor? You're just tired and hot—first day—and too much to drink.

(SHE *puts coins on table, helps him up,* THEY *start to hotel room.*)

DARROW: Worst of it is, I don't know where their prejudices are because I don't know where their loyalties are. You get me?

RUBY: Not exactly.

DARROW: I get the jurors through their feelings, right? Biases—prejudices—passions . . . and I tap into that by knowing their *loyalties*! But are Hawaiians loyal only to Hawaii? Or us? Chinese only to China? Japanese to Japan? Or all of them to us first? And who're the damned mixed bloods loyal to? Quarter white, quarter Chinese—half Hawaiian?

RUBY: You'll figure it out—

(THEY *enter their hotel room.*)

Oh, look what I bought!

(RUBY *immediately sliding into a flowery kimono. Twirling in it, then embracing him.*)

Like it?

DARROW: Sure. Sure—

RUBY: Yours is over there.

(SHE *indicates another kimono. No response.* HE *seems preoccupied.*)

I ordered room service for dinner, Dee—for us!

(DARROW *nods, mind somewhere else.*)

Still worried about that Lady Law and the jurors, huh?

DARROW: Yup!

RUBY (*Helping him out of tie, jacket*): Was just thinking, Dee—our local firm's Oriental Law Clerk—the one who went scouting the neighborhoods for us—he say anything helpful to you?

DARROW: Said: in court down here—jurors are gonna *separate* their own *feelings* from their *logical reasoning,* They'll vote on what they decide are the logical reasons for what happened.

RUBY: That's interesting, Dee.

DARROW: Only I don't understand their feelings—let alone how they reason. So how the hell am I supposed to know how they separate 'em? Jesus Christ!

(RUBY *pours them some lemonade, sits down.*)

(DARROW *disdains lemonade, pours drink from sideboard, downs it.*)

RUBY: No more, Dee. You need to think now. Please?

(HE *puts down glass.*)

Occurs to me though—wouldn't be too hard to get to that jury about a mentally troubled man who—in the moment—*can't* separate his logical mind from his feelings—and goes out of control—irrational with those feelings—so he can't think straight.

DARROW (*Contemplating idea*): I don't think-

RUBY (*Interrupting*): What else did this Law Clerk say—about the natives?

DARROW: Not much—nobody's hostile to our case or me though . . . and everyone's sorry for the family. Feel they got a bad deal first trial. And—they've got special sympathy for Theodie.

RUBY: Anything else?

DARROW: Kalani was a professional prizefighter in Honolulu. But born on another island. Only here a couple years. Known as a hothead newcomer that settled everything with his fists . . . not really accepted—an outcast. The whole gang's transient—from different islands—drifters—only together here a couple months before Theodie's assault.

(*Beat.*)

RUBY: You stop at the D.A.?

DARROW: Lunchtime.

RUBY: And?

DARROW: He corroborated everything about the first case—whats, whens, whys . . .

(*Beat.*)

RUBY: Dee? All this is tremendously in our favor!

(A silence. Then:)

Know what? David *should* know right away how the jurors are gonna think through things logically so he can give the medical testimony in a way that persuades them to go along.

DARROW: How's he gonna do that?

RUBY: No attempts at sympathy for Johnny's condition—only scientific—logical explanations of his mental state that made him behave like he did—

DARROW: You're right. No reason he can't do that, for God's sake! He's a scientific man.

(Lights up STEIN, in Chicago office, as DARROW starts talking on phone, STEIN looks at Darrow, listening to him)

David?

DAVID (STEIN now talks to DARROW): What's going on?

DARROW: Need to tailor your approach on your testimony, David

STEIN: What's "tailor" mean?

DARROW: Give the testimony logically—scientifically—'cause that's how jurors operate here. Keep emotion out of it.

STEIN: What's *that* mean?

DARROW: Emphasize the medical reasons. Physical causes—the science of what happened to Ramsey to make him act like he did—and I'll take it from there!

STEIN: But you operate on feelings—getting sympathy for your client—

DARROW: Don't have to! I'm gonna try a new way now. New ace up my sleeve. Ruby's idea—and I like it.

STEIN: Ruby's making decisions now?

(Beat.)

DARROW: "Ideas," David. I make decisions.

DAVID: Well—I'll try. Clarence?

DARROW: Yup?

STEIN: Only one boat a week down there from Frisco. I think I could manage to be there by the twelfth for you. How's that?

(*Beat.*)

DARROW: Week after, David.

STEIN: That's almost the start of the trial!

DARROW: Time enough for you to examine Ramsey, prep him, then testify.

STEIN: Rather have a few days to settle in—talk with Ramsey—along the lines you want now—

DARROW: Look, David—everyone thinks I'm pleadin' Code of Honor. Waivin' my opening statement too.

STEIN: Why on earth?

DARROW: I'd have to say just *how* I'm pleadin' and *who* I'm pleadin' it for. This way nobody knows. The prosecution starts their case just when you get here. Then? I come in with my Temporary Insanity Plea, calling only the Lieutenant to the stand. Then you testify—loaded with science and fact. And there's no time for the prosecutor to get her psychiatrist to examine the Lieutenant *before* the trial's started. Especially on scientific grounds.

STEIN: But can't she do it at the time?

DARROW: Court here doesn't allow a rebuttal on a witness with *their* psychiatrist *after* trial's underway.

STEIN: Brilliant move!

DARROW: Top of my form, David! Top of my form!

STEIN: Cunning like a fox!

(*Blackout on* STEIN.)

RUBY: Good idea for you to talk to him about the way to go, huh?

DARROW: You were right. And when you're right, you're right!

(HE *kisses her.* THEY *both laugh.*)

RUBY: Here—put this on—

(SHE *helps* DARROW *into kimono.*)

Oh, don't you just look grand!

(*Looking at him, then around the room.*)

Now—soon as room service arrives? We're gonna have dinner, Dee . . .

(SHE *starts lighting candles.*)

By candlelight—by the window—overlooking Waikiki!

End of Act One

❖   ❖   ❖

ACT TWO

(TOM LOU *over mike at a desk in courtroom. Morse code beeps:*)

TOM LOU: Tom Lou at WHLU now reporting from Honolulu. April 15th.
Thursday. Sweltering day predicted, folks—105 by noon. And Honolulu
experiencing an overflow of crowds for the trial! Downtown streets here
jammed with spectacle—pageantry we haven't seen since the days our
Queen ruled. Speaking to you from the courtroom, folks, where the trial
begins shortly.

(RUBY *walks in, taking seat in gallery.*)

Mrs. Darrow is here.

(HE *looks around, then up.*)

Overhead? Courtroom fans only spinning heat—one hundred degrees
in here right now—and—our famous mosquitoes?

(*Swats his arm, then other arm.*)

Everywhere!

(HE *chuckles as* DARROW *enters, sits.*)

Darrow's in.

(*Gavel sounds.* NANILOA, *entering high on level with red lacquered Asian box,
containing objects of evidence. Sets this down.*)

Naniloa here.

(VOICE OF JUSTICE *is an offstage voice. Should surround theater audience as well
as onstage scene. Deep, resonant, authoritative.*)

VOICE OF JUSTICE: ALL RISE! HEAR YE! HEAR YE! THE CITY AND
COUNTY COURT OF HONOLULU, THE TERRITORY OF

HAWAII VS. MRS. KATHRYN MONTEGU AND LIEUTNENAT JUNIOR GRADE JOHN BIRMINGHAM RAMSEY. COURT IN SESSION NOW! MISS CHAN FOR THE PROSECUTION, PLEASE!

TOM LOU: Ramsey-Montegu Trials beginning, folks. Let's listen in:

NANILOA: Gentlemen of the jury, The Prosecution intends to show the Defendants kidnapped Kim Kalani and—when he wouldn't sign a forced confession—murdered him. Now, we will agree, the District Attorney may well have told the defendants: Kalani wanted to confess—privately—and if he confessed—there might well be only an Assault and Battery charge for him in a retrial. And—the other men would be charged with the rape! And we will agree the District Attorney may well have suggested too—Mrs. Montegu's villa might be just such a private place to sign the confession. And—since Kalani reported to probation every day at this courthouse—the courthouse stairs might well be the place to find Kalani leaving each day at around nine o'clock. But—the District Attorney's suggestions—we will show—became only rich fodder for the defendants! Because on these very courthouse steps—the defendants first stalked Kalani—attempted to lure him into the rental car to go to the Villa to sign.

Then when he refused—they came back a second day—kidnapped him to the Villa—tried to force the signed confession. And when they couldn't get it?

They MURDERED Kalani in cold blood!

First evidence of this plan? Witnesses, who—both days in front of this courthouse—saw with their naked eyes—the rented black sedan which hid the Defendants' *real identities*.

We will then introduce further proof with testimony from the car rental clerk—and to put into evidence we have: the receipt from the rental with Lt. Ramsey's signature!

(SHE *pulls receipt from box, displays, puts it back. Hubbub in courtroom.*)

Further—at Mrs. Montegu's Villa—we will prove—they *murdered* Kalani—not an hour later with a .32 caliber Colt. This gun—which testimony from the Barley Hardware and Gun Shop proprietor corroborates under oath—was exactly the kind of gun *Mrs. Montegu* had bought there and signed a receipt for.

(SHE *flashes gun and receipt from box as hubbub again in courtroom.* SHE *puts these back.*)

Next? We will show with police testimony that as the Defendants raced away to throw Kalani's corpse over a cliff—a highway policeman stopped their car for speeding before they could get rid of the corpse. And we intend to prove with the Medical Examiner's testimony—a .32 caliber bullet was found near Kalani's heart, consistent, of course, with bullets used in a .32 caliber Colt! Exactly the type of gun Mrs. Montegu had purchased.

VOICE OF JUSTICE: ALL RISE! COURT WILL RECONVENE 9 A.M. MONDAY, APRIL 19TH. COURT NOW IN RECESS!

(*Morse code beeps.*)

TOM LOU: And so this day in court ends with Naniloa offering intriguing information—displaying the strength, courage, and intelligence all of us in Honolulu have come to admire in her.

(DARROW *still seated, putting papers in briefcase.*)

Court in a four-day recess now, folks—people leaving here—hurrying to swim, boat, relax on their lanais. We'll be back with the trial, Monday, April 19th. Tom Lou, WHLU, your native Honolulu station now signing off—

(*Morse code beeps.* TOM LOU *exits as* RUBY *moves forward to* DARROW.)

RUBY: Where did she get all that evidence, Dee? The car? The gun? The witnesses? I went over everything they sent you in Chicago. *None* of that was there.

DARROW: Ruby, don't worry. Come on—let's go get something to eat.

(HE *gets up, walking,* SHE *follows him.*)

None of this matters to our case at all. It's all just—

RUBY (*Interrupting*): You only had three weeks to prepare everything! We depended on these Honolulu lawyers hook, line, and sinker. And I don't think they ever gave us one piece of that evidence—the car—rental clerk—gun—gun-shop clerk—

(THEY're out of courtroom by Kamehameha's statue.)

DARROW: There're no Discovery Laws down here—I don't think they knew what she'd found! She's showboating! Sounds dramatic as hell—doesn't amount to a row of beans! Everyone's told me she's got no significant evidence at all—that the receipt doesn't prove they killed Kalani. Or the gun or the car or witnesses.

RUBY: They're the same people told you these Hawaiians can't be gotten to emotionally, right? Well, you could hear a pin drop, the jury was so spellbound by her! Emotion all the way!

DARROW: Doesn't matter the jury got entranced a moment or two. That's not hard evidence. Like blood evidence. Now, please? You're making me nervous.

RUBY: I'm not so sure she hasn't got blood evidence, Dee.

DARROW: You remember where that Chinese restaurant was? And the juice stand? I sure could use some cold juice right now—

(HE exits, SHE follows as lights shift to another day. TOM LOU enters courtroom, sits at table, fiddling with mike and wires. Finally, Morse Code beeps.)

TOM LOU: I think we're on?

(HE looks around, pinging mike. NANILOA, very angry, walks into court on high platform. DARROW enters, sits as RUBY sits in gallery, to side.)

TOM LOU: We're on! Afternoon, folks. Tom Lou at WHLU reporting. Sorry about the delay today here, folks—trouble with connections all day—but now it's 2 P.M., folks. Afternoon session and nearly three weeks into the trial.

Most of us believe this may well be the final day for the prosecution's direct case. Let me catch you up on the important events of the morning: Naniloa has offered an array of witnesses—the medical examiner who testified, quote: "Kalani bled very little from the fatal .32 gun wound," unquote. But—her next witness, the official blood lab technician, testified that, quote: "it was determined it *was* Kalani's blood found

TOM LOU (Cont'd):

in the Villa," unquote. Then from police at the murder scene, quote: "Kalani's blood stains were all over Mrs. Montegu's Villa—floor, carpets, towels," unquote—

(NANILOA, *more perturbed, throws open box, holds up bloody bath towels, showing them around for all to see.*)

Finally, the second police officer testified, quote: "Kalani's blood saturated his trousers and undershorts too which we found at the bottom of a clothes hamper! Their flies ripped open with such violence buttons were broken and fabric torn!"

(SHE *holds up pants, shorts, from box, displaying them with rage and disgust, coming closer with articles:*)

NANILOA: WHAT HAPPENED GENTLEMEN?

(*Gavel* SOUND.)

The white, *Haole* police quickly took possession of Kalani's body when they found it. And took it to be examined. Then to the white, *Haole* funeral parlor which Hawaiians never use. Then Kalani's mother's brought in and forced to identify her son—from his casket, sealed neck down! Finally? The body's buried *immediately* at sea!

(*Gavel sounds again. Defiant,* SHE *steps closer, holding out pants, shorts.*)

THIS IS A LYNCHING, GENTLEMEN! CASTRATION "WHITE SOUTHERN STYLE!"

VOICE OF JUSTICE: MISS CHAN TO CHAMBERS! COURT IS IN RECESS!

(*Gavel.* NANILOA *exits.* RUBY, *upset, goes to* DARROW.)

RUBY: SHE'S PUT IT ALL TOGETHER WITH *RACE*! NOW SHE'S GONG TO DRAG THAT FRONT AND CENTER THROUGH HER WHOLE CASE? Why didn't you object, Dee? You focusing on what's going on?

DARROW: Shh! Reporter's probably listening. She was called to chambers. It'll be handled there. Let's go—

(*THEY exit courtroom, walking toward hotel.*)

RUBY: But the jury heard her! You always said that was what was important. And RACE? It's what kept you out of the case first time they asked you here. You only had three weeks to prepare! But *I* went through every scrap—Chester—local lawyers—nothing! No one ever *privately* gave you anything on that Villa did they?

DARROW: Doesn't matter, Rube.

RUBY: Our local lawyers didn't get hold of the report about the bloody clothes at least?

DARROW: That Ramsey went out of his mind is what's important. And that's what I aim to prove. That'll put race at the fringes of the case. And make the blood insignificant too—so calm down and c'mon? I need a nap—

(*THEY exit as TOM LOU comes to desk and mike.*)

TOM LOU: Now? Fourth week of trial with WHLU with Tom Lou. And court about to start, folks. With Mr. Darrow for The Defense!

(*Gavel.*)

VOICE OF JUSTICE: MR. DARROW, PLEASE.

DARROW: I hereby enter for U.S. Navy Lieutenant (j.g.) John Birmingham Ramsey, Commander and Engineer S-43 submarine, Pearl Harbor, Territory of Hawaii, U.S. of A, the plea of not guilty! Reason? Temporary Insanity.

VOICE OF JUSTICE: THE RECORD WILL SO REFLECT.

(*Gavel. NANILOA looks up stunned.*)

NANILOA: I strenuously object. Prosecution was not informed of plea—a customary courtesy here. And—having assumed another plea would be entered, Prosecution has not engaged psychiatrists to examine Defendant, so he may be questioned by them in rebuttal. I hereby move a one-day postponement to allow psychiatrists to examine Defendant.

VOICE OF JUSTICE: DEFENSE DOES NOT HAVE LEGAL OBLIGATION TO INFORM THE PROSECUTION. MR. DARROW, PLEASE.

DARROW: Gentlemen, Miss Naniloa's accused the Defendants of kidnapping, premeditated murder, and—the worst—most bestial crime known to civilized man: castration! What a crude, lurid crime Miss Naniloa imagines in her wild fantasy was committed. "White Southern Style!"

NANILOA: Objection! Argument! Not evidence!

VOICE OF JUSTICE: SUSTAINED!

DARROW: Well then—"evidence"? You see there is good reason for that blood evidence folks: "a second wound!"

(HE's *now very close.*)

Undiscovered! Coroner's stated the autopsy wasn't complete: quote: "exclusive attention only to bullet wound in chest," unquote. And no body to exhume! If we only had that, we'd knock Miss Naniloa's lurid accusation out of the ring! Because we'd find that second bullet wound. Probably in the abdomen, gentlemen. Maybe we'd find even more wounds! Profusely bloody, abdominal wounds—ever see one?

(*Growing very intimate with audience.*)

An ugly sight, profuse blood! But there it was in that villa. Because shots hit Kalani's chest, then abdomen too—when he went turncoat on this poor family—demanding money, jewels, using a gentle lady as his shield, then taunting, humiliating the Lieutenant that he'd rape his wife again—which pushed the Lieutenant beyond reason! Until poor Ramsey fired off two shots at the man. Three? Maybe four?

Sounds crazy—doesn't it? Well—it was! A crazed mental state that overwhelms reason. A state when men sometimes shoot round after round after round—at their own families—the ground—the ceiling—themselves! In shock! Wild! Dazed! CRAZED! Not accountable! Temporarily Insane!—Lieutenant Ramsey's pitiable condition that day, gentlemen. Remembering nothing he did afterwards—when his senses finally returned! I call to the stand now, Lieutenant John Ramsey, please?

(NANILOA *is stunned as* RAMSEY *enters, right hand raised, taking stand as* HE *speaks:*)

RAMSEY: I do solemnly swear to tell the truth, the whole truth, and nothing but the truth, so help me God.

(DARROW *going to him, speaks softly so no one hears:*)

DARROW: You can do it, son—strong, brave man—I know you can do this—

(*To jury:*)

And now, Lieutenant—can you tell us what the District Attorney suggested you do?

RAMSEY: The District Attorney mentioned Kalani reported here every day, for probation—so we would be able to meet him right outside here and see if he was agreeable. And if so, we could arrange a meeting for a subsequent day.

DARROW: What was your response to these suggestions?

RAMSEY: I drove to the courthouse with Mrs. Montegu in the rented car.

DARROW: Can you tell us the reason for renting the car?

RAMSEY: Kalani wanted everything kept from his gang. My car's bright yellow—recognized all over Honolulu from the first trial—as I am. So we rented a car and decided Mrs. Montegu'd talk to Kalani since no one knew her.

DARROW: To your knowledge—did she do that?

RAMSEY: She went to the courthouse steps, then I saw Kalani coming, and saw her speak to him. She came back and said he'd suggested meeting with us the very next day. Same time. Same place. He was anxious to get "a good deal," he said.

NANILOA: Hearsay.

VOICE OF JUSTICE: SUSTAINED.

DARROW: Can you describe for us what happened the following day, Lieutenant?

RAMSEY: We picked Kalani up next day, got to the Villa—but as soon as we were inside—he announced he knew we had "Big Money" and we had to give it to him or he wouldn't sign.

DARROW: So, fair to say he wasn't only after a light sentence—but a payoff too?

NANILOA: Objection!

VOICE OF JUSTICE: SUSTAINED.

DARROW: What happened next?

RAMSEY: I said we didn't have money in the house. Right then he jerked Mother M.'s pearls off her neck and demanded I give him her "big diamonds" too. I said she had none.

DARROW: And then?

RAMSEY: He pulled a knife and dragged her in front of him. Then started threatening if he didn't get what he wanted—he had men who'd followed us, were parked, and knew *my* address. They'd all take us there and gang rape my wife again! In front of us!

NANILOA: Hearsay!

DARROW: The defendant is entitled to tell the facts of what happened as he observed them.

VOICE OF JUSTICE: OVERRULED!

DARROW: All of what happened terrified you. Fair statement, son?

NANILOA: Leading witness!

VOICE OF JUSTICE: SUSTAINED!

DARROW: How did you feel about what Kalani threatened in the Villa, son?

RAMSEY: I started not thinking straight. Panicking. Then he started jerking Mother M. around, screaming to give him her money, diamonds, describing in filthy language what he'd do to her daughter—she seemed about to faint.

DARROW: And then?

RAMSEY *(Starts visualizing this)*: I'm going out of control—trying to keep in focus . . . I see him—he blurs—see him . . . blurs. Scared I'll pass out—she'll faint . . . remember the desk . . . gun . . . get it—inch back to drawer knob—steady hand—open drawer—Gun! He blurs—

(Beat.)

DARROW: Now—if I may—going back to December 3, 1931—a month before the tragedy in the villa—three months after your wife's assault—

RAMSEY: Yes, sir.

DARROW: You were, at that time, trapped in what I'd like to call a "vicious cycle." You'd consulted a private psychiatrist because you'd started blanking out with some frequency and it frightened you. Fair description, son?

NANILOA: Leading witness!

VOICE OF JUSTICE: SUSTAINED.

DARROW: You consulted a psychiatrist privately because of blackout spells. Correct?

RAMSEY: Yes, sir.

DARROW: The psychiatrist analyzed your condition as—let me quote: "stemming from the Lieutenant's deep feelings of humiliation and inadequacy at not getting justice for his assaulted wife," unquote. As you recall—an accurate diagnosis of your mental state a month before the tragedy at the Villa?

NANILOA: Leading witness.

VOICE OF JUSTICE: SUSTAINED.

DARROW: Now son, the psychiatrist recommended you ask navy doctors for transfer on psychiatric grounds. You refused, he gave you sedatives. Your condition worsened—you felt more engulfed by humiliation feelings because of diagnosis, suggestion of transfer, need to take sedatives?

NANILOA: Leading witness. In addition, witness not qualified to give medical opinion.

VOICE OF JUSTICE: SUSTAINED.

DARROW: On December 9, 1931, Lieutenant, and I'm quoting the psychiatrist's notes: "Lieutenant reported seeing flashes of wife's beaten face when he blanked out," unquote. Accurate statement as you recall, son?

RAMSEY: Yes, sir.

DARROW: Psychiatrist strongly urged you report this to Navy. But you said no—didn't know what to do. Fair statement of your condition and attitude then, son?

RAMSEY: I had to be a man! Get justice for Theodie with a second trial! I couldn't be thought of as a coward who ducked out of everything with a weakling's "mental medical transfer"! Or "medication"! I can't tolerate humiliation.

DARROW: And you'd had experiences long before these—blanking, passing out, time lapses—in humiliating circumstances where you couldn't function and do what was expected of you. Fair statement, son?

RAMSEY: At Annapolis.

DARROW: What happened there?

RAMSEY: I failed to perform maneuvers adequately at sea and was dressed down harshly twice in a row. I started panicking, got dizzy, blanked, passed out on duty, on ship. I was in infirmary three months and—and—thought of suicide—I felt worthless. A chaplain pulled me through—

DARROW: Suicide?

RAMSEY: Yes, sir.

DARROW: Can you describe how you felt last December, son, a month before the tragedy at the Villa when you felt you couldn't get justice for Theodie?

NANILOA: Objection! Leading this witness!

VOICE OF JUSTICE: SUSTAINED!

DARROW: Can you describe how you felt last December, son?

RAMSEY: Suicidal! Feelings of helplessness—worthlessness—overwhelming sir. I'm from the Old South—traditions of chivalry—duty—bravery. I felt unworthy of Theodie—my career—a rotten, measly weakling seeing a "head doctor"—taking pills, for God's sake! I cringed at Pearl if anybody saw me—ate alone at mess—then started getting dizzy—blanking out on sub duty—risking my men's lives!

(HE *looks away.*)

DARROW: Go on—

RAMSEY: I began to feel—I wasn't entitled to anything—worthless—like at Annapolis—overwhelmed—sinking—I thought of drowning myself on duty—then got the thought of my gun—

DARROW: When?

RAMSEY: Near Christmas—

DARROW: Less than a month before the meeting at the Villa?

RAMSEY: Sunday—waiting for Theodie to get dressed—for the Admiral's Christmas party. I was scared I couldn't face it! I was trying to relax—build up guts to go. I was reading some kind of cheap newspaper the maid left behind—but I was so overwhelmed—Christmas season—how worthless my life was. I kept reading—and then I hit a scandalous article about Theodie and me! I couldn't focus—newspaper blurring—dizzy—room blanking in and out—

DARROW: Did that phenomenon stop?

RAMSEY: I—came—but had lost time—

DARROW: How did you know?

RAMSEY: I found myself sitting, paper on the floor, fiddling with my gun—Theodie came in—

DARROW (*Patting him on back*): Thank you, son. That'll be all, your honor.

(GAVEL.)

VOICE OF JUSTICE: COURT IN SHORT RECESS!

DARROW (*Quietly*): Brave of you, son—good job.

RAMSEY: I couldn't have done it without you—and Dr. Stein's prep!

(*RAMSEY, NANILOA exit. DARROW sits, going over papers. MRS. MONTEGU enters.*)

MRS. MONTEGU: Mr. Darrow?

DARROW: Ma'am?

MRS. MONTEGU: You must stop this dreadful plea you've shoved forward.

DARROW: The jury's enthralled! Finally, I got 'em! They're buying our case, ma'am, and it's in your favor. We're on our way!

MRS. MONTEGU: By making Johnny publicly repeat every unspeakable detail of our tragedy? That he became a weak, terrified madman? Popping off a loaded gun? Referring to poor Theodie's humiliation again? And-

DARROW (*Interrupting*): We're trying to save your lives! Dr. Stein and I and-

MRS. MONTEGU (*Interrupting*): Stein? I doubt I will ever forgive your going against my husband, the admiral, and my wishes. Why wasn't I told? And how dare you put Theodie up to cajoling me into accepting everything? And secretly taking that poor girl's money for Dr. Stein? She's fragile and you very much took advantage of her.

DARROW: She's legal age. Volunteered her own money. And Johnny approved. He's the one on the stand, after all.

MRS. MONTEGU: Did it cross your mind Johnny's in a fragile state too?

DARROW: And a fragile state of affairs, madam. You too.

MRS. MONTEGU: Yes, I am. I'll never be able to show my face in Oyster Bay again.

DARROW: Especially if you're in Oahu prison, ma'am!

(*Ignores her, pours water from pitcher, drinking.*)

MRS. MONTEGU: I want the plea changed at once!

(DARROW *ignores her, continues drinking. Gavel.* RAMSEY *enters, goes to witness box.* NANILOA *enters with red box, goes to* RAMSEY.)

NANILOA: There's a bathroom directly off the living room in the Villa. Correct, Lieutenant?

RAMSEY: Yes.

NANILOA: Bathroom where Kalani died?

RAMSEY: No.

NANILOA: You remember he didn't?

RAMSEY: I mean Mrs. Montegu told me later.

NANILOA: What?

RAMSEY: He died on the way to the hospital.

NANILOA: When did she say that?

RAMSEY: When we were arrested. I'd come to by then.

NANILOA: Was he in the bathroom?

RAMSEY: No! I mean, I don't remember.

NANILOA: So he could have been in the bathroom?

RAMSEY: I don't remember.

NANILOA: Was he shot in the living room?

(SHE *gets the red lacquered box.*)

RAMSEY: I don't remember—

NANILOA: So it could have been the bathroom?

RAMSEY: I DON'T REMEMBER!

(NANILOA *holds up bloody sheet from box.* RAMSEY *gazes.*)

NANILOA: You remember this sheet from the Villa found wrapped around Kalani's corpse?

RAMSEY: Yes. I saw him wrapped in it after I came to—when we were stopped . . . also . . .

NANILOA: What?

RAMSEY: I remember he was shot in the living room.

NANILOA: You remember that?

RAMSEY: I mean, I was told that.

NANILOA: Do you remember or were you told anything else that happened in the living room?

RAMSEY: That's where I grabbed the gun.

NANILOA: And you remember shooting Kalani there?

RAMSEY: Yes—I mean; no—I mean; I remember being in the living room— going for the gun. I testified to that—then I blanked. Mother M. said he was shot in the living room.

NANILOA: Why was he in the bathroom?

RAMSEY: I don't remember—

NANILOA (*Holding up bloody towel*): These bathroom towels from the villa have his blood on them. And traces of his blood were in the shower drain.

(DARROW *looks up sharply.*)

Was Kalani in the bathroom shower?

RAMSEY: Yes—I mean, Mrs. Montegu told me—we were trying to cleanse his wounds in there, then bandage them—

NANILOA: You and your mother-in-law lifted this seriously wounded heavyweight champ from the living room to the bathroom?

RAMSEY: No!

NANILOA: You didn't lift him?

RAMSEY: NO!

NANILOA: Drag?

RAMSEY: NO!

NANILOA: Roll?

RAMSEY: WALK! He—

NANILOA (*Interrupting*): "Walked"? To the bathroom? You remember that, right? Gun at his head, right? Not shot twice in the living room at all.

DARROW: Conjecture and compound!

VOICE OF JUSTICE: SUSTAINED!

NANILOA: Did you tie his hands behind him in the living room when—gun to his head—he still wouldn't confess?

RAMSEY: NO! I mean; I don't remember!

NANILOA: Did he walk to the bathroom gun at his head?

RAMSEY: I don't remember.

NANILOA: But you just said he walked!

RAMSEY: Not with a gun at his head!

NANILOA: His back?

RAMSEY: I don't remember! And I was *told* he walked. I don't remember!

NANILOA: Did you back him into the shower—shoot him in the heart so he slid down against the back wall—in a sitting position?

RAMSEY: I don't remember any of that.

NANILOA: Any of *what*?

DARROW: Leading witness! Conjecture! Badgering!

VOICE OF JUSTICE: SUSTAINED!

NANILOA: Now you have testified that he walked to the bathroom and was in the shower.

DARROW: He has not!

NANILOA: Did he walk to the bathroom?

RAMSEY: No . . . Yes—I don't know—I keep telling you everything was told to me by Mrs. Montegu!

NANILOA: After you shot him in the shower—while he was still alive—did she hold the gun on him while you ripped these open?

(SHE *pulls bloody pants, undershorts from box.* DARROW *jumps up, disturbed.*)

> Castrated him? Then turn on the spigot to wash the blood down the drain?

RAMSEY: NO! NO! NO!

NANILOA: Afterwards, did you wrap him in the sheet and drag him out?

RAMSEY: NO! THAT WASN'T THE WAY WE-

NANILOA (*Interrupting*): Oh? What was "the way" then, Lieutenant? Why don't you straighten the story out for us?

RAMSEY: I remember nothing. NOTHING!

NANILOA: That will be all, Lieutenant. You are excused.

(*Gavel.* ALL *leave but* DARROW. RUBY *comes in hurriedly.*)

RUBY: Oh, Lord, Dee—he *is* remembering—isn't he?

DARROW: She was badgering him—rattling him—so he wasn't perfect. But nothing damaged him very much.

(DARROW *starts pacing.*)

> He wasn't thinking straight—so how could he remember details straight?

RUBY: I don't know but I don't like it.

DARROW: Well—Stein will take care of it—set everything straight—

RUBY: You sure you're in this all the way, Dee? Thinking it through straight?

DARROW: WHAT?? Johnny's the one we're proving wasn't thinking straight, remember?

(RUBY *exits as Morse Code beeps, as:*)

TOM LOU: FLASH! Dr. David Stein, expert psychiatric witness from Leopold-Loeb trial, is in Honolulu and taking the witness stand now! Let's listen in:

VOICE OF JUSTICE: HEAR YE! HEAR YE! COURT IN SESSION NOW! MR. DARROW, PLEASE!

DARROW: I call to the stand, Dr. David Stein, please.

(STEIN *enters, goes to dock.*)

STEIN: I do solemnly swear to tell the whole truth and nothing but the truth, so help me, God.

DARROW: Now, Dr. Stein, you are currently director of the Chicago Psychiatric Institute. Am I correct?

STEIN: I am.

DARROW: And this hospital is the chief hospital in the Chicago area for the treatment of the mentally ill. Correct?

STEIN: It is.

DARROW: How long have you been affiliated with Chicago Psychiatric?

STEIN: Nine years—

DARROW: And you graduated from Harvard Medical School in 1918. Correct?

STEIN: Yes, sir.

DARROW: Classmate of Karl Menninger's who went on to found the pioneer Menninger Clinic in Topeka, Kansas. For the mentally ill, correct?

STEIN: Eventually. First, we both went from Harvard to residencies in neuropsychiatry at Boston Psychopathic.

DARROW: Can you describe what kind of work that hospital did?

STEIN: They were doing groundbreaking work—first hospital to offer intensive short-term treatment for acute conditions. By which I mean short mental lapses. Hospital held the radical view that mental patients could have short psychotic episodes—which could be chronic—but then go into remission—allowing the patient to recover and return to society.

DARROW: After this residency what did you do?

STEIN: I affiliated at the State Hospital for the Insane in New York City.

DARROW: What kind of philosophy did this psychiatric facility have, Doctor?

STEIN: Another pioneer hospital—breaking from nineteenth-century ideas that no treatment, help, or rehabilitation were possible for mental conditions . . . we treated patients to rehabilitate them.

DARROW: Would it be fair to say you were trained to work with patients who could have sporadic mental lapses, but then get better—or recover?

STEIN: Yes.

DARROW: Turning now to this trial, you have examined Lieutenant Ramsey?

STEIN: I have.

DARROW: And reviewed all his medical and psychiatric records?

STEIN: I have, sir.

DARROW: Please give your diagnosis and opinion then—of the mental state

Lieutenant Ramsey was in when that gun went off in Mrs. Montegu's Villa?

STEIN: The lieutenant was suffering from a condition he had suffered from before—as he has testified. He was experiencing something like "a mental bomb" going off in his head.

(DARROW *looks out to audience not sure they've understood or like what they've heard.*)

DARROW: Could you explain the repercussions of this, Doctor, for the jury's understanding?

STEIN: The condition would create a mental phenomenon that would cause him to lose his capacity for immediate memory recall.

(DARROW *looks again from jury, who aren't comprehending, to* STEIN.)

DARROW: Further explanation of this concept—in logical, scientific terms?

STEIN (*Nodding, trying to explain as* DARROW *wants him to*): Well—to be more scientific—I might explain this as a condition in which one feels a bomb has exploded in one's mind—that is, the lieutenant would have felt a shock—when Kalani betrayed and threatened him. He would have suffered a form of amnesia. Or as it is clinically called. "Shock Amnesia."

(NANILOA *rises*)

NANILOA: Amnesia is not a legal defense!

(DARROW *pauses, disarmed, looks quickly at her, back to* STEIN.)

DARROW: Any other medical interpretations or definitions you can give us, Doctor, for Lieutenant Ramsey's behavior?

STEIN: One could call it "an uncontrollable impulse."

NANILOA: Not a legal defense.

DARROW: Any other way to describe this condition?

STEIN (*Slightly rattled, trying to do it right*): A state under which—that is—a state of—"impaired consciousness," I might say—causing defendant to act in an—"automatic or reflexive manner"—and causing patient to frequently display no concern for the usual social conventions. "Somnambulistic ambulatory automatism," I might say.

NANILOA: Not a legal defense.

(*DARROW glaring at her, then pacing, disturbed at what's happening, looking around.*)

DARROW: It doesn't matter if it's not a legal defense! He is *explaining!* Now—could this definition be simplified for the layman's understanding?
STEIN (*More and more frustrated*): Still *simpler* terms? Yet *medical, scientific* terms? Well—Ramsey was "temporarily insane"—out of his mind for a brief period of time—then returned to a state of sanity.

(*DARROW seeing jury (audience) is not with him.*)

DARROW: But in terms of what happened to him, Doctor—what went on medically to the man?

(*STEIN now struggling:*)

STEIN: He was in a daze—unaware of what was happening—or—his condition could be termed "chemical insanity"—the long period of tension and emotional excitement Ramsey endured—which caused "change in his body chemistry" as controlled by "the ductless glands"—so Ramsey acted "erratically"—when Kalani threatened him—
DARROW (*Interrupting*): That's all!
STEIN: For heaven's sake! I have further testimony prepared. I'd like to provide it for—
DARROW (*Interrupting*): That's all!

(*NANILOA comes forward.*)

NANILOA: Dr. Stein, you were paid quite a handsome fee, weren't you, sir, to leave your position at a large Chicago hospital for over five weeks, and travel halfway round the world?
DARROW: Conjecture!
STEIN: Yes, I was.
NANILOA: Just one further question, Doctor. Your testimony is based on only one assumption—that Lieutenant Ramsey believed Kalani was the one who attacked his wife. True, sir?
STEIN: Yes, of course.

NANILOA: So—if Ramsey didn't really believe Kalani attacked his wife, your
      testimony has *no* value in this case—true?
STEIN *(angry)*: Obviously, madam.
NANILOA: That is all.

(STEIN exits.)

TOM LOU: Court is now in recess, folks.

*(NANILOA looks triumphantly at DARROW, exits. DARROW to courtyard. RUBY
meets him.)*

RUBY: But he was supposed to—
DARROW *(Interrupting)*: He didn't get through to the jury! I had to get him off.
      Every time he opened his mouth it got worse! *(Loudly.)* KISS OF
      DEATH: THE JURY WAS NODDING OFF!
RUBY: Shh! Let's go back to the hotel.

(SHE's trying to push him out without being obvious.)

DARROW: Jury coughing, sneezing—gallery rattling papers . . . hand fans
      going—
RUBY: Control yourself!

(SHE continues pushing him out.)

DARROW: FI-AS-CO!
RUBY: He should've known how to talk to a jury—he's done it before. All that
      gobbledy-gook?
DARROW: I told him to do that. And *you* told me to tell him! You said that was
      the way to go!
RUBY: You're not thinking straight. The Oriental Law Clerk said that.

(SHE takes his arm, THEY start to walk.)

DARROW: And that Hawaiian princess, or whatever the hell she is, rattling him
      to death? And that question at the end? God, I'm in quicksand, Ruby.
      He was my rock!

(NANILOA *suddenly appears in* COURTYARD *on high level [as on steps].*)

NANILOA: The prosecution wishes to make a statement at this time to the neighborhood press.

(TOM LOU *appears, stoops to one knee to get his camera flashing on her.*)

We believe in presenting Dr. Stein, the defense has made a grave error: failed to understand "simple facts" about us. We trust our own, have very little respect for "WESTERN Medicine"—or "WESTERN doctors"! Especially this strange new kind: "the psychiatrist!" Going into people's heads and reading their thoughts!

TOM LOU (*Calling out*): So? In a nutshell?

NANILOA (*Laughs at play on words*): In a "nutshell"? Well—this Dr. Stein offered these diagnoses of the accused:

(SHE *takes out list and rattles these off as the psychobabble they are to her:*)

"Shock amnesia." "Uncontrollable impulse state of impaired consciousness." "Somnambulistic ambulatory automatism." "Chemical insanity." "Shock insanity."
"Body chemistry change." "Ductless glands." "Automatic reflexive actions." "Moving in a walking daze." "No concern for social conventions"!

(SHE *looks toward* TOM LOU.)

So—In a "nutshell? From *these* diagnoses? The neighborhood now offers *their* diagnosis of Dr. Stein: a "Witch Doctor"—with Evil Power—coming straight from hell!!

(SHE *smiles slightly, glances at* DARROW *and* RUBY, *exits. Morse code beeps, as* TOM LOU *goes to desk, typing:*)

TOM LOU: PSYCHIATRIST STRIKES OUT! NANILOA SCORES HOME RUN!

(*As* RUBY, DARROW *walk from area:*)

DARROW: I've got to get to that jury some other way than Stein—somebody else has got to take the stand—somebody who—

(*HE stops.*)

THEODIE!

RUBY: THEODIE?

DARROW: THEODIE!

RUBY: You never wanted her—said she was skittish—nervous like a cat—

DARROW: But she can tell in plain English how he lost his mind—little by little—day by day. Nobody else can do that. She lived with him, for God's sake—saw him blanking out—not remembering—

RUBY: You said she was terrified to take the stand and that you'd never make her.

DARROW: They're all a spoiled, pampered lot. I can't cater to her every whim! And when the words "Not Guilty" are heard in a court, Rube? Be surprised how defendants don't give a tinkers' damn how it happened!

(*Beat.*)

RUBY: Well—let's hope—

DARROW: Whole town has sympathy for her. She's educated—attractive—and I'll coach her. Besides—she's who I've got!

(*Lights on* THEODIE, *enters, right hand lifted, speaking as she comes.*)

THEODIE: And I do solemnly swear to tell the truth, the whole truth and nothing but the truth. So help me, God!

(*SHE enters witness box,* RUBY *exits,* DARROW *braces himself, goes to* THEODIE.)

DARROW: Now, Mrs. Ramsey, your husband grew very thin during the months after the first trial. Not eating at home. Is that true?

THEODIE: He lost twenty pounds in four-months' time.

DARROW: Ever see him so thin before?

THEODIE: At Annapolis, when we were engaged. But after my—my assault— he was much worse.

DARROW: In what way, ma'am?

THEODIE: I'd wake screaming—from a nightmare I'd started having—again and again—I was a little girl back at our summer home in Oyster Bay— and a hooded horseman—on my father's horse—was dragging me . . . horse stomping me—hooded man trying to ra-

(SHE *stops, clenching her fists.*)

DARROW (*Gently*): Go on, if you can . . .

THEODIE: I'd wake screaming. Johnny soothing me. Then he'd pace all night. He couldn't hold down food, either. I got so worried about him. We grew very close . . . loving at that time. He was so sad—sorry for what had happened to me . . . never so caring in his life! Our love bond was perfect . . . after that night at the inn . . .

DARROW: Anything else from your physical or mental condition affect him—to your knowledge?

THEODIE: That we can't have babies—and when they wired my jaw—and I asked him to hold my hand. You could hear me moaning all over the hospital—and I was so sorry for *him*. He was shaking. Later he told me that image of me was what kept flashing before his eyes.

DARROW: Anything else?

THEODIE: Humiliating gossip—all over Pearl—he was a coward only fit for desk jobs stateside. Why wasn't he out getting justice for me himself— instead of waiting on the law?

DARROW: This gossip affect him badly?

NANILOA: Leading witness!

VOICE OF JUSTICE: SUSTAINED!

DARROW: Do you recall how you felt the gossip affected him?

THEODIE: He wouldn't even leave the house! One Sunday we *had* to go to the Admiral's Christmas party—but he told me he couldn't. I said it would look bad not to go. So, he was waiting on me . . . reading some native scandal sheet of the maid's . . . I came in . . . he was so upset . . . that newspaper article . . . it was opened on the floor.

DARROW: That was affecting him?

THEODIE: I could see our picture in that paper—it was the same rotten article I'd read before—

(NANILOA *looks up quickly,* DARROW *notices.*)

DARROW: Yes?

THEODIE: Then I saw his .45 was in his lap . . . and he was fussing with it . . .
    I took and hid it, sir . . .

DARROW: Thank you, ma'am. That will be all.

(*THEODIE sits. NANILOA comes forward.*)

NANILOA: Now, Mrs. Ramsey, The *Honolulu Sun* is the only weekly Sunday
    paper there is. So the newspaper you just brought into testimony—and
    Lieutenant Ramsey brought into testimony—that would've been from
    the native *Honolulu Sun*, right?

THEODIE: Yes, because the maid always leaves it and finishes it on Mondays.

NANILOA: Would the issue be the Sunday, December 19, 1931, issue, if you
    recall?

THEODIE: Well, it would've had to be, wouldn't it—since the Admiral's party
    was the Sunday before Christmas?

NANILOA: And you had read through that paper earlier that day?

THEODIE: Yes.

NANILOA: And recognized the article about you and your husband that lay at
    his feet and the article you'd read as one and the same?

THEODIE: Yes.

(*Beat. DARROW begins rifling briecase for newspaper but can't find it. NANILOA
pulls newspaper from red box.*)

NANILOA: December 19, 1931. *Honolulu Sun*. "Inside the Ramsey Marriage,"
    "Lulu Wonders" column. A picture of you and the Defendant and this:
    quote, "Speculation is rising that Theodora Ramsey was planning a di-
    vorce months before her assault, in-"

THEODIE (*Interrupting*): WHAT?

DARROW: Rumor! Hearsay! Speculation!

(*DARROW enraged.*)

NANILOA: Quote: "In point of fact, Theodora Ramsey had booked hotel space
    from Cook's Travel Honolulu a month before her assault for a six-week
    stay in Reno, Nevada!"

THEODIE: I have friends in Reno!

DARROW: I beg the court! Reconsider! Strike entire line of questioning!

VOICE OF JUSTICE: DENIED!

DARROW: Move for MISTRIAL!

VOICE OF JUSTICE: MOTION DENIED! COUNSEL MAY APPEAL! PROS-
ECUTION MAY PROCEED AT THIS TIME!

(DARROW pacing, glaring from NANILOA to audience, thinking.)

NANILOA: There's further substantiation of your impending divorce, Mrs.
Ramsey.

(DARROW stops, shaken.)

Profile questionnaire from the University of Hawaii. And—

DARROW: Violation of confidentiality!

(Searching briefcase, documents.)

I don't have the questionnaire here—

NANILOA: Subpoenaed, sir. No discovery laws in Hawaii.

(SHE takes document from red box.)

THEODIE: I remember nothing about a questionnaire at all!

NANILOA: From Psychology I course you were enrolled in, July 28, 1931.
Question: "Are you married? Yes or no." But you wrote all over the back,
quote: "Trapped and want out! Married me for my money and Daddy's
advancing his career. They wanted rid of me! Especially DADDY. He
was cruel to me in unspeakable ways. Consult you privately?" Unquote.

THEODIE: Some student must've written that as a prank!

NANILOA: Continuing, Lulu's column, quote: "It was known the Lieutenant
was involved with another sailor's wife. He danced openly with her at
Ala Waii Inn at the Officer's Dance—night of the supposed kidnapping—publicly humiliating his wife. It was in rage at *this* that Mrs. Ramsey stormed out."

THEODIE: That's a lie!

*(During following, DARROW seems distressed. Focusing now on THEODIE, HE
searches intermittently for documents, tapping pen on desk, searching more.*

Papers fall helter-skelter to floor. HE picks them up out of order, crumpled, jams them back in briefcase.)

NANILOA: Now, you testified you were kidnapped when you left the Ala Waii Inn that night?

THEODIE: Yes.

NANILOA: Involved in any kidnap plot before?

(DARROW looking at NANILOA, is acutely shocked, distressed at line of questioning.)

THEODIE: Good heavens, no!

(NANILOA takes document from red box as DARROW rifles papers, angry, frustrated. Pages scattering. HE sinks into chair.)

NANILOA: Long Island police records show you and your then fiancé, Cadet Ramsey, were arrested, taken into custody, jailed. August 24th, 1928, Oyster Bay, Long Island, for kidnapping baby, Megan O'Flaherty, in pram outside store. You sped to Manhattan . . .

THEODIE: The baby slept the whole time!

NANILOA: Checked into Delmonico's Hotel, left infant unattended in hotel room, and were arrested dining formally downstairs!

THEODIE: We were kids ourselves!

NANILOA: Defendant Mrs. Katherine Montegu bailed you both out—and made private settlement to the mother.

THEODIE: Mummer knew it was nothing but harmless summer fun!

NANILOA: Having harmless summer fun when you left the Ala Waii Inn, Mrs. Ramsey?

THEODIE: I went for a walk.

NANILOA: On foot?

THEODIE: ON FOOT!

NANILOA: Didn't you drive your car? Park it down by the beach—then walk across to the Waikiki Dance Pavillion, Mrs. Ramsey?

THEODIE: NO!

NANILOA: To get even with your husband—by flirting with a "Ukulele Music Boy" in the band there?

THEODIE: NO!

NANILOA: Deposition: Suzy Manuu, hatcheck girl, Ala Waii Inn. September 19, 1931. Suppressed from rape trial.

(DARROW *rises, somewhat out of control.*)

DARROW: ARE WE TRYING THE RAPE CASE AGAIN?
VOICE OF JUSTICE: OVERRULED!

(DARROW *leans heavily on table now, to keep his bearings.*)

NANILOA: Quote: "Midnight and the *Haole* woman come to my Hatcheck: 'Give me my scarf!' she say—and she plenty *hu hu*! So? She leave, and drive her yellow car to John Ena Road. I ending job—so I walking John Ena too. *Bimbye*—here come Lieutenant husband quick-march-walking-run—and he plenty *hu hu* too. And *li'di* and *li'dat*—did I see him wife? And I don't answer. Then I go to Pavillion. *Bimbye*—I see wife's yellow car by beach—but see she laughing at Pavilion! Throw off her scarf, shoes! Swing her hips and barefoot and hula plenty fast with this *lolo buggah*: 'Manuello, Ukulele Music Boy.' Then husband coming for her. She grab scarf, shoes, jacket—run in her car driver seat. Husband jump in beside. Down Ala Moana Road they go. WHEE!" Unquote. Now, Mrs. Ramsey—isn't this what really happened that night?
THEODIE: None of it—except I got my fringed scarf from that Hatcheck.

(SHE *toys with it.*)

NANILOA: Continuing Lulu: Quote: "Wasn't Mrs. Ramsey driving and drunk—and weren't they in a screaming fight over the lieutenant's affair and her flirtation at the Pavillion—and didn't he punch her, then sock her so hard—she hit against the car door which flew open—throwing her to the ground—while he took the wheel and raced away?" Unquote. This gossip column was the article that affected the Lieutenant mentally that morning, wasn't it?
THEODIE (*Near breaking*): MY HUSBAND WOULDN'T HAVE BEEN AF-FECTED BY ANY OF THAT GARBAGE AT ALL BECAUSE IT IS ALL SO FAR FROM THE TRUTH AS TO BE COMICAL—IF OUR FAMILY'S GOOD NAMES—AND LIVES WEREN'T AT STAKE HERE!
NANILOA: Kahawaii Hospital records. Suppressed from rape trial. Subpoenaed and released this morning—

(SHE *looks at* DARROW *who can't look back.*)

First, the emergency room: quote: "Patient Theodora Ramsey, admitted. Jaw fractures, bleeding, contusions confirm physical attack. But *Negative* for sexual attack."

Second hospital report—six weeks later: gynecology ward. "Patient Theodora Ramsey: *Negative* for pregnancy."

THEODIE: Those reports have mixed me up with someone else.

DARROW: Objection! Violation of patient-doctor confidentiality.

NANILOA: Didn't both you and your husband lie?

THEODIE: No!

NANILOA: Make a plot to blame *Kalani* for your husband's beating *you*? Even add a fictitious gang rape and pregnancy onto the event so everyone would be thrown further off—and never suspect you either of your wild flirtation with a strange Hawaiian at a public dance pavilion?

THEODIE: I SAID NO!!

NANILOA: Your pact was thrilling, wasn't it? To prove you both could drown your wild behavior and his savagery to you in our clear blue seas? Get away with murder? Then walk off scot-free to your next escapade!

(*THEODIE takes a step to move out of dock.*)

THEODIE: Johnny did nothing to me but love and protect me!

NANILOA: And Kalani was an easy target, wasn't he? Because—by sheer luck—he and the others left that very pavilion—around the very same time you walked over there to flirt around!

THEODIE: I was gang-raped! And beaten! And impregnated by Kalani and his gang! And there is a wealth of real proof for that! Let me see those stupid documents, will you, please?

(*NANILOA hands her the papers.*)

Totally incompetent! Misspelled! Pidgin English! What is it you're insinuating with these anyway? Johnny and I aren't in love? That we harm innocent babies? And plot evil together? That it's your third-rate college and hospital—and trashy scandal sheets that tell the truth?

(*SHE is clutching papers, shaking them in her fist, starts moving out of dock. To* NANILOA:)

I'M AN *AMERICAN WOMAN!* AND THE PROBLEM HERE IS WE HAVE GOTTEN NO JUSTICE IN THIS GOD-FORSAKEN

JUNGLE OF YOURS! THIS KANGAROO COURT! NOT THE RAPE TRIAL AND NOT NOW!

(SHE *glares at* NANILOA.)

I DON'T HAVE TO ANSWER TO YOU!!

(*Shaking, then crumpling and tearing papers.*)

Or about these rotten sheets of garbage!

(*Now indicating audience as if jury before her.*)

Or to your slant-eyed yellow trash jury!

(*Gavel.*)

VOICE OF JUSTICE: WITNESS TO THE DOCK! ORDER IN THE COURT!
THEODIE: ALL YOU'VE DONE IS HEAP YOUR OWN LEPROUS PUS FILTH ON US!

(DARROW *has risen, going toward her, but* SHE *moves farther from dock, toward jury.*)

DARROW: Mrs. Ramsey, please—Mrs. Ramsey—

(RAMSEY *and* MRS. MONTEGU *enter from anteroom,* MRS. MONTEGU *frozen to the spot,* RAMSEY *coming forward toward* THEODIE. *Gavel sounding. Following overlaps as courtroom slides out of control. Gavel continuing to sound.*)

VOICE OF JUSTICE: ORDER IN THE COURT! WITNESS TO THE DOCK! ORDER IN THE COURT!
DARROW: THEODIE! CONTROL YOURSELF! STOP IT! STOP IT!
RAMSEY: FOR GOD'S SAKE! WHAT ARE YOU DOING? FOR GOD'S SAKE!!!
NANILOA: I demand witness be held in contempt of court at this time!

(GAVEL *sounding.*)

VOICE OF JUSTICE: ORDER IN THE COURT OR THE COURT WILL BE CLEARED.

(*Gavel continuing.* THEODIE *starts tearing documents to shreds.*)

THEODIE: THERE! AND THERE! AND THERE!

(*Papers scattering, shredded, to the floor.*)

VOICE OF JUSTICE: CLEAR THE COURT! DEFENDANTS RE-MANDED TO PEARL HARBOR! COUNSEL REPORT TO CHAMBERS!

(THEODIE *continues to shred papers, into smaller and smaller bits.* SHE'S *hysterical.*)

THEODIE: AND THERE ! AND THERE!

(NANILOA *exits.* RAMSEY *moves to* THEODIE, *slaps her face, shaking, shoving her to floor:*)

RAMSEY: BITCH! WRECKING US! SPOILED STUPID BITCH!

(DARROW *goes to* RAMSEY, *restraining him.*)

DARROW: Get hold of yourself!

(RAMSEY *stops.* DARROW *helps* THEODIE *to her feet.* SHE *runs out. A long silence. Then* MRS. MONTEGU *moves forward:*)

MRS. MONTEGU: Theodie should never have been dragged up there to start with, Mr. Darrow.
DARROW: She was the best person I had to corroborate Johnny's instability—which she did. And to gain him some measure of sympathy—which she did not.
MRS. MONTEGU: I doubt she's gained any of us sympathy, Mr. Darrow, tearing up evidence!
DARROW: No one told her to tear up evidence.

MRS. MONTEGU: Well, if you'd've been clever enough to block those lying scandal sheets, and mixed-up hospital reports, she wouldn't have had to tear them up, would she?

DARROW: I beg your pardon?

MRS. MONTEGU: We should never have got you down here to start with. Colonel kept on saying what a risk you were. That we should just keep on doing what we'd done with the first trial: masterminded everything from the sidelines. With Chester. But then we had the District Attorney's help . . . so I was afraid.

DARROW: District Attorney's help?

MRS. MONTEGU: We made a wonderful arrangement with him in the first trial, Mr. Darrow. Almost all that evidence that came in now was suppressed then: Filthy Oriental scandal sheets—sneaky, duplicitous Oriental witness—that Suzy What's-her-name—those third-rate lab reports. The district attorney got it all declared "tainted"—"lost"—"inadmissible"—

DARROW: WHAT ARE YOU TELLING ME?

MRS. MONTEGU: Then he confided we'd never get a conviction in a retrial either. Another racial split would kill it—and not enough hard evidence. We'd need something new, strong to win—like a confession!

(DARROW *turns away.*)

Someone came right up, right then with the idea that all the District Attorney had to say was Kalani'd sent word he wanted to plea bargain and sign a confession.

DARROW: I talked to the District Attorney. He said a native came to him—privately—told him Kalani wanted to confess secretly if-

MRS. MONTEGU (*Interrupting*): How trusting of "words" you still are, Mr. Darrow! Even when I've told you, haven't I, that "words here are so very cheaply bought and sold"!

(*Beat.* DARROW *trying to get a hold of this:*)

DARROW: You set a trap for me down here?

MRS. MONTEGU: Of course for this trial, District Attorney's hands were tied: up for reelection—forced to use that willful half-breed girl as Prosecutor to get himself the yellow vote. And wouldn't one just know she'd sneak her way around the yellow police until she turned up that blood evidence and everything else?

(Beat.)

DARROW: Have you got any idea what you've done to me?

(HE staggers, trying to grasp it.)

> Who the hell do you think you are that you can use me? Manipulate me? Get me cornered like this down here at the edge of the world? My reputation on the line? I'll be ruined—Made a fool of by you! WHO THE GOD DAMN HELL GAVE YOU THE RIGHT TO DO THAT?

(SHE regards him coolly. Whistle blows.)

MRS. MONTEGU: My one regret about any of this, Mr. Darrow? We didn't do what Colonel wanted: string that whole pack of yellow dogs up on trees at the very start!

(SHE exits. A silence. Then:)

RAMSEY: Don't—don't listen to Mother—she means nothing—knows nothing really.

(DARROW regards him.)

DARROW: She means everything! Knows everything! A liar! A dangerous bigot! A vicious KILLER!

RAMSEY: But Mother's not me!

DARROW: You're the ringleader! Mastermind of the rape trial—with Chester, the Colonel, your mother-in-law, and the District Attorney's help! And now—with this trial you're stomping on me, my name, my life's work! GOD DAMN YOU TO HELL!

RAMSEY: I did nothing! Unstable, volatile—but innocent!

(DARROW keeps looking at him.)

DARROW: You are the worst, the most dangerous criminal KILLER of all! You're capable of "impulse insanity violence," all right—but when it's directed at your wife. RIGHT? Or Kalani? Killed by you in premeditated cold blood at that Villa because he wouldn't sign!

(RAMSEY *turns away.*)

You've abused your power! Influence! Entitlements! The honor of the uniform you've got on. And me! I QUIT!

(RAMSEY *whirls around to him.* DARROW *starts packing up briefcase.*)

Your "bought-off" Honolulu lawyers can close with the "Code of Honor" plea. And if that doesn't work, dollars to donuts the Colonel can call President Hoover and get you all "clemency with leniency and mercy"!

(*Whistle blows.*)

They're whistling for you now, Lieutenant, aren't they? To take you to your jail boat?

(RAMSEY *runs out one way,* DARROW *looking after him. Then a beat or two, and* DARROW *packs briefcase. Morse Code beeps. Lights* UP: *Reporter on mike:*)

TOM LOU: And now, folks, after fifty hours of sequestration, the jury has taken their seats. The verdict is in! Judge on the bench!

(*Gavel sounds.*)

VOICE OF JUSTICE: GUILTY! MANSLAUGHTER! IN THE FIRST DE-GREE! SENTENCE: TWENTY YEARS. HARD LABOR. IN OAHU PRISON. WITH NO PAROLE.

(*Gavel sounds.* NANILOA, *triumphant, enters, looking over audience's head, as if speaking to* JUSTICE.)

NANILOA: I request prisoners be remanded to Oahu Prison at once!
VOICE OF JUSTICE: REQUEST NONAPPLICABLE!
NANILOA: What?
VOICE OF JUSTICE: IN CONSIDERATION OF PETITIONS FROM THE GOVERNOR, CONGRESSMEN, AND THE REPRESENTATIVE TO CONGRESS FROM THE TERRITORY OF HAWAII, ALL BEGGING MERCY AND LENIENCY—CLEMENCY HAS BEEN GRANTED! SENTENCE COMMUTED TO ONE HOUR! SERVED

IN GOVERNOR'S OFFICE: IOLANI PALACE! PRISONERS RE-
PORT TO PALACE IN CUSTODY OF HIGH SHERIFF AT ONCE!

NANILOA (*Bewildered, not comprehending, looking out, speaking to the* VOICE OF
JUSTICE, *over the audience*): WHAT'S HAPPENED HERE?

VOICE OF JUSTICE: CLEMENCY! ONE HOUR IN IOLANI PALACE!
CLEMENCY!

NANILOA: Lynch law's legal? The verdict's a farce? There's no righteousness!

VOICE OF JUSTICE: COURT ADJOURNED! HEAR YE!

NANILOA: *"Ua mau ke ea o ka aina i ka pono!"* The people have been betrayed!
And the life of our land!

(*Gavel.* NANILOA *leaves as* DARROW *stands stunned.* RUBY *hurries in.*)

RUBY: Oh Dee!

DARROW: The last straw, huh? One hour in Iolani Palace? Probably with cock-
tails? Everything I stand for, everything I wanted, ripped to shreds? Like
she ripped the evidence? You understand I came down here with an important cause! You're with me on that, right, Rube?

(*Beat.* HE *starts stuffing briefcase, one way then another, papers falling to
floor.*)

RUBY: Right with you, Dee. I'm right here.

(SHE *picks up papers handing them to him. A beat.*)

But listen to me? Even if you didn't establish your plea—somewhere
else—someone else will.

(HE *snaps briefcase shut.* SHE *links her arm in his,* THEY *start to walk.*)

You opened the door a little more . . . raised the possibility there could
legitimately be such a plea . . .

DARROW: But I wanted to *establish* it! Secure the Old Man's Legacy down the
years—

(THEY *stop. Silence.* SHE *looks at him, as he contemplates what he's said.
Then:*)

God, maybe I wanted it *too much*, huh, Rube? Put blinders round my eyes—

(SHE *looks at him:*)

RUBY: Maybe, but your legacy's already secured down the years, Dee. Your reputation—your life's work—it's all right there in place, last time I looked.

(SHE *smiles at him.*)

Now come on—let's start packing. A boat sails for Frisco tomorrow, I think.

(THEY *start walking again.*)

Winter or not—be real good to be back home in Chicago, won't it, Dee?

(THEY *are gone. Blackout. Then very bright lights flood stage. Other times, places, other feelings.* NANILOA *comes forward to audience:*)

NANILOA: An old Hawaiian story goes: when the white man came, he said to us: "Look up to the heavens! And pray to our God! And it will go well for you!" And so we did. And then we looked down—and our land was gone! And half our people dead—syphilis, gonorrhea, smallpox, cholera, influenza—that the white man brought to our Paradise!

(SHE *comes closer to audience.*)

I lobby for our people now—in Washington—for statehood! A tough, uphill battle against American sugar kings, plantation owners, Washington politics, and the Japanese! For the right to control our own water, crops, land! Life! *"Ua mau ke ea o ka aina i ka pono"*! It is only righteousness that perpetuates the Life of the Land!

(SHE *stands proud as* THEODIE *enters area. To audience:*)

THEODIE: I leave Hawaii hours later at Chester's advice. So there'll be no complaining witness for retrial of the rape case. The other men go free. January 6, 1934—Reno, Nevada . . . I divorce Johnny. Two years to the day Kim Kalani was shot . . . strange . . . chilling coincidence—

(SHE *looks down.* MRS. MONTEGU *enters, contained, holding back all feelings.*)

MRS. MONTEGU: July 4, 1937. Whimsy Cottage, Oyster Bay . . . Long Island . . . New York . . . our beloved Theodie's taken her own life . . . this gay holiday weekend . . . cocktail party time on the veranda . . . a scream rings out . . . a bedroom window above . . . in the garden . . . Colonel finds her . . . splayed across a flower bed . . .

(RAMSEY *comes forward to area. To audience.*)

RAMSEY: December 7, 1941. I am on duty—Pearl Harbor—when the Japanese start bombing—our entire naval fleet—

(*Morse Code beeps.* TOM LOU, *older, more established. From his desk, on mike:*)

TOM LOU: Tom Lou, WHLU, reporting. Just back from Pearl Harbor. Shock— chaos everywhere. First casualty lists just posted. *USS Oklahoma.* Among casualties, folks? From the Montegu-Ramsey Trial you may remember from long ago? Captain John Birmingham Ramsey. Killed.

(*Morse Code beeps. Lights down on all except* SPOT *on* DARROW *somewhere else.* HE *seems almost like a portrait.*)

DARROW: I speak and will always speak for the underdog. The wretched, the forgotten of this earth—chased by life, hounded like wolves into dark corners—dungeons from which they can't escape. The wretched of every kind—wretched in body, wretched in spirit—wretched in *mind!* Those who still have some hope, some undying faith remaining in the institutions of this land—to help them!

End of Play

MRS. PACKARD

by Emily Mann
Inspired by a true story

Kathryn Meisle as Mrs. Packard in *Mrs. Packard* at McCarter Theatre Center, Princeton, New Jersey (Photo © T. Charles Erickson)

Much madness is divinest sense
To a discerning eye;
Much sense the starkest madness.
'Tis the majority
In this, as all, prevails.
Assent, and you are sane;
Demur,—you're straightaway
dangerous,
And handled with a chain.

Emily Dickinson

EMILY MANN

Emily Mann's Mrs. Packard *premiered at the McCarter Theatre Center in Princeton, New Jersey, and subsequently was produced at the Kennedy Center, having received a Kennedy Center New Play Award. On Broadway, Mann's play* Having Our Say *won three Tony nominations, toured nationally, enjoyed a South African production, and was adapted by Mann for CBS, garnering Peabody and Christopher awards and a Writers Guild nomination. Other plays by Mann include the award-winning* Execution of Justice; Still Life; Annulla, an Autobiography; *and* Greensboro (A Requiem). *A collection of her work,* Testimonies: Four Plays, *is published by Theatre Communications Group. Additionally, Mann has adapted numerous classics and has received the prestigious Hull-Warriner Award from the Dramatists Guild, where she serves on the council. Artistic Director of McCarter Theatre, she has directed many plays there, including the revival of Edward Albee's* All Over, *for which she received a 2003 Obie Award when the production moved off-Broadway.*

Mrs. Packard held its world premiere at McCarter Theater Centre, Princeton, New Jersey, on May 4, 2007. Emily Mann, artistic director.

Cast:
Elizabeth Parsons Ware Packard . . .Kathryn Meisle
Dr. Andrew McFarland . . . . .Dennis Parlato
Theophilus Packard . . . . .John C. Vennema
Mrs. Bonner . . . . .Fiana Toibin
Mrs. Tenney, Mrs. Sybil Dole . . . . .Julie Boyd
Mrs. Chapman, Miss Sarah
Rumsey, Mrs. Blessing . . . . .Molly Regan
Mrs. Stockton . . . . .Georgine Hall
Dr. J.W. Brown, Mr. Abijah Dole,
Dr. Duncanson, and others . . . . . . .Jeff Brooks

Mrs. Josephus Smith, Mr. Haslet,
Mrs. Blackman, and others . . . . . . .Robin Chadwick
Director: Emily Mann
Set Design: Eugene Lee
Costume Design: Jennifer von Mayrhauser
Lighting Design: Jeff Croiter
Original Music and Sound Design: Rob Milburn and Michael Bodeen

CHARACTERS

ELIZABETH PACKARD

THEOPHILUS PACKARD—Her husband

DOCTOR MCFARLAND—Superintendent of Jacksonville

MRS. BONNER—Matron at Jacksonville

MRS. CHAPMAN—Patient of the 7th Ward

MISS RUMSEY—Witness for the prosecution

MRS. BLESSING—Witness for the defense

MRS. TENNEY—Matron of the 8th Ward

MRS. DOLE—Witness for the prosecution

MRS. STOCKTON—Patient of the 7th Ward

JUDGE

MR. SMITH—Witness for the prosecution

MR. HASLET—Counsel for the prosecution

DR. KNOTT—Witness for the prosecution

MR. LA BRIE—Witness for the defense

MR. BLACKMAN—President of the board of trustees

CLERK

STEPHEN R. MOORE—Counsel for the defense

DR. BROWN—Witness for the prosecution

MR. ABIJAH DOLE—Witness for the prosecution

DR. DUNCANSON—Expert witness for the defense

MR. BLESSING—Witness for the defense

FOREMAN OF THE JURY

ARTHUR—Age five

> *Married women and infants who, in the judgment of the medical superintendent are evidently insane or distracted, may be entered or detained in the hospital on the request of the husband of the woman or the guardian of the infant, without the evidence of insanity required in other cases.*

> *Passed into law on February 15, 1851, in the state of Illinois.*

❖   ❖   ❖

ACT ONE

(Illinois, 1861. A theatrical space that will become many places. A grated window. Bolted doors. Tight white light up on the Judge.)

THE JUDGE: The case on trial at Kankakee City, Illinois. January 11, 1864. Upon the motion of the Hon. Charles B. Starr, presiding, it is ordered that an issue be formed as to the sanity or insanity of Mrs. Elizabeth P.W. Packard and that a jury of twelve men will aid in the investigation of said issue. The court will come to order in the matter of *Packard vs. Packard.*

(Sound of a gavel. Lights change. McFarland's office, the asylum. REVEREND THEOPHILUS PACKARD, *57, with* DR. MCFARLAND, *a good-looking 50.* THEO *is very upset.)*

DR. MCFARLAND: And who will care for your children, Reverend Packard, now that your wife will be confined?

THEOPHILUS: My sister lives near us and though she has children of her own, she—she offered . . . *(DOCTOR: I see.)* And some of the women in my congregation offered to—to help as well, *(Choking.)* and the older children will—

DR. MCFARLAND: Yes . . . I'm sure.

THEOPHILUS: Can you help my wife, Doctor?

DR. MCFARLAND: I will know more after my examination of her . . .

THEOPHILUS: Yes, yes. Of course.

DR. MCFARLAND: But cases like your wife's are a specialty of mine here at Jacksonville. *(THEO [hoarsely]: Really?)* Tell me, though, Reverend, are you quite certain you have tried every avenue with your wife to keep her calm?

THEOPHILUS: I do not know what else to do! It is very difficult for me to leave her here, but I fear for the children's spiritual and—and physical welfare. *(DR. MCFARLAND: I see.)* She flies into rages, Doctor. I can no longer control her, and I fear I now may lose my present church.

DR. MCFARLAND: Your "present church"? Has this happened before, sir?

THEOPHILUS *(Beside himself)*: Oh, yes. We have had to move three times in the last ten years due to my wife's—outbursts. I—I love my wife, Doctor.

Before that, she was a—a good wife and mother and a helpmate to me in my church, but *now* I—I—

(*Knock on the door.* MRS. BONNER, *an Irish matron, sticks her head in.*)

MRS. BONNER: Doctor?
DR. MCFARLAND: Mrs. Bonner.
MRS. BONNER: I have Mrs. Packard with me. Shall I bring her in?
DR. MCFARLAND: Yes, yes . . . Reverend, please remain quiet during my examination of your wife. She may be upset, but let me handle—

(ELIZABETH, *43 and very beautiful, enters, hair flying, in a rage. She pulls away from* BONNER.)

ELIZABETH: Don't you touch me! (*Seeing* THEO, *spitting this at him.*) "Peter, Peter, Pumpkin Eater had a wife and couldn't keep her . . ." (*She continues over.*)
DOCTOR MCFARLAND (*Overlap*): Mrs. Packard?
THEOPHILUS (*Overlap*): Elizabeth, don't . . . (*Gets up.*)
ELIZABETH: Put her in a pumpkin shell
THEOPHILUS (*Overlap*): Stop it.
ELIZABETH: And there he kept her very well.

(*A pause.* SHE *and* THEO *look at each other. Silence.* THEO *turns away.*)

DR. MCFARLAND: Mrs. Packard? I am Dr. Andrew McFarland, superintendent of Jacksonville Insane Asylum.

(SHE *turns* ["Oh?"])

DR. MCFARLAND: I should like to have a discussion with you, Mrs. Packard, with your husband present before he leaves you here with us. (ELIZ: *But Doctor*—) I wish to assure you—you will be quite comfortable here . . . and will in future be in my . . . personal care.

(THEY *meet eyes.*)

ELIZABETH (*Suddenly girlish, almost flirtatious*): Really? I am so glad to hear it—that I would be in your personal care. However, you must surely see

I don't belong here! (DR: *Ah, yes?*) Yes! I don't know why it is, Doctor—it may be merely a foolish pride—but I can't help feeling an instinctive aversion to being called insane. (*A beat.*) Like Peter Peter's wife? She felt the same, I'm sure—living in a pumpkin shell . . .

DR. MCFARLAND (*Unsure, almost a laugh*): . . . Indeed . . . (*Offers her a seat.*) Your husband and I have had a long talk this morning (ELIZ [*bitter*]: *Have you?*) and he tells me that you love to read and write and discuss . . .

ELIZABETH (*Wary*): Yes . . . quite right.

DR. MCFARLAND: Well, I intend for you to enjoy special privileges while you are here with us, (ELIZ: *No, no—*) and I will be sure to furnish you with books of your choosing. (ELIZ: *But Doctor—*) Perhaps you and I will be able to converse together as well. I should like that.

(*A moment. Then* ELIZABETH *bolts, runs toward her husband, starts to whale on him.*)

ELIZABETH: I will not! stay here! I will not stay! Why are you turning everybody against me? Why are you trying to convince anyone who'll listen I am mad?!

DR. MCFARLAND (*Overlap*): Mrs. Packard! Mrs. Packard! Please take your seat. Mrs. Packard . . . !

(*The* DOCTOR *stops her from hitting her husband.*)

Please take a seat and let us finish our interview in a civilized manner.

(*HE sits her back down.*)

ELIZABETH (*Muttering, shaking her head, laughing at the absurdity, spitting it at her husband*): "Peter, Peter Pumpkin Eater—had a wife . . ."

DOCTOR MCFARLAND: Now, then—

ELIZABETH (*Laughing wildly to herself*): The children's favorite rhyme . . .

DR. MCFARLAND: I do hope you slept well and that the plain food of the asylum will agree with you.

ELIZABETH (*Snaps*): No, I am afraid nothing agrees with me here. None of this "agrees with me." (DOCTOR: *I'm sorry . . .*) Quite frankly, my bed is narrow, and hard, and made of straw and I am unused to sleeping alone.

(THEO shifts uncomfortably. The DOCTOR looks up, smiles.)

DR. MCFARLAND: . . . I understand.

ELIZABETH: In fact, when I ceased, only recently, to have the warmth of my once dear husband in bed beside me, I brought the youngest of my children into bed with me so that I could sleep. This my husband well knows. So, no, I did not sleep well, I thank you. I could not.

DR. MCFARLAND: How many children do you have, Mrs. Packard?

ELIZABETH: We have six children, five boys and a girl. *(Tears start to stream.)* The oldest is eighteen years old and the youngest eighteen *months*. *(To THEO.)* All except the oldest were living at home the morning I was abducted.

DR. MCFARLAND: Abducted?

ELIZABETH *(Trying to keep the hysteria and sobs down)*: Yes, abducted! I was having my bath—I—I looked out the window—saw a sheriff . . . and two strong men, two doctors . . . and my husband!—walk—come walking up the path to our front door, up the stairs . . . yelling, pounding on my—my bedroom door! . . . I screamed I—I wasn't dressed. They would not wait! They . . . hacked down the door—with an axe. Completely . . . naked!!! Terrified—as any woman would be . . .

DR. MCFARLAND: Surely.

ELIZABETH: A doctor took my hand. "Her pulse is very quick!" he said . . . And pronounced me insane. The second doctor, the—the same . . . my husband . . . said, "Get dressed. At once!" Then two strong men carried me out of my house . . . onto a . . . a waiting wagon, then onto a—train . . . here. *(Pause.)* I was . . . abducted. . . . Don't you agree?

DR. MCFARLAND *(Nods)*: I see you did not come on your own volition, Mrs. Packard.

(A beat.)

ELIZABETH *(In a small voice)*: Doctor . . . I try—

DR. MCFARLAND *(Gently taking her hand)*: Mrs. Packard, you are here because your husband is concerned about your sanity, and wants you to have professional care.

ELIZABETH . . . Doctor . . . my husband is jealous! *(THEO: Now, wait just one . . .)*: His congregation is dwindling. I—encouraged . . . healthy discussion! . . . The Christ I worship and love would not have an innocent baby *damned at birth*, Theophilus! (*Screaming at* THEO.) It is woman who will crush the serpent's head!

THEOPHILUS: That is quite enough, Mrs. Packard! You see, Doctor? This is what I was telling you. She flies into these fits frequently. This is what I have been living with and—

DR. MCFARLAND (*HE gently signals him to calm down*): Yes, Mr. Packard . . . Mrs. Packard, I understand you . . . flouted your husband in front of his congregation?

(*Long pause.*)

THEOPHILUS: She did.

ELIZABETH (*Very quiet*): . . . I did . . . ask for the congregation and the minister's blessing to leave the church and worship with the Methodists . . .

DR. MCFARLAND (*Amazed, almost amused*): You made this request during Sunday service? Your husband was at the pulpit?

THEOPHILUS: Yes. I was at the pulpit. She exposed her perversity to full public view! (DR: *Ah.*) The entire congregation saw she had gone mad.

ELIZABETH (*Screeching*): Since neither you nor the congregation responded to my request, I left the church and crossed the street to worship with the Methodists! (*Then whispers to the* DOCTOR.) Where my personal beliefs could be respected.

DR. MCFARLAND: How long ago did you interrupt your husband's service, Mrs. Packard?

ELIZABETH: . . . Nine weeks ago.

DR. MCFARLAND: I see. And how long would you say these disagreements about religion have caused—marital strife—between you and your husband?

ELIZABETH: The last year or so, I should think, but it's not only religion, Doctor, it's—

THEOPHILUS (*Interrupting, erupting*): The last *ten* years, at least, Elizabeth!!! (ELIZABETH *looks at him aghast.*) Her mother was mad as well, Doctor, you should know, and Mrs. Packard herself was committed to an asylum once before, when she was young.

ELIZABETH: I was put in hospital for brain fever!—not madness! My father will attest to that. (THEO: *Nonsense.*) And my mother was not mad, Doctor. She had lost four children in infancy, and she did *grieve* for them. (DR: *Of course.*) (*Spitting at* THEO.) She doubtless wept because she'd been taught her babies were damned for eternity!

THEOPHILUS: You see?! . . . As I told you, Doctor, it is a clear case of moral perversity.

DR. MCFARLAND *(Slowly)*: Yes, most insanity starts as such, but often we can find the appropriate treatment, *(To Elizabeth.)* if the patient is willing. *(He rises.)* Reverend, I leave you with your wife to say goodbye . . . *(THEO and the DOCTOR meet eyes.)* Mrs. Packard, let me remind you that you will have every special privilege here while under my watch. *(SHE offers her hand in gratitude. HE holds it for a moment, looking deeply into her eyes.)*

ELIZABETH: Doctor.

DR. MCFARLAND: It has been a . . . very great pleasure to meet you, Mrs. Packard. Truly.

(HE then nods to THEO as HE exits, leaving THEO with ELIZABETH. There is a long silence. Neither speaks. Then with great control:)

ELIZABETH *(Smiling)*: You see, husband? The doctor does not think me mad.

THEOPHILUS: You are wrong there, Mrs. Packard. Believe me.

(Lights change.)

(A man in black testifies.)

CLERK: Mr. Josephus Smith, you have been sworn.

MR. SMITH: I have been in charge of the Bible school at Reverend Packard's church since just before Mrs. Packard was taken to the asylum three years ago. I was elected superintendent of the school for the special purpose of keeping Mrs. Packard *straight*. We all knew—the entire congregation knew—Mrs. Packard was insane. She thought she was the Holy Ghost . . .

(Lights change.)

ELIZABETH *(Quiet)*: Theophilus, how can you *do* this to the mother of your children?

THEOPHILUS: It is for your own good—and quite obviously—for the good of the children.

ELIZABETH: What will the children do without their mother?

THEOPHILUS: My sister will help and Libby will be helpful as well.

ELIZABETH: Libby is only ten years old, Theo. She's a little girl!

THEOPHILUS: I am well aware of her age, Mrs. Packard. The children will be well cared for, and they will soon get used to it.

ELIZABETH: They will not "get used to it" and neither shall I!

THEOPHILUS: You are very ill, Elizabeth, and you are harming the children.

ELIZABETH: I am not *ill*, husband, and well you know it! *(A beat.)* I—I understand. You are angry. It was a great betrayal and a great humiliation, *(Beside herself.)* but—but you never listen!!! or or . . . care to—Or or . . . let me *think*!—and I—I—for *myself*!! and—

THEOPHILUS: Stop babbling.

ELIZABETH: Theo! let us talk at home, in the privacy of our home.

THEOPHILUS: I gave you fair warning.

ELIZABETH: This is a prison, Theo! I am begging you. The matron threw me to the floor this morning! Theo, please. I shall *die* here.

(MRS. BONNER listens outside the door.)

THEOPHILUS: You're hysterical. Sit down. I don't want them to have to restrain you again.

ELIZABETH: Dear God, I shall die without my babies. It's the reason I'm alive, Theo, to be a mother, to care for my little ones. *(HE puts his head in his hands.)* I slept in your bed for twenty-one years, I bore you six beautiful children, I kept a spotless, loving Christian home for you. Please take me home. I will be forever in your debt. I'll do anything, anything. Please, Theo! Theo, I'm begging you. *(SHE looks closer.)* Are you asleep?

THEOPHILUS: I'm sorry. I have been broken of my rest.

ELIZABETH *(Laughing and crying)*: You have been broken of your rest!? *(SHE pulls herself together.)* I see . . .

THEOPHILUS *(Sad)*: I hope some day you will understand . . . I had no recourse. You endanger the souls of your family and yourself as you are now. *(Gently taking her hand.)* As I have told you repeatedly, you may think your own thoughts, Elizabeth, when you are thinking right; and when you are thinking right, you may come home. *(HE thinks of embracing her but she turns from him.)* I sincerely hope . . . you will be cured.

(HE exits. ELIZABETH starts sobbing. MRS. BONNER enters to guard her, watches her turmoil.)

MRS. BONNER: Ye didn't get yer way, didja? You fancy ladies never do.

ELIZABETH: I thank you to keep your opinions to yourself.

MRS. BONNER: Oh, wouldja now?

ELIZABETH: He's the crazy one. Not me.

MRS. BONNER: But he's the one leavin', darling, livin' in the world.

(Lights change.)

(A woman in a black bonnet on the witness stand.)

MR. HASLET: State your name please for the record.

MRS. DOLE: I am Mrs. Sybil Dole, Mr. Packard's sister.

MR. HASLET: Mrs. Dole—did you ever see your sister-in-law behave in a manner that made you think her mad?

MRS. DOLE *(With great indignation)*: Yes. One evening we were sitting at table.

(Bells sounds for breakfast. Women enter pushing on a long table.)

MRS. BONNER: Alright! Come on, ladies. Step to it! *(She takes out a stick from her belt and slams it on the table.)*

MRS. DOLE: Mrs. Packard was talking about religion.

MRS. BONNER: You! The new girl! *(She points to Elizabeth.)* Over there.

(ELIZABETH goes where directed to a table where there are two other women— neat, middle class. MRS. STOCKTON (70) picks at the dry food in front of her, smiles at Elizabeth. MRS. CHAPMAN (40) greets her with a nod. ELIZABETH whispers a question to her.)

MRS. DOLE: She became very excited. When Mr. Packard remonstrated with her, she became extremely angry . . .

MRS. BONNER: No talkin'!

MRS. DOLE: She rose up from the table, said she would have "no fellowship with the *unfruitful work* of *darkness*" . . . took her teacup, and left the room in great violence.

(A WOMAN from the other table, full of WOMEN from ward 8, the violent ward, starts screaming and waving her cup, banging it and waving it. Then she comes running over to ELIZABETH, and tries to hit her with the cup.)

MRS. BONNER: Stop that, ya little tit!

(MRS. BONNER *restrains the woman and starts to beat her and kick her into submission. The others make a racket while she does.*)

MRS. BONNER: Silence! Eat yer food. And sit up straight, alla yas. Or you'll grow hunchbacked like the *auld* ladies sittin' over there! (*Indicates Elizabeth's table.*) You wouldn't want to look like any o' them now, wouldja?

(SHE *laughs.* MRS. BONNER *saunters over to Elizabeth's table, stopping behind* ELIZABETH.)

MRS. BONNER (*To the women at the table for Ward 8*): What do we think of the new girl? She looks a bit weak to me. (*To Elizabeth.*) Are you the *weak* one. Mrs. Packard? (*Pause.*) Don't answer right now. Think on it. We'll talk tomorrow . . . and the day after that. I'll check up on ya . . . Every day . . .

(BONNER *moves on. The* WOMEN *at Elizabeth's table connect to her sympathetically with their eyes.* MRS. CHAPMAN *pats Elizabeth's hand.*)

(ELIZABETH *stares at her.*)

MRS. BONNER: Quiet! Alla yas. Now EAT!

(SHE *slams her stick down.* THEY *eat the dry food in silence. Lights change.*)

(*Continue* MRS. DOLE'S *testimony while Ward 7 gets set up.*)

MR. HASLET: Mrs. Dole, do you believe your sister-in-law was insane? Or is insane?
MRS. DOLE: I do. Mrs. Packard would not think to leave the church *unless* she was insane.
MR. MOORE (the defense) (*Interrupting*): Mrs. Dole, do you believe literally that Elijah went direct up to heaven in a chariot of fire—
MRS. DOLE: I do.
MR. MOORE: That the chariot had wheels, and seats, and was driven by horses?
MRS. DOLE: I do.
MR. MOORE: Do you believe Jonah was swallowed by a whale and remained in its belly three days and then was cast up?!

MRS. DOLE (*With great clarity*): It is in the Bible, sir.

(*LIGHTS change. A week later. The 7th Ward.*)

(*MRS. BONNER enters, pushing in a very large trunk. We hear a WOMAN crying in an adjacent ward.*)

MRS. BONNER: Yer husband sent you this, Mrs. Packard.
ELIZABETH: Oh, thank heavens.

(*SHE runs to the trunk, opens it. SHE rummages through the contents of the trunk.*)

MRS. BONNER (*Laughing*): Judgin' by the size of it, he expects yer stayin' 'til Doomsday!

(*ELIZABETH takes out old "doing her chores" clothes, some rotten fruit. She digs further, frantic.*)

ELIZABETH: Is this some kind of a cruel joke?! (*She digs to the bottom.*) Mrs. Bonner, is this all there is for me? None of my good clothes? . . . No paper or pen?
MRS. BONNER: That's what came last week, whatcha have there.
ELIZABETH: There must be some notes or tokens from my children.
MRS. BONNER: And why would good little children want to be writin' a crazy lady in the nuthouse, Mrs. Packard?
ELIZABETH (*Stung*): Excuse me?
MRS. BONNER: You heard me.
ELIZABETH (*Shaking with anger but with ladylike force*): Mrs. Bonner, may I please have some paper and a pen?!
MRS. BONNER: No . . . No . . . that's all ya got in the wide world, what you have there. Don't know what else to tell ya. . . . He's *your* husband, thank God, not mine! (*SHE exits, amused.*)

(*ELIZABETH goes back to the trunk, continues to look through it. SHE pulls out an old MIRROR, stares at her reflection, sits, humiliated. MRS. CHAPMAN comes over to her.*)

MRS. CHAPMAN: You'll find a way to survive, dear. Give it time.

(*ELIZABETH closes her eyes, shoves away the mirror, and the tears flow.*)

ELIZABETH: How long have you been here?

MRS. CHAPMAN: Three thousand four hundred forty-six days. But who counts days?

ELIZABETH: Nearly ten years? (*Voice rising.*) Dear God.

MRS. CHAPMAN: I would never agree to do what my husband wanted, you see. So he's kept me here. I wouldn't be surprised if I die here.

ELIZABETH: You chose to stay?

MRS. CHAPMAN: Yes, I suppose . . . In the end.

ELIZABETH: Do you have children?

MRS. CHAPMAN: . . . No.

(*ELIZABETH gets up.*)

ELIZABETH: Well, I have to get out of here. My children need me . . . (*Paces again.*)

MRS. CHAPMAN: Of course they do.

(*ELIZABETH looks at her in panic, hair wild, dress buttoned wrong.*)

ELIZABETH: I am not mad.

MRS. CHAPMAN (*An odd laugh*): You see the woman in the corner there sleeping? She's a Spiritualist. She actually foresaw the War Between the States, but she talked about it. She's an Abolitionist. Her husband is not. Mrs. Stockton there?—her husband is a minister, very Old School . . . (*ELIZABETH* [*nodding*]: *Ah . . . Yes . . .*) (*MRS. CHAPMAN takes note.*) She started studying with a Swedenborgenist about ten years ago. Her husband would not have it. And the woman in the corner there?—She and her husband . . . "disagreed" about her property, so . . .

ELIZABETH: But Dr. McFarland does not think *I'm* mad.

MRS. CHAPMAN (*An odd laugh*): Mrs. Packard! Make no mistake, dear. You're here because the doctor has agreed to keep you here. In my experience—

(*DR. MCFARLAND enters with MRS. BONNER.*)

DR. MCFARLAND: Good morning, ladies. Mrs. Bonner will take you to the yard while I treat Mrs. Packard.

(MRS. CHAPMAN *looks to her, alarmed.* BONNER *gathers together the women and takes them out, as* ELIZABETH *tries to compose herself.*)

MRS. BONNER: Step lively, ladies, you heard the doctor! Come on, now! Move quickly, Mrs. Chapman! Or I'll lose my patience with ya. Mrs. Stockton, I'll knock yer carcass from here to kingdom come if ya don't move along. Holy Joseph!! Git on with ye!

(THEY *exit.*)

DR. MCFARLAND: And how are you feeling today?

ELIZABETH: Oh . . . m-much better . . . now that you are with me, Doctor . . . (HE *smiles.*) As you know, . . . I don't belong here.

DR. MCFARLAND: . . . You look a bit calmer than you did on first meeting.

ELIZABETH: . . . Perhaps the shock . . . of my abduction . . . is beginning to wear off . . .

DR. MCFARLAND: Good. Now, what books shall I bring you, Mrs. Packard? I promised you in our interview I would furnish you with books of your choosing.

ELIZABETH: Well . . . though I do enjoy reading a vast . . . array of—of theologians, I—do not think I'll be here long enough to start a new and weighty volume, Doctor, (*In a small voice.*) do you? (HE *smiles.*) . . . Perhaps a newspaper? So I can follow the progress . . . of our Union troops . . .

DR. MCFARLAND (*Surprised, impressed*): Really? Easily done . . . you must know, Mrs. Packard, I have met many intelligent and learned women in my day, but they were rarely married. Rarely mothers.

ELIZABETH: Yes, well . . . my father thought it only just that I have the same opportunities to cultivate my mind as my brothers.

DR. MCFARLAND: You're a fortunate woman.

ELIZABETH: Yes, well, my father is an extraordinary man. When I was a little girl, I would sit outside his study door for hours, and listen to the guests who came to visit—fellow ministers like my father or—or eminent scholars. I love to learn—(*Tears start to stream.*)

DR. MCFARLAND: Yes . . .

ELIZABETH: And I often had lively conversations with my father . . . about these new ideas . . . I always longed to with—(*Stops herself.*)

DR. MCFARLAND: I'm sorry.

(HE *gives her his handkerchief.* SHE *takes it.*)

DR. MCFARLAND: There, there . . . breathe deeply . . . just be still for a moment.

ELIZABETH: I . . . Yes, Doctor.

(Long pause.)

DR. MCFARLAND: I should like to give you a new treatment, Mrs. Packard, to relieve some of your strain. You will feel my hands. Just breathe deeply. Your nervous system has been severely taxed . . .

ELIZABETH: Yes, *(Whispers.)* yes, it has.

DR. MCFARLAND: . . . Breathe deeply, Mrs. Packard . . . That's it . . .

(HE gently starts to place his hands on her back. She has not been touched in weeks. She starts to breathe deeply and enjoys the touch.)

Feel the warmth of my hands . . . (SHE: *Oh* . . .) Yes . . . shhhh . . . shhhh . . . on your back . . . and your neck . . . and your shoulders.

ELIZABETH: Yes . . .

DR. MCFARLAND: You can trust me, Mrs. Packard.

ELIZABETH: Yes . . .

DR. MCFARLAND: Just breathe deeply . . . (ELIZ: *Ah* . . .) And feel my hands on your back and your neck . . .
And your throat . . .
And your chest . . .

ELIZABETH: Ah!

DOCTOR MCFARLAND: Just relax . . .
. . . Your lower back and your chest . . .
You're trembling, Elizabeth . . .

ELIZABETH: Yes . . .

DR. MCFARLAND: Just give in . . . That's it . . .
Just . . . give . . . in . . .
Close your eyes, feel my warmth . . .
Shshsh—shshshsh
There . . . There . . .

ELIZABETH: Ah . . . Ah . . .

DR. MCFARLAND: Yes, yes . . . Yes . . .

ELIZABETH: Ahhhh . . .

(After a long silence.)

DR. MCFARLAND: You may open your eyes now, Mrs. Packard.

(SHE *opens her eyes, looks around dazed, trembling and flushed.*)

    How do you feel now? You look very much better.
ELIZABETH: . . . Yes . . . I feel . . . very much better.
DR. MCFARLAND: Good.

(*A long moment of profound mutual attraction.* HE *kisses her on the forehead.*)

ELIZABETH: . . . Dr. McFarland?
DR. MCFARLAND: Merely a kiss of charity, my dear.
ELIZABETH (*Confused, flushed*): . . . Thank you.

(*A pause.*)

DR. MCFARLAND: You must know, Mrs. Packard . . . it is unusual to find
    a woman of such stimulating intelligence and learning in such a
    charming . . . form.

(ELIZABETH *laughs, blushes.*)

ELIZABETH: How nice of you to say so, Doctor.
DR. MCFARLAND: Your husband is . . . a . . . a fortunate man.
ELIZABETH: Early in my married life I learned the sad truth, Doctor. My hus-
    band does not . . . know me.
DR. MCFARLAND: Ah! I am sorry to hear it, Mrs. Packard.
ELIZABETH: . . . I was thinking just this morning . . . It's strange—I believed in
    and spoke out for the just cause of Abolition . . . And now that I find my-
    self here . . . I . . . realize . . . I'd been speaking about myself . . .
DR. MCFARLAND: Yourself?! Come, come! What do you mean?
ELIZABETH: I wonder . . . if I'd known I would . . . *belong* to my husband . . .
    should I have married at all.
DR. MCFARLAND: Mrs. Packard! That would have been a—a calamitous choice
    for you to have made, I should think, a passionate woman like you!
ELIZABETH (*Flushes*): . . . I . . . I could never, ever regret having my six beauti-
    ful children, don't misunderstand me, but . . . the price to pay is quite
    high, don't you think? I now better understand those women who

choose not to marry. I could never understand them before! Or women who want to *vote?* I'm thinking *very* hard about them at the moment . . .

DR. MCFARLAND *(Horrified but laughing)*: Good heavens! That is certainly not the cure I had hoped you would take away from this institution. Mrs. Packard! My dear, it is quite clear you're an exceptional woman . . . and if I were in the least bit unethical, I'm afraid I'd keep you here forever! I'd never want to let you out of my sight! *(HE laughs, with irony:)* But, sadly, I am a good man. *(THEY both laugh. SHE, uncertain. Pause.)* Now . . . Let's use your prodigious mind . . . to find a solution to your dilemma, and I shall call that solution . . . a cure. *(Looks at her pointedly.)* Do you understand me?

ELIZABETH: . . . I'm not sure . . .

DR. MCFARLAND: Well, then . . . Let's get to the heart of the matter, shall we? What is this about your saying you're . . . *(Finds it in his notes.)* the personification of the Holy Ghost?

ELIZABETH: Wh-what? . . . I never said that. That would be . . . crazy!

DR. MCFARLAND *(With a smile)*: Yes, . . . indeed. And it greatly concerns your husband that you did.

ELIZABETH: No, no! What I said—perhaps it isn't clear—is that the Trinity only makes sense to me if it consists of the Father, the Son, and the Holy Female Spirit. That is, the Son is the fruit of the love between the Father and the Holy Ghost. This idea has been discussed for centuries, Doctor.

DR. MCFARLAND *(Also with a smile)*: Really? And suppressed for centuries as heretical. Mrs. Packard, think! Your husband is a minister of the faith.

ELIZABETH: I don't care! It isn't heresy. The noun in Aramaic for Holy Spirit is *female*. It is a feminine noun.

DR. MCFARLAND *(Taken by surprise)*: . . . Really?

ELIZABETH *(Getting animated)*: Yes! And Jesus of Nazareth spoke Aramaic. Our good Lord Jesus Christ would not eliminate women from every possible interpretation of his Word. He assumed a knowledge of the language.

DR. MCFARLAND: Yes, well . . . *(Clearly fascinated.)*

ELIZABETH: What may be of some confusion is I have said that as a woman, I *represent* the female Spirit in earthly form, just as you, as a man, represent the Father and the Son. You may not agree with this interpretation, but it is not delusional.

DR. MCFARLAND: Yes, well . . . it is even . . . quite interesting, Mrs. Packard. But you must be practical! What you have just said is irrelevent.

ELIZABETH: Irrelevent! Why?! . . . Why not discuss what is clearly interesting?

(*A beat.*)

DR. MCFARLAND: . . . If you and I were to have met under different circumstances, perhaps the two of us could indulge in . . . stimulating dialogue, but I am here to help you return home to your husband and children, post-haste. You must begin by promising me to keep these . . . thoughts to yourself.

ELIZABETH: No. I don't want to.

DR. MCFARLAND: Mrs. Packard, be reasonable! You must see that you cannot hold forth on these ideas in your husband's house.

ELIZABETH: But Doctor, my children—

DR. MCFARLAND: No, no. Sh-sh-sh-sh. I cannot be more clear. You have not given a response acceptable to your husband's teachings, and that must be our prime concern.

ELIZABETH: Then perhaps you should understand my husband's teachings, Doctor.

DR. MCFARLAND: No, no, you are here so I can understand you, Mrs. Packard, not your husband.

ELIZABETH: Then understand what I am up against, Doctor! My husband is not merely "a minister of the faith."

DR. MCFARLAND: How do you mean?

ELIZABETH: . . . My husband was a great sinner in his youth. (DR.: *Really?* . . .) He was a—a drunkard, and a wastrel and a disgrace to his minister father . . . (DR.: *Well*—) One night—hear me out—his little brother, Isaac, who was a sickly child, said to him: "Theo, have you looked after your soul?" . . . And Theo had to answer no, he had not looked after his soul. Isaac said: "Promise me you will *get right with God*, Theo." . . . Those were his last words. Isaac died in Theo's arms.

DR. MCFARLAND: . . . I see . . .

ELIZABETH: Soon after, Theo had a vision and entered seminary, reborn. *Do* you see, Doctor? My husband is obsessed; he thinks only about damnation and is terrified by any deviation from—

DR. MCFARLAND: Then do not deviate! Your task, Mrs. Packard, is to accept your husband's beliefs and find a way for you and your children to live within them.

ELIZABETH (*Suddenly wild-eyed*): But Doctor, a few months ago, he said the children could not have *seconds* at supper!

DR. MCFARLAND (*Nonplussed*): Pardon me?

ELIZABETH (*Beside herself*): My husband locked himself away for hours, praying for their souls, praying because they wanted seconds!—
DR. MCFARLAND: Mrs. Packard! What are you saying?

(*A beat.*)

ELIZABETH (*snaps back*): I have a mind—
DOCTOR MCFARLAND: I know you have a mind, Mrs. Packard—
ELIZABETH: Well, I must use my mind.

(*A beat.*)

DR. MCFARLAND: Perhaps I should bring you paper and pen. . . . Mr. Packard
   says you like to write . . . ?
ELIZABETH: Yes.
DOCTOR MCFARLAND: I encourage you to write down your . . . very interesting
   thoughts, and then perhaps you and I can discuss your musings . . .
   together, at length. I should like that. But what you write is not *ever* for
   your husband's eyes—that would only provoke him—only mine. Understood?

(ELIZABETH *looks at him. A long moment.*)

   I can be of great help to you, Mrs. Packard. I am sure of it . . .

(HE *exits. Lights change.*)

(*A* MAN *on the witness stand and nighttime in Ward 7.*)

MR. HASLET: Dr. Brown, did you make an evaluation of Mrs. Packard's mental
   state?
DR. J.W. BROWN: I did. I visited Mrs. Packard by request of Mr. Packard at their
   house three years ago . . . (*Pleased with his subterfuge.*) She thought I
   was selling sewing machines. We discussed them at length. I found her
   completely rational on that subject. We spoke at length on women's issues, as well. (CHAPMAN *and* STOCKTON *enter to get ready for bed.* MRS. BON-
   NER *resentfully leaves paper, pen and newspaper.*) We did not agree on
   those issues, but I did not think her *completely* insane on that subject.

When we spoke of religion, however, I had no doubt that she was *hopelessly* insane and needed to be committed to the asylum.

(ELIZABETH, *seeing paper and a pen on her bed, starts to write.* CHAPMAN *and* STOCKTON *get ready for bed.*)

MR. HASLET: Can you give us your reasons, Doctor, for diagnosing her insane?

DR. BROWN: I can, sir. (*He takes out his notebook and reads from his notes.*) If you don't mind I should like to read my reasons.

MR. HASLET: Go on.

DR. BROWN: Number one: *she disliked to be called insane.* Number two: she claimed perfection or nearer perfection in action and conduct than her husband! . . . Number three: She believed that to call her insane and abuse her was blasphemy against the Holy Ghost! Number 4: She had an extreme aversion to the Calvinist doctrine of the total depravity of mankind and in the same conversation, she said her husband was a specimen of man's total depravity! Number 5: She likened her marriage to the Civil War, saying she was the North and her husband was the South, and that man's despotism over his wife may yet now prevail, but she had right and truth on her side and ultimately she would prevail! Number 6: She called me a rebel when I went out the door, a copperhead! Believed that some calamity would befall her owing to my being there, and took a great dislike to me. Number 7: She viewed the subject of religion from the (*Stumbling as he tries to read this.*) esoteric standpoint of Christian ex . . . ex-eg-etical analysis, and—and ag . . . glut . . . inating the poly . . . syn—thetical ec . . . toblasts of homo . . . geneous as—ceticism.

MR. HASLET: What? . . . Thank you, Doctor.

(*Lights out on* brown. *Lights up on night in the 7th Ward.*)

(FEMALE INMATE *whimpers behind the door Up Center. Concerned,* ELIZABETH *goes to the door and tries to open it, but it is locked.*)

ELIZABETH: Hello! Hello! Who's there? Are you all right? (*No answer.*) Are you all right? Do you need help?

(MRS. BONNER *runs on, and starts to beat the* WOMAN *behind the door. The* WOMAN *screams. More blows and groans.* MRS. CHAPMAN *and* MRS. STOCKTON *sit up in bed.*)

ELIZABETH: Stop it! Stop it!

MRS. BONNER: Shut up, you!

(Another blow and a groan. The other wards wake up. Cries and bellows.)

ELIZABETH: Oh, Dear God!

MRS. CHAPMAN *(to Mrs. Packard)*: Go to bed, dear. There is nothing you can do. Pray for sleep.

(The ATTENDANT enters with a straitjacket and jackets the WOMAN.)

MRS. BONNER: QUIET! Quiet! Or I'll knock you all to kingdom come! QUIET now!

ELIZABETH *(Pounding on the door)*: Are you all right?!? Answer me!

MRS. BONNER: Jacket 'er.

(BONNER exits to the 8th ward as the ATTENDANT finishes jacketing the INMATE and taking HER off.)

BONNER: Quiet!! I'll skin yas alive! Qui-et!!!

(MRS. STOCKTON puts the pillow over her head and starts to cry. The bedlam builds to an ear-splitting madness, like a prison riot. ELIZABETH prays, terrified. LIGHTS.)

(Early the next morning. Lights fade up slowly.)

(ELIZABETH has fallen asleep, fully dressed, pages of writing around her.)

MRS. BONNER *(off as she enters)*: Alright, ladies. Get moving! Step lively! Special sewin' to do before breakfast.

(MRS. BONNER has a large basket filled with sewing and sewing boxes.)

MRS. BONNER *(Continuing)*: Let's go. Here y'are . . .

(SHE distributes garments to the women as they wake up, exhausted, and throw on dresses. ELIZABETH gathers her papers and gets herself ready.)

MRS. BONNER: Move along now, and make yer sewin' with yer very best hand, ladies. Yer mendin' for the doctor's family today . . . take care.

(*ELIZABETH, surprised, looks at the others to see if they think her statement is un-usual. BONNER looks through the basket, finds something.*)

MRS. BONNER (*Pointedly*): Mrs. Packard, I have a skirt of Mrs. McFarland's for you to mend . . . there—right there, on the waistband.

(*ELIZABETH takes the skirt. It is large. She meets BONNER's eyes. A standoff.*)

ELIZABETH: Thank you.

(*As MRS. CHAPMAN sorts through the basket of clothes needing mending, MRS. STOCKTON sits back down on her bed with a groan, exhausted.*)

MRS. BONNER: Mrs. Stockton! Get up off that bed, or I'll—

(*SHE palms her stick. MRS. STOCKTON struggles up, terrified.*)

MRS. STOCKTON: Yes, yes! . . . I'm . . . sorry.

(*MRS. BONNER exits, slamming the door. A silence.*)

MRS. STOCKTON (*Gathering herself*): At least we'll be doing something quiet and useful . . .
MRS. CHAPMAN: Yes, Mrs. Packard, take note. This is the sunny side of prison life. (*Laughter.*)

(*MRS. CHAPMAN holds up each garment looking for where it needs mending. She passes a garment on to MRS. STOCKTON. Wordlessly, the women look at the garments of what must be a large family of children. When MRS. CHAPMAN holds up a sleeping gown for a 14-to-18-month-old child, ELIZABETH is stricken.*)

ELIZABETH: May I see that for a moment, Mrs. Chapman?

(*MRS. CHAPMAN hands it to her. ELIZABETH looks at it, holds it, then brings it to her face, gets lost in it. The WOMEN watch, understanding. Suddenly aware, SHE hands it back to MRS. CHAPMAN.*)

ELIZABETH (*Quiet*): Thank you.

(*THEY sew. Finally:*)

MRS. CHAPMAN: What is your baby's name?

ELIZABETH: . . . Arthur . . . We have six children . . . (*To Mrs. Stockton.*) And you?

MRS. STOCKTON: Blessedly, my children were already grown and on their own when I came here . . . They write to me . . .

(*THEY sew.*)

ELIZABETH: What happened last night?

MRS. CHAPMAN: . . . Someone was being disciplined for something or other, I should think. They call it "subduing the patient." It happens . . . many nights.

ELIZABETH: Really?

MRS. CHAPMAN: I hope it wasn't too bad for her.

(*THEY sew.*)

ELIZABETH: . . . I was wondering last night . . . Did you ladies know? Would you have done any differently—if you had known . . . the real consequences?

STOCKTON: That is a very good question, Mrs. Packard. . . . Mrs. Chapman? . . .

MRS. CHAPMAN: Would I have done any differently . . . knowing I would end up here? (*After some reflection.*) I don't know, but I think not . . . I think I would have done . . . just what I did . . .

ELIZABETH: Well, (*A beat, wipes away quick tears.*)—I think the torment of being completely cut off from my children—I may not have been quite so outspoken, I think, if I had known the real cost.

MRS. STOCKTON: I tried to go home once . . . but I couldn't be quiet. I kept aggravating him, so I had to come back.

MRS. CHAPMAN: I never considered going home. (*Hatred just under the surface.*) I wouldn't give my husband the pleasure . . . (*THEY sew.*) When I was young, I think I heard tales, sort of mutterings and rumors . . . But it did not seem to have anything to do with me somehow . . . I think I heard about disobedient wives thrown into madhouses—who-knew-where . . . Timbuktu!—but *vaguely*, we heard tell vaguely . . . on the wind almost . . .

MRS. STOCKTON (*Laughing*): Yes . . .

(*THEY sew.*)

ELIZABETH (*A hard question*): Do you ever wonder . . . if your husband is right?
MRS. STOCKTON (*Pointed*): What do you mean?
ELIZABETH: I find myself doubting . . . myself—my very sanity, I suppose—deep down . . . I did make the children nervous sometimes . . .
MRS. STOCKTON (*With force, taking her hand*): You are sane, Elizabeth. Keep saying that to yourself over and over. I am sane, I am sane. Let it become a little ditty in your head: I am sane.
ELIZABETH (*Quiet, wiping away tears*): Yes . . . Thank you, Mrs. Stockton.
MRS. CHAPMAN: Ladies . . . (*She speaks very softly looking to make sure no attendant is around.*) I received a note from the 8th Ward yesterday . . . Mrs. Bonner beat a poor woman nearly to death during the night. She was in such a state, she . . . lost . . . consciousness while she was doing it . . . (*She gets up and holds MRS. STOCKTON.*) It was Mrs. Hosner, I'm afraid. (*MRS. STOCKTON: Oh Dear God.*) (*Handing the note to STOCKTON from a secret pocket under her apron.*) She hanged herself yesterday . . . (*MRS. STOCKTON is stricken, just as:*)
ELIZABETH: What?

(*The DOCTOR enters with MRS. BONNER.*)

DR. MCFARLAND: Ladies . . .
WOMEN: Doctor . . .

(*MRS. STOCKTON hides the note under her apron and tries to regain her composure.*)

ELIZABETH (*Helping cover for the women*): Doctor McFarland! How nice to see you! I have just now finished mending your wife's skirt. It looks lovely, don't you think? (*She holds it up.*) Now, how does this work? Do I give you the bill for it now or later?

(*HE laughs.*)

DR. MCFARLAND: Mrs. Packard, come over here and speak with me in private, please. Mrs. Bonner, you may clear the room.

MRS. BONNER: Come on, ladies. Off with you! And take yer sewin' with ya. Move along, Mrs. Stockton . . . Yer gettin' slower than molasses—(*A malicious warning in her ear.*) Watch yerself.

(*MRS. STOCKTON grabs MRS. CHAPMAN's arm as they leave, upset.*)

DR. MCFARLAND: . . . Tell me, do you enjoy being provocative?

ELIZABETH: . . . Actually, I think I do. When it is warranted.

DR. MCFARLAND: Yes, I think you do, too.

ELIZABETH: I did not realize slave labor was part of the cure here at Jacksonville.

(*HE laughs.*)

DR. MCFARLAND: Yes—your color comes into your cheeks when you are being provocative. It is very attractive.

ELIZABETH: Pardon me?

DR. MCFARLAND: Did you receive the paper and pen I left for you?

ELIZABETH: I did, thank you. I have already put them to good use.

DOCTOR MCFARLAND: Excellent. I thought you might. So . . . Mrs. Packard—I assume you still want to leave Jacksonville . . . do you not?

ELIZABETH: Yes. Of course.

DR. MCFARLAND: As I told you, I shall miss you terribly, my dear, but I have decided not to be selfish. I shall let you go, painful as that is. In fact, you can elect to leave quite soon.

ELIZABETH (*Shocked, happy*): Really? You're going to declare me sane.

DR. MCFARLAND: Mrs. Packard . . . I trust you have given our earlier discussion some serious thought?

ELIZABETH: Oh, yes . . .

DR. MCFARLAND: Good. I expected so. Then . . . I also expect you will submit to sign an affidavit to honor and obey your husband in all things—that you will be his unconditional helpmate and support in his church, in his home, and in his bed. Sign this paper, and I shall send you home, *cured*. Agreed?

(*A beat.*)

ELIZABETH: . . . Do you know what you are saying, Doctor?

DR. MCFARLAND: Oh, yes.

ELIZABETH: That if I submit to all my husband's wishes and opinions, I should be considered *sane*???! (*Laughs.*) I should think it would mean just the opposite.

DR. MCFARLAND: Would you?

ELIZABETH: Yes! (*Getting angry but remaining charming.*) I will not ask you to put yourself in my shoes. Clearly, that would be asking too much, but let us say for just one moment that the tables were turned, shall we? (*Thinking on her feet.*) Pretend for a moment you and I . . . were married . . . (SHE *holds his wife's skirt up to her:* HE *laughs.*) and we both teach at a school of great repute . . .

DR. MCFARLAND (*Amused*): Yes . . . ?

ELIZABETH: You are beloved by students and faculty alike.

(HE *is enjoying this.*)

DR. MCFARLAND: Go on.

ELIZABETH: I am not. In fact, I am feared and despised, and the students fall asleep whenever I lecture! (THEY *laugh.*) Furthermore, you and I clash on simply every major issue facing the school. I decide to have you removed by force and committed to a lunatic asylum until you submit to me in writing that you will agree with me on every single issue we have previously clashed upon, even though during your confinement you realize you are further apart from my views than ever before. Would *you* sign? Would you find that situation acceptable? . . . Would you find my despotic behavior just? (HE *laughs.*) Or rather, would you not find me insane and fit for commitment to this asylum?

DR. MCFARLAND: You are quite a lovely woman . . . Dear God.

ELIZABETH: Doctor . . .

DR. MCFARLAND: Come, come, Mrs. Packard! What you just described is a fairy tale—a charming fairy tale—but a fairy-tale nonetheless. What I am advising you to do is look clear-eyed at the world in which you have been placed, and save yourself, I beg of you.

(*A beat. A radical shift in tone.*)

ELIZABETH: . . . I sign . . . and I keep what I truly believe hidden from my children?

DR. MCFARLAND: Oh, yes. *Especially* from your children.

ELIZABETH (*Almost unable to speak*): I don't know . . .

DOCTOR: Do you remember the healing treatment I gave you when you first arrived?

ELIZABETH: Yes, of course.

DR. MCFARLAND: Did it help?

ELIZABETH: Why, yes. Actually, I was able to sleep that night for the first time since I'd gotten here. I missed my children so much I couldn't bear it . . . I couldn't sleep . . . We all need to be touched, Doctor.

DR. MCFARLAND: Indeed . . . And it seems to me that you must get home to your children—if not your husband—as soon as you can. Do I understand your . . . desire? Or—?

ELIZABETH: No, you understand my desire.

DR. MCFARLAND: Good. (*HE takes her hand.*) However . . . I must admit, unlike you, I have not slept, Mrs. Packard, . . . not since . . . You are a passionate and . . . a beautiful woman. I marvel your husband can bear to be parted from you, even for a night. (*ELIZABETH laughs.*) You cannot thrive here. Let me help you . . . Elizabeth. I would so enjoy . . .

(*THEY almost, almost kiss.*)

ELIZABETH (*A big decision*): . . . Yes. I will . . . let you help me. My children need me. Wh-what do the papers say?

DR. MCFARLAND: What we have discussed, of course. That you will obey your husband . . .

ELIZABETH: Doctor . . . Why not let the papers say you release me . . . because I am sane?

DR. MCFARLAND: Madam?

ELIZABETH (*Continuing*): You must not lie, Doctor; to lie is a sin.

DR. MCFARLAND: I do not—

ELIZABETH: Say: "Elizabeth Packard is not mad". Say: "Elizabeth Packard will not thrive here." Say (*Intimate/seductive.*): "I will release you, Elizabeth, I will protect you, Elizabeth, I will deliver you . . ."

DR. MCFARLAND: Mrs. Packard . . .

(*THEY connect—a long, eroticized moment, then HE is the one to step back. A moment.*)

DR. MCFARLAND (*Continuing*): Perhaps I shall bring you the papers . . . to sign later today, or—or . . . in the morning. . . . It's—best you leave as soon as possible.

ELIZABETH: Doctor—will you bring the papers—as presently written?

DR. MCFARLAND: Yes, of course. (*With an edge.*) There is no other way—to release you, Mrs. Packard.

ELIZABETH: I see. You were not always as you are now, were you, Doctor? You had hoped for more, I'm sure.

DR. MCFARLAND (*Curt*): . . . Good day, Mrs. Packard.

(*HE exits, off balance. Lights.*)

(*DR. CHRISTOPHER W. KNOTT on the stand*)

CLERK: Dr. Christopher W. Knott, you have been sworn.

DR. KNOTT: Sir, I have no doubt Mrs. Packard was insane. I would say that she was insane the same as I would say Henry Ward Beecher, Horace Greeley, or the like are insane. Three-fourths of the religious community are insane in the same manner! Nothing excites the human mind quite so much as religion . . . Though Mrs. Packard is a lady of fine mental abilities, I observed she has a nervous temperament, is easily excited, and has a strong will. Let us remember, gentlemen, the female mind is more excitable than the male mind. Confinement, in any shape, or restraint of any kind, I thought would only make Mrs. Packard's condition worse. Mrs. Packard required complete rest.

(*Lights change.*)

(*That night. The WOMEN are in bed, trying to sleep. Silence. Then blows, a groan from off.*)

MRS. TENNEY (*Off*): She can't breathe! Lizzie! Lizzie! Do you want to drown her?

MRS. BONNER: Ouchhh . . . Alright . . .

(*Gasp. Choke.*)

It woulda been better if I'd killed her.

(*ELIZABETH wakes up with a gasp.*)

MRS. CHAPMAN (*Firm*): Mrs. Packard, pray for sleep.

MRS. BONNER (*Off*): Yer useless!
ATTENDANT (*Off*): Get back here!

(*The door bursts open. A* WOMAN *in elegant attire, wild, wet hair, runs in. Looking to get out. Asking where "out" is.* MRS. BONNER *enters, followed by the* ATTENDANT. SHE *catches her and slaps her across the face, grabs her and starts to drag her off.*)

ELIZABETH: Stop it! Stop it, Mrs. Bonner!

(MRS. BONNER *stops for a moment, looks at* ELIZABETH, *dangerous.*)

MRS. BONNER: I am seekin' satisfaction and I will have it. I will not be abused
    by a patient. (*To the attendant:*) You! Take her back to the screen room
    and jacket 'er. She has the *divil* in her and I'm to beat it out of her.

(*As the* ATTENDANT *takes the* WOMAN *off:*)

ELIZABETH: What has she done?

(BONNER *exits, slamming and locking the door.*)

MRS. CHAPMAN: It doesn't matter, Elizabeth.
ELIZABETH: We have to do something.

(MRS. CHAPMAN *with an odd laugh turns over to try to sleep.* ELIZABETH *gets up, starts to throw on clothes.* MRS. CHAPMAN *sits up.*)

MRS. CHAPMAN: Elizabeth? What—?
ELIZABETH: The doctor's right.—I have to get home to my children—
MRS. CHAPMAN: . . . Has he offered you the papers, dear?

(*A scream stops* ELIZABETH *cold.* SHE *listens.*)

ELIZABETH: Oh, dear God! I can't bear it anymore. I can't, I can't . . .

(SHE *tries to dress more. To* MRS. CHAPMAN:)

    Yes! I'll do anything . . . I'll sign anything . . . The children—

(The scream becomes a screaming spasm, eerie in the still air. ELIZABETH starts to cry then stops herself. SHE makes a decision, races to her trunk, pulls out writing paper.)

MRS. CHAPMAN: Elizabeth, are you all right?

ELIZABETH: Yes, yes. Never mind, Mrs. Chapman. I'm sorry I've disturbed you . . . I—I . . . We can speak in the morning.

(SHE takes her pen and paper, sits, and starts to write. The wails continue as: lights slowly change.)

(MRS. DOLE on the stand.)

MR. HASLET: Was there a time you thought Mrs. Packard was unfit to care for her children?

MRS. DOLE: Yes. One day, Mr. Packard wanted me to take the baby, Arthur, home with me. Now Mrs. Packard consented, so I took the baby up to my house. In a short time, the other children came up and said their mother wanted to take her own child, so I took the child back down. Mrs. Packard's appearance was very wild, and she was filled with spite toward Mr. Packard. She called him a devil, and she defied me to take the child again, and said that she would evoke the strong arm of the law to help her keep it. Later that morning, they took her away. For the sake of the children, I approved of her removal.

MR. HASLET: Thank you.

(Lights slowly shift. It is morning.)

(ELIZABETH is still writing furiously. The other WOMEN are asleep. SHE has been writing all night. SHE blows out the candle as she hears MRS. BONNER in the hallway, banging the doors with her stick and calling to the WOMEN.)

MRS. BONNER: Step lively! Everyone up! Out of bed! Get on with you! *(Repeat.)* Step lively, ladies. Out of bed!

(The WOMEN start to wake up. MRS. CHAPMAN sees ELIZABETH writing, sitting on the floor where she saw her last, ink-stained, looking wild and agitated, almost mad.)

MRS. CHAPMAN: Mrs. Packard, have you slept?

ELIZABETH: No . . .

MRS. CHAPMAN: Mrs. Packard? Elizabeth! (*SHE goes to her.*) What are you doing? My dear . . .

ELIZABETH (*Speaks quickly, manically*): I am his favorite. I am writing him.

MRS. CHAPMAN: What? What do you mean? Whose favorite?

ELIZABETH: The doctor's! He loves me.

MRS. CHAPMAN: Do not believe that, Elizabeth.

(*MRS. STOCKTON approaches.*)

ELIZABETH: But he does! I will use my position for all of us. I'll not just help myself.

MRS. CHAPMAN: Elizabeth, what are you talking about?

ELIZABETH: There is no other way, Mrs. Chapman. I can appeal to the doctor's humanity and his good conscience—(*MRS. CHAPMAN laughs.*) He will pronounce us *all sane* . . . And he will tell our husbands and our children we are sane. (*MRS. CHAPMAN: No, he won't!*) He will change the . . . the degradation he fosters in this institution, or—or—

MRS. STOCKTON: Mrs. Packard! You must never tell a man like Dr. McFarland he is wrong.

MRS. CHAPMAN: He will punish you terribly for criticizing him, I fear, and then you will be of no use to yourself, your children, or any of us. I beg you, you have not had your sleep in weeks and you have written all night, pages and pages of—

ELIZABETH (*Out of control*): Yes! this is my "Reproof." That is what I shall call it. (*She scribbles the title on the front page.*) I shall tell him what is in it personally, and then I shall give him the pages to study so he and I can discuss it later, alone—at length, just as he promised—

MRS. STOCKTON: Mrs. Packard, wait. Get dressed and see him after breakfast. Your nerves are frayed now, my dear. You are exhausted and upset, and in no condition.

ELIZABETH (*Suddenly lucid and quiet*): No! With all due respect, nothing will change if I stay here, as you two have. I have to *do* something. I will see him before breakfast if he is here.

MRS. CHAPMAN: Elizabeth! Sign the papers and go home.

ELIZABETH (*Overlap*) (*Howls*): NO!!!!! *I cannot go home on his terms!* (*Clear again.*) I betray my children if I betray myself! I cannot go home and lie to them, pretending I agree with everything their father thinks and says and *believes*! (*Sobbing.*) I can't do that to them! I can't do it! I can't!!

MRS. CHAPMAN: I understand, but you cannot do this.

(*ELIZABETH breaks away.* SHE *goes to the door, calling:*)

ELIZABETH: Mrs. Bonner! Mrs. Bonner!

MRS. STOCKTON: What are you doing, child?

ELIZABETH: I cannot wait. If I wait, I might lose courage. Mrs. Bonner!

(*MRS. BONNER comes to the door, her face bloated and bruised.*)

BONNER: What are you roarin' about?

ELIZABETH: I should like to speak with Dr. McFarland before breakfast; please. Do you know if he is about?

MRS. BONNER: I seen him earlier.

(*ELIZABETH starts to go.* BONNER *stops her with her stick.*)

You stay here. I'll see if *he* wants to speak to *you*. The rest of ya! Get dressed! Breakfast in five minutes! Step lively!

(*ELIZABETH gets herself ready, straightens her hair and pages and buttons her dress. Half the pages [the copy] she hides in the back of her mirror which she puts back in her trunk.*)

MRS. CHAPMAN: Elizabeth, I beg of you . . .

MRS. STOCKTON: This is suicide.

(*ELIZABETH shakes her head.*)

ELIZABETH: No, this must be done, like Queen Esther in the Bible. She was the king's favorite, I—I . . . In case something happens to me—I have made a copy of the "Reproof." (*MRS. CHAPMAN: What?!*) It is hidden in the back of the mirror. Remember that, will you? . . . He'll listen to me.

MRS. CHAPMAN: No, he will not!

ELIZABETH: I know him.

(*She starts to pace. Under her breath to herself, quickly:*)

I am sane, I am sane. Make it a little ditty in my head: I am sane . . .

(DR. MCFARLAND *enters the room.*)

DR. MCFARLAND: Ladies?
WOMEN: Doctor . . .
DR. MCFARLAND: Mrs. Packard, you wished to see me?
ELIZABETH: Yes . . . Please.
MRS. CHAPMAN: We are going to breakfast, Elizabeth. (*As she leaves.*) Shall we see you there?

(MRS. BONNER *peeks her head in.*)

MRS. BONNER: Let's go then, ladies.

(BONNER *looks at the* DOCTOR *and* ELIZABETH, *suspicious, as* MRS. CHAPMAN *and* STOCKTON *leave, then closes the door.*)

ELIZABETH: Thank you for coming, Doctor.
DR. MCFARLAND (*Subdued, guarded*): Pleasure. Now what can I do for you, Mrs. Packard? . . . Do you wish to sign your papers now?
ELIZABETH: Yes, perhaps I will sign them now, but first I want to give you the opportunity, to uh—I have been writing to you all night.
DR. MCFARLAND: Really?
ELIZABETH: Yes, Doctor. My heart feels as if it's bursting . . .
DR. MCFARLAND: Oh. Well, then . . .
ELIZABETH: I-I . . . I should like to read you some of what I wrote, or rather tell you in my own words what I am thinking and refer to my notes if I must—
DR. MCFARLAND: Of course.
ELIZABETH: —And then give it to you to read so we can discuss it later, in depth—as you once proposed. (DR.: *Yes . . .*) As you can see, I wrote quite a lot to you—for "your eyes only" . . .
DR. MCFARLAND (*Laughs, relieved*): Yes. I see. I look forward to our discussion . . . In depth, as you say.
ELIZABETH: I hope you will let me get to the very end since it is complex; all I have to tell you.
DR. MCFARLAND (*Indulgent*): Do . . . go on.

(ELIZABETH *starts to read.*)

ELIZABETH: . . . Dear Dr. McFarland, in Christ's own expressive language I say: "Come let us reason together."

(HE *smiles and sits.*)

DR. MCFARLAND: Please, continue.

(SHE *sits with him.*)

ELIZABETH (*Hesitating*): Doctor, I would never dream of contradicting you or criticizing you in any way. You are the doctor, I the patient. But . . . there are things you may be ignorant of occurring in this institution th—

DR. MCFARLAND: Pardon me? I must interrupt you. (*Laughing.*) What do you think I could possibly be "ignorant of"?

ELIZABETH: Please, Doctor, let me just get the sense of this out. I am confident you will understand once I do.

DR. MCFARLAND: Perhaps we should discuss this at another time. You look upset this morning and not quite yourself.

ELIZABETH: No, no. Please, Dr. McFarland, please allow me to continue. I have not slept, that is true, but let me continue to—(*Long pause.*)

DOCTOR MCFARLAND: Yes?

ELIZABETH: I—I appeal to your great humanity, your power to heal, care for, and protect the sick and powerless in need . . . You see—(*She stops.*)

DR. MCFARLAND: Mrs. Packard? . . .

ELIZABETH: Your hands calm me, Doctor. May I . . . take your hand? . . .

DOCTOR MCFARLAND: Alright . . .

ELIZABETH (*Taking his hand, steeling herself*): Doctor . . . it is my honest opinion . . . that the principle upon which . . . upon which—

DR. MCFARLAND: Yes?

ELIZABETH: Upon which . . . some of your staff . . . treat . . . some of the inmates of this institution is contrary to reason, to justice, and to humanity, and—

DR. MCFARLAND: Wha—?! What did you say?

ELIZABETH: Please, Doctor. Hear me out—You are a renowned physician and a humane person. Perhaps you do not know what goes on here (DR.: *Excuse me?*) . . . but some of the patients are treated here in your institution in a very insane manner. (DR.: *No wait—*) No human being can be subjec—

DR. MCFARLAND: Mrs. Packard! What are you saying? You of all people should know I (and my staff) are dedicated to healing and caring for those in mental torment. It is my life's work, Mrs. Packard. (*ELIZABETH: Of course.*) I thought you of all people truly understood (me) . . . my position . . . (*ELIZABETH: Yes . . .*) and though I am well known for running a highly disciplined institution, this is essential for the well-being of the patients. (*ELIZABETH: I—I . . .*) Otherwise, there would be . . . mayhem, absolute chaos! and no patient could be treated.

ELIZABETH: Of course. Yes! I *do* understand, and that is why I must tell you— I hear the women through the walls. It is horrifying the trials they must endure. (*DR.: Mrs. Packard, clearly—*) Doctor, if you could hear them, if you could imagine for just one moment your own wife or your daughters going through the beatings these wives and daughters are put through— (*DOCTOR: I—*) if you could picture that in your clear mind—I believe you would change the methods your staff uses to—to tend to the pa—

DR. MCFARLAND: That is quite enough! (*Quiet.*) Mrs. Packard, I am one of the most respected doctors of the mentally ill in this country. My integrity is unimpeachable. Mentally ill patients are not mistreated under my watch, if that is what you are implying. Quite the contrary, as *you* should *well know.* I am sure you misunderstand what you hear.

ELIZABETH: Doctor, you are a loving and compassionate man. I understand you well, sir, just as you understand me.—I felt your warm, healing hands. I know how you kissed me . . . (*Continuing.*)

DR. MCFARLAND (*overlapping*): What are you—(*Stammering.*) insinuating?— wh—

ELIZABETH: And I beg of you!—release the sane inmates. *Declare* us sane. (*DOCTOR: Mrs. Packard—*) Our children need us, Doctor. We have so much to contribute outside of this prison.

DR. MCFARLAND (*Outraged*): Prison?! This is not a *prison,* Mrs. Packard! The women who are patients here must be kept here for their own health and protection and for the protection of their children.

ELIZABETH: No, Doctor. Look calmly at all you do that's good, but also admit that in my ward alone there are sane women who have been held here unjustly for years and years. (*DOCTOR: That is un—*) You are not healing these women; you are merely doing our husbands' bidding. (*DR.: What?! How d—?*) Are you helping Mrs. Chapman, Doctor, or Mrs. Stockton? Are you?? (*DOCTOR: You have no—*) As a sister in Christ, "do unto others as you'd have them do unto you." I speak out of love and respect, in the hopes that you will . . . reform.

DR. MCFARLAND: What a grossly presumptuous statement.

(*SHE says nothing. A long pause.*)

I am extremely—angry, . . . Mrs. Packard.
ELIZABETH: Yes.

(*Another long pause.*)

DR. MCFARLAND: I am an eminent man. A highly respected man. Do you not
    know that?
ELIZABETH: Yes, I know you are . . . And you want to be a good man. (*With pro-
    found emotion.*) Do not turn your back on God. If you do, you'll die.
    You'll die by your own hand.
DOCTOR MCFARLAND (*Long pause*): Good God, woman! What are you . . .
    saying—?
ELIZABETH (*Hoarse, deeply felt, quiet*): I know to love each other is impos-
    sible, Doctor. You are married before God, as am I, but you should
    know, I never gave my heart. It is whole and complete, and I give it now,
    to you.

(*HE stares at her, haunted. SILENCE. THEY lose themselves in each other's gaze.
Finally, HE turns, goes to the door and calls:*)

DR. MCFARLAND: Mrs. Bonner!

(*HE turns back to ELIZABETH.*)

ELIZABETH (*Relieved*): Yes, Mrs. Bonner is one of the worst offenders.

(*MRS. BONNER enters. SHE looks at ELIZABETH, suspicious.*)

MRS. BONNER: Doctor?

(*Startled. HE turns to MRS. BONNER.*)

DR. MCFARLAND (*Quietly, hoarse*): . . . Please escort Mrs. Packard to the yard.
    She is in need of some air.
ELIZABETH: What? No . . .

(*BONNER moves to take her. ELIZABETH stands her ground.*)

No! Doctor!! Please . . . I heard her just last night—she said it would
have been better if she'd killed the patient!

MRS. BONNER (*Under her breath*): Shut yer mouth you. Just shut it.

ELIZABETH: . . . I heard you! I saw you, Mrs. Bonner!

BONNER: She saw nuthin'.

(*ELIZABETH crosses to the DOCTOR, imploring, pulling at him.*)

ELIZABETH: Doctor, I heard her! Don't you believe me? Doctor, please I beg
of you.

DR. MCFARLAND: Quiet her.

(*HE disengages; BONNER grabs for her.*)

ELIZABETH: NO!!! . . . NO!! . . . I will not be *quiet*!! (*ELIZABETH struggles.*) I will
never be quiet!!!

BONNER (*Overlapping ELIZABETH*): Callin' an attendant! Subdue the patient!

ELIZABETH: If you know what goes on here, Doctor, *you* are insane—(*Continuing, sobbing.*)

(*The DOCTOR wheels on her, enraged.*)

DR. MCFARLAND (*Overlapping ELIZABETH*): What did you say?

(*The ATTENDANT enters.*)

ELIZABETH (*Continuing*): Insane!!—for knowingly inflicting pain on powerless people in need, and it warrants imprisonment . . . *for life* as you imprison others!

(*The ATTENDANT throws her to the ground. Shackles her.*)

ELIZABETH (*cont.*): I feel called of God and I shall obey his call to expose your
character and the character of your institution unless you *repent*. (*She
continues on.*)

DR. MCFARLAND (*Overlapping*) (*In real pain*): You . . . you ungrateful—why are
you doing this?

ELIZABETH (*continuing*): I have ability—I have my father—I have God's promised aid—

DR. MCFARLAND (*Overlapping*) (*Betrayed love*): I gave you everything! every possible—Why are you questioning my . . . my integrity—my—

ELIZABETH (*Continuing*): I have friends who will help me . . . break the chains that bind us here—in—in slavery!

DR. MCFARLAND (*Overlap*): Quiet! Quiet her!

ELIZABETH (*Continuing*): . . . Doctor, please . . . I am . . . your truest . . . friend . . .

(*Pause.*)

DR. MCFARLAND (*In turmoil, pain, and rage*): Mrs. Bonner, take Mrs. Packard upstairs to the 8th Ward. Treat her as you do the maniacs. Bring her belongings down to the trunk room. She is to have *nothing*.

(*As* BONNER *drags her off, the* DOCTOR *picks up the pages and starts to read. Sound of a prison door clanging shut.*)

End of Act One

ACT TWO

(Minutes later.)

The 8th Ward. Reveal: Bellowing, screaming mayhem. The ward is filled with maniacs. Mattresses on the floor. The walls are covered with filth and the floors strewn with refuse. The inmates are filthy, not having been bathed in years, and they sit in their own excrement.)

(ELIZABETH enters, pushed on by a jubilant MRS. BONNER. The matron for the 8th Ward, MRS. TENNEY, approaches, a kind, timid woman of middle age. ELIZABETH can barely breathe from the stench.)

MRS. BONNER *(Jubilant)*: Welcome to yer new home, darlin'. *(Unlocks the shackles.)* Mrs. Tenney, this is Mrs. Packard. She's a mad one. Dr. Mc-Farland has removed her from the 7th Ward and wants you to admit her here where she belongs, in the 8th.

MRS. TENNEY: Thank you, Mrs. Bonner. Hello, Mrs. Packard.

(ELIZABETH nods.)

MRS. BONNER: She's to have nuthin'. Nuthin' a-tall. Her belongings have been taken to the trunk room. Doctor's orders.

MRS. TENNEY: Is she violent?

MRS. BONNER *(With a malicious glint)*: Oh, she can be. Sometimes . . .

(ELIZABETH shakes her head, meets eyes with MRS. TENNEY.)

ELIZABETH: How do you do, Mrs. Tenney?

MRS. TENNEY: Leave her with me, Mrs. Bonner. Thank you. I'll take care of her from here.

(MRS. BONNER exits. ELIZABETH wipes her eyes, looks around her, tries to compose herself. After a moment:)

Follow me please, Mrs. Packard.

(THEY *pick up their skirts and step over the filth and refuse on the floor as* MRS. TENNEY *takes* ELIZABETH *over to a bed stand with filthy rags covering it.* ONE OF THE INMATES *watches them, curious.*)

This will be your bed.

(ELIZABETH *closes her eyes, almost dizzy.*)

ELIZABETH: I see. . . . Are there . . . any clean sheets I could have?
MRS. TENNEY: Excuse me? I'm afraid not.

(ELIZABETH *looks around.*)

ELIZABETH: Is there a place to bathe? That is, if one knew how?
MRS. TENNEY: Oh, not really, no.

(*Pause.*)

ELIZABETH: It's practically impossible to breathe.
MRS. TENNEY: Once or twice a week some men come in and shovel it all out.

(*A long pause.*)

ELIZABETH: Like a barn.
MRS. TENNEY: Yes, like a barn.

(*A pause.*)

ELIZABETH: Do the doctors or the superintendent, then, not come here often, Mrs. Tenney?
MRS. TENNEY: Rarely, Mrs. Packard. They rarely come to the 8th Ward, if at all. I have never seen Dr. McFarland here.
ELIZABETH: I see. (*She looks around; her survival instinct starts to kick in.*) What is that bowl over there?
MRS. TENNEY: Oh, yes, that is a bedpan we thought to try on one of the less disturbed patients, but she wouldn't have it near her. So we are sending it back down.
ELIZABETH: Don't do that. It will make a splendid washbowl. And show me

where the facilities are located that *you* use. I should like to use them as well.

MRS. TENNEY: Pardon me?

ELIZABETH: That red ribbon—do you need it? I'm sorry to ask, but perhaps we could . . . tie it around the handle of the bedpan to make it clear to all the attendants that it is mine personally, alright? And they must not handle it. I'll keep it clean. Just show me where to rinse it. Now let us find me some soap and a towel, even a piece of toweling will do. I must bathe once a day, even if it is only a sponge bath. Is that true for you as well?

MRS. TENNEY: Why, yes, it is. I myself bathe daily . . . too. (*Giving her her ribbon. ELIZABETH looks at her, expectant.*) Oh, yes. I will try to find you soap and a towel.

ELIZABETH: Don't try, Mrs. Tenney. Do it. I know you can.

MRS. TENNEY: Yes, yes I-I-will t—. (*She stops herself.*)

(*As ELIZABETH ties the ribbon.*)

Have you angered the doctor, Mrs. Packard?

ELIZABETH: I have, Mrs. Tenney.

(*Finishes trying the bow, exhausted, but discovering a kind of clarity.*)

You know, I am almost relieved to be here?

MRS. TENNEY: Excuse me?

ELIZABETH: At least it's clear now—since I cannot tend my children—what the Lord would have me do. (*She looks around. Silence. Then, she picks up the rags from off the "bed."*) Can you find some buckets and soap . . . Let's boil these. (*Hands them to Tenney.*) In fact, let's strip all the beds, and then we must take all the rotted straw, throw it out, and restuff these mattresses. (*MRS. TENNEY: Wh—?*) They stink. Are there more attendants? (*She throws her mattress to the ground and opens it up.*) Perhaps you and I can scrub and delouse the patients as well. (*She laughs.*) Think of me as a colleague, why don't you? And by the way, I need someone to go to the trunk room and retrieve my mirror for me. It . . . means a great deal to me.

(*MRS. TENNEY, bewildered, watches ELIZABETH work.*)

MRS. TENNEY: . . . Oh, oh . . . Why, yes . . . yes . . . of course . . . I—I—

(SHE *exits.* ELIZABETH *continues to gut the mattresses and tend to the patients, as we dissolve in time.* DR. MCFARLAND *enters.* SHE *sees the doctor but continues cleaning.* HE *watches her, amazed she is cleaning the ward. After awhile, covered:*)

DR. MCFARLAND: Good day, Mrs. Packard.

(*After a long time, with contained fury:*)

ELIZABETH: Doctor, there is always something that can be done for the benefit of others, and since I hadn't the opportunity to do missionary work at home, I thank you for assigning me quite a large missionary field here to cultivate.

DR. MCFARLAND: Yes. Our good works are never enough, Mrs. Packard. We require grace. Did you learn nothing from your husband? . . . Or your father?

ELIZABETH: I should like some paper and a pen.

DR. MCFARLAND: You did forfeit that right.

(SHE *works.*)

ELIZABETH: Why are you here, Doctor? You never visit the 8th Ward, I understand.

DOCTOR MCFARLAND: I wanted to . . . observe today . . . and see how you are . . . getting on.

ELIZABETH: Now you see.

DOCTOR MCFARLAND: Yes.

(SHE *works.*)

ELIZABETH: Why are you still here?

(*No answer.*)

Would you like to talk now—(*With irony.*) in depth? Or help me with the work?

DOCTOR MCFARLAND: I am on my rounds. I have other duties and patients in need besides you, Mrs. Packard.

ELIZABETH: Indeed you have, Doctor. . . . And yet you cannot stay away.

DOCTOR MCFARLAND: Pardon me?

ELIZABETH: Tell me, Doctor, have you slept?

DOCTOR MCFARLAND: No, I have not slept . . . I am too much awake.

ELIZABETH: I'm sorry. Perhaps your soul is not quiet.

(A beat. HE turns, abruptly, to go.)

I will not see you again—at least not soon—will I?

DOCTOR MCFARLAND: No. Perhaps not.

(An INMATE at the other end of the ward attacks another INMATE. Bedlam ensues. ELIZABETH calls for MRS. TENNEY. MALE ATTENDANT and BONNER enter and separate the women, then the ATTENDANT slugs the instigator in the mouth. SHE crumples to the floor, unconscious. HE picks her up and carries her off like a sack of refuse.)

DOCTOR MCFARLAND *(Shaken, covering)*: . . . You see, Mrs. Packard—discipline is utterly necessary for the well-being of the patients.

ELIZABETH: Doctor! Surely you see this is an immense disgrace?

DOCTOR MCFARLAND *(Heatedly, defending himself)*: Mrs. Packard! I do see the world for what it is . . . and I choose to *live* in it. . . . Just as you should.

ELIZABETH: Ah. Yes. Well . . . I had thought better of you. *(A pause.)*

(HE exits. The doors clang shut behind him. Lights.)

(MISS SARAH RUMSEY on the stand.)

MR. HASLET: State your name please for the record.

SARAH RUMSEY: Miss Sarah Rumsey.

MR. HASLET: How do you know Mrs. Packard?

SARAH RUMSEY: I worked for one week in Mrs. Packard's house as a favor to Mr. Packard. When Mrs. Packard found I was going to stay in the house and that the French servant had been discharged, she ordered me into the kitchen! Before that she had treated me kindly as a visitor. I thought it an evidence of insanity for her to order me into the kitchen. She ought to have known I was not an ordinary servant.

(In Ward 8: MRS. TENNEY gives ELIZABETH paper from a hidden pocket in her apron. From a hiding place in the ward, ELIZABETH retrieves pages of writing and gives them to TENNEY who stashes them in her hidden pocket. ELIZABETH writes a note, as MRS. TENNEY goes to tend a patient. Then SHE joins her.)

MR. HASLET: Were you present at the interview when Mrs. Packard ordered the congregants from the church to leave the house?

SARAH RUMSEY: I was. Mrs. Packard was very pale and angry. She was in a sundress and her hair was down over her face. It was 11 o'clock in the forenoon.

MR. HASLET: Did you stay at the house?

SARAH RUMSEY: I did. I stayed at the house. Mrs. Packard came out to the kitchen. She was dressed then. She said she had come to reveal to me what Mr. Packard was. She talked very rapidly; she would not talk calm. Said Mr. Packard was an archdeceiver; that he and members of the church had made a conspiracy to put her into the insane asylum. She wanted me to leave the conspirators. Said she had a new revelation, and that she had been chosen by God for a particular mission. She said that if I would side with her, I would be a chief apostle in the millennium.

MR. HASLET: Thank you, Miss Rumsey.

(Lights change. The ward, cleaner. Months later. ELIZABETH and MRS. TENNEY wash a PATIENT, the woman we saw earlier dressed so elegantly.)

MRS. BONNER *(Off)*: I'll do no more cleanin' up after yer kind! Whoo-hoo! Mrs. Tenney!

(MRS. BONNER enters, shoving on a crying MRS. STOCKTON. Months living in the 8th Ward have taken away MRS. PACKARD's girlishness. She has a steely, hard-won strength.)

MRS. BONNER *(Continuing)* *(delighted with her prey)*: I got a lazy one here for isolation! Hands over your head!

(MRS. BONNER rips MRS. STOCKTON's nightgown off. ELIZABETH looks up, recognizing her.)

ELIZABETH: Mrs. Stockton?

MRS. STOCKTON *(Crying and muttering)*: Oh, Elizabeth, I shall die of shame . . .

ELIZABETH *(To MRS. BONNER)*: How dare you?

MRS. BONNER: Come on with ya. That way.

(As MRS. STOCKTON turns, BONNER smacks her on the rump. STOCKTON, humiliated, runs naked toward the door, BONNER following, laughing.)

ELIZABETH: Stop it! Stop it! How da—?

(MRS. TENNEY *stops* ELIZABETH *as* MRS. BONNER *turns and glares at her [a dangerous moment] then exits after* MRS. STOCKTON.)

MRS. TENNEY: Don't try to stop her, dear. That would be dangerous for Mrs. Stockton. Look to your patient. I'll see after your friend.

(MRS. TENNEY *exits to look in on* MRS. STOCKTON. *Sounds from* MRS. STOCKTON *in distress come from off. The* PATIENT *whom Elizabeth is tending looks up and starts to chant in a little voice,* "Peter Peter Pumpkin Eater had a wife and—"

DR. MCFARLAND *enters in a fury, carrying a sheaf of papers. The ward erupts.*)

DR. MCFARLAND: Leave that patient.

(ELIZABETH, *slowly and defiantly, continues washing the patient. More sounds of distress. The other inmates, alarmed, start to wail.*)

DR. MCFARLAND (*Continuing*): Mrs. Packard! Have I not repeatedly told you that you were not to have pen or paper?

(SHE *looks at him, calmly.* SHE *will not answer. Sounds of* MRS. STOCKTON *choking on the water treatment heard from off.*)

Did I not? (*Still no answer.*) Why have you been pretending you have nothing with which to write? (*No answer.*) For months now, I have forbidden you to write. Why have you been lying, Mrs. Packard? (*Mocking her.*) "To lie is a sin."

(ELIZABETH *is about to answer. Instead, a silent standoff.*)

MRS. TENNEY (*Leaving the isolation room*): She's had enough now, Mrs. Bonner. I'll get you a blanket, Mrs. Stockton.

(MRS. TENNEY *appears. We hear* MRS. STOCKTON *whimpering off.*)

DR. MCFARLAND: Ah, Mrs. Tenney! How did Mrs. Packard get paper and a writing utensil? Did you supply her with them?

(MRS. TENNEY *is about to answer "yes."* ELIZABETH *gets up to stuff another mattress.*)

ELIZABETH *(Icy calm)*: She did not.

DR. MCFARLAND: Mrs. Packard, I will ask you again: how did you get the paper and pen with which to write this document?

(*Before* MRS. TENNEY *can answer:*)

ELIZABETH *(striving to stay quiet and steady)*: Doctor, do you not know that all of the inmates who have any wits about them, as well as much of your staff, except for Mrs. Tenney, of course—want to expose to the world both you and this abomination you call an asylum? They want to aid me in any way they can. They supply me with paper; they inform me about what is really happening inside this institution, and I write it all down. (MRS. BONNER *enters from the isolation room, we hear whimpers from* STOCKTON *off.*) Can you hear that? That is Mrs. Stockton—a woman of seventy years and complete virtue—who is now in your isolation room, naked! after undergoing a torture session from Mrs. Bonner.

DOCTOR MCFARLAND: Mrs. Stockton needed disciplinary action, Mrs. Packard, and is completely safe.

(*Facing him off.*)

ELIZABETH: That's a lie. Are you going to straitjacket and gag the lot of us? You are losing this battle, Doctor. I warned you I would expose you.

(MRS. TENNEY *is terrified.* ELIZABETH *continues stuffing mattresses. Whimpering from off.*)

DR. MCFARLAND *(With contained fury)*: It is unwise of you to declare war on me and my institution, Mrs. Packard. Mrs. Tenney, if I find in future that Mrs. Packard has the use of paper or pen, you will lose your position immediately.

MRS. TENNEY: Yes, Doctor.

DR. MCFARLAND: I don't care how hard it might be to replace you, but replace you I shall. Do you understand me?

MRS. TENNEY: Yes, Doctor.

DR. MCFARLAND: . . . You may go.

(MRS. TENNEY *nods, finds a blanket, and runs to aid Mrs. Stockton.*)

DR. MCFARLAND (*Continuing*): And Mrs. Packard, I shall replace Mrs. Tenney with someone who is not so sympathetic, nor soft, nor kind. Do you understand me? Someone will run this ward whose job it is to make you obey my rules! Mrs. Bonner, I thank you for bringing these . . . ravings to my attention. (BONNER *exits.*) What you wrote here is libelous—lies! Mrs. Packard. Pages and pages and pages . . . all lies! This scribbling only confirms to me your complete and total madness! (*He starts to leave in a rage.*) I should never again let you see the light of day.

ELIZABETH: Doctor, where are the letters from my family? A little bird tells me a pile of mail for me has sat on your desk for months. (*He stops.*)

DR. MCFARLAND (*Turns back*): You have no right to your mail.

ELIZABETH: No right? Why not? I am not a criminal. It cannot be legal for you to withhold my mail.

DR. MCFARLAND: It is perfectly legal. You are in the ward for the hopelessly insane. The inmates do not receive mail here.

(*Shakes her head, almost laughs.*)

ELIZABETH: Well . . . have you sent the letter I wrote to my husband?

DR. MCFARLAND: I will not send the letter you wrote to your husband. Not ever.

ELIZABETH: Why not?

DR. MCFARLAND: You have no right to set conditions to your husband for your release! Only I decide when and if to release you. You write to him he must repent!? (*Laughing.*) You must be joking! Indeed not, my dear lady! *You* are the one to repent, not him and not . . . me. You daily prove to me that you are all that your husband represents you to be, that he is an abused man, a fine minister of the cloth, saddled with a . . . a defiant, troublemaking, and profoundly disturbed wife who refuses the much-needed treatment offered her to get well!

ELIZABETH (*Laughing*): Oh, I see. Signing a document promising to lie was the "much needed treatment offered me to get well"!? Ah! (*Icy clear.*) What is your master plan, Doctor? Can you tell me, or is it criminal? I have nearly been killed twice here in this ward by my "roommates" during the night. Is that what you and my husband want? To either make me into a maniac . . . or kill me?

DR. MCFARLAND: Mrs. Packard! You eschewed the special privileges I was more than willing to give you.

ELIZABETH: I did not!

DR. MCFARLAND (*With great force*): *You most certainly did, madam*!!

ELIZABETH: Oh . . . I see. I am terribly sorry if I hurt you, or . . . shamed you, Doctor. (*Honestly.*) That was truly not my intent.

DR. MCFARLAND (*Explodes*): You—you did not hurt me, Mrs. Packard, nor did you . . . *shame* me! I assure you! And that is completely . . . immaterial in any case. You belong here where I have put you, and you will obey *my rules* in this ward.

ELIZABETH: I see there is no way for me to get out of this institution while you are superintendent.

DR. MCFARLAND: I would be happy for you to be gone from this institution, believe me! You are nothing but an extreme annoyance to me. Worse, a howling fury who will not leave me in peace.

(SHE *continues to stuff straw into the mattress with great force.*)

ELIZABETH (*Quiet intensity almost to bursting*): Well, then, Doctor. Let my *husband* decide whether what he has done to me was right or not! Let him come here and see the hellhole he has exiled me to. Let him stand in this room and see the maniacs . . . (*Trying not to scream at him.*) and that I am NOT a MANIAC . . . and that neither he nor you can make me into a maniac!!! (*The* DOCTOR *shakes his head.* SHE *tries not to cry.*) Let him say how truly *sorry* he is that he threw his dear . . . wife . . . Elizabeth, into these horrifying . . . horrific . . . conditions! Let him admit that I was never deranged!! If he repent, I will return home to him!! I entered this institution a sane woman and I shall leave it as I entered it—*a sane woman*!! And for the sake of my children, you both shall CALL me SANE!

DR. MCFARLAND: Look at you. You're raving. I will state the obvious and this for the last time. Go home to your husband under the conditions I have outlined—in writing—or die here.

(*A pause. She breaks.*)

ELIZABETH (*Quiet, intimate*): Doctor, my husband should be my protector, but he is not. Will you protect me? Please . . . ? Will you be my husband in heaven?

(*SHE tries to embrace him, kiss him. HE brutally disengages from her. Silence. MCFARLAND stares at her, SHE at him.*)

DR. MCFARLAND (*Quiet*): Why must you try to destroy every man who cares for you?

(*MCFARLAND exits. ELIZABETH reels, sits on the bed, begins to rock and cry.*)

ELIZABETH: Oh, dear God, I'm going mad. (*SHE repeats under, overlap.*)

(*Lights shift.*)

ABIJAH DOLE *on the witness stand, upset.*)

HASLET: Mr. Dole, do you need a recess?

ELIZABETH: I am going mad . . .

ABIJAH DOLE (*Choked up*): I—I'm fine thank you.

HASLET: Mr. Dole, when did you know your sister-in-law was insane?

ABIJAH DOLE: I suppose . . . I knew she was insane the morning I found her in the west room still in her night clothes. It was almost noon! She took my hand and led me to the bed. The daughter, Libby, was lying in bed of brain fever. Mrs. Packard's hair was disheveled. Her face looked wild. (*ELIZABETH "I'm going mad . . ."*) The child was moaning and moving her head from side to side. I wondered if she had made the child deranged. Mrs. Packard said: "How pure we are. I am one of the children of heaven." Then she said, "Brother Dole, this is serious business. The woman shall bruise the serpent's head." And she called Mr. Packard a devil.

HASLET: Did you see her soon after that at church?

ABIJAH DOLE: I did. I was then still superintendent of the Sabbath school. Just at the close of school—I was behind the desk—she appeared before me almost like a vision, and told me she pitied me for marrying my wife, who is a sister to Mr. Packard. She said I might find a more agreeable companion! She said that if she had cultivated amorousness, she would have made a more agreeable companion. She then requested to read or deliver an address to the Bible class.

(*MRS. TENNEY enters and places a cool cloth on ELIZABETH's forehead.*)

HASLET: How did she look?

ABIJAH DOLE: Very wild and excited. I did not know what to do. I knew Mr. Packard thought her insane and did not want her to discuss these kinds of things in the Sabbath school, but I did not want to take the responsibility myself so I put it to a vote. I was much surprised when the class allowed that she could read it.

HASLET: What was the content of her address?

ABIJAH DOLE: I can not recall but it was evidence of her insanity. I felt so bad. . . . (*Starts to sob.*) I knew she was mad, but I also knew she needed rest.

(*Lights shift.*)

ELIZABETH: I am sorry to put your position in jeopardy, Mrs. Tenney.

MRS. TENNEY: There, there . . . just breathe deeply now. It's my choice. I am glad to do it.

ELIZABETH: . . . For the sake of my children—I must not go mad . . .

MRS. TENNEY: That's right, Mrs. Packard.

(*After calming her,* MRS. TENNEY *looks around to make sure no one is watching, then pulls paper from a pocket beneath her apron.*)

MRS. TENNEY: Here are testimonies from the ladies in the Fifth Ward. Shall I hide them in your bonnet, Mrs. Packard?

ELIZABETH: Please.

MRS. TENNEY: I've had your trunk brought up so we ladies don't have to sneak down to the trunk room anymore.

ELIZABETH (*With a half-smile*): You've defied the doctor, Mrs. Tenney? . . .

MRS. TENNEY (*Proud*): I suppose I have, Mrs. Packard.

(MRS. TENNEY *uncovers the trunk. It has been under a pile of sheets.* SHE *takes the pieces of paper and hides them in the lining of the trunk and in a bonnet.*)

ELIZABETH: Will you sit with me?

MRS. TENNEY: Why, of course. I forget you are a patient, and that you need care, as well.

ELIZABETH: It's not that I need care, Mrs. Tenney. It is that I am so terribly lonely. I always had my children to speak to at home . . .

MRS. TENNEY: I understand.

ELIZABETH: Until just weeks before he sent me away, my husband left the children entirely to me. I was always with them . . . (*Sits up.*) Mr. Packard knows *nothing* about the children. That's why I'm so frightened for them—(*She wipes away quick tears.*) He worried only about the children's souls. For some reason, he was afraid our little Isaac had been born damned. He'd go into his study for hours on end to pray for him and terrified the children with his constant talk of hellfire and everlasting torment. (*MRS. TENNEY: Tsk, tsk, shame . . .*) (*ELIZABETH folds papers into the bonnet.*) I hated to bring up the children in fear, but I raised the children to honor their father, so—

MRS. TENNEY: Of course . . . (*THEY work.*) Well, at least you hadn't a husband like mine.

ELIZABETH: How do you mean?

MRS. TENNEY: Well . . . mine just jumped into that bottle, and no one could get him out of it.

ELIZABETH: Oh, no . . .

MRS. TENNEY: Oh, yes . . . (*THEY work.*) Why did you marry yours, dear?

ELIZABETH: I suppose I thought I loved him. I barely knew him. (*MRS. T. nodding Mmm . . . hmmm.*) I was a young bride, and he was very much older than I. Mr. Packard was a colleague of my father's, and *my* father respected *his* father so it seemed an auspicious match. (*MRS. T: Surely.*) I worshipped Mr. Packard's piety, I think. (*MRS. T: Hmph.*) I wanted to be just like my mother—the wife of a beloved minister, mother of a large brood of children, and I was happy for a time. Mr. Packard was not beloved by any of his congregations, however—and though I loved motherhood, he was never really a natural husband . . . or father. I don't think I'd be in prison here today if I had married *anyone* else . . .

MRS. TENNEY: Well, don't blame yourself, dear. Lots of women marry the wrong man. I suppose I did, too, but at least I hardly knew mine. He died, very young . . .

ELIZABETH: I'm so sorry.

MRS. TENNEY (*Shrugs*): Oh, perhaps it's a blessing.

(*INMATES become agitated as MRS. BONNER enters with an ATTENDANT and a straitjacket. MRS. TENNEY quickly hides the papers, leaving the bonnet on the bed.*)

MRS. BONNER: Alright, Mrs. Packard. No more naughtiness for you, my dear. It's off to isolation with ya.

ELIZABETH: What?

MRS. BONNER (*To the attendant*): Jacket.

ELIZABETH: What are you doing?

(*ELIZABETH starts fighting them off.*)

MRS. TENNEY: What are you doing to her?!

MRS. BONNER: She's to be in the isolation room three days. (*Crowing.*) No more writin' for you, Mrs. Packard! Dr. McFarland's orders.

MRS. TENNEY: I don't believe Dr. McFarland would do that to Mrs. Packard.

MRS. BONNER (*Viciously turns on her*): Oh, no? Go and ask him yerself.

MRS. TENNEY: I shall go to the doctor, Mrs. Packard. I will try to get you out.

(*SHE exits.*)

MRS. BONNER: Don't struggle, Mrs. Packard. It will hurt ya a whole lot more if ya do.

(*THEY finish straitjacketing ELIZABETH and drag her off.*)

(*The back wall opens to reveal the isolation room. MRS. BONNER shoves ELIZABETH inside. MRS. STOCKTON is huddled in a corner, a blanket around her, muttering and crying. ELIZABETH sees her, tries to run to her.*)

ELIZABETH: It's all right, Mrs. Stockton. Remember, "I am sane, I am sane"— keep your little ditty in your head—I am sane.

(*Grabbing ELIZABETH:*)

MRS. BONNER: I've looked forward to this moment for a long time, Mrs. Packard.

ELIZABETH: I'm certain you have, Mrs. Bonner.

(*MRS. BONNER holds her down in a tub of cold water and then brings her back up, gasping and coughing.*)

(*DOCTOR MCFARLAND enters the ward and listens to ELIZABETH'S punishment.*)

MRS. BONNER: How are ya feeling now, Mrs. Packard?

(*ELIZABETH will not answer.*)

Ochh. You won't say? I see. Well, you have to tell me when to stop, you know. Otherwise I won't. I won't stop.

(*BONNER dunks ELIZABETH again.*)

(*MCFARLAND goes to her bed, rips off the bedclothes, looking for papers. Lights shift. Simultaneous scenes.*)

(*A MAN sits on the stand.*)

MR. LA BRIE: I am the Justice of the Peace.

(*MCFARLAND picks up the bonnet, puts it down.*)

MR. LA BRIE: I live fifteen rods from the Packard house.

(*BONNER pulls ELIZABETH's head up from the water.*)

I saw Mrs. Packard nearly every day—sometimes two or three times a day.

(*BONNER dunks ELIZABETH.*)

MR. LA BRIE: I have seen nothing in the six years I have known her that could make me think her insane. I am not a physician and I am not an expert, but if she be insane, no commonsense man could find it out.

(*BONNER pulls ELIZABETH up brutally. SHE is practically unconscious. Frustrated by his search, MCFARLAND enters the screen room. ELIZABETH sees the DOCTOR. THEY lock eyes.*)

DOCTOR MCFARLAND: Mrs. Bonner, you may go.

(*BONNER exits. DOCTOR MCFARLAND pulls ELIZABETH to her feet.*)

MR. LA BRIE: Of course, we all knew Mr. and Mrs. Packard were having difficulties. It was becoming public knowledge.

(*Lights fade on LA BRIE.*)

SHE *clings to him, sobbing.* HE *holds her tight. A long embrace.* MRS. TENNEY *enters, sees them. The* DOCTOR *quickly covers.*)

DOCTOR MCFARLAND: Take Mrs. Packard to her bed, Mrs. Tenney.

(MRS. TENNEY *nods, takes* ELIZABETH *and helps her off.*)

(*Profoundly disturbed,* DR. MCFARLAND *stares at his own reflection in the water. A moment of self-revelation.*)

(LIGHTS *slowly change.* WALLS *of the isolation room close as lights come up on the ward.*)

(*The ward. Weeks later.*)

(ELIZABETH, *very weak and depressed, lies on her bed in a fetal position.* MRS. TENNEY *covers her with a blanket.* THEOPHILUS *enters. The* INMATES *see* THEO *and become agitated, some start screaming.* ELIZABETH *sees him, turns away.*)

MRS. TENNEY: May I help you, sir? Visitors are not allowed on this ward.
THEOPHILUS: I am Reverend Packard. That is my wife, Elizabeth. Dr. McFarland said I could come up.
MRS. TENNEY (*Surprised*): Did he, really?
ELIZABETH (*Hoarse and depressed*): Mrs. Tenney, tell him to observe where he's exiled his wife . . .

(MRS. TENNEY *does not know what to say.*)

THEOPHILUS: . . . I know you may not wish to speak with me, wife, but I must ask you some questions. (*To Mrs. Tenney.*) Can you possibly stop their . . . howling?

(*The* PATIENTS *become more and more agitated.* THEOPHILUS, *scared, tries not to show it.*)

MRS. TENNEY: I shall try, sir.
THEOPHILUS: Mrs. Packard, I have brought you some warm clothing . . . (*Waits for her to thank him. She does not.*) I have brought you . . . greetings from the children. (ELIZ: *Ah!*) Elizabeth, I have lost my position at

the church. I have lost my congregation. We have no money. We are living on the handouts of former parishioners. I cannot afford to keep all the children with me, and I am moving back to Massachusetts. I am asking your advice on where each child should go . . . The littlest ones can stay with my sister. Toffy and Samuel can be on their own. That leaves Isaac and Libby. Libby is not well. She takes after your mother. She cries and weeps all day. I don't know what to do with her.

ELIZABETH: Oh, dear God, Theophilus . . . What have you done to the children?

THEOPHILUS (*A broken man*): What have I done—?? Wife, your . . . illness has ruined us.

ELIZABETH (*Shakes her head*): Have you seen the letter I wrote you?

THEOPHILUS: I have received no letters from you.

(*Long pause.*)

ELIZABETH: Nor I from you . . . or the children.

(*Pause.*)

THEOPHILUS: What was in the letter?

ELIZABETH: If you repent, I will come home. And *I* will care for the children.

THEOPHILUS (*Bewildered*): Repent?

ELIZABETH: Oh, Theophilus. I once did care for you. And you for me. Admit sending me here was wrong. Ask my forgiveness and we will try again. I will try to forgive you.

THEOPHILUS: That is impossible. I cannot allow you near the children.

ELIZABETH: And why is that exactly?

THEOPHILUS (*Tears in his eyes, he explodes*): You know why!

(*The* INMATES *start to get upset.* MRS. TENNEY *calms them.*)

Here. (*HE puts down the bundles on the bed.*) I am leaving you some warm clothes and some writing paper. I know how much you like to write.

(*SHE almost thanks him. After another long pause, answering her question:*)

God forgive me, Elizabeth . . . you frighten me . . . so very much. (*HE sits.*)

ELIZABETH (*sad*): I know, dear. (*She puts her arm around him.*) . . . And I know you are quite certain what you believe is right, but there are many people, many intelligent people, who think you wrong. I am merely one of them.

THEOPHILUS: Have you no advice for me about the children?

ELIZABETH: You will not take my advice. Please tell the children their mother loves them, to never doubt how much she loves them.

(*SHE gets up and pulls out sewing from her trunk. She pulls out letters sewn inside the garments.*)

Perhaps you will deliver these to the children. I will not have to smuggle them out if you do. And please ask the doctor to mail my letters in future. I know you have asked him not to and that I am to receive none. And I have not. I have received not one letter from family or friends since I arrived here . . . I suppose you poisoned my dear Papa against me, too, didn't you?

THEOPHILUS: Your father understands you belong in the asylum, Elizabeth. He was the one who committed you the first time.

ELIZABETH: He was mistaken to commit me! He thought it was a hospital he was sending me to. He admitted this to me years ago.

THEOPHILUS: Really? Well, not to me. In fact, quite the contrary, I'm afraid.

ELIZABETH: What? What do you mean?

THEOPHILUS: He told me only recently he believes he was right to have committed you when you were young.

ELIZABETH: Wh—? I don't believe you!

THEOPHILUS: He was going to write you, but when I told him what you had done, he agreed with me. You belong here, Elizabeth.

(*She sits, devastated.*)

ELIZABETH (*Pause, hoarse*): Have you asked the doctor about . . . my progress, Theophilus?

THEOPHILUS: Yes . . .

ELIZABETH: He says I have worsened, has he not?

THEOPHILUS: I do not wish to upset you further, Elizabeth.

(*One last try:*)

ELIZABETH: Look around you, Theophilus! That's all I ask of you. Do I in any way resemble these poor women? *You* decide.

THEOPHILUS: Elizabeth, if you could only see yourself . . .

ELIZABETH: I am your wife. Take me *home*!

(*SHE goes to him, embraces him.*)

THEOPHILUS: I-I—

(*THEO is deeply upset as DOCTOR MCFARLAND enters. ELIZABETH manages to hide some of the paper under her blanket.*)

DR. MCFARLAND: Reverend Packard—There you are!

THEOPHILUS: Doctor—

DR. MCFARLAND: Where did you get that paper, Mrs. Packard?

ELIZABETH: Mr. Packard gave it to me. I am sure he thought it an innocent amusement for me to write here, knowing I loved to write when I was at home.

DR. MCFARLAND: Let me see it.

(*SHE hands it to him.*)

DR. MCFARLAND: I will take care of this. Reverend Packard, why did you give paper to your wife?

THEOPHILUS: As Elizabeth said, for her comfort and amusement.

DR. MCFARLAND: You must not do that. (*He swallows his rage.*) If you ever attempt to interfere again with my management and discipline of your wife, you shall have the liberty of taking her away, forthwith. Do you wish to do that? Do you wish to take her away with you now?

(*A terrible silence. Will THEO take her home? A long moment. The DOCTOR and ELIZABETH watch him. Then: THEO submits, silently.*)

DR. MCFARLAND: Come with me, sir. You should not be here.

(*The MEN exit. ELIZABETH collapses on the bed. MRS. TENNEY approaches.*)

MRS. TENNEY: I overheard, of course . . . (*Long pause.*) Lie! Mrs. Packard, just lie. Women have been doing it since the beginning of time . . .

ELIZABETH (*Hoarse, depressed*): But . . . I can't . . . do it . . . And you heard him—he'll never let me near the children again . . . I've lost them . . .

(SHE *curls into a fetal position.*)

MRS. TENNEY (*Tough*): Do not lie down in that bed. Come on, up with you.

ELIZABETH: What? I cannot. I cannot just now, Mrs. Tenney.

MRS. TENNEY (*Tough caring*): Then I shall help you. Come on . . .

ELIZABETH: Please, just let me stay here a little while longer. I am so . . . tired. (*She throws her arm over her head.*)

MRS. TENNEY: I've seen it too often, Mrs. Packard. A patient wants to stay in bed for a little while and then another little while, and then after awhile she never gets out of bed.

ELIZABETH: What's the difference? Perhaps Mr. Packard and Papa are right about me. I don't really care anymore, Mrs. Tenney.

MRS. TENNEY (*With urgency*): Well, I *do* care, Mrs. Packard! Come on. Up with you! If you remain in this bed, you will die in this bed. I have seen it before. Come on, up you go . . .

(MRS. TENNEY *gets her up with difficulty as:*)

(*Lights change.*)

(A *distinguished* MAN *with a Scots accent is on the stand.*)

DR. DUNCANSON: I am Dr. Robert Duncanson. I have earned advanced degrees in both theology and medicine from the University of Glasgow and Anderson University. Mrs. Packard's explanation of woman representing the Holy Ghost, and man representing the male attributes of the Father, and that the Son is the fruit of the Father and the Holy Ghost is a very ancient theological dogma, sir, and entertained by many of our most eminent and learned men. (*Laughs.*) It is by no means a mark of lunacy.

(*Music. The Lunatics' Ball six months later.* MRS. CHAPMAN *and* MRS. STOCKTON *enter with* BONNER *and sit. The* WOMEN *from Ward 8 are dancing. Simultaneous scenes:*)

DR. DUNCANSON (*Continuing*): I spoke with her three hours. With every topic I introduced, she was perfectly familiar and discussed them with an intelligence that at once showed she was possessed of a good education and a strong, vigorous, and healthy mind.

(ELIZABETH enters, pale and depressed, shaky, escorted by MRS. TENNEY. SHE *sees* MRS. CHAPMAN *and crosses to her.)*

> I did not agree with all of her thoughts, but I do not call people insane because they differ from me, nor even from a majority of people.

ELIZABETH *(Very subdued)*: Mrs. Chapman, how good to see you. *(THEY take hands.)*

DR. DUNCANSON: You might as well with as much propriety call Galileo mad; or Newton; or Jesus; or Luther; or Morse who electrified the world!

MRS. CHAPMAN: We hear you are having a difficult time, dear.

ELIZABETH: Some days are better than others, but Mrs. Tenney helps me a good deal. She insisted I come to the ball tonight. *(THEY laugh.)*

DR. DUNCANSON: With Mrs. Packard, there is wanting every indication of insanity that is laid down in the books. I pronounce her a *sane* woman, and wish we had a *nation* of such women.

(Lights fade on DUNCANSON.*)*

ELIZABETH *(Conspiratorial)*: I'm not supposed to leave the 8th ward. Doctor McFarland's orders.

MRS. CHAPMAN *(looks at her piercingly)*: Oh, Elizabeth. Promise me you will not end up like our dear Mrs. Stockton.

ELIZABETH: What do you mean?

ELIZABETH *(Sees* MRS. STOCKTON*)*: Mrs. Stockton, how good to see you.

(No answer. MRS. STOCKTON *looks blankly ahead.)*

> Mrs. Stockton?

MRS. CHAPMAN: She has not spoken a word since she came back from the isolation room months ago.

ELIZABETH: Oh, no . . . NO! . . .

(SHE kneels down in front of her and tries to look into her eyes.)

> Mrs. Stockton? . . . Hello, dear . . . Mrs. Stockton!?

(MRS. STOCKTON just sits there. Tears stream down her cheeks, but SHE looks vacantly ahead of her. ELIZABETH sees MRS. STOCKTON has lost the battle. Her mind is gone.)

. . . I'm so sorry, dear.

(*ELIZABETH buries her head in* MRS. STOCKTON's *lap.*)

MRS. CHAPMAN: Elizabeth, no crying now. (*Seeing* BONNER, *bitter.*) Do not give
   that woman the pleasure.

(CHAPMAN *and* BONNER *meet eyes.* MCFARLAND *enters, leading a group of prosper-
ous-looking* MEN. HE *is giving a tour.* MRS. CHAPMAN *and* MRS. TENNEY *see him and
shield* ELIZABETH *from the doctor's sight.*)

DR. MCFARLAND: The Lunatics' ball is held twice a year in this auditorium. It is
   a welcome break from our institutional routine. Even some of the local
   townspeople enjoy coming!

(*Two of the* MANIACS *dancing start a fight.*)

MRS. BONNER: Stop that now, ladies! Stop it! Behave yourselves! (*Shoos them
   away.*)

(DR. MCFARLAND *brings the* TRUSTEES *downstairs as one* INMATE *starts to sing "Mine
Eyes Have Seen the Glory."*)

(*The* DOCTOR *and the* TRUSTEES *enter.* DR. MCFARLAND *stops the* TRUSTEES *at* MRS.
CHAPMAN's *group, not noticing* ELIZABETH.)

DOCTOR MCFARLAND: Gentlemen, perhaps you have met Mrs. Tenney. And
   this is Mrs. Chapman from our 7th Ward. Our best ward. Mrs. Chapman, some of our trustees!
MRS. CHAPMAN: How do you do?
DR. MCFARLAND: This way, gentlemen—

(*The* MEN *smile and nod and start to move on.* ELIZABETH *sees her last chance
and quickly extends her hand to the man who looks like he is in charge. Highly
adrenalized:*)

ELIZABETH: How do you do? I am Elizabeth Packard from the 8th Ward.
   (DR.: *Gentlemen, shall we—?*) The ward for the violent and hopelessly insane. I have been working since my incarceration there to clean it and

clean the inmates and make a healing atmosphere for treating the sick. I do so hope you can see it on your visit.

MR. BLACKMAN, CHAIRMAN: Really? . . . How extraordinary. I am chairman of the board, and I have never seen that ward.

ELIZABETH: Oh, then you must come. It has been transformed.

MR. BLACKMAN: Yes . . . Did you say you worked here, Mrs.—?

DR. MCFARLAND: Yes, Mrs. Packard has been a very helpful patient during her cure.

ELIZABETH: Yes, you see, I am actually *still sane*—and I do hope you will give me just ten minutes of your time so I may demonstrate my sanity to you.

MR. BLACKMAN: Well . . . You certainly are a charming and articulate creature, Mrs. Packard. I should think we could arrange . . . ten minutes. Doctor?

DR. MCFARLAND: Mrs. Packard has been placed in the proper ward for her treatment and should not be disturbed.

MR. BLACKMAN (*A man used to running things and getting his way*): Nonsense. Ten minutes would be fine, I should think. . . . Tomorrow morning after breakfast, Mrs. Packard?

DR. MCFARLAND: Mr. Blackman, I really must insist—

MR. BLACKMAN: In your office, Doctor? I look forward to it.

DR. MCFARLAND (*Angry, covers*): Yes, of course, come this way, gentlemen. Good evening, ladies. Mrs. Packard.

(*The* TRUSTEES *move on.* ELIZABETH *meets eyes with* MCFARLAND, *then* HE *exits, following. The ball continues then off, as lights slowly change.*)

(MR. BLESSING *on the stand.*)

MR. BLESSING: I am Mr. William Blessing. My wife and I live eighty rods from the Packard house. I have known Mrs. Packard since she moved to Manteno. She visited at my house often. She attended the Methodist church for a while after the difficulties commenced, and then I saw her every Sunday. I never thought her insane. After the word was given out by her husband that she was insane, she claimed my particular protection. I thought her husband was insane if anyone was. I—I regret . . . I assured Mrs. Packard her husband could not commit her to a lunatic asylum without first proving her insane in a court of law. The morning I looked out my window and saw the men carry Mrs. Packard out of her house, I ran across the street to try to stop them. The sheriff informed me that Mr. Packard had every right to do what he was doing and I had

better step back. Later, we tried to visit her at Jacksonville. I even wrote
to the governor, but I learned there was nothing we could do to help her.

(*Lights change.*)

(*The next morning.* MCFARLAND's *office.*)

(*The* TRUSTEES *and* THEOPHILUS *gather inside the office. Low* LIGHT. DOCTOR MC-
FARLAND *waits for* ELIZABETH *outside, nervous, pacing.* ELIZABETH *enters, her arm
gripped by* MRS. BONNER.)

MRS. BONNER (*Off*): Move quickly, Mrs. Packard, or ye'll be losing yer time . . .

(HE *greets them:*)

DR. MCFARLAND: Mrs. Packard! Ready for the meeting? I should like to escort
    you in myself.

(SHE *stops.*)

ELIZABETH: Would you?
DR. MCFARLAND: I think it would be a nicer entrance than if you were to enter
    on Mrs. Bonner's arm, don't you?
ELIZABETH: . . . Perhaps.

(*Pulls her close, conspiratorial:*)

DR. MCFARLAND: I trust you're going to take a good whack at Calvinism, Mrs.
    Packard—explicate your more *radical* views to the trustees?
ELIZABETH: Surely, you know I am.

(HE *guides her into the office. The* MEN *rise. Lights come up.* ELIZABETH, *not having slept, nervous, strives for control.*)

MR. BLACKMAN: Good morning, Mrs. Packard.
ELIZABETH (*Charming to them*): Good morning. Gentlemen, (*Cold, surprised
    to see* THEO.) Mr. Packard . . . Thank you for agreeing to meet with me
    today. I know you are busy men, and I shall not go past my time.
MR. BLACKMAN: Please, have a seat.

ELIZABETH: Thank you, sir. (*She sits, nervous, suspicious of* THEO'S *presence: a deep breath.*) I am the wife of . . . Reverend Theophilus Packard, invited here today, I assume, by . . . Dr. McFarland?

DR. MCFARLAND: Indeed . . .

THEOPHILUS: That's right.

DR. MCFARLAND: Yes.

ELIZABETH: Let me begin by saying my husband would have me incarcerated here because I . . . do not believe any longer in his Old . . . to my mind his *perversely* Old School Calvinist teachings. As the scales of bigotry have fallen from my eyes, gentlemen, I have found a great deal of truth and—and wisdom in other faiths—the Methodists, the Universalists, and even—

MR. BLACKMAN: I see, yes . . . however, I must warn you, Mrs. Packard, we are all Presbyterian. Some of us devout Calvinists from the Old School, like your husband.

ELIZABETH: I . . . thank you for your warning, sir. (*She looks at* MCFARLAND.) However, I still beg you to listen to my thoughts . . . Though I may have differing beliefs from you or my husband, I hope you will see . . . I am not insane. (*Holding on to her fury.*) Dr. McFarland thinks his charge is to keep me here until I am quiet and docile and accept all that my husband believes. Since I cannot ever believe again in what I consider to be my husband's narrow views of Christ (*Suddenly mischievous, to* BLACK-MAN.)—or perhaps even your narrow views of Christ, sir—does that mean I must stay shut up in an insane asylum for the rest of my life?

(*MR. BLACKMAN and* ELIZABETH *meet eyes. The other* TRUSTEES *exchange looks.*)

MR. BLACKMAN: Mrs. Packard, tell me—in what ways do you differ with the church, my dear? Do you have visions or hallucinations? Bouts of uncontrollable ravings? Do you speak in tongues?

ELIZABETH (*Laughs*): No, not in the least. May I describe to you in specific detail my disagreements with my husband's Calvinism—or Puritanism—and my defense of Christianity?

MR. BLACKMAN: Yes, yes, please go ahead.

DR. MCFARLAND: Yes, Mrs. Packard. Please inform the trustees of your . . . very interesting views.

ELIZABETH: Gentlemen, my husband accuses me of teaching my children doctrines . . . ruinous to their spiritual well-being, practices that will endanger their souls for eternity. But, gentlemen, I teach my children

Christianity; my husband teaches the children Calvinism. Christianity upholds the authority of salvation and *God*; Calvinism upholds the authority of damnation and the *Devil*. (THEO [*outraged*]: *"Where do you—"*) Please, hear me out.

MR. BLACKMAN: Mrs. Packard, are you not being needlessly provocative?

DR. MCFARLAND (*smiling with pleasure*): Of course she is! She cannot resist.

ELIZABETH: No, no. The intellectual and theological argument will become clear, I promise you, and I think—as men of immense intelligence—you may even find these ideas . . . intriguing, at the very least, sir. (*MR. BLACK-MAN: I see . . .*) Dr. McFarland did.

(DR. MCFARLAND *sputters: What? I—I—*)

MR. BLACKMAN (*Flattered by her*): Well, go on, Mrs. Packard.

ELIZABETH: Calvinism teaches us that our very natures are sinful. Is not this true in your church?

(*The* TRUSTEES *nod and agree.*)

MR. BLACKMAN: Why, yes, of course.

ELIZABETH: From childhood, we are all taught to overcome evil with evil—that is, the very first step toward becoming better is to believe we are (*Mock scolding.*) very, very *bad*! Is this not so? (BLACKMAN *smiles, almost laughs, charmed.* THEO *is appalled.*)

MR. BLACKMAN: Yes, surely.

ELIZABETH: But Christ taught us to "overcome evil with *good*," to *do* good, to take care of our fellow creatures. In fact, he believed our *true natures* are good. Do you follow me?

MR. BLACKMAN (*Not agreeing but indulgently allowing her to continue*): Well . . . yes, continue.

ELIZABETH: Yet my husband preaches that only "the elect" are good! or good enough to be saved, that election is predestined, and that everyone who is not "of the elect" will burn in hell for eternity. (*Passionately felt.*) Gentlemen, Jesus taught us that we are *all God's dear children*, and there is no *limit* to God's *mercy*!

MR. BLACKMAN (*Smiling, shaking his head*): And where does it tell us this in the scriptures, Mrs. Packard?

ELIZABETH: I have studied Acts, sir. Chapter two, verse twenty-one: "And it shall come to pass, that whosoever, WHOSOEVER, shall call upon the name of the Lord, our God . . . *shall be saved."* Therefore, repentance always remains a condition of pardon . . . In other words, we can *all* enter the Kingdom of Heaven *together.*

MR. BLACKMAN (*Gruff*): I see . . .

ELIZABETH: Gentlemen, I believe Christ's Word is simple. Our God is a *nurturing* God—like a mother's love—rather than a punishing God, and *this* is what I have taught my children . . . (*Tears streaming.*) Simply this . . . (*Pause.*) I am not mad; I merely disagree with my husband, as many sane wives often do. (*SHE and BLACKMAN almost laugh together.*) I do not ask my husband to change his beliefs, sir, merely to allow me the right to follow my own . . . (*Quits while she's ahead.*) And I—thank you, so very much, for hearing me today.

(*Alarmed,* THEO *and the* DOCTOR *exchange glances. The* DOCTOR *moves in.*)

DR. MCFARLAND: Is that all you have to say, Mrs. Packard?

ELIZABETH: Yes, that should suffice, Doctor.

DR. MCFARLAND: Mr. Blackman, I—

MR. BLACKMAN (*Gesturing to the doctor to wait*): I should like to thank you, Mrs. Packard. Though I cannot for one moment sanction your characterization of Calvinism, or Puritanism, you have presented a cogent and (*With irony.*) *mostly* rational treatise on the subject. (*TRUSTEES are amused.*) (*DR: Mr. Blackman, I—*) Gentlemen, I cannot but say Mrs. Packard appears to me far from violent or hopelessly insane. She is certainly emotional—perhaps passionate is more the word—but she is also logical, in her own way (*THEY laugh.*), much like my own wife. If this is the cause of her confinement here, I for one cannot support her staying here . . . (*ELIZABETH holds her breath;* DR. *and* THEO *exchange glances.*) Don't you concur, gentlemen?

A TRUSTEE: Yes, yes . . . I agree, Mr. Blackman.

DR. MCFARLAND: Mr. Blackman, with all due respect—

MR. BLACKMAN: My own wife, I'm afraid, has been reading far too much for her own good, like Mrs. Packard, and has come up with notions I find to be crackpot, but I should not like to live without her! (*THEY laugh.*) Dr. McFarland, I think she should be sent home, though I do not altogether envy the poor Reverend's living situation. (*More laughter.*) He must try to preach one doctrine in his church while his wife preaches another at home and across town! (*More laughter.*)

THEOPHILUS: Pardon me, gentlemen. May I say *one word*?

MR. BLACKMAN: Of course, Mr. Packard. First, though, I should like to finish the discussion with your wife, without interruption. Then we can speak together, at length.

THEOPHILUS (*Nods, angry and humiliated*): I see.

MR. BLACKMAN: Mrs. Packard, is there anything more you should like to add?

ELIZABETH: Only this: I am so very grateful to you, gentlemen, for recognizing my sanity; and thank you, Doctor, for allowing me to present some of my more (*With veiled irony.*) . . . "radical" views to the trustees.

DR. MCFARLAND (*Acidly to ELIZABETH*): Indeed. (*To TRUSTEES.*) Gentlemen, perhaps we could have a private conference before we speak further with the Packards? Mrs. Packard's illness can be difficult to detect, and she has not accurately described her more—

MR. BLACKMAN (*Piercing, to the doctor*): No, I think not, Doctor. Incarceration seems to have been obtained in consequence of Mrs. Packard *using* her reason, and not as reported, by her *losing* her reason. Reverend Packard . . . I should like to hear your thoughts regarding your wife's presentation.

THEOPHILUS: The questioning of doctrine is not worthy of discussion.

MR. BLACKMAN: Well . . . Reverend, as you can see, it does not seem appropriate to me nor to the rest of the trustees here to keep your wife at Jacksonville in either the violent ward or the 7th Ward any longer. (*Pointedly.*) Doctor McFarland agrees. *Do you not, Doctor?*

DR. MCFARLAND (*Choosing his words extremely carefully*): I think the kind of cure Reverend Packard seeks—did rightly seek—is not possible to attain in this instance.

THEOPHILUS: You concede defeat, Doctor?

DR. MCFARLAND: I am afraid I must, Reverend. I am sorry. I could not reach her.

MR. BLACKMAN: Could you not, Reverend, find a way to make peace with your wife—agree to let her think her own thoughts—these . . . liberal thoughts, as wrongheaded as you may find them—but confine her speaking about them to the privacy of your own home? We could make it a condition of her release that she must agree not to speak out publicly.

THEOPHILUS: I am afraid that is not good enough. She endangers the salvation of the children, gentlemen! May I remind you that intellectual and moral perversity are forms of insanity and require confinement?

MR. BLACKMAN: Mr. Packard—

THEOPHILUS: Sir, my wife still holds fast to her heretical ideas. You have heard, unfortunately, only a very few of her less radical views. May I describe some of them to you, *please*?

MR. BLACKMAN: That will not be necessary, sir. (*THEO: Gentlemen, my wife believes—*) Your wife seems to all of us far from violently insane, and no liberal religious views—as silly as they are—will change my mind.

THEOPHILUS: Gentlemen, understand—I am a minister of the old school. My wife did destroy my congregation . . . She did destroy the very foundation of our marriage and family life. Furthermore, if the kinds of ideas she has adopted in the past few years—these "liberal ideas" as you call them—are allowed and encouraged to flourish, they will endanger, I fear, the very foundation of this *country*! May I remind you, gentlemen, that our country was *founded* on exactly those princip—

MR. BLACKMAN: Mr. Packard! (*HE puts up his hand to calm him.*) Indeed . . . However, may we return, to the question of your children? For their sakes, Reverend—

(*THEOPHILUS rises.*)

THEOPHILUS: No, no . . . For the sake of my children, sir, I will protect them from their mother's moral degeneracy. As a man of God, I will not, as you seem to want me to do—I will not allow her heretical ideas to infect my home, and I will not *live* a lie. Shame on you, gentlemen. *Shame*.

(*Lights change.*)

(*A WOMAN testifies.*)

MRS. BLESSING: I lived across the street from the Packards, and it was a madhouse—doors locked, children crying—shameful! One day after Mrs. Packard came back from the asylum, little Isaac came to my house crying "they are killing my mother." I rushed over there with him and tried to see her, but Mr. Packard refused to let me in. I never thought Mrs. Packard was insane. I thought Mr. Packard was insane, if anyone was. Mrs. Packard claimed the right to live with her family and considered herself more capable of taking care of her children than any other person. I thought she should divorce, but she knew she would lose her children if she did, and she could not live with that. She said she "wanted protection in her own home, not a complete divorce *from* it."

(Lights change.)

(The nursery in the packard home. THEOPHILUS *nails the window shut from the inside. It is winter, freezing.* ELIZABETH *is wrapped in a shawl to keep warm.)*

ELIZABETH *(quiet):* The irony is not lost on me, husband, that I have left one prison only to be thrown into solitary confinement in my own home on my release. And in the empty nursery . . . *(HE pounds with the hammer, will not speak to her.* SHE *gets up.)* Theo, there is no fresh food in the house. Let me go to the market, or send one of the older children. *(HE pounds.)* They are hungry. *(Refuses to answer.)* Husband! Please. Let me speak to the children. They know I am here, Theophilus. *(No response.)* Why won't you speak to me? They want their mother.

(The following are the first words HE *says to her in days. They tear out of him. The pain is almost unbearable.)*

THEOPHILUS: Stop . . . chattering! *(Between gritted teeth.)*

*(*ARTHUR, *age five, starts to cry for his mother behind the door.)*

ARTHUR *(Off):* Momma, Momma?
ELIZABETH: Arthur, is that you?

*(*THEO *turns to her in a fury, almost in tears, then takes an enormous key chain out of his pocket.)*

THEOPHILUS: There is no money for fresh food.
ELIZABETH: Theophilus, how are we to *live*?

(HE just stares at her, opens the door. ARTHUR *is there, tries to run to his mother.)*

THEOPHILUS: Come on, Arthur. Come with me. You cannot see your mother now. *(Gently.)*
ARTHUR: Are you my Momma?

(As THEO *takes him off, locks the door:)*

ELIZABETH: Yes! I'm your Momma . . . !

(We hear ARTHUR *off, calling for his mother. A knock on the door. Then a sheet of paper, a letter, slips under the door.)*

LIBBY: Read this. You have to read this. Mummy . . . ?

ELIZABETH *(To the door, quiet)*: Yes, yes. I have it. Thank you, darling.

THEOPHILUS *(Off)*: Libby! Libby! Get away from that door! Now! . . . I am warning you.

*(*ELIZABETH *picks up the letter and reads.* SHE *can't believe it.)*

ELIZABETH *(To herself)*: Oh . . . dear . . . God . . . *(*LIBBY *cries.)* Don't cry now. Libby, wait here one moment!

*(*ELIZABETH *grabs a pen from the window seat, scrawls on the envelope.)*

THEOPHILUS: Libby, get away from that door! Do I have to come and get you?

LIBBY: Coming, Pa! Coming!

(Slipping the envelope under the door:)

ELIZABETH *(To* LIBBY*)*: Take this message to Mrs. Blessing across the street, alright?

LIBBY: Yes, I will . . .

ELIZABETH: Thank you, Libby dear. You did well. Very well . . . Go on.

*(*SHE *hears a commotion in the house, doors slamming, drawers slamming.* THEOPHILUS *screams at the* CHILDREN*:)*

THEOPHILUS *(off)*: Who has been rifling through the mail on my desk?! Isaac!? Libby?

THE CHILDREN *(Off)*: It wasn't me, it wasn't me . . .

THEOPHILUS *(Off)*: Whoever has stolen a letter from my desk will be severely punished.

(Finally we hear THEOPHILUS. HE *unlocks the door and enters, looks around, frantic.)*

ELIZABETH: Looking for this? *(*SHE *picks up the letter.)*

(*THEOPHILUS stops.*)

THEOPHILUS: Where did you get that? Who—

ELIZABETH: I don't think that is the proper question to ask, husband. And I would not tell you if I knew. The real question is in regards to the content of this letter. When did you and your sister plan to have me committed to (*SHE reads.*) the Northampton, Massachusetts, Asylum for the Insane . . . ? (*No answer.*) I see. How were you planning to do it, just out of curiosity? Bind and gag me and carry me from Illinois to Massachusetts in a private railway car perhaps? No, too expensive. And you have no money. Perhaps trick me somehow into thinking all was forgiven, move to Massachusetts, set up a sweet home near the asylum, and repeat the same kind of kidnapping you did here? Whatever your scheme, I am sure you and your sister had great fun dreaming it up, and you reveled in the idea that this time you might be able to get away with it completely.

THEOPHILUS (*Tears in his eyes, enraged*): What do you want from me, Elizabeth? Clearly—God *forgive* me—I've failed to save you.

ELIZABETH: Oh, is that what you wanted to do?

THEOPHILUS: Yes! That is what I want to do. Do you want to make *me* mad? Is that your goal? You have succeeded in utterly destroying me, the children, and what little professional and family life I managed to maintain in your absence.

ELIZABETH: Self-pity is an ugly emotion, Mr. Packard. Practice to rid yourself of it. You did make your own destruction.

THEOPHILUS (*Clear truth*): Perhaps, but who did make the children's destruction, Elizabeth? You have hurt the children, I fear, beyond repair. (*She cannot answer. Long pause.*) Libby cries and frets all day and cannot sleep at night. The boys are . . . uncontrollable! You are a selfish and a worthless mother. Can't you see the children are better off without you?

(*SHE is wounded to the quick. THEOPHILUS starts to the door.*)

ELIZABETH (*In pain and rage, hoarsely quiet*): God sees you, Theophilus. God hears you, and God will judge you for a *liar*! What an awful doom awaits you on Judgment Day.

THEOPHILUS: How dare you speak to a man of God in such a manner?

ELIZABETH: A man of God? Whose God?! There is not an ounce of compassion in you. You do not believe for one instant that I am mad. Admit it.

THEOPHILUS: I will not admit to a lie.

ELIZABETH: Nor will I. My mother always thought you cold. Little did she know how *very* cold.

(Long pause.)

THEOPHILUS *(Quiet)*: Your mother . . . was mad . . . just as you are.

(THEOPHILUS exits, slamming the door and locking it. ELIZABETH sits in the rocker and rocks.)

(Lights change.)

JUDGE: Doctor McFarland, you may read your letter into evidence.

DOCTOR MCFARLAND *(Reads)*: Your Honor: It is the opinion of the medical faculty of the Illinois State Hospital for the Insane at Jacksonville that Mrs. Elizabeth P.W. Packard is hopelessly insane. Though she can at times appear rational, she is in fact delusional and has torn Mr. Packard's life to pieces. It is my opinion that Mrs. Packard is beyond hope of being cured, and I will *never* take her back . . . We shall not ever . . . readmit her to Jacksonville. My colleagues and I have so signed.

(Lights change.)

(THEO enters carrying her coat.)

THEOPHILUS: What have you done? What have you done? Will you ruin everything I touch? Do I count for nothing?

ELIZABETH: What? What's happened?

THEOPHILUS: It seems you somehow, Elizabeth, got a message—delivered to Mrs. Blessing across the street?? . . . Is this true?

(SHE smiles.)

ELIZABETH: Oh, yes . . .

THEOPHILUS: Well, it appears Mrs. Blessing delivered your message to a *judge!* I have been issued a *writ of habeas corpus.* You and I must appear before a judge in two hours time. *(HE throws her coat at her.)* Get dressed.

(*HE exits. As* SHE *puts on the coat:*)

(*Lights change.*)

JUDGE: Gentlemen of the jury, let me remind you—though it is legal for a man to commit his wife to a lunatic asylum without proof of insanity, it is illegal to imprison a woman in her own home unless she is proven insane in a court of law. Mrs. Packard, I have granted your request to read a short statement to the jury.

(*ELIZABETH turns.*)

ELIZABETH: Your Honor . . . Gentlemen of the jury, you have heard all the evidence. I beg you to follow the dictates of your own conscience, God's secretary within you. It is almost by accident that I appear before you. How mysterious are God's ways and plans! . . . God saw that suffering for my opinions was necessary to confirm me in them. And the work is done, and well done, as all God's work always is. I am not now afraid of being called insane if I avow my belief that Christ died for *all* mankind. Can I ever believe God loves his children less than I do mine? Further, because I view Doctor McFarland and my husband differently from how they wish to view themselves, should I therefore be silenced? In America we are a free people, and every citizen living under this government has a right to form his own opinions, and having formed them, he has a right to express his individual opinions wherever he may think proper. In America, we do not lock up those with whom we disagree. And whosoever seeks to do so is a traitor to our flag and the cause which it represents. Gentlemen of the jury, for those of you who love liberty and for those of you who love women, I entrust my *life* to your good judgment and your manly protection.
JUDGE: Gentlemen, the quality of your service is reflected in your judgment.

(*Gavel. Lights change.* ARTHUR *runs to* ELIZABETH *and buries himself in his mother's arms*)

ARTHUR: Momma! (*HE murmurs to her as* SHE *rocks him.*)
ELIZABETH: Oh, my darling boy! A last, at last . . .

(*THEO comes forward to take the child.* ELIZABETH *hugs him tight, meets eyes with* THEOPHILUS.)

ELIZABETH (*To THEO*): He says you are taking him away. Where are you taking him?

THEOPHILUS: I am taking him *home*, Mrs. Packard. Come along, Arthur.

ELIZABETH (*Into ARTHUR's eyes*): Remember, Momma loves you, always. I will be with you . . . as soon as I possibly can . . .

THEOPHILUS: Come away from your mother. You are in my charge.

ELIZABETH: Go with Papa, dear, go on . . . it's all right.

(ARTHUR *takes* THEO's *hand.* ELIZABETH *tries not to cry.*)

THEOPHILUS: I shall . . . always pray for your soul, Elizabeth . . .

(*THEY exit.*)

JUDGE: Has the jury reached a verdict?

FOREMAN: We have, Your Honor.

JUDGE: The defendant will rise. Mr. Foreman, you may read the verdict.

(ELIZABETH *rises, shaky and uneasy.*)

FOREMAN OF THE JURY: We, the undersigned jurors in the case of *Packard vs. Packard*, having heard the evidence, are satisfied that said Elizabeth P.W. Packard . . . is sane.

(ELIZABETH *gasps.*)

JUDGE: It is hereby ordered that Mrs. Elizabeth P.W. Packard be relieved of all restraints incompatible with her condition as a sane woman and is now at liberty.

(*Gavel. The court exits.* DR. MCFARLAND *approaches* ELIZABETH.)

DR. MCFARLAND: My congratulations, Mrs. Packard.

ELIZABETH (*Nods, icy*): Doctor . . . (*A long pause.* THEY *regard each other. Finally:*) I was surprised at your veracity on the stand.

DR. MCFARLAND: Pardon me?

ELIZABETH: One of your statements was in fact correct.

DR. MCFARLAND: Oh? And what statement was that, Mrs. Packard?

ELIZABETH: "Mrs. Packard is beyond hope of being cured." That is quite accurate, Doctor. Since I was imprisoned for speaking out, the cure was to silence me, and you failed. I am *in*-curable . . . and grateful for it. Now if you will excuse me, I need to see my children—

(SHE *starts to exit.*)

DR. MCFARLAND: Mrs. Packard, Mr. Packard wanted you to have this.

(HE *hands her a letter.*)

ELIZABETH (*Suddenly alarmed*): Do you know what's in it?
DR. MCFARLAND (*Sad*): Oh, yes.
ELIZABETH (*With dread*): Be merciful. Tell me what it says.

(SHE *steels herself.*)

DR. MCFARLAND: Mr. Packard has left for Massachusetts with the children and all your household goods. (SHE *starts to go.*) No, no. You cannot stop him; he has only taken what is his. The house will be sold. He has left your trunk from the asylum there . . . so you can have some things.

(*Hands her the letter.*)

ELIZABETH (*Nodding*): He has robbed me of everything, except my life. Except my life. (*Struggling.*) To have God's approval is now my sole ambition . . . Rest assured, Doctor, I shall put the contents of my trunk to good use.

(*A beat.*)

DR. MCFARLAND: Perhaps we shall make peace in heaven, Mrs. Packard.

(SHE *reaches out and takes his hand;* HE *gently pulls away, exits.*)

Lights change. A bare stage save for the trunk. ELIZABETH *moves to it with purpose, opens it, takes out the mirror and bonnet. Tears streaming,* SHE *takes out clothes, rips seams, pulls out pages of writing from the linings of clothes and the lining of the trunk, as the* COMPANY *enters:*)

MRS. CHAPMAN: It took Elizabeth nine years to gain custody of her children. She and her husband never lived together again.

MRS. STOCKTON: Mrs. Packard died at the age of eighty-one.

MRS. TENNEY: Until the end of her life, she worked for the rights of the mentally ill and partnered with the abolitionists to fight for the emancipation of married women. Her father publicly supported her in her work.

MRS. STOCKTON: Due to her efforts and the influence of her books, thirty-four bills were passed in various legislatures. "No woman of her day," her obituary read, "except possibly Harriet Beecher Stowe, exercised a wider influence in the interest of humanity."

MR. BLESSING: Mrs. Packard succeeded in having Jacksonville Insane Asylum investigated for negligence and abuse.

MR. BLACKMAN: Though the investigators recommended the firing of Doctor McFarland, the trustees chose not to ask for his resignation.

MRS. STOCKTON: Mrs. Stockton . . .

MRS. CHAPMAN: and Mrs. Chapman . . .

MRS. STOCKTON: died at Jacksonville.

MRS. BONNER: Mrs. Bonner was committed to the poor house for the criminally insane.

THEOPHILUS: Theophilus Packard remained a minister, but never again had his own church. He died at the age of eighty-three. Of all his children, only Samuel lived a long life and was a practicing Calvinist. Arthur and Isaac committed suicide . . .

LIBBY: Libby lived with her mother until her mother died. Libby died a year later, in an insane asylum.

(The DOCTOR enters.)

DR. MCFARLAND: Dr. McFarland and Mrs. Packard never saw each other again. In 1891, Dr. McFarland . . . hanged himself.

(We hear the ghostly, remembered sound of a prison door clang shut. ELIZABETH looks up.)

End of Play

NO CHILD . . .

by Nilaja Sun

Nilaja Sun in her play *No Child* . . . at the Barrow Street Theatre in New York City
(Photo: © Carol Rosegg)

SPECIAL NOTE

Anyone receiving permission to produce NO CHILD . . . is required to give credit to the Author as sole and exclusive Author of the Play on the title page of all programs distributed in connection with performances of the Play and in all instances in which the title of the Play appears for purposes of advertising, publicizing or otherwise exploiting the Play and/or a production thereof. The name of the Author must appear on a separate line, in which no other name appears, immediately beneath the title and in size of type equal to 50% of the size of the largest, most prominent letter used for the title of the Play. No person, firm or entity may receive credit larger or more prominent than that accorded the Author. The following acknowledgments must appear on the title page in all programs distributed in connection with performances of the Play:

No Child . . . received its World Premiere by
Epic Theatre Center, New York, NY in May 2006.

Originally produced off-Broadway in New York
at the Barrow Street Theatre
by Scott Morfee and Tom Wirtshafter.

Permission for use of Our Country's Good by Timberlake Wertenbaker was
granted by the Estate of Thomas Keneally and Timberlake Wertenbaker.
First presented at the Royal Court Theatre, London on September 10, 1988.

NILAJA SUN

Nilaja Sun is the solo writer and performer of the off-Broadway smash No Child . . . , *which concluded its New York run in 2007 and garnered her the Lucile Lortel, Outer Critics Circle, and Theatre World awards, and an Obie. In addition she was honored with the John Gassner Playwriting Award, and* No Child . . . *was named the best one-person show at the U.S. Comedy Arts Festival. Sun has toured the play throughout the country, garnering a Jeff Award as well as a Black Theatre Alliance Award, and an Irne Award. As a result of her long-term relationship with New York's Epic Theatre Center, where* No Child . . . *was developed, she was named Epic's first artistic associate. As an actor, Sun's New York credits include roles in* Huck and Holden (*Cherry Lane Theatre*), The Cook (*INTAR*), and The Adventures of Barrio Grrrl! *by Quiara Alegría Hudes. As a solo performer, Sun's solo projects embrace* Blues for a Gray Sun *(INTAR),* La Nubia Latina, Black and Blue, Insufficient Fare, Due to the Tragic Events of . . . *and* Mixtures. *Recipient of a Princess Grace Award, Sun has worked as a teaching artist in New York City for ten years.*

Note: This play may be performed with one actor or with as many as sixteen actors. The play takes place in several locations but is best staged in a fluid style with lights and sounds suggesting scene changes.

CHARACTERS
(in order of appearance)

JANITOR BARON—80s, narrator
MS. SUN—30s, teaching artist
MS. TAM—20s, teacher
COCA—16, student
JEROME—18, student
BRIAN—16, student
SHONDRIKA—16, student
XIOMARA—16, student
JOSE—17, student
CHRIS—15, student
MRS. KENNEDY—School principal
SECURITY GUARD—Any age
PHILLIP—16, student
MRS. PROJENSKY—Substitute teacher
MR. JOHNSON—Teacher
DOÑA GUZMAN—70s, grandmother to Jose Guzman

PLACE

New York

TIME

Now

Scene One

(School. Morning. JANITOR *enters, mopping floor as he sings.)*

JANITOR: *Trouble in mind.*
I'm blue.
But I won't be blue always.
Cuz the sun's gonna shine
In my back door someday.

(To audience.) Hear that? Silence. Beautiful silence, pure silence. The kind of silence that only comes from spending years in the back woods. We ain't in the back woods (though I'm thinking 'bout retirin' there). It's 8:04 A.M.—five minutes before the start of the day. And, we on the second floor of Malcolm X High School in the Bronx, USA. Right over there is my janitor's closet, just right of the girls' bathroom where the smell of makeup, hair pomade and gossip fills the air in the morning light. There's Mrs. Kennedy's room—she the principal. For seventeen years, been leading this group of delinquents—Oh I'm sorry, academically and emotionally challenged youth. She got a lot to work with! Seventeen feet below my very own, lay one hundred-thousand-dollar worth of a security system. This include two metal detecting machines, seven metal detecting wands, five school guards, and three NYC police officers. All armed. Guess all we missing is a bomb-sniffing dog. Right over there's Ms. Tam's class, she one of them new teachers. Worked as an associate in the biggest investment firm in New York then coming home from a long dreary day at work, read an ad on the subway—y'all know the ones that offer you a lifetime of glorious purpose and meaning if you just become a New York City teacher. Uh-huh—the devil's lair on the IRT. I adore Ms. Tam, she kind, docile, but I don't think she know what she got herself into. See, I been working here since 1958 and I done seen some teachers come and go, I said I seen teachers come and go. Ah! One more time for good luck, I seen teachers come and go and I do believe it is one of the hardest jobs in the whole wide world. Shoot, I don't gotta tell you that, y'all look like smart folk! The most underpaid, underappreciated, *underpaid* job in this crazy universe. But for some miracle, every year God creates people that grow up knowing that's what they gonna do for the rest of they life. God, ain't He sometin'! Now, you might say to me, "Jackson Baron Copeford the Third. Boy, what you doin' up dere on dat stage? You ain't no actor." That I know and neither are these kids you about to

meet. *(He clears his throat.)* What you about to see is a story about a play within a play within a play. And a teacher (or as she likes to call herself—a teaching artist—just so as people know she do somethin' else on her free time). The kids call her Ms. Sun and in two minutes from now she gonna walk up them stairs towards the janitor's room and stop right at Ms. Tam's class. She gonna be something they done never seen before. Now I know what you're thinking: "Oh, Baron. I know about the public schools. I watch Eyewitness News." What I got to say to that? HUSH! You don't know unless you been in the schools on a day-to-day basis. HUSH! You don't know unless you been a teacher, administrator, student, or custodial staff. HUSH! Cuz you could learn a little sometin'. Here's lesson number one: Taking the 6 train, in eighteen minutes, you can go from Fifty-ninth Street, one of the richest congressional districts in the nation, all the way up to Brook Ave. in the Bronx, where Malcolm X High is, the poorest congressional district in the nation. In only eighteen minutes. HUSH!

Scene Two

(Before class.)

MS. SUN *(On the phone, hallway.)*: Mr. Pulaski! Hi, it's Nilaja Sun from Bergen Street. 280 Bergen. Apartment four? Hey! Mr. Pulaski, thanks for being so patient, I know how late my rent is . . . By the way, how's your wife Margaret? Cool. And your son Josh? Long Island University. That's serious. Oh he's gonna love it and he'll be close to home. But yes, I apologize for not getting you last month's rent on time, but see the IRS put a levy on my bank account and I just can't retrieve any money from it right now. Well, it should be cleared by Tuesday but the real reason why I called was to say I'm startin' a new teaching program up here in the Bronx and it's a six-week-long workshop and they're paying me exactly what I owe you so . . . what's that? Theatre. I'm teaching theatre. A play actually. It's called *Our Country's Good* . . . Have you heard of it? Well it's about a group of convicts that put on a play . . . So the kids are actually gonna be doing a play within a play within . . . What's that? Ah, yes, kids today need more discipline and less self-expression. Less "lulalula" and more daily structure like Catholic school during Pope Pious the Twelfth. On the flip side of the matter, having gone to Catholic school for thirteen years, I didn't even know I was black until college. *(She roars her laughter.*) Sir? Sir, are you still there? (*Bell rings.*) I gotta go teach, sir. Are we cool with getting you that money by the twenty-fifth? How about the thirtieth? Thirty-first? I know, don't push it. You rock. Yes, I'm still an actor. No, not in anything right now. But soon. Yes, sir, happy Lent to you too, sir.

Scene Three

(*Classroom.*)

MS. TAM: Ms. Sun? Come on in. I'm Cindy Tam and I'm so excited to have your program here in our English class. Sorry we weren't able to meet the last four times you set up a planning meeting but so much has been going on in my life. Is it true you've been a teaching artist for seven years? In New York City? Wow. That's amazing. I'm a new teacher. They don't know that. It's a *challenge*. The kids are really *spirited*. Kaswan, where are you going? Well, we're going to be starting in a few minutes and I would strongly suggest you not leave. (*Listens.*) OK, but be back in five minutes, um, Veronica, stop hitting Chris and calling him a mother-fucker. I'm sorry, please stop hitting Chris and calling him a mother-fucker. Thanks, Veronica. Sorry, like I said, very excited you're here. Where is everyone? The kids usually come in twenty to thirty minutes late because it's so early. I know it's only a forty-one-minute class but I've been installing harsher penalties for anyone who comes in after fifteen. After five? OK, we'll try that. Well, what we *can* do today is start the pro-gram in ten minutes and wait for the bulk of them to come in, eat their breakfast, and . . . You wanna start now? But there are only seven kids here. The rest of them will ask what's going on and what am I gonna say to each late student? (*Scared out of her wits.*) OK. Then, we'll start. Now. Class! Please welcome Ms. Sun. She's going to be teaching you a play, and teaching you about acting, and how to act and we're gonna do a play and it's gonna be fun.

COCA: Fun? This is stupid already. I don't wanna act. I wanna do vocabulary.

JEROME: Vocab? Hello, Ms. Sun. Thank you for starting the class on time. Since we usually be the only ones on time.

BRIAN: Niggah, you ain't never on time.

JEROME: Shut up, bitch motherfucker.

MS. TAM: Jerome, Brian? What did I tell you about the offensive language?

JEROME: Yo, yo. We know. Pork-fried rice wonton coming up.

MS. TAM: I heard that, Jerome.

JEROME: Sorry, Ms. Tam.

BRIAN (*Accent*): Solly, Ms. Tam.

MS. TAM: Go on, Ms. Sun! (*Beat.*)

MS. SUN: Ah, well, I'm Ms. Sun and I will be with you all for the next six weeks and by the end of those glorious weeks, you would have read a play, analyzed the play, been cast in it, rehearsed it and lastly performed it. It's gonna be a whirlwind spectacle that I want you to start inviting your parents and friends and loved ones to come see . . . What's that? No, it's not *Raisin in the Sun* . . . No, not *West Side Story*. It's a play called *Our Country's Good*.

COCA: Ew. This is some patrionism?

MS. SUN: Patriotism? No. It's a play based in Australia in 1788 and it's written by a woman named Timberlake Wertenbaker.

BRIAN: Yo, Justin Timberlake done wrote himself a play. "Gonna rock yo' body. Today. Dance with me."

MS. TAM: Brian, focus?

BRIAN: "People say she a gold digga, but she don't mess with no broke niggas."

MS. TAM: Brian!!! Put down the Red Bull.

BRIAN: Beef-fried rice.

MS. TAM: Brian.

BRIAN: Vegetable-fried rice.

JEROME: Ay yo! This some white shit. Ain't this illegal to teach this white shit no mo'?

MS. SUN: Are you done?

JEROME: Huh?

MS. SUN: Are you done?

JEROME: What?

MS. SUN: With your spiel? With your little spiel?

JEROME: Yeah.

MS. SUN: Because I'm trying to tell you what the play is about and I can't when you keep on interrupting.

JEROME: Oh my bad. Damn. She got attitude. I like that.

SHONDRIKA: I don't. What's this play about anyway?

MS. SUN: Well, what's your name?

SHONDRIKA: Shondrika.

MS. SUN: Well, Shondrika . . .

SHONDRIKA: Shondrika!

MS. SUN: Shondrika?

SHONDRIKA: Shondrika!!!

MS. SUN: Shondrika!!!

SHONDRIKA: Close enough.

MS. SUN: Ah-hah . . . *Our Country's Good* is about a group of convicts.

XIOMARA: What are convicts?

JEROME: Jailbirds, you dumb in a can. Get it? (*Laugh/clap.*) Dominican! Dominican!

MS. SUN: . . . And they put on a play called *The Recruiting Officer.* You'll be reading . . .

COCA: We gotta read?

JEROME: Aw hell no.

MS. TAM: Yes, you'll be reading, but you're also gonna be creating a community.

JEROME: Ay yo! Last time I created a community the cops came.

(*Latecomers enter.*)

MS. TAM: Kaswan, Jose, Jennifer, Malika, Talifa, Poughkeepsie, come on in, you're late. What's your excuse this time, Jose?

JOSE: Sorry, Miss. But that faggot Mr. Smith was yelling at us to stop running to class. Fucking faggot.

MS. SUN: ENOUGH!

JOSE: Who? Who this?

MS. SUN: Hi. I'm Ms. Sun. Take your seats *now.* And as of today and for the next six weeks, when I'm in this classroom, you will not be using the word faggot or bitch or nigga or motherfucker or motherfuckerniggabitchfaggot. Anymore. Dominicans shall not be called and will not call each other dumb in a cans or platanos.

COCA: *Ah, y pero quien e heta? Esa prieta?*

MS. SUN: *La prieta soy yo, señorita.* (COCA *is speechless.*)

BRIAN: Shwimp fwy why! Shwimp fwy why!

MS. SUN: We will respect our teacher's ethnicity.

BRIAN: Shwimp fwy why??? (*No one else laughs.*)

MS. SUN: Ladies will not call each other heifers or hos.

SHONDRIKA: Shoot! That's what I'm talkin' about.

MS. SUN: We will start class on time. We will eat our breakfast beforehand. And from now on we are nothing but thespians.

XIOMARA: Lesbians? I ain't no Rosie O'Donnell.

MS. SUN: No, no! Thespian! It means actor, citizen, lover of all things great.

XIOMARA: I love that hard cash, that bling-bling.

MS. SUN: Say it with me, class, thespian.

XIOMARA *(Bored)*: Thespian.

MS. SUN: Thespian!

JEROME *(Bored.)*: Thespian.

MS. SUN: Thespian!

COCA: Thespian, already, damn!

MS. SUN: Now, let's get up and form a circle.

SHONDRIKA: Get up? Aw hell no!

JOSE: Miss, we not supposed to do exercises this early.

MS. TAM: Come on guys, stand up. Stand up.

COCA: Miss, this is mad boring.

MS. SUN: Boredom, my love, usually comes from boring people.

BRIAN: OOOOOOOOOOOOH!

COCA *(Dissed)*: What's that supposed to mean?

BRIAN: That's O.D., yo! Oh she played you, yo!

JEROME: Ay yo, shut yo trap! Miss, I could be the lovable and charming leading man that gets all the honies' numbers?

MS. SUN: We'll see.

JEROME: Miss, can I get your number? *(Beat.)* Nah, I'm just playing. Let's do this, yo. Get up. *(They get up.)*

MS. SUN: OK, thank you . . .

JEROME: Jerome!

MS. SUN: Jerome. Great circle! Let's take a deep breath in and out. In . . .

BRIAN: Ohm! Nah! I'm just playing. Keep going. Keep going. Keep going. Keep going.

MS. SUN: . . . and out . . . In . . .

COCA: I'm hungry. What time it is?

MS. SUN: . . . and out . . . stretch with me, will you? Now, who here has ever seen a play? *(No one raises their hand . . . but CHRIS.)* Really? Which show?

CHRIS: *Star Wars.* It was a live reenactment.

MS. SUN: Was it in a theater?

CHRIS: Yeah. We all wore outfits and costumes and acted alongside the movie.

JEROME: Damn, Chris, you like SupaDupaJamaicanNerdNegro.

CHRIS: And for that, I zap you. *(To Ms. Sun.)* You really gonna make us act onstage?

MS. SUN: Yup.

CHRIS: I'm scared.

MS. SUN: Yeah, well guess what? Before I walked in here, even with all my acting and teaching experience, I was scared and nervous too, but you get
over it once you get a feel for the audience and you see all of your parents and your friends and your teachers smiling at you. Did you guys
know that public speaking is the number one fear for all humans—even
greater than death?

JEROME: What? They ain't never lived in the hood.

JOSE: But, Miss, you should be scared of this class, cuz we supposed to be the
worst class in the school.

MS. TAM: It's true. They are.

MS. SUN: Really, well, in the past thirty-five minutes, I've met some pretty
amazing young adults, thinkers, debaters, thespians . . .

BRIAN: Lesbians.

MS. SUN: Keep breathing! *(Bell rings.)* Oh no, listen, read scenes one through
five for the next time. Thanks guys, you are great.

MS. TAM: Wow. That was amazing. You're really great with the kids. *(Beat.)*
Just to let you know. They're probably not going to read the play and
they are probably going to lose the handout and probably start to cut
your class and their parents probably won't come to the show. Probably.
OK, bye.

MS. SUN: Bye. *(She watches her leave.)* For all our sake, Ms. Tam, I hope you're
probably wrong.

Scene Four

(School hallway.)

MRS. KENNEDY: Ms. Sun, hi, Mrs. Kennedy—the principal, so glad to meet
you. Sorry about the attendance, Ms. Tam is a new teacher and we need
all these kids to pass five Regents exams in the next two months. The
pressure's on. Let me know when you'll be needing the auditorium.
There are four schools in this building and it's like fighting diseased lions
to book a night in it. But, you're priority. We've given you one of the most
challenging classes. But I believe in them. I believe in you. Tyesha, can
I have a word? *(She walks off. Security guard stops Sun.)*

SECURITY GUARD: Y'ave pass ta leave. I said do you have a pass to leave? Oh,
you a teaching artist? Oh. Cuz you look like one a them. Well, excuse me
for livin'! *(To other guards.)* Just trying to do mi job. I don't know the dif-

ference 'tween the teachers, teaching artists, parents, Board of Ed people and these animals comin' in here. I don't know da difference. Just
tryin' to do mi job. (*To student.*) Girl, girl! Whatcha t'ink dis is? You can't
go in wifoot goin' tru da detector. I don care if you just walked out and
now you come back in. Rules are rules. Put ya bag in and yo wallet and
your selfish phone.
   (*Beep.*) Go back. Ya belt.
   (*Beep.*) Go back. Ya earrings.
   (*Beep.*) Go back. Ya shoes. Don't sass me!
   (*Beep.*) Go back. Ya hair . . . t'ings.
   (*Beep.*) Go back. Ya jewelry. Oh, oh I don' have time for your attitude.
Open your arms, spread your legs. Oh, oh I don' care about your science
class. Should know betta' than to just waltz in 'ere ten minutes 'fore
class. Got ta give it one whole hour. Lemme see yo I.D. Don' have? Can't
come in. Excuse?!!! What ya name is? Shondrika Jones! I don' care about
ya Regents. Go, Go, Go back home. Next time don' bring all dat bling
and don' bring all dat belt and don' bring all dat sass. Who ya t'ink ya is?
The mayor of New York City? Slut! (*To another student.*) Boy, boy, don't
you pass me! (*Light shift.*)

JANITOR (*To audience*): Your tax dollars at work! As Ms. Sun makes her way
   back home on the train, she thinks to herself.

Scene Five

(*Subway car.*)

MS. SUN: What will these six weeks bring? How will I persuade them to act onstage? (*Beat.*) Why did I choose a play about convicts? These kids aren't
   convicts. The kids in Rikers are convicts. These kids are just in tenth
   grade. They've got the world telling them they are going to end up in jail.
   Why would I choose a play about convicts? Why couldn't I choose a play
   about kings and queens in Africa or the triumphs of the Taino Indian?
   This totally wouldn't jive if I were white and trying to do this. How dare
   I! Why would I choose to do a play about convicts?

Scene Six

(*Classroom.*)

JEROME: Because we treated like convicts every day.

MS. TAM: Jerome, raise your hand.

JEROME (*Raises hand.*): We treated like convicts every day.

MS. SUN: How do you mean?

SHONDRIKA: First, we wake up to bars on our windows.

COCA: Then, our moms and dads.

SHONDRIKA: You got a dad?

COCA: Yeah . . . so? Then our mom tells us where to go, what to do, and blah, blah, blah.

JEROME: Then, we walk in a uniformed line towards the subways, cramming into a ten-by-forty-foot cell (*Laughs.*) checking out the fly honies.

BRIAN: But there ain't no honies in jail, know what I'm saying?

JEROME: Unless, you there long enough, what, what!

MS. SUN: Then, class, you'll walk into another line at the bodega at the corner store, to get what?

XIOMARA: Breakfast.

MS. SUN: And what's for breakfast?

XIOMARA: Welch's Orange and a Debbie snack cake.

MS. SUN: Exactly, then what?

SHONDRIKA: Then, we go to school.

CHRIS: . . . Where a cool electronic object points out our every metal flaw.

JEROME: Damn, Chris, you read way too much sci-fi!

SHONDRIKA: Then we go to a class they tell us we gotta go to, with a teacher we gotta learn from and a play we gotta do.

MS. SUN: And now that you feel like prisoners . . . open to page twenty-seven. Phillip says, "Watkin: Man is born free, and everywhere he is in chains." What *don't* people expect from prisoners?

JOSE: For them to succeed in life . . .

MS. SUN: But, in the play . . .

COCA: They succeed by doing the exact opposite of what people expect.

MS. SUN: And so . . . how does that relate to your lives?

SHONDRIKA: Shoot, don't nobody expect us to do nothing but drop out, get pregnant, go to jail . . .

BRIAN: . . . or work for the MTA.

XIOMARA: My mom works for the MTA, nigga. Sorry, Miss . . . NEGRO.

SHONDRIKA: So, dese characters is kinda going through what we kinda going through right now.

MS. SUN: Kinda, yeah. And so . . . Brian . . .

BRIAN: By us doing the show, see what I'm saying, we could prove something to ourselves and our moms and her dad and Mrs. Kennedy and Ms. Tam that we is the shi . . . shining stars of the school, see what I'm saying?

MS. SUN: Great, turn to Act One, Scene Six. Can I have a volunteer to read? (*Sun looks around.*)

SHONDRIKA: Shoot, I'll read, give me this: "We are talking about criminals, often hardened criminals. They have a habit of vice and crime. Habits . . ."

JOSE: Damn, Ma, put some feeling into that!

SHONDRIKA: I don't see you up here reading, Jose.

JOSE: Cuz you the actress of the class.

SHONDRIKA (*Realizing she is the "actress" of the class*): "Habits are difficult to BREAK! And it can be more than habit, an I-nate—"

MS. TAM (*Correcting*): Innate . . .

SHONDRIKA: See, Ms Tam why you had to mess up my flow? Now I gotta start from the beginning since you done messed up my flow. (*Class sighs.*)

BRIAN: Aw. Come on!!!

MS. TAM: Sorry, Shondrika.

SHONDRIKA: Right. "Habits are difficult to break. And it can be more than habit, an innate tendency. Many criminals seem to have been born that way. It is in their nature." Thank you. (*Applause.*)

MS. SUN: Beautiful, Shondrika. And is it in your nature to live like you're a convict?

SHONDRIKA: No!

MS. SUN: Well, what is in your nature? Coca?

COCA: Love.

MS. SUN: What else? Chris?

CHRIS: Success. And real estate.

MS. SUN: Jose, how about you?

JOSE: Family. Yo. My brother and my *buela*.

MS. SUN: Brian?

BRIAN: And above all, money, see what I'm sayin', know what I mean, see what I'm saying?

MS. SUN: Yes, Brian, we see what you're saying . . . and now that you know that you actually *can* succeed, let's get up and stretch!

COCA: Get up? Aw—hell no!

JOSE: This is mad boring.

XIOMARA: I just ate. I hate this part.

JEROME: Can I go to the bathroom? *(Bell rings. Lights shift.)*

JANITOR: Not so bad for a second class. Although, due to discipline issues, attention problems, lateness and resistance to the project on the whole, Ms. Sun is already behind in her teaching lesson. And, the show is only four weeks away. Let's watch as Ms. Sun enters her third week of classes. The show must go on! (I'm good at this. I am!)

Scene Seven

(Classroom.)

COCA: Miss. Did you hear? Most of our class is gone for the day . . . They went on an important school trip. To the UniverSoul Circus. There's only five of us here.

MS. SUN: That's OK, Coca. We'll make due with the five of us, including Ms. Tam.

MS. TAM *(Tired)*: Ewww . . .

MS. SUN: So, we will start the rehearsal section for *Our Country's Good.* We have the lovely Xiomara as Mary Brenham.

XIOMARA *(Deep voice.)*: I don't want to be Mary Brenham, I want to be Liz . . . the pretty one.

MS. SUN: I think I can make that happen. Chris as the Aborigine.

CHRIS: It's good.

MS. SUN: And Phillip as . . . Phillip as . . . Ralph! Phillip, do me a favor, go to page thirty-one and read your big monologue about the presence of women on the stage.

PHILLIP *(Inaudibly)*: "In my own small way in just a few hours I have seen something change. I asked some of the convict women to read me some lines, these women who behave often no better than animals." *(Pause.)*

MS. SUN: Good, Phillip, good. Do me a favor and read the first line again but pretend that you are speaking to a group of a hundred people.

PHILLIP *(Inaudibly)*: "In my own small way in just a few hours I have seen something change."

MS. SUN: Thank you, Phillip. You can sit down now. *(She goes to work on an-*

other student.) No, Phillip, get back up. Someone is stealing your brand new . . . what kind of car do you like, Phillip?

PHILLIP *(Inaudibly)*: Mercedes LX 100, Limited edition.

MS. SUN: That! And, you have to, with that line there, stop him from taking your prized possession. Read it again.

PHILLIP *(Inaudibly)*: "In my own small way I have seen something change."

MS. SUN: Now open your mouth . . .

PHILLIP *(Inaudibly but with mouth wide.)*: "In my own small way . . ."

MS. SUN: Your tongue, your tongue is a living breathing animal thrashing about in your mouth—it's not just lying there on the bottom near your jaw—it's got a life of its own, man. Give it life.

PHILLIP *(Full on)*: "In my own small way I have seen something change!" *(The bell rings.)*

MS. SUN: That's it. That's it. Right there . . . *(She is alone now.)* God, I need a Vicodin.

Scene Eight

(School. Night.)

JANITOR: It may not look it, but this school has gone through many trans-formations. When I first arrived at its pristine steps, I marveled at the architecture . . . like a castle. Believe it or not, there were nothin' but Italian kids here and it was called Robert Moses High back then. Humph! See, I was the first Negro janitor here and ooh that made them other custodians upset. But I did my job, kept my courtesies intact. Them janitors all gone now . . . and I'm still here. Then came the 60s, civil rights, the assassination of President Kennedy right there on the TV, Vietnam. Those were some hot times. Italians started moving out and Blacks and Puerto Ricans moved right on in. Back then, landlords was burning up they own buildings just so as to collect they insurance. And, the Black Panthers had a breakfast program—would say "Brotha Baron! How you gonna fight the MAN today?" I say "With my broom and my grade D ammonia, ya dig?" They'd laugh. They all gone, I'm still here. Then came the 70s when they renamed the school Malcolm X after our great revolutionary. I say, "Alright, here we go. True change has got to begin now." Lesson number two: Revolution has its upside and its downside. Try not to stick around for the downside. Eighties brought

Reagan, that goddamn crack ('scuse my cussin') and hip-hop. Ain't nothing like my Joe King Oliver's Creole Jazz Band but what you gonna do. And here we come to today. Building fallin' apart, paint chipping, water damage, kids running around here talking loud like crazy folk, half of them is raising themselves. Let me tell ya, I don't know nothing about no No Child, Yes Child, Who Child What Child. I do know there's a hole in the fourth-floor ceiling ain't been fixed since '87, all the bathrooms on the third floor, they all broke. Now, who's accountable for dat? Heck, they even asked me to give up my closet, make it into some science lab class cuz ain't got no room. I say, "This my sanctuary. You can't take away my zen. Shoot, I read *O* magazine." They complied for now. Phew! Everything's falling apart . . . But these floors, these windows, these chalkboards—they clean . . . why? Cuz I'm still here!

Scene Nine

(Classroom.)

COCA: Miss, did you hear? Someone stole Ms. Tam's bag and she quit for good. We got some Russian teacher now.

MRS. PROJENSKY: Quiet Quiet Quiet Quiet Quiet Quiet Quiet. Quiet!

MS. SUN: Miss, Miss, Miss. I'm the teaching artist for . . .

MRS. PROJENSKY: Sit down, you.

SHONDRIKA: Aw, snap, she told her.

MRS. PROJENSKY: Sit down, quiet. Quiet, sit down.

MS. SUN: No, I'm the teaching artist for this period. Maybe Miss Tam or Mrs. Kennedy told you something about me?

JEROME *(Shadowboxes)*: Ah, hah, you being replaced, Russian lady.

MS. SUN: Jerome, you're not helping right now.

JEROME: What?! You don't gotta tell me jack. We ain't got a teacher no more or haven't you heard? *(HE flings a chair.)* We are the worst class in school.

MRS. PROJENSKY: Sit down! Sit down!

MS. SUN: Guys, quiet down and focus. We have a show to do in a few weeks.

COCA: Ooee, I don't wanna do this no more. It's stupid.

CHRIS: I still want to do it.

JEROME: Shut the fuck up, Chris.

JOSE: Yo man, she's right. This shit is mad fucking boring yo.

COCA: Yeah!

XIOMARA: Yeah!

BRIAN: Yeah!

SHONDRIKA: Yeah!

COCA: Mad boring.

JEROME: Fuckin' stupid.

MRS. PROJENSKY: Quiet! Quiet! Quiet!

MS. SUN: What has gotten into all you? The first two classes were amazing, you guys were analyzing the play, making parallels to your lives. So, we missed a week when you went to go see, uh . . .

SHONDRIKA: UniverSoul Circus.

MS. SUN: Right! But, just because we missed a week doesn't mean we have to start from square one. Does it? Jerome, Jerome! where are you going?

MRS. PROJENSKY: Sit down, sit down, you! Sit down!

JEROME: I don't gotta listen to none of y'all. (*He flings another chair.*) I'm eighteen years old.

BRIAN: Yeah, and still in the tenth grade, nigga. (*Brian flings a chair.*)

MS. SUN: Brian!

JEROME: I most definitely ain't gonna do no stupid-ass motha fuckin' Australian play from the goddamn seventeen-hundreds!

MS. SUN: Fine, Jerome. You don't wanna be a part of something really special? There are others here who do.

JEROME: Who? Who in here want to do this show, memorize your lines, look like stupid fucking dicks on the stage for the whole school to laugh at us like they always do anyhow when can't none of us speak no goddamn English.

MS. SUN: Jerome, that's not fair, no one is saying you don't speak English. You all invited your parents . . .

COCA: Ooee, my moms can't come to this. She gotta work. Plus the Metrocard ends at seven.

XIOMARA: My mom ain't never even been to this school.

JEROME: That's what I'm sayin'! Who the fuck wanna do this? Who the fuck wanna do this?

MS. SUN: I'll take the vote, Jerome, if you sit down. Everyone sit down.

MRS. PROJENSKY: Sit down!

MS. SUN: Thank you, ma'am. OK, so, who, after all the hard work we've done so far building a team, analyzing the play in your own words (that is not easy, I know), developing self-esteem *y coraje* as great thespians . . .

BRIAN: Lesbians.

MS. SUN: Who wants to quit . . . after all this? (*She looks around as they all raise their hands . . . except for Chris.*) I see.

CHRIS: Miss. No. I still wanna do the show.

JEROME: That's cuz you gay, Chris. Yo, I'm out! One. Niggas. (*Pause. Ms. Sun is hurt.*)

MS. SUN: OK . . . Well . . . Ms?

MRS. PROJENSKY: Projensky.

MS. SUN: Ms. Projensky.

MRS. PROJENSKY: Projensky!

MS. SUN: Projensky.

MRS. PROJENSKY: Projensky!!!

MS. SUN: Projensky!!!

MRS. PROJENSKY: Is close.

MS. SUN: Do they have any sample Regents to take?

MRS. PROJENSKY: Yes, they do.

MS. SUN: Great. I'll alert Mrs. Kennedy of your vote.

PHILLIP (*Audibly*): Ms. Sun?

MS. SUN: Yes, Phillip, what is it?

PHILLIP: Can I still do the show? (*Beat.*)

Scene Ten

(*Principal's office.*)

MRS. KENNEDY: So they voted you out? Well, Malcolm X Vocational High School did not get an eight-thousand-dollar grant from the Department of Education of the City of New York for these students to choose democracy now. They will do the show. Because I will tell them so to-morrow. If they do not do the show, each student in 10F will be suspended and *not* be able to join their friends in their beloved Great Adventures trip in May. The horror. Look, I understand that they consider themselves the worst class in school. News flash—They're not even close. I know that they've had five different teachers in the course of seven months. I also can wrap my brain around the fact that seventy-nine percent of those kids in there have been physically, emotionally, and sexually abused in their tender little sixteen-year-old lives. But that does not give them the right to disrespect someone who is stretching them to give them something beautiful. Something challenging. Something Jay-Z and P Diddly only *wish* they could offer them. Now, I will call all their parents this weekend and notify them of their intolerable behavior as well as invite them to *Our Country's Good*. Done. See you next Wednesday, Ms. Sun?

MS. SUN: Yes, yes. Thanks! Yes! . . . Uh, no, Mrs. Kennedy. You won't be seeing me next Wednesday. I quit. I came to teaching to touch lives and educate and be this enchanting artist in the classroom and I have done nothing but lose ten pounds in a month and develop a disgusting smoking habit. Those kids in there? They need something much greater than anything I can give them—*they need a miracle* . . . and they need a miracle like every day. Sometimes, I dream of going to Connecticut and teaching the rich white kids there. All I'd have to battle against is soccer moms, bulimia, and everyone asking me how I wash my hair. But, I chose to teach in my city, this city that raised me . . . and I'm tired, and I'm not even considered a "real" teacher. I don't know how I would survive as a real teacher. But they do . . . on what, God knows. And, the worst thing, the worst thing is that all those kids in there are *me*. Brown skin, brown eyes, stuck. I can't even help my own people. Really revolutionary, huh?

It seems to me that this whole school system, not just here but the whole system is falling apart from under us and then there are these testing and accountability laws that have nothing to do with any real solutions and if we expect to stay some sort of grand nation for the next fifty years, we got another thing coming. *Because we're not teaching these kids how to be leaders.* We're getting them ready for jail! Take off your belt, take off your shoes, go back, go back, go back. We're totally abandoning these kids and we have been for thirty years and then we get annoyed when they're running around in the subway calling themselves bitches and niggas, we get annoyed when their math scores don't pair up to a five-year-old's in China, we get annoyed when they don't graduate in time. It's because we've abandoned them. And, I'm no different, I'm abandoning them too. *(Beat.)* I just need a break to be an actor, get health insurance, go on auditions, pay the fucking IRS. Sorry. Look, I'm sorry about the big grant from the Department of Ed but perhaps we could make it up somehow next year. I can't continue this program any longer, even if it is for our country's good. Bye! *(Light shift.)*

JANITOR *(Sings)*:
> *I'm gonna lay. Lay my head*
> *On some lonesome railroad line.*
> *Let that 2:19 train—*

Scene Eleven

(Outside of school.)

MS. SUN *(Sings.)*:
> *Ease my troubled mind—*

JEROME: Ms. Sun?

MS. SUN: Hi. Jerome.

JEROME: You singing? *(Beat.)* We were talking about you in the cafeteria. Had a power lunch. *(He laughs.)* Most of us were being assholes . . . sorry . . . bad thespians when we did that to you.

MS. SUN: You were the leader, do you know that, Jerome? Do you know that we teachers, we have feelings. And we try our best not to break in front of you all?

JEROME: Yeah, I know, my mom tells me that all the time.

MS. SUN: Listen to her, sweetheart, she's right. *(Beat.)* Look, the show is off. I'll be here next year, and we'll start again on another more tangible play, maybe even *Raisin in the Sun*. Now, if you'll excuse me, I have an audition to prepare for. *(She turns to leave.)*

JEROME: Ms. Sun, "The theatre is an expression of civilization . . ."

MS. SUN: What?

JEROME: I said, "The theatre is an expression of civilization. We belong to a great country which has spawned great playwrights: Shakespeare, Marlowe, Jonson, and even in our own time, Sheridan. The convicts will be speaking a refined, literate language and expressing sentiments of a delicacy they are not used to. It will remind them that there is more to life than crime, punishment. And we, this colony of a few hundred, will be watching this together. For a few hours we will no longer be despised prisoners and hated gaolers. We will laugh, we may be moved. We may even think a little. Can you suggest something else that would provide such an evening, Watkin?" *(Beat.)* Thank you.

MS. SUN: Jerome, I didn't know . . .

JEROME: . . . that I had the part of Second Lieutenant Ralph Clark memorized. I do my thang. Guess I won't be doing it this year though. Shoot, every teacher we have runs away. (*Beat.*)

MS. SUN: Listen, Jerome, you tell all your cafeteria buddies in there, OK, to have all their lines memorized from Acts One and Two and be completely focused when I walk into that room next week—that means no talking, no hidden conversations and blurting out random nonsense, no gum, and for crying out loud, no one should be drinking Red Bull.

JEROME: Aight. So you back?

MS. SUN: . . . Yeah, and I'm bad. (*She does some Michael Jackson moves.*)

JEROME: Miss, you really do need an acting job soon. (*Light shift.*)

JANITOR: Things are looking up for our little teaching artist. She got a new lease on life. Got on a payment plan with the IRS. Stopped smoking, ate a good breakfast, even took the early train to school this mornin'.

Scene Twelve

(*Classroom.*)

COCA: Miss, did you hear? We got a new teacher permanently. He's kinda . . . good!

MR. JOHNSON: What do we say when Ms. Sun walks in?

SHONDRIKA: Good morning, Ms. Sun.

MR. JOHNSON: Hat off, Jerome.

JEROME: Damn, he got attitude! (*Beat.*) I like that!

MS. SUN: Wow, wow. You guys are lookin' really, really good.

MR. JOHNSON: Alright, let's get in the formation that we created. First, the tableau.

MS. SUN (*Intimate*): Tableau, you got them to do a tableau.

MR. JOHNSON (*Intimate*): I figured you'd want to see them in a frozen non-speaking state for a while. Oh, Kaswan, Xiomara, and Brian are in the auditorium building the set.

MS. SUN (*Intimate*): Wow. This is amazing. Thank you.

MR. JOHNSON: Don't thank me. Thank Mrs. Kennedy, thank yourself, thank these kids. (*To class.*) And we're starting from the top, top, top. Only one more week left. Shondrika, let's see those fliers you're working on.

SHONDRIKA: I been done. "Come see *Our Country's Good* cuz it's for your *own* good."

MS. SUN: Beautiful, Shondrika. Let's start from the top. *(Sound of noise.)* What's all that noise out in the hallway?

BRIAN: Ay, yo. Janitor Baron had a heart attack in his closet last night. He died there.

COCA: What? He was our favorite . . .

JEROME: How old was he, like a hundred or something?

SHONDRIKA: I just saw him yesterday. He told me he would come to the show. He died all alone, y'all. *(Long pause.)*

MS. SUN: Thespians, I can give you some time . . .

JEROME: Nah, nah, we done wasted enough time. Let's rehearse. Do the show. Dedicate it to Janitor Baron, our pops, may you rest in peace.

MS. SUN: Alright, then, we're taking it from the top. Chris, that's you, sweetheart.

CHRIS: "A giant canoe drifts onto the sea, clouds billowing from upright oars. This is a dream that has lost its way. Best to leave it alone." *(Light shift.)*

JANITOR: My, My, My . . . them kids banded together over me. Memorized, rehearsed, added costumes, a small set, even added a rap or two at the end—don't tell the playwright! And, I didn't even think they knew my name. Ain't that something? I think I know what you saying to yourselves: I see dead people. Shoot, this is a good story, I wanna finish telling it! Plus, my new friend up here, Arthur Miller, tells me ain't no rules say a dead man can't make a fine narrator. Say he wish he thought of it himself. Meanwhile, like most teachers, even after-hours, Ms. Sun's life just ain't her own.

Scene Thirteen

(Sun's apartment. Night.)

MS. SUN *(On phone)*: Hi. This is Ms. Sun from Malcolm X High. I'm looking for Jose Guzman. He's a lead actor in *Our Country's Good* but I haven't seen him in class or after-school rehearsals since last week. My number is . . . *(Light shift. On phone:)* Hi. This is Ms. Sun again from Malcolm X High. I know it's probably dinner time but I'm still trying to reach Jose or his grandmother, Doña Guzman . . . *(Light shift. On phone:)* Hi. Ms. Sun here. Sorry, I know it's early and Mrs. Kennedy called last night, but the show is in less than two days . . . (*Light shift. On phone:*) Hi. It's midnight. You can probably imagine who this is. Does anyone answer this phone? Why have a machine, I mean, really . . . Hello, hello, yes. This is Ms. Sun from Malcom X High, oh . . . Puedo hablar con Doña Guzman. Ah Hah! Finally. Doña Guzman, ah ha, bueno, Ingles, OK. I've been working with your grandson now for six weeks on a play that you might have heard of. (*Beat.*) Un espectaculo . . . ah ha, pero Ingles, OK. I haven't seen him in a week and the show is in twenty-four hours. Mañana actually . . . Como? His brother was killed. Ave Maria, Lo siento, señora . . . How? Gangs . . . no, no, olvidate, forget about it. I'll send out prayers to you y tu familia. Buenas. (*She hangs up. Light shift.*)

JANITOR: Chin up now!

Scene Fourteen

(*School auditorium.*)

JANITOR: Cuz, it's opening night in the auditorium . . . I'm not even gonna talk about the logistics behind booking a high school auditorium for a night. Poor Mrs. Kennedy became a dictator.

MRS. KENNEDY: I booked this auditorium for the night and no one shall take it from me!!!

JANITOR: The stage is ablaze with fear, apprehension, doubt, nervousness, and, well, drama.

MR. JOHNSON: Anyone seen Jerome?

MS. SUN: Anyone seen Jerome?

COCA: His mom called him at four. Told him he had to babysit for the night.

MS. SUN: But, he's got a show tonight. Couldn't they find someone else? Couldn't he just bring the brats? Sorry.

MR. JOHNSON: What are we going to do now? His part is enormous.

PHILLIP: Ms. Sun?

MS. SUN: What, Phillip?

PHILLIP: . . . . I could do his part.

MS. SUN (*With apprehension*): OK, Phillip. You're on. Just remember . . .

PHILLIP: I know . . . someone is stealing my Mercedes LX one hundred Limited Edition.

MS. SUN: And . . . ?

PHILLIP: . . . Let my tongue be alive!

DOÑA GUZMAN: Doña Guzman, buenas. Buenas. Doña Guzman. The abuela de Jose.

MS. SUN: Jose, you made it. I'm so sorry about your brother.

JOSE: Yeah, I know. Where's my costume at? Buela, no ta allí.

DOÑA GUZMAN: Mira pa ya, muchacho. We had very long week pero he love this class. He beg me "mami, mami, mami, Our Country Goo, Our Country Goo, Our Country Goo." What can I do? I say yes. What I can do, you know.

MS. SUN: Oh señora. It's parents like you . . . thank you. Muchissima gracias por todo. Sit, sit in the audience, por favor.

MRS. KENNEDY: Ms. Sun, everyone is in place, there are about seventy-five people in that audience, including some parents I desperately need to speak to. We're glad you're back. Good luck!

SHONDRIKA: Miss, you want me to get the kids together before we start?

MS. SUN: Yeah, Shondrika, would you?

SHONDRIKA: Uh huh.

JANITOR: Now, here's a teacher's moment of truth. The last speech before the kids go on!

MS. SUN: Alright. This is it. We're here. We have done the work. We have lived this play inside and out. I officially have a hernia.

COCA (*Laughing*): She so stupid. I like her.

MS. SUN: We are a success . . . no matter what happens on this stage tonight. No matter which actors are missing or if your parents couldn't make it. I see before me twenty-seven amazingly talented young men and women. And I never thought I'd say this but I'm gonna miss you all.

SHONDRIKA: Ooh, she gonna make me cry!

MS. SUN: Tonight is your night.

COCA: Ooee, I'm nervous.

PHILLIP: Me too.

MS. SUN: I am too. That just means you care. Now let's take a deep breath in and out. In . . .

BRIAN: OHM! Nah, I'm just kiddin'. Keep going. Focus Focus.

MS. SUN: . . . and out. In and out.

SHONDRIKA: Miss, let's do this for Jose's brother and Janitor Baron.

MS. SUN: Oh, Shondrika, that's beautiful. OK, gentlemen, be with us tonight! PLACES. (*Light shift.*)

CHRIS: A giant canoe drifts out onto the sea, best to leave it alone.

COCA: This hateful hary-scary, topsy-turvy outpost. This is not a civilization.

XIOMARA: It's two hours, possibly of amusement, possibly of boredom. It's a waste, an unnecessary waste.

PHILIP: The convicts will feel nothing has changed and will go back to their old ways.

JOSE: You have to be careful OH DAMN. (*Nervously, he regains his thought.*) You have to be careful with words that begin with IN. It can turn everything upside down. INjustice, most of that word is taken up with justice, but the IN turns it inside out making it the ugliest word in the English language.

SHONDRIKA: Citizens must be taught to obey the law of their own will. I want to rule over responsible human beings.

PHILIP: Unexpected situations are often matched by unexpected virtues in people. Are they not?

BRIAN: A play should make you understand something new.

SHONDRIKA: Human beings—

XIOMARA: —have an intelligence—

BRIAN: —that has nothing to do—

JOSE: —with the circumstances—

COCA: —into which they were born.

CHRIS: THE END. (*Raucous applause. Light shift.*)

JANITOR: And the show did go on. A show that sparked a minirevolution in the hearts of everyone in that auditorium. Sure, some crucial lines were fumbled, and some entrances missed and three cell phones went off in the audience. But, my God, if those kids weren't a success.

Scene Fifteen

(*Backstage.*)

COCA: Miss, I did good, right? I did good? I did good. I did my lines right. I did my motivations right. I did good, right? I did good? I did good? I did good? (*Assured.*) I did good. I did good. I did good. Oh, Miss. I been wantin' to tell you. You know I'm pregnant, right? . . . Oh don't cry . . . Damn. Why do everyone cry when I say that? No, I wanted to tell you because my baby will not live like a prisoner, like a convict. I mean we still gotta put the baby-proof bars on the windows but that's state law. But that's it. We gonna travel, explore, see somethin' new for a change. I mean, I love the Bronx but there's more to life right? You taught me that.

"Man is born free" right . . . I mean, even though it's gonna be a girl. *(Beat.)* I know we was mad hard so thank you.

JOSE: Ms.? I don't know but, that class was still mad boring to me.

PHILLIP *(Audibly)*: Ms. Sun?! I wanna be an actor now!

SECURITY GUARD: O, O! We gotta clear out the auditorium. You can't be lolly-gagging in here. Clear it out. Clear it out. Clear it out! By the way, I never done seen dem kids shine like they did tonight. They did good. You did good. Now, you got ta clear it out!

MS. SUN *(To herself)*: Jerome . . . Jerome. *(Beat.)* "And we, this colony of a few hundred, will be watching this together, and we will no longer be despised prisoners and hated gaolers. We will laugh, we may be moved. We may . . ."

JEROME *(Gasping)*: ". . . even think a little!"

MS. SUN: Jerome? What are you doing here?

JEROME *(Panting)*: Mom came home early. Told me to run over here fast as I could . . . *(He realizes.)* I missed it. I missed it all. And I worked *hard* to learn my lines.

MS. SUN: Yes, you did, Jerome. You worked very hard. *(Long beat.)*

JEROME: You gonna be teaching here again next year?

MS. SUN: That's the plan. But, only tenth-graders again. Sorry.

JEROME: Oh no worries. I'm definitely gonna get left back for you. Psyche . . . Lemme go shout out to all them other thespians. You gonna be around?

MS. SUN: No, actually I have a commercial shoot early tomorrow morning.

JEROME: Really, for what?

MS. SUN *(Slurring)*: It's nothing . . .

JEROME: Aw, come on you could tell me.

MS. SUN: Really, it's nothing.

JEROME: Lemme know. Lemme know. Come on, lemme know.

MS. SUN: It's for Red Bull, damnit. Red Bull.

JEROME: Aight! Ms. Sun's finally getting paid. *(Light shift.)*

Scene Sixteen

JANITOR: And on to our third and final lesson of the evening: Something interesting happens when you die. You still care about the ones you left behind and wanna see how life ended up for them. Ms. Tam went back to the firm and wound up investing 2.3 million dollars towards arts in education with a strong emphasis on cultural diversity. Phillip proudly works as a conductor for the MTA. Shondrika Jones graduated *summa cum laude* from Harvard University and became the first black woman mayor of New York City. Alright now. Jose Guzman lost his life a week after the show when he decided to take vengeance on the Blood that killed his brother. Jerome. I might be omnipresent but I sure as heck ain't omniscient. Some of the brightest just slip through the cracks sometime. Do me a favor—you ever see him around town, tell him we thinkin' about him. And Ms. Sun. Well, she went on to win an NAACP Award, a Hispanic Heritage Award, a Tony Award, and an Academy Award. She was also in charge of restructuring of the nation's No Child Left Behind law *and* lives happily with her husband, Denzel Washington. His first wife never had a chance, poor thang. She still comes back every year to teach at Malcolm X High; oh, oh, oh, recently renamed Saint Tupac Shakur Preparatory. Times—they are a-changin'! (*He grabs his broom and sings. Lights shift as he walks towards a bright light offstage.*)

>*Trouble in mind*
>*It's true*
>*I had almost lost my way*

(*Offstage light brightens as if the heavens await. He knows to walk "into" it.*)

>*But, the sun's gonna shine*
>*In my back door someday*
>*That's alright, Lord. That's alright!*

End of Play

HOT 'N' THROBBING

by Paula Vogel

Rebecca Wisocky and Tom Nelis in the Signature Theatre Company
production of *Hot 'n' Throbbing* (Photo: © Carol Rosegg)

Some plays only daughters can write. Hot 'n' Throbbing *was written on a National Endowment for the Arts fellowship—because obscenity begins at home.*

PAULA VOGEL

Hot 'n' Throbbing *was produced in an outstanding New York revival at Signature Theatre company in 2004–05, when Vogel was playwright in residence in a season devoted to her work.* Vogel is best known for How I Learned to Drive, *which received the 1998 Pulitzer Prize for Drama, the Lortel, Drama Desk, Outer Critics Circle, and New York Drama Critics awards for best play, and also won her a second Obie Award.* Her new play, A Civil War Christmas, *was developed at Long Wharf Theatre during 2008.* Other plays include The Long Christmas Ride Home, The Mineola Twins, The Baltimore Waltz, Desdemona, And Baby Makes Seven, *and* The Oldest Profession. *Among her many honors are the 2004 Award for Literature from the American Academy of Arts and Letters, the Rhode Island Pell Award in the Arts, the Hull-Warriner Award, the Laura Pels Award, the Pew Charitable Trust Senior Award, a Guggenheim, an AT&T New Plays Award, the Rockefeller Foundation's Bellagio Center Fellowship, several National Endowment for the Arts fellowships, a McKnight Fellowship, a Bunting Fellowship, and the Governor's Award for the Arts. She is a fellow of the American Academy of Arts and Sciences. For many years Vogel directed Brown University's M.F.A. playwriting program. Currently she heads the playwriting department at the Yale School of Drama.*

Hot 'n' Throbbing by Paula Vogel was produced on March 28, 2005 by Signature Theatre Company in New York City, James Houghton, artistic director.

Cast:
CHARLENE . . . . .Lisa Emery
LESLIE ANN . . . . .Suli Holum
CLYDE . . . . .Elias Koteas
VOICE . . . . .Tom Nelis
CALVIN . . . . .Matthew Stadelmann
VOICE-OVER . . . . .Rebecca Wisocky
Director: Les Waters
Set Design: Mark Wendland
Costume Design: Ilona Somogyi
Lighting Design: Robert Werzel
Sound Design: Darron L. West

CHARACTERS

LESLIE ANN (aka Layla)—About fifteen.

CALVIN—About fourteen.

Both CALVIN and LESLIE ANN are voyeurs, as teenagers are, hooked on watching—TV, Nintendo, music videos, parents. They watch the live action.

CHARLENE—Over thirty-four. Wears Lina Wertmüller glasses. On-again, off-again member of Weight Watchers and Al-Anon.

CLYDE—Over thirty-four. Holes in dungarees. Almost a beer belly. (Note to actor: you've got to go gangbusters on this role. The bigger the asshole you are, the more we'll love you. Trust me on this.)

VOICE-OVER—Hard to tell her age under the red lights. VOICE-OVER narrates the script that CHARLENE is writing. She's CHARLENE's inner voice. She is a sex worker; at times bored with her job; at times, emphatically overacting, hoping to land a job in a legitimate film. Sometimes she dances. Her voice is amplified through a microphone. Her voice is sensual and husky.

THE VOICE—The first level—he's a character in CHARLENE's screenplay, a detective. At times he's a client in the strip joint, watching the VOICE-OVER with appreciation or jaded. His voice is also amplified through a microphone. He waits for the coroner to arrive and the forensics squad. While he waits, he reads CHARLENE's books—Irish dialects, or not—maybe just a flat Baltimore dialect. Sometimes he's the DJ—spinning the score of the play. He becomes CLYDE's alter ego. And he's also the director of a Gyno film gone bad.

SET

There are two play worlds in this piece. The stage lights and the red lights—reality, constructed as we know it, and a world that sometimes resembles the real, as we fantasize about it.

In the red light, the living room becomes the film set of Gyno Productions, a strip joint, a dance hall. The red light sets and the living room have this in common: they are stages for performance, for viewing.

Don't believe anything that happens in the red light.

The living room should look like the living room of a townhouse that cost $129,900 ten years ago. On a 9½% mortgage, no deposit down. Although we never see the upstairs, we know there are two bedrooms, one bath; downstairs there is a half bath. These preconstructed developments are called "empty nesters."

A few pieces. A sofa which folds out, in a tweed. Scotchgarded. A matching armchair. A coffee table. Television set, which may or may not be running erotica or police shows. The set is on constantly.

The door to the half bath. A front door. On the lower stage left, a large white office desk complex, with a secretary, holding a computer and printer. Along the wall behind this office island, where the dining room was supposed to be, is the ubiquitous sliding patio doors, looking out onto the parking lot in a Maryland suburb. Curtains premade, cream that sort of matches the tweed. And oh yes. Wall-to-wall shag.

An area outside the house for LESLIE ANN's class.

TIME

Ten years ago and the present.

Music notes:
I wrote this play in 1993 to several soundtracks: Janet Jackson's *Control* (particularly "Nasty") and Kaoma's *World Beat*. Also *Thriller* and *Silence of the Lambs*. Soundtapes from horror movies and Frank Sinatra. The main thing is that the music changes from erotic to terrorific.

In 1999 I wrote this to *Red Hot + Blue*.

Two props: **red light** where indicated. And music. Music always helps to get it up.

❖   ❖   ❖

*(In a growing **red light**, we see* LESLIE ANN *dressed in very tight pants and a hal-ter top, making suggestive stripper or vogue-ing movements. At end of* VOICE-OVER, *we see an older woman sitting at a computer screen, typing. Living room.)*

V.O.
"CUT TO: INTERIOR. NIGHT—VOICE-OVER:
   She was hot. She was throbbing. But she was in con-trol. Control of her body. Control of her thoughts. Control of . . . him.
   He was hot. He was throbbing. And out of control. He needed to be restrained. Tied Down. And taught a Lesson.
   But not hurt. Not too much. Just . . . enough. She would make his flesh red all over. She would raise the blood with her loving discipline. And she would make him wait. Make him beg. Make them both wait . . . until she was ready."

CHARLENE and VOICE-OVER: And she would make him wait. Make him beg.
CHARLENE *(Types)*: Sounds too male-bashing—"Make him ask?" Oh, fuck it. "Make him beg. . . . Make them both beg . . ."

*(Suddenly the bathroom door slams open in **stage light.** LESLIE ANN stands in front of the sink dressed as above.)*

LESLIE ANN *(Screams)*: MAAHM! WHERE'S YOUR EYELINER?
CHARLENE: ON THE TOP SHELF! NEXT TO THE BEN GAY!
CHARLENE *(Back to the flat narrative tone at the computer)*: "Until she was ready. Ready to release them both at the end of a long, hard night. Ready to heave herself to the other side of her love throes, ready to give it up—"
LESLIE ANN: MAAHM! CAN I USE YOUR MASCARA!!
CHARLENE: Sounds like upchucking. "Ready to pant, ready to scream, ready to die in each other's arms . . ."

(CHARLENE stops; calls out:)

   Leslie Ann! What are you doing?
LESLIE ANN: Puttin' on some make-up.

CHARLENE: Why are you putting on make-up.

LESLIE ANN: I already told you.

CHARLENE: No you did not tell me.

LESLIE ANN: I Did. So.

CHARLENE: Why are you wearing make-up.

LESLIE ANN: I'm Going. Out.

CHARLENE: Out Where?

LESLIE ANN: Out. To Lisa's. To Spend the Night.

CHARLENE: This is the first time I've heard about it.

LESLIE ANN: I Told You!

CHARLENE: I don't want you going to Lisa's.

LESLIE ANN: But Why?!

CHARLENE: Because.I.said.so.

LESLIE ANN: I'm goin'.

CHARLENE: Her parents do not supervise that young lady. You are not going to Lisa's.

LESLIE ANN: But all the girls will be there!

CHARLENE: You are not all the girls.

(*LESLIE ANN slams the bathroom door. We hear the water running. From offstage:*)

LESLIE ANN (*Off*): I'MM GOING!

(*CHARLENE sighs. Types.*)

(**Red light.** THE VOICE *and* VOICE-OVER *simulate/dance with the monologue below;* CALVIN *enters, sits on the sofa, reading a thick book while watching the* TV. LESLIE ANN *emerges from the bathroom in her tight pants. She slumps next to her brother, watching the* TV, *blasé and waiting.*)

V.O.

"VOICE-OVER CONTINUED:

He wanted to take her downtown and book her. Spread her, cuff her, and search every inch. He wanted to penetrate her secrets with his will. He wanted to gently pry open that sweet channel that leads to joy, and fill her with his passion until the dull pain faded into pleasure. Until her hips locked into a rhythm to match his. Together they would rock each other, clinging to each other as the tempo got faster, faster, faster and faster, faster and faster and faster, faster . . ."

(*THE VOICE and VOICE-OVER break and retreat to the background;* **lights** *go back to normal. CALVIN slumps on the sofa, LESLIE ANN confronts CHARLENE:*)

LESLIE ANN: You just don't care. You want me to stay in this boring house until I rot like you and four-eyes on the sofa over there.

CHARLENE: Leslie Ann, I am behind my schedule. I've got to get out forty pages by the first mail tomorrow morning, and I'm on page twenty-six.

LESLIE ANN: Layla. I am not answering to a dumb-shit name like Leslie Ann.

CALVIN (*Singing the Eric Clapton riff, and*): "LAY-LA!! YOU'VE GOT ME ON MY KNEES."

LESLIE ANN (*Appealing to her mother for help against Calvin*): MAH-HM.

CHARLENE (*Still typing*): I'm sorry, sweetie. Layla.

CALVIN: "LAY-LA! I'M BEGGING DARLIN' PLEASE."

LESLIE ANN: Shut up, creep!

CALVIN: Are you going out in those tight pants?

LESLIE ANN: What business is it of yours?

CALVIN: Those pants are so tight you can see your P.L.'s.

LESLIE ANN: Shut up.

(*CHARLENE looks up from typing with interest.*)

CHARLENE: What are P.L.'s?

(*No answer.*)

LESLIE ANN: Nothin'.

(*CHARLENE back to typing.*)

CALVIN: Hey, as long as I don't have to walk you up the aisle for some shotgun wedding, you trouncing around with your P.L.'s hanging out . . .

CHARLENE: P.L.'s?

LESLIE ANN: Why don't you just go beat-off in your room, you little pervo . . .

CHARLENE: Those pants are too tight. Did you spray-paint them on?

LESLIE ANN: Betcha wish you had my thighs, huh, Ma?

CHARLENE: We are not discussing the subject of my thighs. You are not leaving the house dressed like that.

LESLIE ANN: Huh. That's funny. Coming from you.

CHARLENE: What's that supposed to mean?

LESLIE ANN: Nothin'.

CHARLENE: I could kill your father for telling you kids a thing like that. I do not write *pornography*. There's a mile of difference between that and . . . *adult entertainment*. He wouldn't know the difference.

CALVIN: I think it's cool.

LESLIE ANN: Shut up, Toady. *(To CHARLENE:)* So what's the difference?

CHARLENE: What?

LESLIE ANN: What's the big difference between porno and—

CHARLENE: It's only pornography when women and gays and minorities try to take control of their own imaginations. No one blinks an eye when men do it.

LESLIE ANN: Uh-huh. So it's okay that you objectify my body because you happen to be female?

CHARLENE: Who have you been talking to?

CALVIN: It was in her Problems of Democracy class this week.

LESLIE ANN: Your movies are filled with girls my age as sex objects. Why don't you use women your own age?

CALVIN *(To his sister)*: 'Cause no one would pay to see that.

CHARLENE: You're going out of the house dressed like that and you blame me for making you a sex object?!

LESLIE ANN: That's right, that's right, blame the victim!

(CHARLENE counts to ten.)

CHARLENE: I know what you're doing. Using this as a ploy for me to lose my temper. And it's not working, Leslie Ann. You are not going to Lisa's. You are staying home and reading a book.

(LESLIE ANN stalks to her mother's bookshelves; THE VOICE suddenly gets interested. He'll start to peruse the books.)

LESLIE ANN: Books like the porno you read?

CHARLENE: I'd rather have you read Henry Miller or D.H. Lawrence than watch *Texas Chain Saw Massacre*.

LESLIE ANN: *Texas Chain Saw Massacre* is a lot less boring.

V.O.
Come on, Charlene. Twenty-six pages.

CHARLENE: This is not about me. You will not fling . . . the way I. make. a. living into my face every time I. give. you. a. directive. The way I put food on the plate, and Nikes on the feet. You are not leaving this house, period, young lady. I want you to go upstairs to your room and do some homework for a change. Your grades last quarter were a disgrace.

LESLIE ANN: Calvin gets to go out.

CHARLENE: Calvin has a 3.75. Calvin can go out all he wants on a Friday night. You are staying home and opening up a book. You'll like it. *Moby-Dick.* I loved that book.

CALVIN: Her book report's due Monday.

V.O.
(*Calling*)
Charlene.

CHARLENE: You children can read quietly in your rooms. I've got to get this section done. Go on upstairs and open up your books.

CALVIN: The only thing Leslie Ann wants to open is her P.L.'s

CHARLENE: Calvin! Quit picking on your sister!

LESLIE ANN: Get your little tattletale nose out of my P.L.'s, you creep!

CHARLENE: I'VE HAD IT! What are you talking about? Leslie Ann?

LESLIE ANN: Ask Calvin. Go ahead, little brother, tell Mom what you've been calling me.

CHARLENE: Calvin?

(*No response.*)

I asked you a question.

CALVIN: P.L.'s are a name for a girl's . . . you know.

LESLIE ANN: It's not very nice. You know, for an honor-roll creep, you sure use some nice language.

CHARLENE: When I was growing up, I didn't have a room of my own. And so I was determined that my children would each have their own privacy. Your mother sleeps on a convertible sofa that has to be made up each morning so you can have your own space. I want you both to go upstairs to your rooms, if you can't be quiet and act normal down here.

LESLIE ANN: Some privacy. The walls are paper-thin. How can I concentrate when all I can hear is four-eyes beating off?

CALVIN: I do not! You have the mouth of a slut, Leslie Ann!

LESLIE ANN: You beat off! In the catcher's mitt Daddy gave you for Christmas! I can feel the walls shaking!—

(*VOICE-OVER tosses a leather catcher's mitt to* THE VOICE.)

CHARLENE (*Suddenly interested, making notes*): Catcher's mitt. Open Window. Show Clipboard. Notes: Leather Catcher's mitt—

CALVIN: Mind Your Own Business!

LESLIE ANN: That's not what Dad meant when he said practice. Catching pop-up flies—

CALVIN: Shut up!—

LESLIE ANN: That's why you wear glasses, Calvin. Nobody else in this family does, little brother. 'Cause you violate yourself.

CALVIN: Mom wears glasses!

(*Startled, the two teenagers suddenly look at their mother with a horrifying new idea.* CHARLENE, *oblivious, stares into her computer screen, typing with a vengeance.* THE VOICE *fists the catcher's mitt. The siblings stop and erupt in laughter.*)

LESLIE ANN: Shut up, pervo!

CALVIN: Musta learned it from you, P.L.—

LESLIE ANN: Quit calling me that. Little brother. Little brother.

CALVIN: Quit it.

LESLIE ANN: Hey, little brother. Help me with my book report, will you?

CALVIN: Uh uh. I'm engrossed in my own book.

(*LESLIE ANN looks at the title.*)

LESLIE ANN: "I'm engrossed in my own book."

(*Looks at the book, loses his place.*)

Ulysses. Heavy. Come on, you've already read *Moby-Dick*.

CALVIN: Last year. For AP English.

LESLIE ANN: Five pages.

CALVIN: No. I'm not supposed to write it for you.

LESLIE ANN: You scratch my back, little brother, and . . . and I might just learn you something interesting—

CALVIN: Yeah?

(THEY *both look at their mother, deep into her typing.*)

LESLIE ANN: Yeah. So you won't haveta hang in the bushes outside the house. You do, don'tcha?

(CALVIN *is suddenly quiet, beet red.*)

(*Yeah. I thought that was you.*)

(LESLIE ANN *suddenly wrestles her brother into a lock on the sofa, on top of him, his arm twisted.*)

CALVIN (*Hissed*): Shit!

LESLIE ANN (*Whispered*): Watching me undressing. In the bushes. Straight-A student. Little Freak Fairy reading *U-lysses*. . . . I'm going to teach, you, a, lesson—

(CHARLENE *types on.*)

CALVIN: You're.An.Asshole!

LESLIE ANN: What.Did.You.Call.Me?

CALVIN: Stop it!

LESLIE ANN: I'll stop when I. feel. like. it.

(THE VOICE *finds a passage in one of the books and reads it to* VOICE-OVER *as* LESLIE ANN *torments her brother.*)

THE VOICE: "Lolita, light of my life, fire of my loins. My sin, my soul. Lo-lee-ta."

(*There is the sound of an automobile horn. Loud.*)

THE VOICE: "Lo. Lee. Ta."

(The horn imitates THE VOICE. *Three times.* LESLIE ANN *jumps up from the sofa.)*

LESLIE ANN: That's my ride! Mom! I've got to go.

CHARLENE: You are not leaving this house. Young lady.

LESLIE ANN: You said I could!

CHARLENE: When! When did I say that?

*(*VOICE-OVER *lights a cigarette, bored. She puffs.* THE VOICE *reads.)*

LESLIE ANN: Last night. I asked you. And you said you didn't care what I did.
So I told Lisa yes.

CHARLENE: Is that Lisa outside? I don't like you riding with her. Go out and
tell her I. said. no.

*(*LESLIE ANN *stomps to the door, pulls it open. We hear loud angry music from
Lisa's car:)*

LESLIE ANN *(To car)*: Gimme. Five! I'll be right there!

*(*LESLIE ANN *closes the door.)*

You said you need peace and quiet. I'm going to give you some. It's an
overnight. A slumber party. I'll be back tomorrow.

V.O.
Bye Bye.

CHARLENE: We are going to have a little chat. Right here. Right now.

LESLIE ANN: Can this wait?

CHARLENE: No. It cannot. I want you to answer a question: where do you
think you will be in ten years' time?

LESLIE ANN: God, Mom. I don't know. Someplace.

CHARLENE: Do you imagine some glamorous job? At the mall? At minimum
wage? Because that's all you're going to get if you don't graduate high
school and go to college.

LESLIE ANN: I don't care; as long as it's far away from here.

CHARLENE: Leslie Ann, you have a mind. And I just want you to use it. You can
do anything you want to do if you put your mind to it. You want to go far
away from here? Read the goddamn book that's due on Monday. *Moby-
Dick.*

LESLIE ANN: Are we through now with our mother/daughter moment?

CHARLENE: You march upstairs. Right. this. minute. You are not leaving this house—

(*Once more, the car horn trumpets: Lo-lee-ta.*)

LESLIE ANN: I'll see you!

(*LESLIE ANN rushes to the door, exits, and slams it behind her. There is a pause. CALVIN watches CHARLENE. She returns to her computer.*)

CHARLENE: Oh, Jesus. I could use a cigarette.
CALVIN: You quit smoking.
CHARLENE: I know. I miss it at times like this. Jesus Christ. Page . . . twenty-seven.

CALVIN:	V.O.
Thirteen to go.	Thirteen to go.

CHARLENE: What's on your agenda for tonight?
CALVIN: I'm staying here with you, Mom.
CHARLENE: Nothing's going to happen.
CALVIN: I know.
CHARLENE: Because if you want to go out, you should just go ahead—
CALVIN: I don't wantto. I'm just going to sit here, quietly, and read *Moby-Dick* again, all right?
CHARLENE: I don't want you to write Leslie Ann's book report for her.
CALVIN: All right.

(*CHARLENE stares at the computer screen. CALVIN stares at her. CHARLENE looks up and sees him staring.*)

V.O.
"What are you looking at?"

THE VOICE: What are you—

V.O.
"looking—"

THE VOICE:—looking at?

(*CALVIN looks down at his book, quickly. CHARLENE goes back to the screen. CALVIN stares at her again. CHARLENE tentatively starts to type. Stops. Starts again. Stops.*)

V.O.
"What are you looking at?"

CALVIN: Writer's block, Mom?

CHARLENE: I'm running out of words.

CALVIN: How about . . .

THE VOICE (Whispered):—Throbbing—

CALVIN: —Throbbing?

CHARLENE: Don't make fun of me, son. My writing puts food in your mouth.

CALVIN: I wasn't making fun! I was just trying to help!

CHARLENE: I know. I'm sorry. Maybe after you go to college, you'll be able to be a real writer.

CALVIN: You're the writer in the family.

CHARLENE: Oh Lord. Not this—this is just . . . junk.

CALVIN (*In a rush*): No, it's not—I really like—

(*CALVIN covers his mouth.*)

CHARLENE: Calvin Lee Dwyer. Have you been reading the files on my personal computer? That's not for you to read!

(*Beat.*)

How did you get my password!

CALVIN: I just wanted to read it.

CHARLENE: There is no privacy in this house.

(*She can't help herself.*)

Do you really think—it's any good?

CALVIN: I really like the detective, Mama. He's cool.

CHARLENE: I'm kinda proud of the detective.

CALVIN: Mama, I think you can really write.

CHARLENE: Oh honey—not really. Not yet. Someday, maybe, when you kids are all taken care of—someday. I'd like to think I have one good book in me.
  . . . You could be a writer too.

CALVIN: I don't want to be anything. And I'm not going to college.

CHARLENE: We'll see.

CALVIN: To Prince George's Community? With all the geeks?

CHARLENE: That's where I went, remember. But I meant maybe somewhere far away from home. It would be good for you to get away.

CALVIN: Leslie Ann's the one who wants to go away.

CHARLENE: I worry sometimes that she'll get as far as the backseat of a car.

CALVIN: I don't think so. I think she's scared to death . . .

CHARLENE: Why?

CALVIN: No reason.

(*Pause.*)

CHARLENE: Okay.

Page twenty-seven . . . I need some words that pack a punch.

CALVIN: So how about throbbing?

CHARLENE: I've got throbbing all over the page. There are just so many ways to say throbbing . . .

V.O.
—"Pulsating—"

THE VOICE:—"Beating—"

V.O.
"Heaving—"

THE VOICE:—"Battering—"

CHARLENE: Wait a moment! Cut—Cut—Cut!! That's it, Charlene—"Cut To—"

(**Light** *changes to* **red**. THE VOICE *stands with a catcher mitt.*)

V.O.
"CUT TO: EXTERIOR. In the bushes outside the house. Nighttime. We see a YOUNG BOY, not yet old enough to shave. He is peering up through the bushes at:"

"CUT TO: BOY's POINT OF VIEW. We see an attractive older WOMAN, full hipped, through her bedroom window, looking at herself in the mirror. The WOMAN removes her glasses, and gazes at her image."

(CHARLENE *removes her glasses at the computer.* CALVIN *stares at her.*)

V.O.
"CUT TO: THE YOUNG BOY. Standing now. He watches as she strokes her face. We see him raise his hand, which holds a baseball mitt. He strokes the leather with his free hand, softly feeling the texture."

(THE VOICE *follows the instructions of* VOICE-OVER.)

V.O.
"CLOSE-UP. On the mitt. THE BOY fists it several times, then raises the glove to his face, breathing in the leather."

(CALVIN *stares at* THE VOICE *hypnotically.* THE VOICE *tosses the catcher's mitt to* CALVIN, *who dons it and follows the* VOICE-OVER.)

V.O.
"CUT TO: THE WOMAN, who begins to feel her own body.
     CUT TO: YOUNG BOY, who begins to run the glove across his chest.
     CUT TO: THE WOMAN, who closes her eyes and runs her fingers over her rounded hips, and down into her waist-line."

(*Bored,* THE VOICE *picks up* Moby-Dick *from the coffee table.*)

V.O.
"CUT TO: CLOSE-UP on leather mitt, rubbing up and down THE BOY'S blue-jeaned thighs—
     CUT TO:—"

(THE VOICE *begins to read from* Moby-Dick; CHARLENE *types wildly from his dictation.*)

THE VOICE: "Yes, Ishmael, the same fate may be thine. Yes, there is death in this business of whaling—. But what then? Methinks that what they call my shadow here on earth is my true substance."

(**Lights** change back. CALVIN sits on the sofa, fondling his catcher's mitt.)

CHARLENE: What the heck was that? Shoot. I've lost it. "Cut to—Cut to . . .
    cut to . . ."
CALVIN: Something wrong, Mom?
CHARLENE: I don't know. I'm distracted, I guess. Other voices are coming in
    over the airwaves.

V.O.
(*Smoking*)
"Cigarette. Lo-lee-ta. Cigarette."

CHARLENE: Concentrate, Charlene. "Cut to—"

V.O.
"Do the dishes. Dishes. Dishes."

CHARLENE: Oh, God. Time for a break. Save—Shut Down. Ah.

(CHARLENE crosses to Calvin and sits beside him.)

CHARLENE: You're not worried, are you Calvin?
CALVIN: Nope.
CHARLENE: Because I can take care of myself.
CALVIN: Uh-huh.

(CHARLENE brushes the hair back off his forehead.)

CHARLENE: I'm sorry you saw . . . what you saw.
CALVIN: Yeah. But it was a good thing I was there.
CHARLENE: Yes. It was. A very good thing. But it's never going to happen again.
CALVIN: I know.

(CHARLENE goes to hug him; he stiffens, moves away, embarrassed.)

CHARLENE: How did you get to be so big so fast? You know what I miss? I miss
    the times when you would come inside the house, as a little boy, with a

scraped knee or in some . . . pain . . . and you'd come in, crying, and let
me hold you. Boys grow up into men so quickly and we never get to just
hold you. Now you always squirm away.
CALVIN: God, Mom.

(*Pause.*)

CHARLENE: Calvin?
CALVIN: Yeah?
CHARLENE: Where does your sister go on weekends?
CALVIN: Ya know. Out.
CHARLENE: Out where? Where does she go with Lisa?

(**Red light** *strikes the area outside of the sliding doors.* LESLIE ANN *and* VOICE-
OVER *do a slow, expert teasing dance for an imaginary male clientele.* CALVIN *parallels their movements.*)

CALVIN: Well . . . see, first they hitch to Mount Pleasant with some suburban
father-type in his Volvo station wagon. Then they hop on the No. 42 bus
to the Corner of Florida and Connecticut. They get off by the bus stop,
and walk two blocks east. They check to make sure they're not being followed. Then they duck into this joint, it's all red brick on the front, with
the windows blacked out, except for the Budweiser sign. The door is
solid metal. They nod to the bouncer, who always pats Leslie Ann on the
fanny. They trot behind the curtains in back of the bar, quick, see, so the
clientele won't see them in their street clothes. And backstage, Al, who's
the owner, yells at 'em for being late.
     And they slip into this toilet of a dressing room, where they strip off
their jeans and sweats in such a hurry, they're inside out, thrown in the
corner. And they help each other into the scanty sequins and the five-
inch heels.
     And they slink out together in the red light as the warm-up act, and
wrap their legs around the poles. And Al keeps an eye out on the guys,
who haven't got a buzz on yet, so they're pretty docile, 'cause the girls are
jailbait. And Leslie Ann and her best friend Lisa shake it up for only one
set. And before you know it, the twenty minutes are up, just a few half-
hearted grabs, and they're doing full splits to scoop up the dollar bills
that will pay for the midnight double feature at the Mall and the burgers
afterwards at Big Bob's.

(**Red light** out on LESLIE ANN and VOICE-OVER. CHARLENE, who has been mesmerized, breaks out of her reverie.)

CHARLENE: Calvin!

CALVIN: Jesus, mom. You're not the only one who can make up stories. Take a joke, will ya? She probably hangs out at Lisa's being dumb.

(Pause.)

CHARLENE: Don't you have a nice girl you can take to the movies tonight?

CALVIN: I don't know any nice girls.

CHARLENE: Well, how about calling up some of your friends and doing something with them?

CALVIN: All the boys in school are creeps.

CHARLENE: But it's Friday night!

CALVIN: So?

CHARLENE: Calvin, sweetie, it's not right for you to spend every weekend in the house.

CALVIN: Am I bothering you?

CHARLENE: That's not the point. You're never going to meet someone slumped on the sofa.

CALVIN: I'm not slumping.

CHARLENE: You are. Sit up straight; you're wearing the springs down that way. When I was your age—

CALVIN (Agonized): What.Do.You.Want From me?

CHARLENE: I just want you to have some *Fun*.

CALVIN: I'm going.

CHARLENE: Where?

CALVIN: What does it matter? I'm going. Out. I can't even sit in the privacy of my own home—

CHARLENE: Now wait, sweetie, I don't want you to take it like that—

CALVIN: Jesus. I'm gone.

(CALVIN stalks to the door, opens it, and slams out.)

CHARLENE (Guiltily): Have a nice time! Don't stay out. Too late . . .

(CHARLENE goes back to the computer and turns it on.)

Boot up. Password.

(CHARLENE *waits. Pauses.* CHARLENE *stealthily unlocks her desk drawer, takes out a pack of cigarettes. Waits. Carefully selects one. Fishes out matches from the drawer.*)

CHARLENE AND VOICE-OVER:
Our little secret, Charlene.

(CHARLENE *lights up. Starts to type.*)

V.O.
"CUT TO: CLOSE-UP:
She tentatively licked the tip, a gentle flick of the tongue, before perching it on her lips. Her head instinctively reared back, before its acid taste. She gently sucked, letting it linger in her mouth—she gently sucked—"

(CHARLENE *pauses, reads what she wrote, inhales and exhales.* THE VOICE *reads* Moby-Dick *aloud:*)

THE VOICE: "The Red Tide—"

V.O.
"She . . . sucked . . . the tip . . . she . . ."

THE VOICE: "The red tide now poured from all sides of the monster like brooks down a hill."
      "His tormented body rolled not in brine but in blood, which bubbled and seethed. . . . Jet after jet of white smoke was shot from the sphiracle of the whale. . . . Hauling in upon his crooked lance, Stubb straightened it again and again, then again and again sent it into the whale . . ."
CHARLENE: Jesus. I can't use that crap. Erase. "Cut to—"

V.O.
"CUT TO: EXTERIOR. THE BOY, in the bushes, watches THE WOMAN smoke. His tongue gently flicks his own lips in response."

(*We see* CLYDE *at the picture window, easing himself against the sliding glass window, watching Charlene.*)

V.O.
"CUT TO: INTERIOR. THE WOMAN, in front of the mirror, oblivious to being watched. She arches her throat and releases a jet of smoke."

(CLYDE *at the window disappears.*)

V.O.
"CUT TO: EXTERIOR. Now we see THE BOY begin to manipulate himself with the gloved hand.

CUT TO: INTERIOR. THE WOMAN hears a noise, and turns to the window.

CUT TO: THE BOY begins to grow urgent in his need, and begins pounding the cupped glove—"

(*There is a pounding at the door;* CHARLENE *is puzzled.*)

V.O.
"Pounding, pounding the cupped glove—"

(*The pounding at the door grows louder.*)

CHARLENE (*With some fear*): Who is that?
CLYDE (*Offstage*): Special Delivery! I got a package for you, Charlene—
CHARLENE: CLYDE?!! Goddamn you—I'm calling the police—

(CHARLENE *races to her Trimline on the desk; she dials 911 but we hear nothing but clicks.*)

CHARLENE: Shit! What did you do to the phone?
CLYDE (*Offstage*): You don't need the phone, baby. I'm here to reach out and touch someone—
CHARLENE: Goddamn! You're drunk again, aren't you? Get away from here, Clyde.

CLYDE (*Pounding, offstage*): Open the fuckin' door. Now. I wanta talk to you.

(CHARLENE, *with a grim calm, reaches into the desk drawer and pulls out a gun. She checks the ammo. We hear a click—possibly amplified.*)

CHARLENE: I'm working.
CLYDE: I asked! Nicely!

(*We hear the door being violently kicked.* CHARLENE *sits back down at her computer, and waits.*)

V.O.
(*Urgently*)

"CUT TO: EXTERIOR. THE BOY thrusts himself against the front door—you can get out of this—

CUT TO: INTERIOR. THE WOMAN, on the other side of the door, presses against it—stay calm, keep your eyes open, stay calm—"

CLYDE (*Offstage*): —I'm Coming! I'm Coming In—

(*With another savage kick, the door flies open.* CLYDE *flies in, disheveled, drunk.* CLYDE *grins, sings.*)

"I hear you KNOCKIN' But You Can't Come In!"
CHARLENE: Get out of here, Clyde. Your last chance.

(CHARLENE *pretends to type.*)

CLYDE: I'm here to audition. To Give You. New Material. The E-Rot-icly Un-Employed. To get your undivided attention. Write this up, Baby.
Oh my god! Is that a doorknob in my pocket or am I just happy to see you?
Baby? Stop looking at the goddamn screen. Look. At. Me.

(*Before* CHARLENE *can stop him,* CLYDE *pulls the computer plug from the outlet.*)

CLYDE: Ta-DA! And Now! The Burlesque Theatre of Langley Park! Presentin'! SEX—ON—WELFARE!

(CLYDE *begins to strip and grind, taking off his T-shirt, and unzipping his dungarees, while singing the trumpet "stripper theme."*)

CLYDE: "BWAH-BWAH-BWAH!!! BWAH-BWAH-BWAH-BWAHHH!!! BWAH-BWAH-BWAH!! BWAH-BWAH-BWAH-BWAH—bwah— **BWAHH!!**—bum-bum **BWAHH!!**—bum-bum **BWAHH**—bum-bum **BWAHH**—bum-bum . . ."

(*At this point,* CLYDE *has turned his back on Charlene, and has lowered his pants and underwear, mooning her.* CHARLENE *stands, calmly, with the gun in her hand.*)

CHARLENE: I want. you. to stand. Very Still. Don't move, Clyde. Don't. Move.

(CLYDE, *seeing the gun, stops, still bent over, exposed.*)

CHARLENE: I don't want to kill you. By accident. I'm just going to shoot you just enough to send you to the hospital.

(CLYDE, *panicked, begins to rush for the door.*)

CLYDE: Jesus Christ—Char-LENE!!

(**Red lights on.** *There is the sound of an amplified gunshot. Very slowly, in stylized motion,* CLYDE *grabs his behind, and writhes, a slow, sexual grind of agony. A male porn star* VOICE *dictates:*)

THE VOICE: He was Hot. He was throbbing. He was Hot He was Throbbing. He was Hot He was throbbing He was hot and throbbing He was hot He was throbbing He was hot and throbbing He was hot He was throbbing He was hot and throbbing He was hot He was throbbing—

(CHARLENE *hides the gun. When the* **regular lights** *come up,* CLYDE *is lying on his stomach on the sofa.* CHARLENE, *holding towels, stands over him.* CLYDE *is crying.*)

CLYDE: Jesus H. Jesus H. Christ. I can't believe it. My own wife. I can't believe—

CHARLENE: Hold still. Calm down and quit wiggling like that. I can't see anything with you moving around—

CLYDE: Am I gonna haveta be in a wheelchair? For Life?

CHARLENE: I said. hold. still. I don't want any blood on the couch.

(CHARLENE *regards the wound.* CHARLENE *regards Clyde's butt.*)

CHARLENE: Yup. I gotcha, all right. A flesh wound. How does it feel?

CLYDE: How does it feel? How does it *feel*?! Like someone rammed a poker in
my flesh! That's how it feels!

CHARLENE: Don't move.

V.O.
—"Don't—"

THE VOICE:—"Don't Move."—

V.O.
(*Seductive whisper*)
FLASHBACK—FIVE YEARS AGO.

(**RED LIGHT** *comes on.* CLYDE *turns on his back, and* CHARLENE *straddles him.* THEY
begin to make out. THE VOICE *turns into* THE DETECTIVE.)

THE VOICE: It's a Friday Night. And it's the first heat wave in the nation's capital. Oh yeah—And it's a full moon. There's just two things to do on a
night like this: make like cats in heat under the AC on high, or shoot
somebody. And so the crime index climbs as high as the humidity.
The waiting's the worst part. Bodies and Mess. Mess and Bodies. 'Cause
I'm the dumb sucker who turns up first on the scene, and then waits
around until the lab guys show up to pick up the bodies and clean up the
mess.

V.O.
(*Back to her screenplay/dominatrix voice*)
"CONTINUING:—"

(*Abrupt **lighting change**: back to bright stage light.* CHARLENE *stands over*
CLYDE, *now on his stomach again, with bandages, tape and antiseptic.*)

CHARLENE: I said Don't Move! You're gonna mess up my sofa! Thank God for Scotchgard . . . There. That's better. You might not need stitches.

THE VOICE (*Reading*): "The red tide now poured from all sides of the monster like brooks down a hill."

(*CHARLENE pours on liquid from the bottle; CLYDE roars.*)

CLYDE: AAHHH!!

CHARLENE: It's a Flesh Wound! It's not supposed to sting like that—

CLYDE: Don't. You. Tell. Me. How It Feels! You Ain't My Butt!!

CHARLENE: I can't do anything with you when you get in moods like this.

(*CHARLENE efficiently bandages him; tears the tape with her teeth. She whiffs the air.*)

CHARLENE: Hooey! God, Clyde. You can't afford ta buy yourself BVD's, but you can throw it away on alcohol.

CLYDE: It's my money.

CHARLENE: I'm getting you some coffee before we go to the hospital. Sit up slowly. And sit on the towel.

(*Like a man missing a limb, CLYDE tentatively feels his behind. Slowly, he pulls up his underwear. He tries to pull up his jeans, winces, and leaves himself undone. He sits up penitently, like a little boy, on the towel, favoring his good cheek.*)

CHARLENE (*Offstage*): There's no milk in the house! So you haveta drink it black!

(**Red light.** *While THE VOICE speaks, CLYDE slowly reaches into the back of his pants, wetting his hand with the blood. Hypnotically, he stares at the red on his hand, either getting faint or aroused. CLYDE closes his eyes, bringing his hand closer to his face. He breathes in the scent of the blood, and then almost tastes his hand. He wipes his hand on the sofa.*)

THE VOICE: What the TV dramas don't show you is that we spend most of our days sitting on our butts, drinking stale coffee. And when we do get to the crime scene, the trails and traces are so stupid a kid could tell you who done it. And the action has come and gone long before you turned up. And so you feel like one big limp dick. That's why some of the guys round up the usual suspects who didn't do it, take 'em downtown, and backhand them—to feel some warm flesh on your flesh, the hot blood on the back of your hand—because a crime scene is a cold, cold place.

(*THE VOICE commands:*)

Action!

(*CHARLENE hands coffee to Clyde.*)

CHARLENE: Jesus! How did you get blood all over?
CLYDE: I guess I sprayed a bit when . . . the shot . . . hit me.
CHARLENE: Drink this. Slowly. Then we'll go.
CLYDE: Okay.

(*CLYDE and CHARLENE sit at opposite ends of the sofa, sipping their coffee.*)

CLYDE: Good coffee.

(*CHARLENE looks suspiciously at him.*)

CLYDE: You're looking good. Filling out a little bit?
CHARLENE: I've quit smoking. Or I'm trying to—
CLYDE: It looks good on you . . . really . . . So—this is like old times, huh? Us sitting up, drinking coffee—
CHARLENE: Forget it, Clyde. Whatever you're thinking, forget it.
THE VOICE: CUT! Take two.
CLYDE: So this is like old times, huh. Us sitting up, drinking coffee—
CHARLENE: Forget it, Clyde. Whatever you're thinking, forget it.

(*Pause.*)

How does it feel?
CLYDE: The more coffee I drink, the more it throbs.
THE VOICE: I want you to—
CHARLENE: "I want you to *feel* it. Maybe then you'll—"
THE VOICE: —*listen.*"

(CHARLENE *just hears what she has said.*)

V.O.
Jesus. That sounds like something he would say.

(*Pause.*)

CLYDE: Say, uh, what happened to the—?

CHARLENE: Don't worry about the gun. Just behave yourself, and it won't go off.

CLYDE: Call me old-fashioned but I prefer the days when havin' protection in the house meant your supply of birth control.

CHARLENE: You're a laugh riot tonight.

CLYDE: Seriously, Charlene, I don't like to think about you havin' guns 'n' shit in the house—

CHARLENE: It's my house.

(CLYDE *stands with some pain.*)

CHARLENE: Where are you going?

CLYDE: I can't talk to you when you're like this.

THE VOICE: CUT! Take three.

CLYDE: I came to talk and you're shutting me out.

CHARLENE: You're about ten years too late.

THE VOICE: Jump Cut!

CLYDE: So. How's work?

CHARLENE:	V.O.
I'm behind deadline.	She's behind deadline.

CLYDE: How are . . . the "gals?" At work?

CHARLENE: The women?

CLYDE: Right. Are you starting to turn a profit at—? I don't remember the name of your production company.

CHARLENE: Gyno Productions.

CLYDE: Right. I knew it rhymed with wino. I never can remember it.

CHARLENE: It's the root for "woman."

V.O.
In Greek.

CLYDE: I can see that's important. But it's still hard to remember.

CHARLENE: Yeah. It is. But we just designed a new logo, for our stationery and business cards—want to see it?

CLYDE: Sure.

(CHARLENE *goes to her desk, opens the middle drawer, and takes out a business card, which she gives to* CLYDE.)

CLYDE: Wow. Charlene Dwyer. Story Editor, Gyno Productions. They promoted you. That's really nice, Charlene.

CHARLENE: No, not that—what do you think of our new mascot?

CLYDE: Well, I'm not sure—what is that thing on here? What is it doin'—it's dancing?

CHARLENE: It's a Rhinoceros—"Rosie the Rhino." She's dancing.

CLYDE: Uh-huh. That's cute. But, don't you. think. Those pink . . . pasties . . . are goin' a bit far?

(CLYDE *looks closer.*)

CLYDE: And the G-String? A Rhino in a G-string does not inspire me.

CHARLENE: I like the G-string.

V.O.
It was my idea.

CHARLENE: And it's supposed to be . . . funny. For women.

(*Beat.*)

Are you done with your coffee?

CLYDE: Look, do you want to talk? Talking involves disagreement. If I don't tell you what I'm thinking, even if it's ignorant, how can I learn anything about what you're doing when you say you're working.

CHARLENE: Yeah? Like what do you want to know?

CLYDE: Well—do you ever think you're gonna run out of words when you're writing like that?

V.O.
She thinks about it all the time.

(CHARLENE stares at Clyde.)

CHARLENE: I think about it all the time.

(Beat.)

    Can I have my business card back, please?
CLYDE: I'd like to keep it, if I may. As a . . . memento. I know it has . . . your
    work number on it—but I won't use it. Okay?
CHARLENE: Right.

V.O.
Shit, that was dumb, Charlene.

(CHARLENE sits, tensely.)

CLYDE: Just relax, will ya? So where do all these words come from?
CHARLENE: I don't know. When I really get going, it's like a trance—it's not me
    writing at all. It's as if I just listen to voices and I'm taking dictation.
THE VOICE: Sometimes when I'm waiting for the body bags, I'll think—she's
    young enough to be my daughter, or maybe she's someone's mother—
    And they talk to me. Frankly, it scares the shit out of me.
CLYDE: Doesn't that spook you? I mean, whose voices are these? Who's in
    control?

V.O.
But she was in control.

(THE VOICE and VOICE-OVER stare at each other, aroused.)

CHARLENE: Well, they're the characters speaking. They kind of . . . sit in the
    living room and talk to me. I mean, I know it's me, but I have to get into
    it. Right now I'm writing something with this detective who goes to in-
    vestigate a homicide and he meets a woman. And there's this incredible
    physical attraction that happens at the crime scene.

(THE VOICE and VOICE-OVER start to make out behind the sofa.)

CLYDE: Uh-huh. I used to think that porno flicks were all pictures and no
    words—

CHARLENE: Look, Clyde, I don't write *porno*. I didn't appreciate you telling
　　Leslie Ann that.

CLYDE: Well, what do you call it? What was the title of your last opus? *Pulp
　　Friction?!* So what is that—Bergman?

CHARLENE: It's my homage to Uma Thurman.

CLYDE: Uh-huh.

CHARLENE: Gyno Productions is a feminist film company dedicated to pro-
　　ducing women's erotica.

CLYDE: Erotica is just a Swedish word for porn, Charlene.

CHARLENE: What's the use?

CLYDE: Look, this is what happens every time I challenge you. You
　　just.shut.down. As if I'm bullying you. And it's just my way. It's the way
　　men learn to argue through contact sports. As if words were body grease,
　　so you gotta grab hard to pin your opponent. And I'm stuck here, feeling
　　stupid and cut off, because you won't explain things in plain English.
　　You speak in a code. A code designed for signals between members of
　　the female sex. Well, pardon me, but I did.not.go.to.college.

V.O.
He's.An.Asshole.

CHARLENE: In plain English: I am not a pornographer. I write erotic entertain-
　　ment designed for women.

CLYDE: Yeah. So to return to what I was askin': what's the big difference?

(THE VOICE *and* VOICE-OVER *begin to make orgiastic noises when Charlene says*
"aroused.")

CHARLENE: For one thing, desire in female spectators is aroused by cinema in
　　a much different way. Narrativity—that is, plot—is emphasized.

CLYDE (*Stares at her*): Yeah. There are lots more words. So what else?

CHARLENE: The "meat shots" and "money shots" of the trade flicks are not the
　　be-all and end-all of Gyno Productions.—Why are you laughing?

CLYDE: I seen one of your movies—and it had tits and ass just like *DEEP
　　THROAT*.

CHARLENE: Physical expression is the culmination of relationships between
　　characters. Most importantly, we try to create women as protagonists in
　　their own dramas, rather than objects. And we try to appreciate the male
　　body as an object of desire.

CLYDE: Now you're talking!

(*In his enthusiasm,* CLYDE *moves too much and flinches.*)

—Oh, suffering Jesus on the cross!
CHARLENE: Is it bad?
CLYDE: Yeah.

V.O.
Awwww.

CHARLENE: Come on, let's go—
CLYDE: No, wait a minute, wait a second. I'm a . . . little woozy. Do you have anything in the house. For the pain?
CHARLENE: Whatd'ya mean, for the pain?
CLYDE: I could use a shot of something.
CHARLENE: You want me to give you a drink, Clyde? Are you insane?
CLYDE: One drink is not gonna hurt. In fact, it will dull the throbbing in my butt. And since it is your bullet that's in my butt, I think you owe me. One.
CHARLENE: You get mean when you drink. I don't want to participate in enabling behavior.
CLYDE: Goddamn Oprah Winfrey! Just get me something, will ya, Charlene? My Butt is bitchin' . . .
CHARLENE: One shot. That's all. I'll get some for me.

(CHARLENE *exits. While she is out of the room,* CLYDE *quickly searches under the sofa pillows and cushions for the gun. She returns with a bottle and two shot glasses.* CHARLENE *pours them drinks and hands Clyde his glass.*)

CLYDE: Wow. That's nice.
CHARLENE: It's Remy.
CLYDE: It's been a while . . . since I had Remy. Well—let's toast. To love and success and a long film career—to you.
CHARLENE: To . . . to you. To you, Clyde.

(*They sip. Pause.*)

THE VOICE: Jump Cut!

CHARLENE: You've got to let go now. It's over.

CLYDE: I . . . kinda lost my head when I got that restraining order today, Charlene. Some things will never be *over*. Like everything you taught me.

CHARLENE: What did I teach you?

CLYDE: You taught me about desire. That's not over. I think about you all the time. I have since high school.

CHARLENE: You're not thinking about me—you're obsessing about me.

CLYDE: No—because you can never understand what's going on inside a man's head, you imagine the worst.

V.O.

Charlene. Get him out of the house.

THE VOICE: Jump Cut!

CLYDE: I'm gonna put myself together—get retrained in something. Maybe go back to school like you did. It really changed you, Charlene, when you went back to school.

CHARLENE: I think that would be wonderful. You've got to believe you can change the story line.

CLYDE: I believe that some things are meant to be.

CHARLENE: Some things are meant to change.

CLYDE (*Carefully*): Maybe that's true for you.
      For me—I have to work out my "karma." Because I really fucked it up in this lifetime. And I have to pay for that by trying.

CHARLENE: I don't believe in "karma."

CLYDE: I do. I believe in it. There's no other way to explain stuff like high school proms . . .

(CHARLENE *laughs, relaxes.* CLYDE *smiles, and moves a little closer.*)

CHARLENE: I forget sometimes how unique you are. When you're not drinking.

THE VOICE (*As* DETECTIVE): Where the hell is the Medical Examiner? And after the third or fourth hour on the scene, you start to take inventory of your life: a joke of a job, no fuckin' family, no wife. This is when the job can get to you, when you start counting it all up and you come up with nothing.

CLYDE: You're everything to me.

(CHARLENE *pours another round of Remy.*)

V.O.
You've had enough for one night, Charlene.

THE VOICE: Jump Cut!
CHARLENE: I . . . think about you. I try to figure it out. All the time. Why I
stayed with it so long. It's funny—I always asked why I stayed—I never
thought to ask how you could act that way. And then one day, I realized
that every dish in the house had been replaced with plastic ones. Part of
me got off, living on the edge like that. I kept saying, I can handle this, I
can take this—but I was losing control.
THE VOICE: Jump Cut!
CLYDE: I never stop thinking about it. It's this tape loop. It's torturing me. I'm
standing outside my body, watching this actor doing that to you. A stunt-
man who's got my face.
CHARLENE: You want to work out your karma? Then let go. Find another
woman, and make her life lucky. Break the cycle. It will be better, the
next time.

V.O.
"She can . . . smell . . . his sweat. So warm, she can smell—"

THE VOICE: "So close, she can almost taste—"

V.O.
"Smell. His.—"

THE VOICE: "Sweat."

(A **red light** *fills the stage again. There is a rustling at the sliding glass window.*
We see CALVIN *against the glass, watching.* HE *stretches his arms against the*
frame.)

CLYDE: It will never be as good as it is with you.
THE VOICE: "CUT TO: INTERIOR. THE WOMAN closes her eyes."

(CHARLENE *closes her eyes.*)

THE VOICE: "CLOSE UP on her lips as she kisses THE MAN, hard, on the mouth."

(CHARLENE *sits by* CLYDE *and gently kisses him. They look at each other. Then they kiss again—a long, hard kiss, breathing each other in.*)

V.O.
"VOICE-OVER: What are you doing, Charlene?"

THE VOICE: "THE MAN and THE WOMAN look at each other for a long time."

V.O.
"VOICE-OVER CONTINUED: This is not a movie, Charlene."

THE VOICE: "THE MAN and THE WOMAN move toward each other, lips parted."

V.O.
(*Urgent*)
"CUT TO: EXTERIOR. We see the door of the house burst open and—"

THE VOICE (*cutting in*): "THE WOMAN begins to breathe, quicker; THE MAN moves closer and presses against her, urgent now—"

V.O.
(*Trying harder*)
"CUT TO—CUT TO: EXTERIOR! We see THE WOMAN run from the house—"

THE VOICE: "THE WOMAN sighs; THE MAN reaches out and strokes her hair—"

V.O.
(*Insistent*)
"Get out of the house!"

THE VOICE: "LONG SHOT. EXTERIOR. THE BOY watches through the window."

*(There is a freeze. CLYDE and CHARLENE on the sofa; CALVIN, stretched on the window. The **red light** changes to the **stage lights**. CLYDE starts unbuttoning Charlene's top.)*

CHARLENE: What about your—?—No, wait—
CLYDE: Shhh! Don't Talk. Not now.

(CLYDE and CHARLENE resume. Just then the door flies open violently; CALVIN flies into the room.)

CALVIN: I AM. GONNA. *KILL* YOU!!
CLYDE: What the fuck—?

(In a fury, CALVIN throws himself on top of the couple. CLYDE and CALVIN roll onto the floor. CLYDE screams.)

CLYDE: SHIT! AAAAH!
CHARLENE: CALVIN! NO! STOP! Watch out for his butt!

(CLYDE and CALVIN wrestle. They stand. CALVIN, from behind, gets CLYDE in a lock, one hand pinned and twisted; CALVIN's arm is locked around CLYDE's throat, choking him.)

CLYDE *(In a squeezed voice)*: It's getting harder to . . . be a . . . family man . . . these days.
CALVIN: You leave her alone. Understand?
CHARLENE: Calvin. It's not. As it looks.
CALVIN: You don't live here anymore. Get it?
CLYDE *(Appreciatively, in the same squeezed voice)*: You're getting . . . mighty big, son.

(And just as quickly, CLYDE slips around and out of Calvin's grip, quickly kneeing him in the groin. CALVIN gasps and falls into a fetal position on the rug.)

CHARLENE: Jesus Christ, Clyde!
CLYDE: He's playing with the big boys now.

(CALVIN *says nothing. His face, beet red, presses into the rug.*)

CHARLENE: Calvin—
CLYDE: Don't touch him. He'll be all right.

(*Pause.*)

Son? You all right?

(CLYDE *offers his hand to* CALVIN, *who refuses it and who slowly gets up.*)

CLYDE: I'm sorry. Reflex action. No man likes to injure the family jewels.
CHARLENE: Calvin—
CALVIN: What's he doin' here?
CHARLENE: Your father . . . just . . .
CLYDE: Dropped in. For a little adult conversation.
CALVIN: That's not what it looked like to me.
CHARLENE: Honey, I can appreciate your concern, but he's still your father—
CALVIN: What's he doin' here?
CLYDE: Look, maybe I should just call it a night.
CHARLENE: No, wait a minute, Clyde. No matter what's happened between you and me, you and Calvin have to learn how to talk to one another. I will not be used as an excuse for getting in the middle of the two of you. Do you both hear me? I want you to both act civilized to each other in my living room for at least sixty seconds.

(*Beat.*) I'm putting on a fresh pot of coffee.

(CHARLENE *exits.*)

CLYDE: Whatta night, huh?

(*As* CLYDE *hobbles past Calvin to sit on the sofa:*)

CALVIN: Hey, what happened to your butt?
CLYDE: Your poor, defenseless mother shot me.
CALVIN: Mom? Mom? She shot you?

(CALVIN *starts to laugh.*)

CLYDE: I don't see anything particularly amusing about it. Men might hit you in the balls, but they do it to your face. Women—they shoot you in the butt.

CALVIN: You musta deserved it.

CLYDE: This is something private between your mother and me.

(Pause.) So—how's school?

CALVIN: Okay.

CLYDE: And life? In general.

CALVIN: Okay.

CLYDE: Still got your nose stuck in the books? Instead of watchin' the live action?

CALVIN: Real men can read books.

CLYDE: Right, right.

(Another pause.)

So—how's your sister?

CALVIN: Okay, I guess.

CLYDE: You guess? You don't know? You gotta keep an eye on her, son. She's at . . . that age. Know what I mean?

(CLYDE punches Calvin in his arm. CALVIN rubs his arm.)

CALVIN: Yeah, sure I do.

CLYDE: That's right. You're the man of the house, now. Blood of my blood, Flesh of my flesh. Best thing to do is just lock her up for a couple a years. She's gonna cause a lot of men heartbreak. You gotta watch her, son.

CALVIN: I do. I watch her all the time.

CLYDE: I mean, it's not her fault, right? But that body of hers . . . you know what I mean? You got to control her.

CALVIN: She's a little hard to control.

CLYDE: Girls' bodies at her age . . . they should be *licensed*.

*(**Red light** stage left of glass door. VOICE-OVER begins to work to the music. LESLIE ANN watches her work, shyly. CLYDE and CALVIN enjoy the show.)*

CLYDE: Where is . . . your sister?

CALVIN: She said she was goin' to some sleepover.

CLYDE: And your mother believes that crap? We don't believe that crap, do we?

(*The two share a laugh, settle back, and watch with glazed attention.*)

THE VOICE:
(*LESLIE ANN starts to join in from her spot, hesitantly at first. CLYDE hands his son a dollar bill, and shows him how to offer it to VOICE-OVER. THE VOICE becomes engrossed in* Moby-Dick, *which really does read like a triple-X flick.*)

"Spread yourselves, give way. . . . Lay back! There!—there!—there again! There she blows right ahead boys!—lay back! Pull, pull, my fine hearts, pull, my children, pull, my little ones. Why don't you break your backbones, my boys? What is it you stare at? So; so; there you are now, that's the stroke, that's the stroke . . . hurrah for the gold cup of sperm, my heroes!"

(**Red lights** out. VOICE-OVER *goes back upstage, and* LESLIE ANN *disappears as* CHARLENE *enters with a tray, a coffee pot, two mugs, a plate of cookies. And a tall glass of milk.* CHARLENE *pauses, watches them. She sets the tray down on the coffee table.*)

CHARLENE: You two are just . . . chattering away like magpies.
CLYDE: We've been talking. Right?
CALVIN: Yup.
CLYDE: Man talk.
CALVIN: You just caught us during the pause.
CHARLENE: I've fixed us a late-night snack. A last cup of coffee before I drive your father to the hospital.
CLYDE: I don't think that's . . . necessary, Charlene.
CHARLENE: This is nothing to fool around with, Clyde. Let me see how it's doing. Turn over.
CLYDE: Not in front of the boy, goddamn it.
CHARLENE: For Christ's sake, he's your own flesh and blood. Turn over.

(*CLYDE turns his wounded cheek toward her. She carefully lowers his pants and examines the wound critically.* CALVIN *peeks.*)

CALVIN: Wow.
CHARLENE: It's still bleeding. Not as bad as before, though. It needs stitches and a fresh bandage.

(*Pause.*)

CALVIN: Mom? Didja really shoot Dad?
CHARLENE: Yes.
CALVIN: Cool. Mom?
CHARLENE: Calvin, we're not going to discuss it.
CLYDE: Why don't you just drink up your milk and go to bed . . .

(CALVIN *stares with disbelief and disgust at the glass of milk.*)

CALVIN: You have got to be shittin' me . . .
CLYDE: Lucky for you this is your mother's house. I'd turn the strap on ya for
    language like that . . .
CALVIN: Mom! Milk?!! MILK!?
CHARLENE: Well, sweetie, it's too late for you to be drinking coffee, and I saved
    the last glass of milk to go with your cookies.
CALVIN: I'm not drinking that shit.
CLYDE: Growing boys need their milk. Right?
CHARLENE: Let's just drop it, Clyde.
CLYDE: Only wusses are scared of milk. A real man can drink milk.
CALVIN: You drink it.
CLYDE: Okay, son—I'll show you how it's done. How a real man drinks milk—
CHARLENE: Stop it. Stop it. I hate this.

(CLYDE *abruptly grabs the milk, and guzzles half the glass. It dribbles down his
chin and shirt.*)

CLYDE: Num, num. A man who can't drink milk can't love women. Is that a
    problem for you, son? Are you that kind of man?
CHARLENE: Why does everything turn into a horror movie around here?
CLYDE: Show your old man. Drink the milk.

(CLYDE *presses the glass into* CALVIN'S *face. They freeze.*)

THE VOICE: "There's the mark of his teeth still where he tried to bite the nipple
    I had to scream out aren't they fearful trying to hurt you—"

(*End freeze.*)

CLYDE: Drink the milk.

CALVIN: No. Shit! Get out of my face.

CLYDE: It's just Milk. What are you scared of? Milk can't hurt you—

(*The two tussle with the milk; it splashes them both.*)

CALVIN: You're. An. Asshole!

(CHARLENE *and* CALVIN *instinctively flinch. A moment's pause.*)

CLYDE (*Quietly*): What.did.you.call.me?

CHARLENE:—Enough!

(CALVIN *goes to Charlene, scared.*)

CALVIN: You don't scare me. This is not your house. You keep away from us. Stop thrusting yourself on Mom, You.Hear.Me?

CLYDE: I wasn't thrusting myself on your mother. Quite the opposite. Did I thrust myself on you on the sofa, Charlene? Did I?

CHARLENE: I'm taking you to the hospital. Now.

CLYDE: Your mother kissed me. First.

CHARLENE (*Together with Calvin*):   CALVIN (*With Charlene*):
    (—This is getting ridiculous.   That's a lie! Isn't it, Mom?

CHARLENE: We're ending this conversation. Now.

CLYDE: Tell him. You kissed me.

CALVIN: Did.You.Kiss.Him? Mom? After all he's done?

THE VOICE: "and his heart was going like mad and yes I said yes I—"

CHARLENE: Calvin—honey—it's hard to explain.

CALVIN: I DON'T BELIEVE YOU!

CHARLENE: For God's sake, Calvin, I'm a human being, too—I have needs—

CALVIN: I'm Getting Out.Of.Here—

CLYDE: When your mother kisses a man, it's like your heart gets squeezed.

CALVIN: ARGGHHH!!

(*Holding his head,* CALVIN *rushes for the door, opens it, and runs out into the night, screaming:*)

I AM SO FUCKED UP!

(*Door slam.*)

THE VOICE: "She kissed me. I was kissed. All yielding she tossed my hair.
    Kissed, she kissed me.
    Me. And me now."

(CLYDE *and* CHARLENE *sit, weary and tense.*)

CHARLENE: Why do you always do that?
CLYDE: Do what?
CHARLENE: Oh, you know. You know very well.
CLYDE (*Getting angry*): Christ!

(CLYDE *and* CHARLENE *look at each other.* **Red light.**)

V.O.
FLASHBACK—FIVE YEARS AGO.

(CLYDE *strikes* CHARLENE *hard on the face; in slow motion, it almost looks like a caress.* CHARLENE *falls back on the sofa.* CLYDE *continues toward* CHARLENE:)

V.O.
"CONTINUING—"

(*Abrupt* **lighting change:** *back to bright stage lights.* CHARLENE *stands, scared.*)

CHARLENE (*Trying to be composed*): Calm down.
CLYDE: Calm down—I don't have a job, I've got no fuckin' family, no wife—
    I've got shit for a life!
CHARLENE: Maybe you should go now.
CLYDE: Christ, Charlene. I just wish—shit, I just wish we could go back, ya
    know? Before college, before I got fired, before everything started bust-
    ing apart. I wish I could just close my eyes and you'd be coming home
    through the door in your uniform, after your night shift.
CHARLENE: Oh God, I hated that fucking uniform.
CLYDE: You'd come in, tired but sweet. I'm under the covers. First you flip on
    the coffee in the kitchen, and the aroma comes up to me before you
    reach the bed. And then I feel your hands on my stubble, stroking it, and

then I hear the sound of your shoes hitting the floor, one by one. And the zippers. The sound of the uniform sliding down your slip. And then the next thing I know, there's your warmth in bed. And your voice urging me up to work. Already slipping into sleep.

   And every morning I went to work with a hard-on. It was great.
CHARLENE: Great.

(CHARLENE *stares into nothing as she slowly pours the coffee as a trickle into a cup.*)

And every night I would stand in the middle of the ward and think, "I can't do this any longer." Holding another bed pan,

V.O.
swimming with someone's fluids. Bodies and mess. Mess and Bodies. Minimum wage. Cleaning up messes.
   This is where a high school diploma gets you, Charlene.

CLYDE: But then you came home. To me and the children.
CHARLENE: Where I cleaned up your mess for free.
CHARLENE: Now I close my eyes and see beautiful, strong, bodies touching each other,

V.O.
coupling with each other. And we write down these words.
And the words become flesh.

(*Beat.*)

CHARLENE: And the pay's much better, too.
CLYDE: I could kill that little faculty fruit at P.G. Community—
CHARLENE: Gil encouraged me; he let me in on the market. This writing is saving my sanity. I'm never going back.

(*Pause.*)

CLYDE: So where's Leslie Ann at tonight?
CHARLENE: She's spending the night with a friend.

CLYDE: A friend, huh.

CHARLENE: Yes. A girlfriend. She asked my permission.

CLYDE: It's your house.

CHARLENE: Don't you dare start implying—

CLYDE: What? Who? Who's implying—?

CHARLENE: I work very hard at being a good mother.

CLYDE: You're a great mother.

CHARLENE: I try, that's all.

CLYDE: Leslie Ann's just at . . . that age, is all. You know.

CHARLENE: No, I don't know. What age is that?

CLYDE: You can't be too careful. Look, I'm hardly the one to give you advice . . . seeing how my backseat activities got me into messes.

CHARLENE: I know exactly where my children are. I know exactly where Leslie Ann is, right now.

V.O.

"CUT TO: INTERIOR. In the rec room of Lisa's house. Night."

(*On the ramp,* LESLIE ANN, *now in an oversized T-shirt, huddles in her sleeping bag, addressing her best friend Lisa.* LESLIE ANN *and* VOICE-OVER *speak to each other.*)

LESLIE ANN: You're my best friend, Lisa. You.know.that. Since Seventh Grade. And you're gonna be my best friend long after I get married and have kids. If it wasn't for the fact.that.I get to see you for homeroom and lunch, I woulda stopped goin' to that stupid school a long time ago.

V.O.

Uh.huh. Is your sleeping bag warm enough?

LESLIE ANN: I feel like there's nothin' you couldn't tell me. You know? I would die before one'a your secrets would roll out.of.my.mouth.

V.O.

Me too. You could tell me—anything.

LESLIE ANN: That's good. Are the other girls . . . asleep? Do you—do.you—

> V.O.
>
> What? Come on, you can tell me anything—

LESLIE ANN: I've never said this to anyone else before. I'll kill you if you—

> V.O.
>
> —You can tell me. Anything.

LESLIE ANN: Well. Do you . . . do you . . . think of boys a lot?

> V.O.
>
> (*Giggling*)
> All the time.

LESLIE ANN: But I mean do you think about . . . think about . . .

> V.O.
>
> What? What? About . . . doing it?

LESLIE ANN: Yeah, but not just that—

(*In a rush.*)

I mean, I think of that, too, but sometimes . . . do you think of them, like, "hurting" you? Well, I don't mean like hurting you, but like, you're tied down and you can't stop them and they do things to you that hurt you, that make you scream but you can't and you wouldn't really want it to happen in real life, you would really get hurt, but when you close your eyes, you see it and it makes you get hot only it's 'cause it's not for real?

(*Pause.*)

Lisa? Lisa? Are you asleep?
THE VOICE: Action

(**Lights** *back up on living room.*)
CHARLENE: Leslie Ann is still a child. And I want her to have every second of childhood that she can get.
CLYDE: A child, huh? Have you looked at your daughter lately?

CHARLENE: There's too much pressure on her, already. Lectures on safe sex, birth control, condoms. I want.her.left.alone.

CLYDE: Okay, okay. You're her mother. But have you walked out of your front door lately: Seen the world? There's no childhood left.

CHARLENE: It's not the world outside I'm worried about her seeing.

CLYDE: What's that supposed to mean?

(Pause.)

CHARLENE: I think we should go now. I'll drive you.

CLYDE: I can drive myself.

CHARLENE: Let's go, then.

CLYDE: I'm not ready.

THE VOICE: Cut! Take two.

CHARLENE: It's late. I want you out of here.

CLYDE: I just got here.

CHARLENE: Don't.

CLYDE: What am I doing? Having a cup of coffee?

CHARLENE: You can't stay, Clyde. I need you out of here.

THE VOICE: Cut! Take three.

CHARLENE: I want you out of here.

CLYDE: Are you going to make me?

CHARLENE: If I have to.

CLYDE: Ooooh.

CHARLENE: Don't mock me, goddamn you—

(There is the sound of door keys, loud heavy metal music and a door slam. LESLIE ANN enters. They all blink at each other.)

CLYDE: Hi, baby girl.

LESLIE ANN: Daddy!

(To Charlene.)

You didn't tell me he was gonna be here.

CHARLENE: What are you doing here?

LESLIE ANN: I came back for somethin'—Lisa's waiting outside—

CHARLENE: Why don't you just go back out to the car and Lisa—

LESLIE ANN: —Why didn't you tell me my father was coming tonight?

CHARLENE: Did you notice the knob is off the front door?
CLYDE: Don't I get a kiss anymore?

(*LESLIE ANN runs to her father and hugs him. Sits in his lap.*)

> That's more like it. . . . My God, you're getting big.

(*HE buries his nose into her head; embarrassed,* LESLIE ANN *jerks her head away.*)

LESLIE ANN: Don't. Dad.
CLYDE: Your hair smells . . . different. It doesn't smell like you—
LESLIE ANN: What? I've bought my own shampoo, that's all.
CLYDE: It doesn't smell like little girl hair anymore.

(*Beat.*)

> So, what you are you doing tonight, princess?
LESLIE ANN: I'm doin' a sleepover at Lisa's—she's my friend in the car. Do you
    want to meet her?
CLYDE: No—that's okay. What do you girls do together?
LESLIE ANN: We're watching movies, mostly. *Friday the 13th, Halloween*—

V.O.
(*À la horror movie*)
"Get out of the house! Get out of the—"

CHARLENE: I don't know how you can watch those.
LESLIE ANN: They're just movies, Mom.

(*To Clyde.*)

> Are you coming back home?
CHARLENE: No! He was just leaving—we were on our way out—
LESLIE ANN: I just got here!
CHARLENE: Leslie Ann, your father and I are in the middle of something—
LESLIE ANN: —Lay-la. Where's Calvin?
CLYDE: He left after a little chat.
LESLIE ANN: Are you gonna be here when I get back?
CHARLENE: No.
LESLIE ANN: You just came over for a visit, Daddy?
CLYDE: I wanted to try to talk to your mother, that's all.

(CLYDE *hands* LESLIE ANN *five dollars.*)

LESLIE ANN: Good luck. She's hard to talk to.
CHARLENE: Okay. That's enough. Go on with Lisa—

V.O.
(*Whispered*)
Don't Go.

LESLIE ANN: Why don't you two just try to talk it out? Daddy, you've got to give
up drinking, that's all. And get another job. It's no big deal. I don't see
why you two can't work it out.
CLYDE: Well, I'd like that, Layla.
CHARLENE: It's a little more complicated than that, honey.
LESLIE ANN: I'm gonna tell Lisa to go on without me.
CHARLENE: No. You are going. With Lisa. And have a nice time.
LESLIE ANN: Everybody gets to talk to him but me!

(*There is the sound of a car horn. Three times. "Lo-lit-ta."*)

THE VOICE: Daddy's girl.

(LESLIE ANN *goes to the door and yells.*)

LESLIE ANN: Go on without me, okay?!

(*There is the sound of a car horn, again, with* THE VOICE *echoing.*)

THE VOICE: Lo-lee-ta . . .
LESLIE ANN: I wanna stay here and talk.

V.O.
(*Whispered*)
Don't Go.

CHARLENE: Not tonight. I mean it.
LESLIE ANN: I can't even talk to my own father!! Why can't we be like other
families?
Don't I even get a chance? Where's my fucking 4-H Club! When did
we ever say grace at the dinner table?! I'm a fucking statistic from a

broken home! A goddamn teenage statistic without enough money for a fucking double feature at the mall who has to lie that my mother's a secretary and that my father's a secret agent so no one finds out I've got a pervo for a mother, a drunk for a father, and a four-eyed geek for a brother who beats off in his catcher's mitt! FUCK!

(*LESLIE ANN slams out of the house. Pause.*)

CHARLENE: I'm not a mean woman. But I'm really going to enjoy watching her when she has children of her own.

CLYDE: I don't remember talking to my mother like that. And my father . . .

CHARLENE: The only reason Leslie Ann thinks the sun shits out of your ass is 'cause I've lied to her all these many years. She thinks I'm just . . . clumsy.

CLYDE: Yeah, well you are.

CHARLENE: I wasn't "clumsy" until after we got married. Running into doors, falling down the stairs—I want to protect her from knowing. It's too late for Calvin. That last fight—he saw it.

CLYDE: Part of becoming a man is accepting your parents' imperfections.

CHARLENE: Imperfections, yes—broken ribs, no.

CLYDE: Okay, Charlene. I've ruined your life. Okay? I'm fucked-up as a husband and a father, and I've ruined whatever fucking chance at happiness you and my children have in this lifetime.

CHARLENE: I'm not asking you for that, Clyde.

CLYDE: What do you want from me?

CHARLENE: What do *I* want? Why'd you come over?

CLYDE: I . . . wanted to see you.

CHARLENE: Why? What is it you want?

CLYDE: I want . . . I want . . . what's the use.

(*CLYDE gets up to go.*)

CHARLENE: Just tell me the truth. Okay? I'm listening.

CLYDE: You'll hate me if you know . . .

CHARLENE: I can't hate you more than I have for the past ten years.

CLYDE: Well. It's . . . it's a fuckin' Friday night. Right?
    And so what do we do, Friday night? Go out, drink some beer, and . . . ya know . . . cruise the strip. I mean, if you're a guy who's alone, that's what there is to do in this town on a Friday.

CHARLENE: I'm with you so far.

CLYDE: Right. So I . . . take a shower, you know, spruce up a little bit. And I count out the change I have left. And it's not much. And that gets me a little depressed, but I think, okay, shit, I'll economize, I'll buy a six-pack for the truck, and I won't drink out, you know? So I go downtown, and hit the streets . . . and I go into a few . . . places . . . but mostly there are minimums. So I think, fuck, I can't even watch the live action.

CHARLENE: You gotta have money to be a player.

CLYDE: So . . . so . . . so I go into a corner bookstore, and it's packed. And I change a five into quarters, and slip into the booth . . . and I—

CHARLENE: —You watch—

CLYDE: Right. And all it does is get me even more agitated. I'm thinking, this is not what I want, on A Friday Night, the feeling of my own fist in a booth—I'm like numb to that by now—and so I get back into my own truck, and I drink a few beers to get my nerve up—and I empty out my pockets . . . I check the dash and under the seats, and I count—and I come up with a lousy eighteen dollars and thirty-seven cents.

CHARLENE: Well, that's better than nothing.

CLYDE: Are you being . . . funny?

CHARLENE (*Quickly*):

No, I'm not. . . . Go on.

CLYDE: Well, I think you know, times are hard, maybe some working girl will consider it—you know? Maybe I'll get lucky, or I'll hit someone green on the street—so I crank up the engine, and start to drive it slow, down the side streets. And I see them, it's warm out tonight, and they're there, in groups—laughing, wearing next to nothing, and they're so close, they're laughing at me, calling out to me—

CHARLENE:—So why didn't you ask someone?

CLYDE:—I don't know. They were all together. I couldn't get one off by herself; I thought they'd laugh—I couldn't just call out, you know, "How about $18.37?" I just . . . just lost my nerve, I was so . . . down by then . . . then . . . and then I just kept driving and the truck kind of drove here by itself.

CHARLENE (*Quietly*):

So you're telling me that you drove to your ex-wife's house because you couldn't afford a prostitute.

CLYDE: Jesus, Charlene, don't make it sound like that!

CHARLENE: I'm not taking offense, Clyde. I'm a grown woman. I can take the truth. In fact, I prefer it.

CLYDE: I mean, the truth is . . . the truth is . . . that lately nothing really seems to do it for me. I don't know what . . . what's happening to me . . . but all the usual . . . uh . . . escapes . . . turn me on but they don't work anymore—I just get more and more depressed and anxious—like what if it just won't work at all, I mean, it happens, sometimes to men, and something's happening in . . . in my head—well, frankly, it scares the shit out of me. And it's building into a big problem now.

CHARLENE: I don't understand.

(CLYDE *starts to shake, ever so slightly, trying not to cry.*)

CLYDE: I mean like magazines, or girls in the booth, you know? I'll try to watch them, to use them but . . . something's changed . . . I start thinking, she's young enough to be my daughter, or . . . I'll bet she's married, or she's someone's mother . . . the words I read in the books I buy, I start to wonder if some woman's writing them, the way you do, to pay the rent for her kids . . . and . . . I think I'm really, really fucked up. I'm sorry—I don't mean to do this to you, I know you've got problems of your own, but I just miss—just talking to you—you know?

(CLYDE *is crying, quietly, openly.*)

CHARLENE (*Softly*): Oh my God, what have we done to each other?

(*Pause.* THEY *sit quietly beside each other on the sofa.* CHARLENE *makes a decision.*)

CHARLENE: How are you feeling? Does it still hurt?

CLYDE: Huh? Oh, that—no, I barely feel it. I think it's stopped bleeding.

CHARLENE: Okay—listen. I'm just a woman on a Friday night, okay? I've come down on my price for you—just once—just for tonight—for $18.37. You've hit the jackpot, mister. I am not your wife—or anyone's mother right now. Just this once, Clyde—we've got to be quick, before the kids come back. Make the sofa bed up, okay? The sheets are already on it, you've just got to take the cushions off and pull it out. I'm going . . . to change into something.

(CLYDE *has a hard time talking.*)

CLYDE: You don't have to . . .

CHARLENE: I know I don't.

CLYDE: I'm not sure if I can . . . if I—

CHARLENE: Then we'll just hold each other and talk. All right? Quick now, before I change my mind. I'll be right back.

(CHARLENE *exits into the bathroom.* CLYDE, *unable to believe his luck, sits for a few moments on the sofa. He notices the cognac bottle, picks it up, and guzzles the cognac. Then slowly, he gets up, in pain. He draws the blinds closed. He begins to take the cushions off the sofa. When he turns his back to the audience, we can see that his jeans are soaked in blood. He sees that he has drenched the cushion, and quickly turns the bloody side to the wall.*)

(*Meanwhile,* THE VOICE *has become an actual* DETECTIVE. *He examines the doorway, looking at the frame for signs of forced entry. He draws out a handkerchief, and finds a bullet casing on the floor. Using his handkerchief, he picks up and examines each glass and coffee cup, looking for prints, etc.*)

CLYDE: Charlene! Uh—Charlene—!

CHARLENE (*Offstage*): What!

CLYDE: I don't have . . . anything on me . . . you know? In case—

CHARLENE (*Offstage*): That's okay. I've got some protection in the house.

(*Laughs.*)

Not protection as in guns. Protection as in condoms. A girl scout is always prepared . . .

(CLYDE *stops, scowls. Angrier.* **Red light** *starts to blend in with the stage lights, slowly.* THE DETECTIVE *finds a condom on the floor.*)

THE VOICE: What is she doing with fuckin' condoms in the house?

V.O.
"Your failure to Obey this order may subject you to mandatory arrest and criminal prosecution which may result in your"

THE VOICE: "Incarceration for up to seven years for criminal contempt and/Or may subject you to family court prosecution . . ."

V.O.

"Now therefore, it is hereby ordered that John Doe observe the following conditions of behaviors:"

THE VOICE: "Stay at least 500 feet away from A) Jane Doe; B)"

V.O.

"Home of Jane Doe"

THE VOICE: "C) Business of Jane Doe"

V.O.

"Refrain from assault, harassment, menacing, reckless endangerment—"

THE VOICE: "Disorderly conduct"

V.O.

"Intimidation"

THE VOICE: "Threats or any criminal offense against Jane—"

V.O.

"—Doe . . ."

(*Increasingly angry,* CLYDE *begins to make up the bed. He pulls out the sofa bed, and sees something under the frame of the sofa: he picks it up. It is a gun. He stops, checks the ammunition. He folds down the bed. He tucks the gun under his shirt in his waistband. He sits on the bed.*)

CLYDE: Ya know, Charlene—maybe if I go back to school, I'll try my hand at screenplays!
CHARLENE (*Offstage*): What?
CLYDE: I said, I could write some screenplays! 'Cause I've got all these pictures—these voices—in my head, too . . .

(*No answer from* CHARLENE *in the bathroom. To himself.*)

Yeah. I'd like to write a screenplay where the porno movie director goes beserk in the middle of the movie, and . . .

(CLYDE's *screenplay starts to play.* THE VOICE *becomes a porn director.*)

THE VOICE: Jump Cut!
CLYDE: Yeah . . .

V.O.
"She was hot. She was throbbing. But she was in control.
Okay. Now we separate the men from the little boys . . ."

THE VOICE:—Cut! Listen, there's been a change in the script—

V.O.
What change?

THE VOICE: Clyde says he wants the bondage in reverse. Okay?

V.O.
That's not what we rehearsed . . .

THE VOICE: Since when are movies made by screenwriters? Directors make the movies. Not some broad sitting on her ass. Improvise, can't you? Your dialogue has gotta be as good as the dumbass writer . . .

V.O.
But I thought—

THE VOICE: Do we pay you to think? You're a professional, aren't you? Do you want the role or don't you—we're wasting overtime—

V.O.
Okay. The show . . . must go on.—Hey, guys, wait, these handcuffs are on awfully tight—

THE VOICE: Come on! Let's finish this take . . . Ready, lights, camera, action—

V.O.
(*Bad acting*)
"Please don't hurt me . . ."

THE VOICE: I'm not gonna hurt you, baby . . . I'm just gonna teach you a little lesson . . . a lesson you'll remember . . .

(There is the sound of a whiplash.)

V.O.
(Pain)
Shit! Wait a minute, guys—that really hurt. Larry— stop the
camera—Larry? Where's Larry?

(There is the sound of a whiplash.)

THE VOICE: We told Larry to take a walk.

V.O.
(Scared)
I don't know any of you guys . . . are you guys with Gyno Pro-
ductions?

THE VOICE: This is not your screenplay.

V.O.
I don't understand.

THE VOICE: Ever hear of snuff films?

*(Just then, the bathroom door opens, and CHARLENE, in a peignoir, reenters the
room. With a well-developed animal instinct, she stands stock-still, smelling the
change in the air. CALVIN and LESLIE ANN have appeared as well, pressed against
the window glass. CALVIN cries as he watches the live action, but LESLIE ANN stands
still and expressionless.)*

THE VOICE: What are you—
CLYDE: What are you looking at?
CHARLENE *(Scared)*: Nothing. Maybe this was a stupid idea.
THE VOICE: You look . . . great.
CLYDE: You look . . . great.
THE VOICE: Really great.
CLYDE: Really great.
CHARLENE: Really? Worth $18.37, huh?
THE VOICE: Ya gotta have money to be a player.
CLYDE: Let me . . . hold you. Come here.
THE VOICE: Lights, camera, action!

(*CHARLENE goes to* CLYDE; *they embrace.*)

CHARLENE: This feels good.
CLYDE: You smell good.

V.O.
Get out of the house!

CLYDE: I've been thinking—ya know, trying to figure out women. What turns
    them on. And I think tonight I've found the answer.
CHARLENE: Let's not talk.
CLYDE: Is it our smell? Our torso? Our butts?
CHARLENE: Let's not bring that subject up.

(*CHARLENE gently strokes Clyde's wounded behind and stops at the wetness.*)

CHARLENE: Hey—wait a moment—
CLYDE: I think women really get turned on to men in pain. That's what they
    like—

(*CHARLENE breaks away; in fear she examines her hand, now bloodied.*)

CHARLENE: Oh my god—Clyde, you're—

(CLYDE *reaches into the back of his pants, and rubs* CHARLENE's *face with his
blood.*)

CHARLENE: Oh my god—

(*CHARLENE looks for the hidden gun;* CLYDE *pulls it out from his pants.*)

CHARLENE: Clyde—listen—
CLYDE: You.Goddamn. Whore!

(CLYDE *savagely hits* CHARLENE. *A condom flies out of her hand.*)

THE VOICE: "The red tide now poured from all sides—"

(*As soon as Clyde strikes Charlene, in the next section,* CLYDE *and* CHARLENE *lip-
synch the voices which are provided by* THE VOICE *and* VOICE-OVER. *The lip synch*

should be very crude; we watch their mouths move like puppets, mechanically and exaggerated.)

CLYDE:	THE VOICE:
(Lip-sync)	*(Live)*
"Do you remember the last time?"	Do you remember the last time?

(CHARLENE starts to cry in elaborate pantomime; the VOICE-OVER sobs into the microphone.)

CLYDE:	THE VOICE:
(Lip-sync)	*(Live)*
"I asked you a question. Do.You.Remember. the last time."	I asked you a question. Do.You.Remember. the last time.
CHARLENE:	V.O.
(Lip-sync)	*(Live)*
"When . . . we . . . made love?"	When . . . we . . . made love?
CLYDE:	THE VOICE:
(Lip-sync)	*(Live)*
"No. When I beat you to within an inch of your life. You didn't learn did you?"	No. When I beat you to within an inch of your life. You didn't learn did you?
CHARLENE:	V.O.
(Lip-sync)	*(Live)*
"No."	No.
CLYDE:	THE VOICE:
(Lip-sync)	*(Live)*
"I.can't.hear.you."	I.can't.hear.you.
CHARLENE:	V.O.
(Lip-sync)	*(Live)*
"No!"	No!
CLYDE:	THE VOICE:
(Lip-sync)	*(Live)*
"I'm going to have to teach you all over again."	I'm going to have to teach you all over again.

CHARLENE:	V.O.
(Has difficulty breathing	*(Live)*
and only shakes her head)	Please—stop—
CLYDE:	THE VOICE:
(Lip-synch with difficulty)	*(Live)*
"Get.On.The.bed."	Get.On.The.bed.
CHARLENE:	VOICE-OVER:
(Live, simultaneous)	*(Live, simultaneous)*
Please—	Please—
CLYDE:	THE VOICE:
(Lip-synch)	*(Live)*
"On.the.bed!"	On.the.bed!

(CLYDE backhands CHARLENE and she falls on the bed.)

THE VOICE:	
(Whisper)	
Now.don't.move.	
CHARLENE:	V.O.
(Live)	*(Live)*
Don't.	Don't.
CLYDE:	THE VOICE:
(Live)	*(Live)*
Don't Move.	Don't Move.

THE VOICE *(Taking over)*:

What makes you think, with your big butt and fat pig thighs, that you're worth eighteen bucks? What man would pay for that?

(CLYDE erupts into crying:)

CLYDE: You're the one making me do this, Charlene. You shouldof never— never gotten that restraining order—kicked me out of the house! Jesus Christ, Charlene—why did you do that? Why?

(CHARLENE reaches up to touch Clyde's face.)

CHARLENE: Don't cry—don't—

(*CHARLENE tries to embrace Clyde.*)

(*As* CLYDE *unbuckles his belt, draws it from the loop, and wraps it around Charlene's throat,* THE VOICE *steps forward, reading from his own notes:*)

THE VOICE: "911 received a call at 9:30 A.M. from victim's neighbor. Arrived at the house approximately at 9:52. Victim: Charlene Dwyer, age 40."

THE VOICE (*Simultaneous whisper with* VOICE-OVER): "Pending coroner's report, strangulation appears to be cause of death. Time of death: 8–12 hours previous. Signs of forced entry. Alleged Perpetrator, Clyde Dwyer, age 42, found dead in bathroom of self-inflicted gunshot wound to the head. Pending forensic report, preliminary judgement: murder/suicide."

V.O.
(*Whispered simultaneous with* THE VOICE)

(*Get to the door can you keep calm—no—you can get out of this—no—keep fighting try to get—ask him with your eyes—no theres no air left—no for the kids stay calm stars put your arms around him keep your eyes open ask no to say no my god no no air I can't no*)

V.O.
It doesn't—have to—end like this—

(*With a muffled shout,* CLYDE *redoubles his grip in answer. As* CLYDE *kills* CHARLENE, *we hear a tape recording of* THE VOICE, *as* THE VOICE *and* VOICE-OVER *exit.*)

THE VOICE: "I asked him with my eyes to ask again yes and then he asked me would I yes to say yes my mountain flower and first I put my arms around his yes—"

(*The tape recording slows down, warped, breaking down.*)

". . . and drew him down to me so he could feel my breasts all perfume yes and his heart was going like mad and yes I said yes I will Yes."

(*Lights change to very real light.* CLYDE, *dazed, sees* CHARLENE *on the bed. Some awful sound emerges from his throat. For a moment, he cradles the body. The stage is empty save for the two of them.* CLYDE *rocks* CHARLENE's *body, then lays the body down on the bed. He picks up the gun, checks it again, and exits to the bath-room.)*

(There is a flash of light. We hear a gunshot, which reverberates as lights dim on the body of CHARLENE *strewn across the bed.)*

(A beat.)

(The front door opens, and LESLIE ANN *walks in. She sees the body of Charlene. She stands still. She walks to the bed, and touches the body. The touch tells her immediately.)*

(Then, as the lights dim on Charlene's body, there is a bright spotlight outside the house, outside the playworld, into which LESLIE ANN *steps. She takes off her clothes, down to her slip. Slowly, sensuously, she moves to music—something from the nineties that transposes into music on the radio now. But she is not dancing. She is dressing, slipping on a conservative dress. She steps into sensible heels. She smooths her stockings. She sweeps her hair up and ties it back.)*

(If this play were a film script, we would see Leslie Ann age before our eyes. Her body becomes more worn, more protected from our gaze, her bones become less light, her face more determined.)

(Oh yes. She wears glasses. Just as she is about to speak to us, the recorded voice of CHARLENE *cuts in:)*

CHARLENE'S VOICE-OVER
VOICE-OVER CONTINUED: FLASH-FORWARD.
Ten Years later. Leslie Ann finishes a lecture.

LESLIE ANN: And with that, we conclude our discussion of *Lolita*. At the end of class today you may collect your papers on *Ulysses* in my box. Two weeks from today your essays on Nabokov will be due in class.

I must say, your papers showed improvement. My thesis advisor thought this seminar was too ambitious for freshmen, but I'm glad to say you've proven him wrong. You can do anything you want to do if you put your mind to it.

LESLIE ANN: Next week we will continue our seminar on the literature of obsession with our reading of *Moby-Dick*—

My brother, who is becoming a screenwriter, claims that *Moby-Dick* is the one book that cannot be adapted successfully by Hollywood. Be that as it may, many Ahabs in LA have tried . . .

In the next four weeks, we will discuss not only Melville's masterpiece, but the criticism of *Moby-Dick*, which is as obsessive as the novel itself. We will examine how the book was first positioned as American, in contrast to English; literature by its juxtaposition of high and low culture, and its wild and erratic mixture of genres. During the Melville Revival, critics saw his similarity to modern writers, such as Joyce and Nabokov in Melville's use of ambiguity, doubleness, the unreliability of the narrator, and stream of consciousness.

CHARLENE'S VOICE-OVER
—You're going out of the house dressed like that and you blame me—

(*LESLIE ANN tries to concentrate.*)

LESLIE ANN: —And we will sample the formalist, culturally materialist, deconstructivist, and posthumanist—

CHARLENE'S VOICE-OVER
—You want to go far away from here? Read the goddamn book that's due on Monday. *Moby-Dick.*

(*LESLIE ANN can't shut it out. For a moment it appears as if LESLIE ANN will lose control in front of her class. She closes her eyes, and tries to gain composure.*)

LESLIE ANN: —Excuse me. I can get very emotional when I talk about *Moby-Dick.*

(*Beat. She takes a breath, and then moves to dismiss her class:*)

Okay. Your papers on *Moby-Dick* will be due four weeks from today. As always, I expect you to be in control of your arguments, in control of your words, and in control of your—

(*But CHARLENE again breaks into her daughter's stream of consciousness:*)

CHARLENE'S VOICE-OVER
(Whispered)
—thoughts.

(LESLIE ANN DWYER freezes at the sound of her mother's voice.)

End of Play

ABOUT THE EDITORS

Alexis Greene is an author, editor, and theater critic. Her books include *The Story of 42nd Street*, with Mary C. Henderson; *Women Writing Plays: Three Decades of the Susan Smith Blackburn Prize*; the biography *Lucille Lortel: The Queen of Off Broadway*; *Women Who Write Plays: Interviews with American Dramatists*; and *The Lion King: Pride Rock on Broadway*, with Julie Taymor. In 1986 she co-founded Literary Managers and Dramaturgs of the Americas and served as its first president. Dr. Greene has taught dramatic literature and theater history at Hunter College, New York University, Marymount Manhattan College, and Vassar College. She holds a Ph.D. in theater from the Graduate Center of the City University of New York, is on the board of the League of Professional Theatre Women, and is a member of PEN and of the Authors Guild.

    Shirley Lauro's play, *Clarence Darrow's Last Trial*, has been honored with a National Endowment for the Arts "Access to Excellence Award" and was an 2006 Carbonell nominee as Best New Play in Florida, where it enjoyed its world premiere at New Theatre. Lauro's latest play, *Madame Marie Sklodowska Curie* has received an EST/Sloan Commission, while another new play, *All Through the Night*, was an 2006 Jeff nominee as Best New Play in Chicago and will premiere in New York in fall 2009. *A Piece of My Heart* opened Manhattan Theatre Club's 20th Anniversary Season, enjoyed over one thousand productions around the world, and recently was selected by V.W. Veterans, Inc., as "the most enduring American play about the Vietnam War." *Open Admissions*, which marked Lauro's Broadway debut, garnered a Tony nomination, two Drama Desk nominations, a Theatre World Award, and the Dramatists Guild's Hull Warriner Award. Lauro subsequently adapted the play for CBS, starring Jane Alexander. Her novel, *The Edge*, was published by Doubleday, Dell in the United States and by Weidenfeld & Nicolson, Ltd., in the United Kingdom. A Guggenheim Fellow, twice recipient of a National Endowment for the Arts Grant and a New York Foundation for the Arts Award, Lauro has served twelve years on the Dramatists Guild's Council and Steering Committee, and is a director of the Dramatists Guild Fund. Affiliations: Ensemble Studio Theatre (Members Council), Actors Studio (Playwrights Unit), PEN, Writers Guild of America, Authors Guild, League of Professional Theatre Women.

PERMISSIONS

Plays in order of their appearance in book:

The Exonerated by Jessica Blank and Erik Jensen. Copyright © by Jessica Blank and Erik Jensen. Reprinted by permission of Farrar, Straus and Giroux, LLC and Faber and Faber Ltd.

Elliot, a Soldier's Fugue by Quiara Alegría Hudes. Reprinted by permission of the author.

Words of Choice by Cindy Cooper. Reprinted by permission of the author.

Clarence Darrow's Last Trial by Shirley Lauro. Reprinted by permission of the author.

Mrs. Packard by Emily Mann. Reprinted by permission of the author.

No Child . . . by Nilaja Sun. Reprinted by permission of the author.

Hot 'n' Throbbing by Paula Vogel. Copyright © by Paula Vogel. Reprinted by permission of William Morris Agency, LLC on behalf of the author.

CPSIA information can be obtained
at www.ICGtesting.com
Printed in the USA
FSHW01n1950160718
50585FS